45

CW00407705

# Wiltshire Record Society

(formerly the Records Branch of the Wiltshire
Archaeological and Natural History Society)

VOLUME XL

FOR THE YEAR 1984

**Impression of 500 copies**

# WILTSHIRE DISSENTERS' MEETING HOUSE CERTIFICATES AND REGISTRATIONS 1689–1852

EDITED BY

J.H. CHANDLER

DEVIZES
1985

© Wiltshire Record Society

ISBN 0 901333 17 4

Produced for the Society by
Alan Sutton Publishing Gloucester

# CONTENTS

# PREFACE

Mrs Nancy Steele retired from the post of Honorary Secretary to the Society at the Annual General Meeting in July 1984 after thirteen years of working for the Society. All members of the Society are indebted to her, not least for the many successful Annual General Meetings which she organized, but perhaps only members who have served on the Committee can fully appreciate how much she has done for the Society. Happily the Committee still has the benefit of her help and advice. The new Honorary Secretary is Dr John Chandler, who is also the editor of this volume.

Dr Chandler wishes to acknowledge the help and advice given by two previous general editors of the Society, Dr D.C. Cox and Miss Janet Stevenson. He also wishes to thank the archivists responsible for the documents calendared here for their unfailing courtesy and guidance, especially Miss K.P. Stewart; Mr K.H. Rogers and the staff of the of the Wiltshire Record Office; Miss M.E. Williams and the staff of the Bristol Record Office; Mr D.J.H. Smith and the staff of the Gloucestershire Record Office; and Mr G. Toop of the Public Record Office. The librarians of Bristol Baptist College, Dr Williams's Library, the University of Bristol Library and the Library of the Wiltshire Archaeological and Natural History Society have allowed him access to published works in their care, and his colleagues on the staff of the Wiltshire Library and Museum Service have assisted him in many ways. To all of them he offers his thanks.

For permission to publish these documents in calendar form the Society is grateful to the Bishops of Salisbury, Gloucester and Bristol, the Controller of Her Majesty's Stationery Office, and the Wiltshire County Council.

J. L. KIRBY

# INTRODUCTION

## The Legislative Background

The documents calendared in this volume resulted from the Toleration Act which received the royal assent on 24 May 1689,[1] and which continued in force (with alterations) until repealed on 30 June 1852.[2] This act[3] opened a new chapter in English nonconformity by removing from the established church the monopoly of legal forms of religious worship, and by enabling the dissenting denominations to progress from small bands of persecuted enthusiasts to a respectable, powerful and significant minority in English life.[4]

Owing to the large number of strange sects which had emerged during the comparatively tolerant years of the Civil War and the Commonwealth and Protectorate the Restoration Parliament was generally hostile to toleration, and a number of disabilities were imposed upon nonconformists; but in 1672 King Charles II himself attempted to remove some of these disabilities. His Declaration of Indulgence[5] was issued without the sanction of Parliament and thus without the force of law. Central to this indulgence was permission to hold religious meetings, or conventicles, and this required a system of licensing and registration. The surviving body of records of this brief period of toleration (it lasted a little under one year, from 15th March 1672), therefore, is a precursor to later registration, and the Wiltshire records have been included in this volume as an appendix.

After this brief respite, brought to a close by the recall of Parliament in 1673, protestant nonconformists were sufferers from the near universal hostility towards and mistrust of Roman Catholic recusants, and therefore of all religious dissidents, engendered at the close of the decade by talk of a 'Popish plot' to instal the Catholic James II on the throne in place of his brother. Their own antagonism towards Catholics only made matters worse, since it embittered Charles II against them. A Toleration Bill of 1680/1 passed through all its stages and only failed when the king refused to give his assent and then dissolved Parliament.[6] The dissolution of Parliament – it was not recalled in Charles's lifetime – ushered in a period of more severe persecution, which

---

[1] *Lords Journal*, vol. 14, p. 217.

[2] *Lords Journal*, vol. 84, p. 421.

[3] 1Wm&M, ch. 18, *An act for exempting their Majesties' protestant subjects dissenting from the Church of England from the penalties of certain laws.* Part of the text is in *English historical documents, 1660–1714,* ed. A. Browning, 1953, pp. 400–3.

[4] The best modern treatment is by Watts, M.R. *The dissenters: from the reformation to the French revolution,* 1978.

[5] Printed in *Eng. Hist. Docs. 1660–1714,* pp. 387–8.

[6] It received its Commons second reading on 24th November 1680: *Commons Journal,* vol. 9, p. 661, and a conference about its not receiving the royal assent was in session when Parliament was dissolved: *Lords Journal,* vol. 13, pp. 756–7).

came to an end only with the reign of James II, 1685–8, who favoured toleration only because it applied primarily to Catholics.

James, like his brother, issued a declaration of indulgence, in April 1687; as in 1672 provision was made for the registration of meeting houses, but this time notification was to be made to local ('some one or more of the next justices of the peace') rather than to central government.[7] No records of registration under this declaration appear to survive in Wiltshire, if indeed any were ever made.[8] The effect of this declaration was beneficial to protestant nonconformists in two ways: at face value it sanctioned their activities and reinforced religious liberties; but the storm of protest it provoked, on account of its permissiveness towards Catholics, found Church of England and many protestant nonconformists marshalled on the same side against the Catholic threat. Thus the way was opened for the toleration of protestant dissent.

Legislation touching nonconformity had to concern itself with three matters: the kinds of nonconformity that were to be permitted; the activities in which nonconformist leaders and their adherents might or might not engage; and the places where nonconformists might hold their meetings. Only the last of these is our concern in this volume, and is considered here. The Toleration Act of 1689 stipulated that:

> no congregation or assembly for religious worship shall be permitted or allowed by this Act until the place of such meeting shall be certified to the bishop of the diocese, or to the archdeacon of that archdeaconry, or to the justices of the peace at the general or quarter-sessions of the peace for the county, city or place in which such meeting shall be held, and registered in the said bishop's or archdeacon's court respectively, or recorded at the said general or quarter sessions; the register or clerk of the peace whereof respectively is hereby required to register the same, and to give certificate thereof to such person as shall demand the same, for which there shall be no greater fee nor reward taken, than the sum of six pence.[9]

The provisions for registering meeting houses enacted in 1689 were to remain in force virtually unaltered until 1812. They were not compulsory in the sense that transgressors could not be penalised under the act for infringement. The Toleration Act merely set out conditions which had to be met before nonconformists became immune from prosecution under earlier statutes forbidding such activities, which were not repealed. A congregation neglecting to have its meeting house registered under the 1689 act laid itself open to prosecution, or more likely harassment, from magistrates by virtue of Elizabethan and later legislation.

The 18th century, although it witnessed several attempts at nonconformist

---

[7] Text in *Eng. Hist Docs. 1660–1714*, pp. 395–7. Use of magistrates to register meeting houses was first envisaged in a bill introduced in February 1673, which however failed to receive a final reading in the Lords: *Lords Journal*, vol. 9, pp. 252–81 *passim*.

[8] Welch, E. 'The registration of meeting houses,' in *Journal of the Society of Archivists*, vol. 3(3), 1966, pp. 116–20, comments (on p. 116) that absence of state papers makes it difficult to decide whether registration was carried out. But local quarter sessions records, the registering authority, may provide the answer.

[9] 1Wm&M, ch.18, s.9: *Statutes at Large*, vol. 3, p.427.

legislation, not all successful, brought only one change to the registration of meeting houses. In 1791 an act extended to Roman Catholics many of the benefits of toleration, including the opportunity to have meeting houses registered, although this could only be done by quarter sessions.[1] Revision of the Toleration Act, which became an issue after 1800, was precipitated not by dissatisfaction with the procedure for registering meeting houses, but with concern at the regulation of itinerant preachers, whose numbers had burgeoned under the impetus of the late-18th century evangelical revival. A bill introduced into the Lords in 1811 generated massive opposition from the nonconformist lobby, and failed. A second bill, the Dissenters' Relief Bill, 1812, also failed, although its aim of overhauling the 1689 act was regarded sympathetically by the Lords.[2] A third attempt was more successful, and with little opposition a new Toleration Act received the royal assent on 29th July 1812.[3]

The Toleration Act of 1812 made several alterations to the procedures for registering meeting houses. Registration (by the same authorities) became compulsory for any religious assembly, 'at which there shall be present more than twenty persons besides the immediate family and servants of the person in whose house or upon whose premises,' the assembly was held. Arrangements were also made for the registering authorities to notify each other annually of all registrations relevant to each other's jurisdiction made during the previous year. The fee for procuring a licence was to become two shillings and sixpence; and the penalties imposed on an occupier for failing to register were set at between £1 and £20, at the magistrates' discretion.

Further legislation followed which, although it did not affect the registration procedures, had a bearing on meeting houses. In 1813 an act extended to Unitarians the same rights as their Trinitarian counterparts;[4] in 1833 meeting houses were exempted from church rates and poor rates;[5] and in 1837, with the establishment of the General Register Office, the Marriage Act conferred on certified meeting houses the right to solemnize marriages, provided that application had been made to the Superintendent Registrar, and a certificate delivered, 'signed in duplicate by twenty householders at the least, that such building has been used by them during one year at the least as their usual place of public religious worship.'[6]

The existence after 1837 of a central government bureaucracy to handle registration matters, the creation of a second procedure for registering meeting houses, and the general evolution of nonconformity since 1689, made it inevitable that the old order would eventually be ended. It was in fact the bishop of Salisbury, Edward Denison, who on 14th May 1852 re-introduced

---

[1] 31 Geo III, ch.32.
[2] *Parliamentary Debates*, 1st series, vol. 23, col. 887–92.
[3] 52 Geo III, ch. 155: *An act to repeal certain acts, and amend other acts relating to religious worship and assemblies. . . .* See also *Parliamentary Debates*, 1st series, vol. 23, col. 1105–10.
[4] 53 Geo III, ch.160.
[5] 3&4 Wm IV, ch.30.
[6] 6&7 Wm IV, ch.85, s.18.

part of a bill which had failed in 1845, and which brought the system of registration to an end. In his speech to the House of Lords, moving the bill's second reading, he reiterated the history of the legislation and its original purpose, which, 'the lapse of time and change of circumstances,' made no longer necessary. He objected especially to the implication that places of worship 'licensed' by the bishop had in some sense gained the Church's approval, which was therefore seen to be condoning erroneous teaching.

> And this feeling was further strengthened by the very indefinite sense in which the words 'Protestant Dissenters' were used. The Socialists registered the places in which they disseminated their doctrine of infidelity and immorality under the title of 'Protestant Dissenters.' The strange and impious fanaticism of the Mormonites was designated in the same manner. He had himself lately, in two instances, in different parts of his diocese, found himself to be the subject of reproach, under the idea that he had 'licensed' persons as Mormonite teachers.[7]

Denison had envisaged that responsibility for registration should pass to the clerk of the peace (quarter sessions), but in its passage through Parliament the bill was amended, so that the Registrar General, through his Superintendent Registrars, became the sole registering authority. The superseded authorities were required to make a return of all meeting houses registered by them since 1689, and deliver it within three months to the Registrar General, who would thereafter be required to publish an annual list of all existing certified places of worship. The bill passed hurriedly through all its stages in both houses in a little over six weeks, and received the royal assent on 30th June 1852, shortly before Parliament was dissolved.[8] The old authorities completed their returns, and these survive, but no list was ever published. The Registrar General did however prepare a report and statistical tables, which were published in 1853 as a Parliamentary Paper.[9]

## Meeting House Certificates

*Definitions.* The process of informing authority of the existence of a meeting house so as to conform with the legislation just described is variously known as certifying, licensing or registering. Consequently confusion often occurs when describing the documents resulting from this process. In this volume certificate, licence and registration all have distinct meanings. A document produced by or on behalf of a dissenting congregation certifying that premises are used, or are to be used, for religious worship is a certificate. The authority's reply, sent to the congregation on receipt of a certificate, and sanctioning such use, is a licence. It was common practice for the licensing

---

[7] *Parliamentary Debates*, 3rd series, vol. 121, pp. 680–3. The progress of the bill can be traced through *Lords Journal*, vol. 84, pp. 151–421 *passim*.
[8] 15&16 Vic. ch.36.
[9] *List of returns made to the Registrar General of the names of certified places of religious worship of protestant dissenters*, 1853 (1852/3, ch.lxxviii).

authority to copy some or all of the information contained in the certificate
into a register; this copy, therefore, is a registration.

Since both the licence and the registration are derived from the certificate it
is the certificate that has been preferred in preparing this edition. Until 1812,
however, it seems to have been the practice of the bishop's administration to
destroy certificates after registration had taken place; for this and various other
reasons described below only the registration may be available, and in one
instance (**309**) the licence alone has been found. After 1812 a fourth document,
the annual return of registrations made by one authority to the other (the
bishop to quarter sessions and *vice versa*), can act as a finding aid and a check on
certificates, and in a few cases, along with the 1852 return to the Registrar
General, may be the only source of information, both certificate and registration having disappeared.

In general certificates survive for the periods 1689–1745 and 1812–38 for the
whole of Wiltshire, and from 1838–52 also for all except north Wiltshire
parishes transferred to the diocese of Gloucester and Bristol. Between 1745 and
1812 and in north Wiltshire after 1838 the registrations have been used. The
position is complicated, however, by the records of peculiars, borough quarter
sessions and other stray certificates and registrations; the status of each entry in
the calendar may be discovered by referring to the list of sources.

*The wording of the certificate.* The 1689 Act did not stipulate the precise
wording in which a meeting house certificate was to be couched. Considerable
variations occur, therefore, in phrasing and terminology, and this uncertainty
about correct form evoked an occasional apology from the writers of
certificates (**279, 1587**). Rarely were their efforts rejected, however (so far as
can be known), and then only because the place-name was ambiguous (**1003**)
or the document was unsigned (**1228**). One irregularly drafted certificate was
rewritten and submitted afresh (**846**). The bishop's registrar seems to have
been ready with advice about the form of words (**893**); and several early
certificates (e.g. **163–5**) appear to have been written by a clerk at quarter
sessions, presumably from information supplied by the signatories in person.[1]

Typical of the certificates submitted to quarter sessions in the 18th century is
the following (**120**):

> To his Ma'ties Justices of the peace att the Generall Qarter Sessions of the peace
> now holding att Marlbrough in the County of Wiltes on tuesday the seventh day
> of October in the year of our Lord one thousand seven hundred and one.
> We whose names are hereunto subscribed doe Certify that the dwelling house of
> Henry Milsum situate in Kington St. Michael in the said County is sett apart and
> from henceforth intended to be used as a Meeting house for the exercise [*of*]
> Religious worr'pp by Protestant Dissenters Witness our hands – William Edall
> William Heath.

Following the overhaul of the procedures by the 1812 Act printed forms
came into use. The first occurrence in Wiltshire dates from February 1813

---

[1] Welch, *op. cit.* p. 117 note 10, cites an example of this practice from Leicester.

(**749**). During the five years 1820–4 printed forms were submitted to the bishop's registrar in 32 out of 168 cases (19%); in 1830–4 the number had risen to 49 out of 132 (37%). They were used by all the main denominations, and several different versions may be identified by minor variations and on typographical grounds. But these differences do not appear to be of value in establishing the denominations using them. Manuscript certificates continued in use until 1852, but many were evidently copied from the printed form. Because of this no attempt is made in the calendar to indicate which certificates are printed and which are manuscript.

The wording of a typical printed certificate is as follows (manuscript insertions are printed in italics) (**1101**):

> To the Right Reverend the Lord Bishop of Salisbury and to his Registrar I *Walter Hutchings* of *Netherhampton In the County of Wiltshire* do hereby certify, that *a dwelling House now in my Occupation in the Aforesaid Village* is intended forthwith to be used as a place of religious worship by an Assembly or Congregation of Protestants; and I do hereby require you to register and record the same according to the provisions of the Act passed in the 52d year of the reign of his Majesty King George the Third, intituled 'An Act to repeal certain Acts, and amend other Acts, relating to Religious Worship, and Assemblies, and persons teaching or preaching therein;' and hereby request a certificate thereof. Witness my hand this *Twenty fourth* day of *January* 18*25 Walter Hutchings.*

From these two examples it will be clear that the basic information found in a certificate is the date, a description of the premises, and one or more signatures. In addition the name of the denomination is given in nearly half (45%) the certificates, although there are marked variations in practice before 1750 (14%), between 1750 and 1810 (82%), and after 1810 (40%).

Most certificates and registrations after 1750 carry two dates, the date on which the certificate was signed and the date on which it was registered and the licence issued. Very often, especially when a Salisbury minister was involved or the meeting house was close to Salisbury, a certificate might be signed and registered on the same day. It was not uncommon, however, for several weeks, months, and in one case (**628**) nearly three years to elapse between the two dates. To what extent such delays were the fault of an inefficient registrar is not clear; in some cases the certificate may not have been presented for registration immediately, either on account of a circuitous journey to Salisbury, or because of a postponement in the opening of a meeting house. Occasionally the date from which the certificate was to take effect was also stipulated (e.g. **1485, 1488**). In six instances (**342, 343, 623, 1121, 1405, 1422**) the date of registration appears to precede the signing date, and clearly one or other date must be wrong.

Certificates submitted to quarter sessions may also carry two dates, the date of signing and the date of the sessions. In many cases, however, only one date is present, and some documents carry no date at all. If still enrolled on the appropriate great roll the lack of a date presents no problem (e.g. **14–22, 31–4**), but once detached from their context such certificates cannot be securely dated (**44–6, 94, 173, 207, 210–1, 242, 262–3, 274**). Many certificates submitted to the bishop after 1842 carry only the date of signing, the registrar adding the date of registration only intermittently.

Four elements are commonly present in the description of the premises: the type of building; its ownership and/or occupier; the parish in which it was situated; a more precise location within the parish. Some certificates, however, reveal only the type of building and the parish, and in one instance (**149**) even the parish name has been omitted. Stalwart nonconformists may perhaps be excused a certain haziness about parish boundaries; very commonly a chapelry or township is incorrectly described as a parish, in one instance (**779**) the writer of the certificate admits his uncertainty, and several places are assigned to the wrong parishes (e.g. **500, 547, 1005**). Such errors did not always go uncorrected. A certificate for a house at Lockeridge in Fyfield (**857**) was rewritten three weeks later with the correct parish, Overton, substituted (**859**). Even more conscientious was Joshua Russell, who in 1840 misspelled Snarlton Lane, Melksham, and a week later sent a further half-crown and a fresh certificate to correct his mistake (**1552, 1554**). Fortunately, very few place-names cannot be identified with certainty. The homonymous pairs of Bishopstones and Charltons may sometimes be distinguished by examining process notes (**931, 1181**), and the enigmatic 'Chitton' (**1286**) can be shown to be Chittoe. 'Mounton' (**136**) and 'Purton Dorset' (**1584**) remain problematical.

By contrast some premises are described in great detail, as in a title deed. Such precision is a trait of Marlborough certificates (**233, 232, 233, 760, 1034**), although it occurs also at Sherston (**1131**) and Sopworth (**1132**). One late Marlborough certificate (**1618**) gives the house number within the street.

Apart from the signatures and the denominations, which are discussed below, a few further points about the form of the certificate must be noted. Several documents presented in 1827 and 1828 were written in duplicate (**1172, 1176–7, 1195, 1219–20**), probably in the expectation that the registrar would return one copy as the licence. Printed forms of this period envisage such a procedure. The same thinking may explain a much earlier pair (**243**). In four instances two certificates for different premises have been written on the same paper or parchment (**59/60, 755/6, 943/5, 1000/1**). More importantly, no fewer than 23 documents certify more than one building apiece. The latest (**313**) dates from 1760, and most are earlier than 1710. The exceptional Quaker certificate of 1690 (**24**) cites a total of 22 meeting places. 89 premises altogether, mostly Quaker, are certified by these 23 documents.

*Signing the certificate.* The business of writing a meeting house certificate was very frequently undertaken, not by the occupier or chapel leaders who would sign it, but by another person, lawyer or nonconformist minister, more adept at the skills of writing. In one instance (**972**) a marginal note tells us the fee, 3s 6d, for writing the certificate; in another (**1724**) a solicitor appears to sign as a witness to the signatures. Doubtless the tradition of detailed descriptions found in some Marlborough certificates, noted above, owed much to involvement by the legal profession. For the same reason names are often found to have been spelled differently in the certificate and the signature. Such expert help was clearly needed in many cases, where some or all of the signatories were illiterate. In two extreme examples from Enford (**490, 499**) all six and seven signatories respectively sign with a mark. A certificate from Cricklade (**1328**) carries seven 'signatures' all written by the same hand.[2]

Four early certificates (**24, 53, 100, 262**) were submitted and accepted without a signature. An unsigned certificate in 1828, however, (**1228**) was rejected by the registrar and returned for the sender to sign. Once printed forms were introduced several examples may be found of a certificate signed by someone other than the person named in the text as certifying. Such irregularities are not, however, commonplace. Most certificates were signed by one person, usually the occupier of the premises or a nonconformist minister, or by a small group of individuals, who may be assumed in most cases to be leading members of the congregation. Men's names predominate, but there are numerous examples of women's signatures. Ministers are frequently identified, since they had special obligations under the Toleration Acts, and other signatories might add their occupations, or some other distinction, such as junior, senior, widow, esquire. In many cases equal weight was given to all the signatures, but often one person was regarded as the signatory, and anyone else was described as 'witness.' This practice became prevalent after the introduction of printed forms, since these were couched in a manner that required only a single signature. Three certificates (**449, 831, 1547**) have twenty or more signatures, and a further eighteen, mostly from the period 1785–1812, have more than ten.[3] In two of these instances (**1227, 1232**) the list is not in fact of signatories, but of occupants. Shorter lists of trustees occur in several 19th century certificates.

Few celebrities of more than local interest have found their way into this volume. David Saunders, 'the shepherd of Salisbury Plain,' made famous by Hannah More's book,[4] signed at Littleton Pannell in 1785 (**384**), and in the following year William Cunnington the archaeologist,[5] whose home was at Heytesbury, signed at Sutton Veny (**390**). Both were Independents. Several important figures in late 17th century nonconformist history signed early certificates, including Andrew Gifford (**6, 19**), Benjamin Flower (**28–30**) and Compton South (**22, 144–5**). In the 18th century the missionary activity of John Cennick in the 1740s has left little trace, and his name does not appear on any certificate, but his protégé, Cornelius Winter, signed at Wilcot in 1784 and 1786 (**381, 389**). Charles Maggs, the notable Melksham Wesleyan (**620, 932, 942**) and Samuel Heath, who brought Primitive Methodism to Wiltshire (e.g. **1141, 1143–4**), are two of the many prominent Methodist figures represented.[6]

[2] A similar case, from Basingstoke, Hants., is reproduced by Willis, A.J. *A Hampshire miscellany, 3: Dissenters' meeting house certificates 1702–1844*, 1965, p. 112.
[3] They are **300, 386, 409, 417, 419, 426, 472, 474, 521, 540, 576, 612, 627, 714, 732, 751, 1227, 1232**.
[4] More, H. *The shepherd of Salisbury Plain*. Bath: Binns *ca.* 1810, and later editions.
[5] See Cunnington, R.H. *From antiquary to archaeologist: a biography of William Cunnington 1754–1810*. Princes Risborough: Shire, 1975.
[6] Jones, T.R. *The departed worthy: a narrative of the religious life and labours of Mr Charles Maggs . . .* Alexander Heylin, 1857; Tonks, W.C. *Victory in the villages: the history of the Brinkworth circuit.* Aberdare: 1907.

*Delivering the certificate.* In the 19th century the most active signatories were the nonconformist leaders of Salisbury. William Sanger signed 71 certificates and is mentioned on another seven, between 1810 and 1828. A Methodist or Wesleyan Methodist at first, he began to certify Independent Methodist premises in 1821, but seems to have courted the New Jerusalem church in Salisbury in 1825 (**1145**) and ultimately to have returned to the Wesleyan fold (**1229**). During his apostasy many Wesleyan certificates were signed and presented to the registrar by resident circuit ministers, such as William Gilpin (twenty certificates, 1820–3) and Isaac Bradnack (six certificates. 1825). The Independents also made frequent use of their resident Salisbury minister, John Everett Good, who between 1821 and 1831 signed or delivered 46 certificates. In many instances (e.g. **979, 981, 997**) the presence of his name, as a process note or an endorsement, is the sole indication of the certificate's denomination. The Baptist cause was represented at Salisbury by John Saffery, a notable evangelist,[7] who was involved in ten certificates between 1813 and 1823, and possibly others.

The work of agents such as these, so important during the second and third decades of the 19th century, continued to the close of the period of registration described in this volume; it had probably begun when the bishop's registrar, and hence Salisbury, became the focus of most registration in the 1760s, but it can only be detected in full after 1812. This is because most of the evidence takes the form of marginal notes and endorsements on the original certificates, which before 1812 do not in general survive. Nor was it restricted to Salisbury. After parts of north Wiltshire were transferred to the diocese of Gloucester and Bristol in 1837, Gloucester nonconformist ministers fulfilled the same function for north Wiltshire congregations (**1538–9, 1675, 1734, 1780**). In Salisbury tradesmen as well as ministers might act as agents (**778, 1002, 1121, 1125, 1497**), not necessarily, one suspects, because of a strong nonconformist commitment, but simply as a favour to an acquaintance or a customer.

It is not hard to see the attraction of using an agent. Registration involved payment of a fee (nearly two days' labouring wages after 1812) and there was an understandable reluctance to entrust such a sum to the postal service. The ministers of the several denominations encountered their colleagues at regular meetings, and these, one assumes, afforded opportunities for the safe transmission of certificates, licences and half-crowns. As might be expected, this kind of informal arrangement seldom figures on certificates (**1357**), but another reason for using an agent is much more apparent. This was the fear that a certificate sent directly to the registrar might not receive prompt treatment. The commanding figure of William Sanger to bully the registrar's clerk into meeting a deadline was useful in this respect and was generally successful. Thirteen of Sanger's certificates and eighteen others include marginal notes about timing, and they range from the polite, 'Mr. Sanger will be obliged to Mr. Lush to let him have this in a day or two (**862**),' to the domineering, 'Mr.

---

[7] *VCH, Wilts,* iii, 137.

Lush will let ws have this on Saturday (**913**).' His entreaties were not always obeyed, however (**886**). The use of an agent occasionally led to mistakes, such as assigning a place to the wrong parish (**857/9; 1005/7**), or duplication; in 1818 Sanger certified a chapel at Winterbourne Gunner four weeks after its licence had been issued (**881/7**), and on a day in 1828 the registrar, deliberately or otherwise, licensed the same house in Poulshot twice, having received certificates from two different quarters (**1228/9**).

Agents in Salisbury notwithstanding, many congregations did make use of the postal service, coaches or carriers to take their certificates to Salisbury, and the evidence of process notes and marginalia provides an interesting sidelight on the problems of rural communications before the development of an efficient postal network. Until the 1830s there is little evidence that the official postal service was used to any great extent. It is mentioned in only one 18th century certificate (**280**); between 1760 and 1812, as noted above, such evidence would not survive, but even thereafter references to the post are very few. One problem was that it did not serve every village; the congregation at Upton Scudamore, for instance, had to arrange for their licence to be left in Warminster (**1338**). After 1830 postmarks occur more frequently, and postage stamps and money orders might be used to pay for registration (**1706, 1721–2**). Hitherto the network of common carriers was perhaps regarded as a more trustworthy means of transmitting money, and it may be significant that Thomas Maffey of Shrewton in 1818 was happy that the licence should be sent by the Sarum post, but he would send the money by the Sarum carrier (**893**).

References to carriers (also described as drovers and newsmen) occur in more than 60 certificates, and coaches and coachmen in a further ten. Most are mentioned in notes written at the time of delivery by the registrar's clerk to remind him who would collect the licence and when, and whether or not the fee had been paid. At least seventeen carriers were recorded, occasionally with a note of their destination or the inn which was their Salisbury terminus. Ten occur only once, but several were used many times. Gould of Donhead delivered eight licences to places in south-west Wiltshire between 1824 and 1831, Silcox from Bath was used twelve times at about the same period for the Trowbridge and Bradford on Avon areas, and 'the Devizes coachman' delivered nine. George George, the Marlborough carrier, was involved in at least fifteen registrations between 1817 and 1832. All but two were for places beyond Marlborough, including Cricklade (**855**), Highworth (**1155**) and Wootton Bassett (**1326**). For these a further journey by another carrier would have been necessary. Carriers appear to have charged 2d (**1289, 1318**) or 4d (**905, 965, 1350**) for their services. They operated weekly, arriving in Salisbury on Monday afternoons, and returning on Tuesday mornings; consequently certificates arriving by a carrier were nearly always registered on a Monday or a Tuesday. Thus a certificate signed at Coate, near Swindon, on Thursday 30th October 1828 (**1239**) had arrived in Marlborough (probably by the Saturday carrier from Swindon)[8] in time for George George to take it to

---

[8] George Alexander in 1830: *Pigot's directory*, 1830, sv. Marlborough.

Salisbury on the following Sunday night and Monday, 2nd–3rd November, and it was registered on Tuesday 4th November. The licence presumably returned to Marlborough on the same day, and was ready for the carrier to take it back to Coate on the following Saturday, 8th November. The entire process need have taken only nine days.

## The Licensing Authorities and their Records

The legislation required that meeting houses should be certified to the relevant bishop, archdeacon or quarter sessions, who would register the certificate and issue a licence. In practice the archdeacons of Sarum and Wiltshire, who between them had jurisdiction over all parishes in Wiltshire except Salisbury and the peculiars, seem never to have acted as registering authorities. The diocesan registrar, in a letter to the Registrar General in 1852 accompanying his return, observed that, 'as no such places have been certified to the Archdeaconry Courts, I have no return to make from them.'[9] A few certificates were in fact addressed to an archdeacon (e.g. **1692**), but were registered with the bishop. In England and Wales 43 archdeaconries reported nil returns in 1852, and in only nine dioceses were archdeacons accustomed to register meeting houses.[1]

Registration by the bishop was normal after 1750, and nearly 80% of known Wiltshire certificates were certified to the bishops of Salisbury. In 1837 parishes in north and north-west Wiltshire lying in the deaneries of Cricklade and Malmesbury were transferred to the diocese of Gloucester and Bristol, whose bishop became, therefore, the appropriate registering authority. Certificates from such places, however, might still be sent to Salisbury, and as late as 1844 the bishop's registrar was licensing meeting houses in parishes over which he no longer had any jurisdiction (**1511, 1596, 1638–9, 1646**). A few Wiltshire places lay in other dioceses. West Wellow, part of which fell in Wiltshire until 1894, was in Winchester diocese, and one certificate has been included (**545B**).[2] Most of Minety formed a detached part of Gloucestershire until 1844, and two of the three certificates found were presented to the bishop of Gloucester (**730, 970, 999B**). They have all been included. Marston Meysey, a Wiltshire parish in Gloucester diocese, appears never to have certified a meeting house. Several parishes or parts of parishes now in Berkshire were formerly detached parts of Wiltshire. They have been included unless specifically described as Berkshire. Kingswood, a detached part of Wiltshire near Wootton-under-Edge in Gloucestershire, has also been included, as has Shalbourne, most of which lay in Berkshire until 1895. Other border parishes,

---

[9] PRO RG31/4, archdeaconries of Sarum and Wiltshire. Printed in *List of returns . . .* 1853, p. 21.
[1] *List of returns . . .* 1853. Paradoxically Salisbury was one of the nine, as the archdeaconry of Dorset (transferred from Bristol in 1836) had registered meeting houses.
[2] It has been published before, in Willis, *op. cit.* p. 130. A later certificate for the same place, described in PRO RG31/5 as being in Hampshire, has been omitted.

formerly in neighbouring counties and not in Salisbury diocese (e.g. Kilmington) have not been considered.

Some 48 Wiltshire places lay in sixteen peculiar jurisdictions.[3] Four of these, the Prebend of Chute and Chisenbury, the Dean and Chapter, the Precentor and the Treasurer, have preserved certificates or registrations, 24 in all. All but two date from the period 1790–1810 (**23, 315**). Their competence to license meeting houses is doubtful. Peculiars were not mentioned in the 1689 act, and no return of registrations was asked of them in 1852. Before 1790 and after 1810 places in their jurisdiction were licensed by the bishop, as indeed were places in other peculiars at all times. A certificate of 1790 (**420**) was registered by both the bishop and the relevant peculiar, and another (**654**), of 1807, was addressed to the peculiar but registered by the bishop.

With only five exceptions (**23, 233, 252–3, 284**) all surviving certificates registered before 1750 were presented to Wiltshire quarter sessions. As might be expected early nonconformists found it more palatable to seek the magistrates' rather than the bishop's approval for their religious meetings. But quarter sessions met only four times a year, and so a delay of up to three months might occur before registration could take place. It has been suggested that convenience – the possibility of immediate registration on demand – prompted the unpalatable switch from quarter sessions to the bishop in the 18th century.[4] No quarter sessions certificates have been found between 1745 (**304**) and 1784 (**377**), and very few thereafter. In addition to the county quarter sessions Devizes, Marlborough and Salisbury held their own sessions, and could therefore register meeting houses. Salisbury responded to the Registrar General's enquiry in 1852 with a nil return, and no protestant meeting house registrations have been discovered.[5] No records of the Devizes quarter sessions before 1842 survive, but a single registration of 1792 was reported to the Registrar General (**434**). Devizes alone of the twenty Wiltshire boroughs asked to complete the 1852 return responded positively. All the others replied with a nil return. Marlborough, however, which was one of these, had in fact registered three certificates at its court of quarter sessions, and these survive (**233, 252–3**).

*Documents among Wiltshire quarter sessions records.* For the first decade of registration, 1689–99, most certificates remain enrolled on the appropriate great roll (WRO A1/110). The existence of these certificates, 91 in all, does not appear to have been noticed hitherto. The earliest 22 are all enrolled on the great roll for Trinity sessions, July 1689, the first sessions after the 1689 act had become law. All the great rolls from Trinity 1689 to Michaelmas 1700 (four rolls per annum) have been examined. Most are bundles of files, and in many cases meeting house certificates are found filed with sacrament certificates. Two certificates (**17,21**) have been damaged, with the loss of significant information. Unfamiliarity with the registering procedure may have resulted

---

[3] Stewart, P. *Diocese of Salisbury: guide to the records. . .* : Wiltshire County Council, 1973, pp. 139–40.
[4] Welch, *op. cit..* p. 117.
[5] There is however a Roman Catholic registration dated 11th January 1799.

in the loss of other certificates; the extraordinary Quaker document of 1690 (**24**), which should have been enrolled, was returned to the certifiers and is now with other Quaker records. A process note on the next certificate (**25**) may have been chiding the clerk for this error.

The majority of certificates submitted to quarter sessions, 223 in all, exist now in two bundles, part of WRO A1/250. The order of both has been disturbed, and so context cannot be used to assign firm dates to undated certificates. So far as can be known certificates in the first bundle all date from 1705/6 or earlier; the earliest certificate in the second bundle is dated 1706, and the latest is 1745. Parchment predominates for the earlier documents, but most later certificates are written on paper. Many show signs of having once been filed, and it is possible that other certificates remain to be discovered still filed on great rolls of this period.

No fewer than eight certificates were presented to quarter sessions during the first four months of 1745, but then no more have been found until 1784. Random examination of great rolls throughout the period 1745–84 has not uncovered any certificates, and none was entered in the quarter sessions order book, 1737–54 (WRO A1/160/7), nor the minute books 1745–81 (WRO A1/150/20, A1/150/21). Between 1784 and 1849 26 certificates (excluding Roman Catholic certificates) are known to have been registered by quarter sessions. Nineteen of these have survived, eight filed on great rolls (the latest – **1112** – dates from 1825), and eleven as a third bundle, part of WRO A1/250. The remaining seven, all before 1800, are known only from the quarter sessions minute book, 1782–95 (WRO A1/150/22). This and later books, until the series ends in 1824, have been checked in their entirety (WRO A1/150/23–6). In 1852, in response to the Registrar General's request, the clerk of the peace returned details of 23 protestant certificates, the earliest dating from 1784, and commented: 'All the books of proceedings at the Quarter Session for the county, from 1688 to the present time, were carefully examined, but no entry appears of any certificate having been filed before 1784.'[6] His return was deficient by at least 306 certificates, a salutary warning to users of the statistical tables in the published report. The clerk of the peace retained a copy of his return and the published report (WRO A1/255) alongside copies of annual returns he submitted to the bishop of Salisbury for the years 1815, 1816, 1823 and 1850, and annual returns he received from the bishops of Salisbury and (from 1846) Gloucester and Bristol. These returns are considered below.

*Documents among the records of the bishops of Salisbury.* So far as is known no certificates were presented to the bishop before 1742, and no Wiltshire certificate (except **409**, discussed below) has survived before 1806 (**643**).[7] (Throughout the period 1742–1836, when Berkshire was transferred to Oxford diocese, Wiltshire and Berkshire certificates were treated in exactly the same way, but the following relates only to Wiltshire certificates.) Until 1806/7 certificates appear not to have been retained, but were copied exactly

---

[6] *List of returns* . . . 1853, p. 15.
[7] All the relevant bishops' registers, 1689–1852 (WRO D1/2/24–34) have been examined.

into the bishop's registers. Six occur in the register for 1728–57 (WRO D1/2/26), 50 in the register for 1757–76 (WRO D1/2/27), 61 in the register for 1777–89 (WRO D1/2/28), and no fewer than 199 in the register for 1790–1807 (WRO D1/2/29). Between 1807 and 1812 a few certificates survive, but most (76 altogether) were registered in two parchment books, running from 1807–10 and 1810–12 (WRO D1/9/2/4). The standard of transcription seems to have been quite high, many errors and idiosyncratic spellings being retained in the transcript, underlined to draw attention to the mistake. However, users of this edition must bear in mind that for the period 1750–1812 they are usually seeing the evidence at third hand, rather than the second hand of most of the remainder of the volume. Misreadings of names may occasionally be detected (e.g. **439, 729**); more worrying is the failure to register a Highworth certificate of 1788 (**409**), which appears to have been erroneously returned to the congregation. Only by the accident that it has been reproduced in facsimile in a publication has it been included here, since it is not in a record office.[8]

All certificates known to have been presented to the bishop's registrar after 1812, and a few earlier ones, survive together (WRO D1/9/2/1). This collection, of about 1,000 Wiltshire certificates, forms by far the largest and most important single group calendared in this volume. They have in recent years been unfolded and arranged in order of date of registration, in eight bundles, covering the years 1806–15, 1816–9, 1820–3, 1824–6, 1827–9, 1830–3, 1834–9 and 1840–52. Many have the place-name and date pencilled at the head, and a slip index of places, now in the Wiltshire Record Office, has been compiled. They are generally in good condition, and many, as has already been noted, are on printed forms. A few annual returns of quarter sessions registrations from the clerk of the peace to the bishop are also included. Before 1836 many certificates for Berkshire places, and after 1836 some from Dorset are interspersed with the Wiltshire certificates.

Details of the certificates of this period were entered into two paper books, covering the years 1812–38 and 1838–52, which now form part of WRO D1/9/2/4; they provide a useful check on the completeness of the surviving certificates. Another check is provided by the annual returns of registrations sent by the bishop's registrar to quarter sessions, and surviving for every year 1813–51 among quarter sessions records (WRO A1/255). Copies of some of these annual returns, as well as returns sent to Berkshire quarter sessions, 1815–22, 1828, were kept by the registrar (WRO D1/9/2/2); this bundle also includes a single return from Wiltshire quarter sessions to the bishop, 1822. Finally there exists a copy of the return sent in 1852 to the Registrar General (WRO D1/9/2/3). It begins, as already noted, in 1742, the registrar admitting that he, 'cannot satisfactorily account for the Return containing no entry previous to the year 1742.'[9]

*Documents among the records of the bishops of Gloucester and Bristol.* Apart from

[8] Beck, R.A. *Highworth United Reformed Church: a short history 1777–1977.* 1977, p. 4; and more recently transcribed in Highworth Historical Society *A history of Highworth*, part 1, 1980, pp. 97–8.

[9] *List of returns . . .* 1853, p. 11.

those for Minety (**730, 999B**) described above, no Wiltshire certificates appear to have been presented to the bishop of Gloucester until after the see was amalgamated with Bristol and the deaneries of Cricklade and Malmesbury transferred to it in 1837. Thereafter a total of 50 registrations has been found, but no original certificates.[1] 36 of these were entered into a book among the Gloucester diocesan archives at Gloucester (GRO GDR350), which also has registrations for Gloucestershire places from 1824. The last entry in this book dates from September 1847, and from then until the end of registration in 1852 nothing more has been found among the archives at Gloucester. The deficiency may be made up from two sources, the bishop of Gloucester and Bristol's consistory court's annual returns to Wiltshire quarter sessions, which exist for 1846, 1847, 1850 and 1851 (WRO A1/255) and the 1852 return to the Registrar General (PRO RG31/2). Details of seven registrations, 1850–2, have been preserved in both sources, and a further five in the 1852 return alone.

Two stray Wiltshire registrations (**1667, 1723**) of 1845 and 1849 exist among the Bristol diocesan archives in the Bristol Record Office. The certificates appear to have been sent to the office of the archdeacon of Bristol, and were registered in a miscellaneous volume (BRO EP/A/45/3) alongside many others for Bristol and south Gloucestershire. This volume has been checked in its entirety along with previous and later volumes (BRO EP/A/45/2, EP/A/45/4) for the period 1837–52.

*Other documents.* Of the other record-keeping authorities little more need be said. Only three (**23, 556, 605**) of the 24 certificates known to have been registered by peculiars have survived; the remainder were registered either in the court act books (WRO D24/7, D25/6), subscription books (WRO D26/3) or on their own (WRO D24/2). The return sent by the Registrar General in 1852 to registering authorities for completion was a printed form in eight columns. Completed returns were bound into large volumes which have in recent years been transferred from the General Register Office to the Public Record Office (Chancery Lane), where they comprise part of class RG31. Details of 1,453 Wiltshire certificates were returned,[2] 81% of the total included in this volume; the earliest dates from 1742 (**284**). Only seven (**730, 999B, 1579, 1584, 1717, 1772, 1780**) appear not to have survived either as certificates or registrations among local archives.

## The Incompleteness of the Record

The meeting house certificates and registrations calendared in this volume do not represent the total number of meeting houses certified in Wiltshire between 1689 and 1852, still less do they describe every building used for nonconformist worship during this period. This can be proved by comparing the known certificates with extant (or recently extant) datable chapels. An

---

[1] A bundle of certificates, 1784–1838, (GRO N2/1) includes none from Wiltshire.
[2] According to the *List of returns . . .* 1853.

architectural description of Wiltshire published in 1963 lists at least ten precisely dated chapels to which no certificate appears to correspond.[3] In view of their vulnerability these survivors must be regarded as only a proportion (and probably a small proportion) of the total of apparently uncertified chapels which has existed.

One reason for incompleteness may be that certain congregations never in fact certified their premises, either, like the Moravians,[4] on grounds of principle, or because there was no necessity to do so. Under the 1689 act, as we have seen, registration was not compulsory, although failure to register exposed a congregation to the force of earlier statutes; after 1812 registration was compulsory, but only for gatherings in excess of twenty people.

A second explanation is the fallibility of those operating the registration system. Two certificates (**24, 409**), potentially lost through human error, have already been cited; a third seems to be hinted at in the note, 'also one for Steple Ashton,' appended to a certificate of 1828 (**1247**). As further nonconformist deposits come into record offices, and as more research is carried out on nonconformist records in general, stray certificates may come to light.

A third, and potentially far more serious, reason for incompleteness is that whole collections of documents may have been lost, destroyed, or never properly kept. Most worrying are the absence of any registrations among the bishops of Salisbury's records before 1742, and the abrupt break in the quarter sessions sequence in 1745. There may, of course, have been a deliberate decision on the part of the two authorities to refer from one to the other all nonconformist registration at these dates. In Ely diocese a complaint in 1761 led to an instruction that no more licences were to be granted without express orders from the bishop, and, 'to tell such people as apply to the bishop's office for licences for meeting houses, to apply to the justices at the quarter sessions.'[5] Perhaps the bishop of Salisbury's registrar obeyed a similar instruction until 1742, about which we know nothing. But if this was not the case, then some early certificates could have been lost. The neighbouring diocese of Winchester had registered 98 meeting houses before 1740, and Gloucester diocese had registered 35.[6] On the other hand Salisbury diocese was not the only late starter: Exeter returned no registrations before 1730, and only nineteen before 1780; Peterborough diocese appears to have begun registering only in the 1770s; only one Staffordshire meeting house, so far as is known, was certified to an ecclesiastical court before 1791.[7] The bishop of Salisbury's registers are

---

[3] Pevsner, N. *Wiltshire.* Harmondsworth: Penguin, 1963. The ten are Bradenstoke 1777, Calne 1836, Chapmanslade 1788, East Tytherton 1745, Ford (in North Wraxall) 1815, Hindon 1810, Lacock 1783, Malmesbury 1802, Staverton 1824 and Wootton Bassett 1838. Others could be added to this list using *VCH, Wilts.*

[4] Welch, *op. cit.* p. 118

[5] PRO RG31/2 Ely diocese.

[6] PRO RG31/5 Winchester diocese; PRO RG31/2 Gloucester diocese. The Winchester certificates have been printed in Willis, *op. cit.*

[7] PRO RG31/2 Exeter diocese; PRO RG31/4 Peterborough diocese; Donaldson, B. *The registrations of dissenting chapels and meeting houses in Staffordshire 1689–1852*, Staffs. Record Soc., 4th series, vol. 3, 1960, p. xxiii.

complete throughout the period of possible registration, and it is in these that the earliest registrations occur. If meeting houses were certified to the bishop before 1742, either no details were kept, or a separate register was maintained which has since been lost. Both these possibilities would seem to be unlikely, since registration was a requirement imposed on the registrar in the 1689 act, and the records of the bishops of Salisbury have in general been well kept; probably therefore, no records have been lost in this way.

The records of quarter sessions are a different matter. The sequence ends suddenly in 1745, no copy was made in order or minute books of the certificates which survive, and even the survivors had been mislaid at the time of the 1852 return. Suspicions are confirmed by the existence of the licence (**309**) of 1756 for which no certificate survives, either as part of a bundle or filed on the relevant great roll. The most likely explanation is that a bundle of certificates, beginning *ca.* 1745 and ending before 1784, has been lost. If this has happened, only a vague estimate of the number of documents involved can be attempted. At the national level there can be no doubt that the trend in the mid-18th century was veering away from quarter sessions towards the ecclesiastical courts. The intermittent and infrequent use made of Wiltshire sessions in the 1780s and later may have continued a practice begun in 1760 or even earlier. Oxfordshire quarter sessions returned only one registration in the 1750s and none at all in the 1760s or 1770s; Somerset returned over one hundred between 1750 and 1759, thereafter the decadal totals to 1800 were 40, four, five, three.[8] The national totals of registrations by all authorities, according to the 1852 returns, suggests that the nadir was reached between 1720 and 1770;[9] comparison with Wiltshire registrations suggests that at most periods Wiltshire corresponds quite closely with the national trend, and that the shortfall between 1745 and 1784 may be fairly small. A reasonable estimate of the number of quarter sessions certificates lost might be between ten and 40, or 0.5% − 2.0% of those surviving.

It may be reasonably assumed that no major collections of certificates or registrations are absent from this volume. A few may have perished with the borough records or peculiars, or may remain to be found; some have been lost at Gloucester, but these are known from the 1852 return. All things considered this volume probably comprises details of at least 95%, and perhaps 99% of all certificates ever presented for Wiltshire meeting houses.

### The Dissenters and their Premises

An eloquent and perceptive account of the history of Wiltshire nonconformity has already been published.[1] The comments which follow are restricted to

---

[8] PRO RG31/7 Oxfordshire and Somerset.
[9] Summarised in Gilbert, A.D. *Religion and society in industrial England,* Longman, 1976, p. 34. It should be borne in mind, of course, that the statistics are derived from the very class of records that we are showing to be defective, and so the argument is in a sense circular.
[1] Reeves, M. 'Protestant nonconformity,' in *VCH, Wilts,* iii, 99–149.

statistical and geographical matters which meeting house certificates serve to illustrate, and to miscellaneous observations derived from them.

Dissent touched every part of Wiltshire, and no area was devoid of certified meeting houses. 42 of the county's 312 ancient parishes, however, are not represented in this volume.[2] Most were very small, and have since disappeared as administrative units; five are no longer in Wiltshire. Nevertheless fourteen parishes with populations (in 1811) in excess of 150 appear to have had no meeting houses between 1689 and 1852.[3] Six of these lay in the extreme north of the county, and four more in the Marlborough-Pewsey area. Most seem to fall into the classic 'closed village' mould,[4] in which all or nearly all the land belonged to a single owner; such squirearchies might not welcome the dissenting evangelists. By contrast 'open villages' comprising many small freeholders, and parishes which included several distinct settlements remote from the parish church, tended to be more favourably disposed towards nonconformity. At Stratton St Margaret in 1744 the inconvenience of a long walk to church was made the excuse for certifying a meeting house (**292**). The ancient parish of Downton, of nearly 12,500 acres and many small owners, figures in 40 certificates; other examples of a disproportionately large number are Brinkworth, the Donheads, Highworth, Kington St Michael and East Knoyle. Brinkworth is interesting as an example of a village which twice witnessed a nonconformist awakening. Proselytised by Presbyterians, Quakers, Independents and Moravians in the 18th century and before, it became a hotbed of dissent. 'Our parish a few years ago swarmed with sectaries,' wrote the rector in 1783, 'at present they are few in number.'[5] But 40 years later Brinkworth became the centre of Primitive Methodist activity for an area extending over much of Wiltshire and neighbouring counties.[6] A particularly noticeable feature is the prominence in nonconformist life of villages – many of them not separate parishes – close to towns. Thus Crockerton (in Longbridge Deverill), near Warminster, Quidhampton (in Fugglestone St Peter) between Salisbury and Wilton, Ogbourne St George near Marlborough, Westport St Mary on the outskirts of Malmesbury, Seend (in Melksham) between Melksham and Devizes, Bratton (in Westbury), and Southwick (in North Bradley), close to Trowbridge.

Meeting house certificates are not a good indicator of nonconformist adherence, but they do offer some of the best evidence available for nonconformist evangelism. They therefore portray the 'active' side of nonconformity and may be compared with the 'passive' side, depicted in censuses of nonconformist allegiance in 1676, 1829 and 1851. For instance, there was no

[2] Based on tables in *VCH, Wilts*, iv, 339–61.
[3] In order of size (most populous first): Kemble, Mildenhall, Stourton, Latton, Compton Chamberlayne, Bishopstrow, Manningford Bruce, Long Newnton, Stanton Fitzwarren, Marston Meysey, Ham, Marden, Eisey, Draycot Cerne.
[4] e.g. Latton and Marden: see *Abstracts of Wiltshire inclosure awards and agreements*, ed R.E. Sandell, Wilts. Record Soc., vol. 25, pp. 92, 38–9.
[5] *Wiltshire returns to the bishop's visitation queries 1783*, ed M. Ransome, Wilts. Record Soc. vol. 27, 1972, p. 45.
[6] Tonks, *op. cit.*

procedure for de-registration, but clearly many of the certificates for dwelling-houses foreshadowed chapel building; when the chapel opened the dwelling-house was no longer required for worship. In March 1851, according to the ecclesiastical census, there were 372 nonconformist meeting houses in Wilt-shire (excluding Roman Catholics), or about 20% of the total number of premises (1,839) which we know to have been registered up to that date.[7] In very crude terms, therefore, four out of every five buildings certified were no longer being used for worship in 1851. Returns to an enquiry about noncon-formity in 1829, which survive in the Wiltshire Record Office,[8] enable us to explore this pattern of wastage further, before the evangelical revival of the 18th and early 19th centuries had begun to subside. Comparison between these returns and the documents calendared here confirms that licensed dwelling-houses were ephemeral, but purpose-built chapels were more permanent. In Malmesbury hundred, for example, twelve chapels and nine licensed houses were used for worship in 1829, whereas only eleven chapels but 73 houses are known to have been licensed. The pattern is repeated elsewhere: in Selkley hundred (around Marlborough) three chapels and five houses were in use, but six chapels and 41 houses had been licensed.

The chronological arrangement employed in this volume permits us to gauge the pace of registration and to compare it with national trends. From a peak of about ten around 1700 yearly registrations fell erratically to almost nil in 1760, but then climbed steadily to attain about twenty in 1800 and 35 around 1825, sliding dramatically thereafter, to about ten by 1850. The Wiltshire totals follow national trends fairly closely, generally representing slightly less than one-twentieth of the total for England and Wales. But there are three anomalies: between 1695 and 1745 Wiltshire forms a considerably larger proportion than one-twentieth (perhaps nearly one-twelfth between 1695 and 1705) – this is possibly accounted for by defects in the national totals derived from the 1852 return. Between 1745 and 1775 Wiltshire dips more emphatical-ly than the national figure; it is suggested above that some Wiltshire certificates have been lost at this period. The third anomaly occurs between 1798 and 1800, when far more meeting houses were registered than might be expected. The reason for this – a pamphlet controversy which led to fears that registration would be curtailed – has been well described.[9]

The denominations of rather more than three-quarters of the certificates are known or may be surmised, and there are few surprises. Most belong either to the so-called 'old dissent,' the 'new dissent,' or Methodism.

The old dissenting tradition, represented by Presbyterians, Quakers and Baptists, had a near-monopoly of assignable certificates before 1750, some 200

[7] *Report on the census of religious worship in England and Wales, 1851*, 1853 (1852/3, ch.lxxxix), pp. 47–9. The total of 1,839 is achieved by allowing for certificates which include more than one meeting house, but subtracting those certified after 30th March 1851.

[8] WRO A1/752. Wiltshire is apparently one of the few counties for which these returns exist.

[9] Jeremy, D.J. 'A local crisis between establishment and nonconformity: the Salisbury village preaching controversy, 1798–1799,' in *Wilts. archaeological and natural history magazine*, vol. 61, 1966, pp. 63–84.

divided fairly equally between them. Geographically they were concentrated in areas of Wiltshire where nonconformity had been strong before toleration,[1] in and around the west Wiltshire manufacturing towns, with outlying clusters in and to the west of Salisbury, around Marlborough, and between Malmesbury and Wootton Bassett. Salisbury Plain, the Vale of Pewsey and the Marlborough Downs are hardly represented. By 1750 the old dissenting tradition had almost burnt itself out. Only four Quaker and three Presbyterian certificates occur between 1750 and 1800, and none thereafter. The Baptists appear to continue unabated, although the simple term 'Baptist' applied to certificates before and after 1750 masks a serious doctrinal rift, the Baptists of the old dissent veering towards Arminian or General Baptist principles, and in some cases to Unitarianism, the new dissenting Baptists more Calvinist in outlook, often describing themselves as Particular Baptists.

The main thrust of chapel building and evangelism in the fifty years after 1770 lay with the Independents and the Methodists. The Independents (or Congregationalists – now usually United Reformed) were in a sense successors to the old Presbyterian tradition. In all nearly 400 certificates may be assigned to them, most dating 1770–1820, but with substantial numbers before and after. They cast their net more widely than their predecessors, but were still noticeably fewer in the Swindon-Marlborough-Ludgershall areas, on Salisbury Plain and in the extreme south-east, around Downton. Their progress was mirrored by the Baptists, with about one hundred certificates between 1770 and 1820. The areas covered were much the same, although evangelising groups in Melksham, Shrewton and Downton resulted in clusters of certificates in these areas. In a few instances (**612, 623, 640, 644, 682, 736, 761**) Baptists and Independents jointly certified a meeting house.

The first Methodist registration occurred for Bradford on Avon in 1756 (**309**), and by 1800 45 are known; but Methodism's main impetus came in the 19th century, with more than 500 assignable certificates of all Methodist persuasions. Arminian and Calvinistic Methodists certified in 1808–9 (**666, 669, 670**), and from 1817 the appellation 'Wesleyan' began to appear (**862**) to distinguish the mainstream connexion from its factions. Of these the Independent Methodists (sometimes described as Tent Methodists), who registered 25 meeting houses between 1821 and 1825, and two 1840/2, and the Primitive Methodists (181 certificates from 1825 onwards) were the most important. The Wesleyans were most active between 1810 and 1830, evangelising a great tract of country from Warminster and Bradford on Avon in the west, through Devizes and the Vale of Pewsey to the Marlborough-Swindon area in the east, with a second centre of activity around Salisbury and the south-east corner. After 1830 the limelight was stolen by the Primitive Methodists, who from bases in Brinkworth, Chippenham, Wootton Bassett and Salisbury tackled the remainder of Wiltshire, the northern clayland villages and the north-east, the

---

[1] Deduced from a list of conventicles in 1669 (Wiltshire portion printed by Webb, E.D. in *Transactions of the Salisbury Field Club*, vol. 1, 1890–3, pp. 36–44); the indulgence licences of 1672 (printed here as an appendix); and the Compton census of 1676 (Wiltshire portion printed by Ruddle, C.S. in *Wilts. notes and queries*, vol. 3, 1901, pp. 535–8).

Savernake-Chute eastern fringe, the valleys west of Salisbury, and a foray into the industrial west.

Apart from the main dissenting traditions, a number of smaller sects may be identified, including the Sandemanians in Trowbridge (**335**), Peculiar Calvinists in Marlborough (**649**), 'New Lights' in Westbury (**854**), New Jerusalemites in Salisbury (**1145, 1221, 1277, 1414, 1452, 1557, 1657**), and a Catholic Apostolic group in Melksham (**1445**). The Mormons appear to have registered anonymously at least nine meeting houses between 1845 and 1850 (**1673–1745,** *passim*), giving point to the bishop of Salisbury's remarks quoted earlier. Of the 407 certificates to which no denomination has been assigned, a number might be identifiable through detailed local or denominational knowledge; they may include the five Plymouth Brethren communities returned in the 1851 census. Doubtless a proportion offered allegiance to no denomination, such as those planted by the Marlborough ironmonger and non-denominational evangelist Joseph Phelps between 1837 and 1850,[2] or the Salisbury Temperance Society, who certified their premises in 1845 (**1668**). A group in Bradford on Avon went so far as to certify a room for use 'by persons protestant and not dissenting from the established church.' (**1070**). And what are we to make of the bishop's assertion that Socialist groups registered their meeting places under the guise of protestant dissenters? If this is true many of the unassigned certificates of the late 1830s and 1840s might in fact belong to Chartists. Indeed one Trowbridge certificate of 1839 (**1536**) corresponds to the so-called 'Democratic Chapel' allegedly licensed for the Chartists;[3] six weeks later a room was certified in Bradford on Avon (**1541**) by Gideon Allen, a leading figure in the Bradford Working Men's Association.[4]

The number of occupations mentioned in the certificates (about 200, excluding carriers) is far too small to draw any conclusion about the social groups from which adherents were recruited, except to note a good mixture, of labourers and farmers, schoolmasters and carpenters, shepherds and clothiers. This diversity is reflected too in some of the premises which were registered. Most were described simply as houses, dwellinghouses or chapels, with a number of barns, schoolrooms and inns. Sometimes individual rooms within a building were specified (e.g. **189, 410, 523**), or adjoining buildings, such as outhouses, workshops and yards. In the case of a chapel a certificate might name also the burying ground (**563, 575, 1643**) or the vestry (**642, 1267**). Industrial premises of various kinds were also brought into use as makeshift meeting houses, including malthouses (**238, 413, 939, 1075**), a brewery (**1073**), a warehouse (**1105**) and a silkhouse (**1268**), as well as premises adjoining a papermill (**365**), a slaughterhouse (**344**), a factory (**999A**) and a stable (**1469**). When a congregation had outgrown a private house but had no chapel a hall might be taken over for worship, such as the Shoemakers' Hall in Salisbury (**310**), Trowbridge barracks (**984**), or Salisbury Masonic Hall (**1443**); even Marlborough Town Hall was commandeered (**248**). Meetings out of doors or in tents might also be certified, in fields (**888, 1044**), an orchard (**1040**) and a

---

[2] *VCH, Wilts*, xii, 159. He earlier signed as a Methodist (**941**) and a Primitive Methodist (**1379**).
[3] R.B. Pugh in *Chartist Studies* ed. A. Briggs, 1959, p. 192.
[4] *VCH, Wilts*. vii, 11.

garden (**1041**). Perhaps the most unlikely place to find in use as a licensed meeting house was a parsonage house, certified by Methodists at Whiteparish in 1798 (**508**).

The process of building or acquiring a meeting house is occasionally illuminated by these documents. An existing building might be fitted up for religious use (**370, 571**); or a new building might be certified even before possession had been taken from the contractor (**1776**). Extensions to an existing chapel might require that a new licence be obtained (**426, 1492**), and while the meeting house was being repaired alternative premises might be needed (**307**). Several congregations found a disused meeting house which had been built for a different denomination, and took it over for their own use (e.g. **575, 1149, 1566**); this practice occurred as early as 1728 (**254**). The most spectacular example of re-use (if indeed all the references are to the same place) is the suite of rooms attached to the George Inn, Salisbury. Licensed for Baptists in 1817 (**853**), the Tent Methodists had it in 1823 (**1053**), it accommodated the New Jerusalem Church in 1825 (**1145**), the Primitive Methodists in 1829 (**1262**), the New Jerusalemites again in 1836 and 1840 (**1452, 1557**), and finally the Mormons in 1850 (**1735**).

## Editorial Method

In calendaring these documents all significant information and, so far as is possible, the character of the original, has been retained, whilst the details have been rearranged in a consistent order eliminating common form. In general the guidelines for editors laid down by Dr. Hunnisett have been followed;[5] but instead of appearing as footnotes annotations have been consigned to square brackets immediately after the information to which they relate. Where both certificate and registration survive the certificate has been used; where the certificate has been lost the registration has been used in preference to the annual or 1852 return; in a few cases where both certificate and registration are missing the annual and the 1852 returns if both exist have been cited with a note of discrepancies between them. The only Wiltshire meeting-house certificates and registrations intentionally omitted from this edition are those relating to Roman Catholics, those relating to a few places formerly in another county (described above), and those submitted to the Registrar General under the legislation of 1837, 1852 and later. The parts of the entry are described below in the order of citation.

*Dates, and ordering of entries.* All dates are cited according to new style reckoning. A date not enclosed in brackets is one which appears on the certificate (or registered copy) as the date of signing. A date in round brackets is the date of registration or the issue of a licence. Many certificates do not carry the latter; some have only the date of registration, or none at all. Where

---

[5] Hunnisett, R.F. *Editing records for publication*, British Records Association, 1977; *Indexing for editors*, British Records Association, 1972.

there is none an approximate date has been supplied in square brackets, based on the context in which the document was discovered. The reasoning may be apparent from the source (e.g. a document enrolled on WRO A1/110 T1689, the great roll for Trinity sessions, 1689, is likely to date from July 1689) or it may be explained after the date. Entries are arranged in a single numerical sequence in chronological order of signing. Two or more entries bearing the same date are arranged in alphabetical order of place. Late discoveries have been inserted in their correct places with a suffix (e.g. **999A, 999B**). A notable group of eight certificates (**77B–77J**), all presented to Easter 1699 Quarter Sessions, was discovered by chance at a late stage when a guard-book entitled 'Wiltshire Records' compiled by C.R. Everett (died 1945) was transferrred to the Wiltshire Record Office from the prints and drawings collection of the Wiltshire Archaeological & Natural History Society in April 1985. The collection was found to contain various Quarter Sessions documents, including eight meeting house certificates, which have now been replaced in their original context on the appropriate great roll. Impossible dates, where registration appears to precede certification, have been retained, but '[*sic*]' has been added after the date of registration.

*Place, and description of premises.* After the date comes the statement of place. This may be an ancient parish or smaller settlement – township, chapelry, tithing – within a parish, or an extra-parochial place. Ecclesiastical parishes within towns are not specified at this point. If the place was extra-parochial, that fact is noted, in square brackets if not stated in the document. Townships, chapelries and tithings are followed by the names of the ancient parishes in which they lay, as stated in the document. If the document gives no parish, or wrongly describes a place as a parish, or gives an incorrect parish, the correct ancient parish is supplied, queried in cases of doubt. The current forms of place-names are used in the text,[6] but all variants are recorded in the index entries. Interesting and unusual forms, however, follow the modern names in round brackets. In the case of ambiguous place-names (e.g. 'Donhead,' 'Codford') both alternatives are given; if there are three or more possibilities no attempt is made to identify which is correct, but if there are good reasons for preferring one to the others this is given, with a query. Unidentifiable place-names are left as found, enclosed within inverted commas. Homonymous places are identified where possible. If the document was signed in another parish this fact is noted.

After the place statement the description of the premises is given. Spelling and punctuation have been modernised and made consistent, redundant words and phrases have been omitted, and occasionally a sentence has been re-ordered for the sake of economy or to improve the sense. The description of the premises may include personal names, such as the owner, occupier or trustees. The spelling of surnames is retained, even if spelled differently elsewhere on the same document. The description may also include a more precise address than that given in the place statement; the spelling of street

---

[6] Authorities: *The place-names of Wiltshire* (English Place-Name Society), 1939; *VCH, Wilts.* iv, 339–61.

names, minor names and urban parishes has been modernised where iden-
tification is not in question. Most certificates continue by describing the
legislation which gave rise to their existence; this and other common form has
been omitted, but more interesting or eccentric formulae have been included.

*Denomination.* Some certificates give the denomination of the meeting
house. Others ascribe a denomination to one or more signatories, and in some
cases the denomination is apparent from a contemporary process note or
endorsement (e.g. 'Revd. G. Gillard, Methodist Chapel, Salisbury'). In all
such cases (some 45% of the total) the denomination is printed without
brackets. Spelling of the names of denominations has been standardised, but a
few interesting or unusual forms have been preserved. By comparing the
signatories of other, more explicit, certificates it is often possible to establish
the denominational allegiance of individuals, and hence of all the certificates
they sign. In such cases the denomination is supplied, queried where appropriate, with a reference to another certificate. The affiliation of several hundred
certificates has been established in this way. In cases where one of the
following names whose allegiance is well known occur the denomination is
given in square brackets followed by an asterisk: Isaac Bradnack (Wesleyan
Methodist); George Gillard (Methodist); William Gilpin (Wesleyan Methodist); John Everett Good (Independent); John Saffery (Baptist); William Sanger
(Methodist, Independent Methodist, see above p. xix); Mr. Thring of Wilton
(Independent, probably James Thring). Other denominations have been
identified from published local and denominational histories and archival
sources. These are followed by an abbreviated reference. It must however be
emphasised that supplied denominations are not part of the original documents
and should not necessarily be trusted.

*Signatures.* After the denomination statement (or after the description of
premises if no denomination is given) follow the signatures. These may be
found in an orderly list or may occur haphazardly. In the former case the order
is preserved in the calendar, but elsewhere the most prominent signatures are
printed first, and the others in no particular order. If only the registration
survives the copyist's order is preserved. Common forenames have been
standardised, but surnames are spelled as they occur in the documents; variant
spellings are however grouped together in the index. Illegible or partially
illegible names are denoted by a query, a series of dots, or both; illiteracy is
signified by 'the mark of . . .' Signatures are often qualified, either by a word
such as junior, widow, esquire, or by an occupation or a place of residence.
These are all (except the word 'witness') included, but spelling, punctuation
and order of words may be modified, and there is one important exception.
Quite a common formula following the signatures is 'housekeepers (or
inhabitants) dwelling in the parish of . . .' Such information has been included.
But often the formula runs 'housekeepers (or inhabitants) dwelling in or near
the parish of . . .' The addition of 'or near' renders the information useless,
since it would be reasonable to assume that the congregation of any meeting
house was drawn from the immediately surrounding area. In such cases the
information has been omitted.

*Process and other notes, and sources.* Following the signatures may be placed information of a very miscellaneous nature. All significant marginal notes and endorsements are recorded here, transcribed as found, within inverted commas and with an indication of where on the document they occur. Peculiarities of the document itself, or its relationship with other documents, are noted. Finally, in round brackets, is given the source, or location of the document calendared. With one exception the document is in a record office, and the appropriate bundle or piece number is given. A list of all the classes of documents used is given below.

# SOURCES AND ABBREVIATIONS

*Manuscript sources*
BRO (Bristol Record Office),
    EP/A/45/3, registrations
GRO (Gloucestershire Record Office),
    GDR350, registrations
PRO (Public Record Office, Chancery Lane),
    RG31/2, 1852 return
    RG31/4, 1852 return
    RG31/5, 1852 return
    RG31/7, 1852 return
    RG31/8, 1852 return
WRO (Wiltshire Record Office)
    854/14, certificate
    1103/42, licence
    A1/110, certificates
    A1/150/22, registrations
    A1/250, certificates
    A1/255, annual returns
    D1/2/26, registrations
    D1/2/27, registrations
    D1/2/28, registrations
    D1/2/29, registrations
    D1/9/2/1, certificates
    D1/9/2/2, annual returns
    D1/9/2/4, registrations
    D7/2, certificate
    D24/2, certificates or registration (see p.xxv)
    D24/7, registrations
    D25/6, registrations
    D26/3, registrations
    G22/1/122 certificate
    G22/1/123 certificate
    G22/1/124 certificate

*Published secondary works*

Antrobus, A. *History of the Wilts. and East Somerset Congregational Union prepared for the triple jubilee, 1797–1947*, 1947
Atley, H. *A topographical account of Market Lavington, Wilts, its past and present condition. . . ,* 1855

Beck, R.A. *Highworth United Reformed Church: a short history, 1777–1977*, 1977

Blackford, J.H. *The manor and village of Cherhill. . .* , 1941

Cooper, F.W. *Broughton Road Baptist Church, Melksham, founded 1669: a short history*, 1970

Davis, H.E. *A history of Bromham*, 1965 [typescript]

Doel, W. *Twenty golden candlesticks! or a history of Baptist nonconformity in western Wiltshire*, 1890

Gordon, A. *Freedom after ejection: a review (1690–1692) of Presbyterian and Congregational nonconformity in England and Wales*, 1917

Gunn, H.M. *History of nonconformity in Warminster*, 1853

Hall, J. *The Wesleyan Methodist itinerancy. . .* , 1873

Haynes, J.J. *The beginnings of Congregationalism at Ebbesbourne*, 1953

HOOCCW. *History of the Old Congregational Church, . . . Westbury, Wilts*, 1875

HPCURCS. *A history of the Presbyterian Congregational United Reformed Church in Salisbury, 1662–1978*, 1979

Jones, T.R. *The departed worthy: a narrative of the religious life and labours of Mr. Charles Maggs. . .* , 1857

Miles, E. *Tisbury (past and present)*; 2nd ed, 1920

Murch, J. *A history of the Presbyterian and General Baptist Churches in the west of England. . .* , 1835

Oliver, R.W. *The Strict Baptist Chapels of England, vol. 5. the chapels of Wiltshire and the west. . .* , 1968

Rogers, K.H. *The book of Trowbridge*, 1984

Sheard, N. *The history of Hindon*, 1979

Stribling, S.B. *History of the Wilts and East Somerset Congregational Union for the century after its commencement, 1797–1897*, 1897

Tonks, W.C. *Victory in the villages: the history of the Brinkworth Circuit*, 1907

VCH. *Victoria history of Wiltshire*, 1953– in progress

Webb, E.D. 'Conventicles in Sarum diocese, AD 1669,' *Transactions of the Salisbury Field Club*, vol. 1, 1893, 36–44.

WF. *Wiltshire folklife*, 1976– in progress

*Wiltshire register for 1827*, 1827

WNQ. *Wiltshire notes and queries*, 8 vols, 1893–1916

# WILTSHIRE DISSENTERS'
# MEETING HOUSE CERTIFICATES
# AND REGISTRATIONS 1689–1852

**1**   9 July 1689. Ramsbury. Mr Henry Dent of Ramsbury, minister of the gospel, keeps a meeting in the house of John Osbourne alias Carpenter. [*Presbyterian*: VCH 12, 45]. Thomas Knackston, Joseph Mabberly?, John Staples, Jain? Banks, Ambrose Tomson, William Smith, Jacob Noe?, John Ballard junior, Thomas Smith. (WRO A1/110 T1689)

**2**   19 July 1689. Little Ashley in Bradford on Avon. A barn now in the possession of Francis Yerbury. [*Presbyterian*: see **29**. *Unsigned*]. (WRO A1/110 T1689)

**3**   23 July 1689. Erlestoke. The dwellinghouse and barn of John Axford. [*Baptist*: Doel 222]. Edward Froud, John Alldridge. [*At foot*] 'To be reade att Saturday next.' (WRO A1/110 T1689)

**4**   30 July 1689. Market Lavington. The dwellinghouse of Thomas Plank, chandler. [*Presbyterian?*: VCH 3 107 (Flower)]. Thomas Planke, John Bell. [*In another hand*] 'Mr Ben. Flower, att a barne of Frances Yerbury maulster att Little Ashely in the parish of Bradford.' [see **2**]. (WRO A1/110 T1689)

**5**   30 July 1689. Trowbridge. The dwellinghouse of Edward Davis, gent. [*Presbyterian*: Webb]. Baruch Nowell, Jeremiah Wayt, Eliamas Tissan?. [*In another hand*] 'The preacher not known.' [*A note about the Erlestoke meeting (**3**) in a different hand is appended*]. (WRO A1/110 T1689)

**6**   30 July 1689. Trowbridge. The dwellinghouse of Edward Grant, clothier. [*Baptist*: Doel 101]. Richard Collier, Isaac Chanter, Andrew Gifford. (WRO A1/110 T1689)

**7**   30 July 1689. Westbury. The barn of Richard Mattock. [*Baptist*: Doel 93]. Roger Cater, William Humphry, John Belton. (WRO A1/110 T1689)

**8**   31 July 1689. Berwick Bassett [*and elsewhere*]. The dwellinghouse of Mary Goddard in Berwick [*Bassett*], the house of Henry Hammons in Brinkworth and the house of John Daye in Lyneham. [*Presbyterian and Independent*: Webb]. Robert Rowswell, Thomas Lewen. (WRO A1/110 T1689)

**9**   31 July 1689. Castle Combe. A barn of James Organ, clothier. [*Presbyterian?*: Webb]. James Organ, Thomas Berry, John Blake. (WRO A1/110 T1689)

**10**   31 July 1689. Chippenham. An outhouse or barn belonging to Mr Walter Scott. [*Presbyterian*: see **11**]. John Greenwood, William Hobbs. (WRO A1/110 T1689)

**11**   31 July 1689. 'Gouges' in Corsham. A barn. [*Presbyterian*]. Nicholas Gore, William Little. [*A separate sheet following this certificate reads*] 'Mr Flower in Chippenham. Mr Flower, a barne of Walter Scott in Chippenham, a barne in the parish of Corsham at Gorridges.' [*Benjamin Flower of Chippenham was Presbyterian*: VCH 3 107]. (WRO A1/110 T1689)

**12**   31 July 1689. Willesley in Sherston. The dwellinghouse of Alice Francklyn and John Watts. [*Presbyterian*: Gordon 242]. William Conway, Jo[*seph?*] Watts. (WRO A1/110 T1689)

**13**   31 July 1689. Westport St Mary. A house of Mary Smith, widow. [*Presbyterian*: Gordon 242]. William Conway, Thomas Evans. (WRO A1/110 T1689)

**14**   [?July 1689]. Bradford on Avon. The dwellinghouse of the widow Miller. [*Baptist*: Doel 222, Oliver 69]. John Morrell?, Richard Hedly, John Plurett [*preceded by* Florett, *struck through*], preacher. (WRO A1/110 T1689)

**15**   [?July 1689]. Donhead St Andrew (*Nether Dunhead*). A house now in the possession of Robert Grove, esquire. [*Presbyterian*: Webb]. Samuel Wells. (WRO A1/110 T1689)

**16**   [?July 1689]. North Bradley. The barn of Richard Greenhill. [*Baptist*: VCH 8 231 (Lawes)]. John Lawes, Alexander Hillmon. (WRO A1/110 T1689)

**17**   [?July 1689]. Sedgehill and East Knoyle. The houses in the possession of Isaac Hilgrove and Philip . . . ford [*the document is torn and part is missing*] in Sedgehill (*Sedgwell*) and Thomas Williams in East Knoyle. [*Baptist*: Doel 222]. John Williams, John Guyer. (WRO A1/110 T1689)

**18**   [?July 1689]. Tisbury. A house now in the possession of John Fezard. [*Presbyterian*: see **15**]. Samuel Wells. (WRO A1/110 T1689)

**19**   [?July 1689]. Trowbridge. The house of Joseph Houlton senior. [*Baptist*: Doel 101]. Edward Grant, Edward Morttymore, Mr Gifford. (WRO A1/110 T1689)

**20**   [?July 1689]. Upton Lovell (*Loushills Upton*). A house now in the possession of Edmund Moudy. [*Presbyterian?*: Gunn 22]. Christopher Stanshell. (WRO A1/110 T1689)

**21**   [?July 1689]. Warminster. . . . in the possession of Chr . . . [*the document is* *torn and part is missing*]. [*Baptist*: Doel 222]. John Urrill?, John Whereatt. (WRO A1/110 T1689)

**22** [?July 1689]. Warminster. A house now in the possession of John Butler. [*Presbyterian*: Murch 86]. Compton South. (WRO A1/110 T1689)

**23** 3 Aug. 1689. 'Wicke' in Bishops Cannings. A house newly erected in a close called the Quakers burying place. [*Quaker*: WNQ 2, 165]. John Withers, John Clarke senior, Samuel Noyes, Edward Gilbert, William Coole. (WRO D24/2)

**24** 15 Jan. 1690. Charlcote in Bremhill [*and elsewhere*]. The house of the widow Joan Hall at Charlcote in Bremhill, the house called the meeting house in Calne, the house of William Hitchcocke in Marlborough, the house of Margaret Shennione in Purton Stoke [*in Purton*], the house of William Player at Foscote in Grittleton, the house of John Gingall in 'Kinton,' the house called the meeting house in the Green at Devizes, the house called the meeting house in Chippenham, the houses of Hester Marshman and Thomas Bevin in Melksham, the house called the meeting house at Slaughterford in Biddestone (*Slatenford in Bitson*), the house called the meeting house in Bromham, at their respective meeting houses in Lea [*in Lea and Cleverton*] and Brinkworth, the house called the meeting house at Cumberwell (*Comerwell*) in Bradford on Avon, the house of William Smith at Holt in Bradford on Avon, the house of Giles Spicer in Alderbury, the house of Leonard Upjohn in Stapleford, the house of Isaac Selfe in [*Market*] Lavington, the house called the meeting house in Warminster, the house of James Abbott in Fovant, the house called the meeting house at Corsham. [*After most entries in this list is added*] 'or at their respective meeting houses.' Quaker. [*This certificate is unsigned. It appears to have been used as a licence, as it was returned to the certifying congregations.*]. (WRO 854/14)

**25** 15 July 1690. Colerne. The house of Joan Hooke, widow. Zachariah Millerd, Anthony Drewett, Peter Drewett, the mark of Thomas Grinway, Richard Aust?, David Grinway, Obadiah Cheltenham, Henry Jones, Daniel Grinway, John Jones. [*In a different hand*] 'Draw a certificate of this and keepe this and send the cert hither.' (WRO A1/110 T1690)

**26** [1691]. Downton. The dwellinghouse of William Michell called New Court. William Michell. (WRO A1/110 H1691)

**27** 11 Jan 1692. Ramsbury. The house that was lately Mr Freeman's. Mr William Turton, minister of the gospel, to be preacher there. [*Presbyterian*: see **1**]. Thomas Smith, Stephen Knackstone, Daniel Sparvill, Matthew Freeman, John Pincke, John . . . , Joseph Smith. (WRO A1/110 H1692)

**28** 6 April 1692. Bradford on Avon. A barn called Kelsons Barn in the possession of Frances Yerbury. [*Presbyterian*: VCH 3, 107]. Benjamin Flower. (WRO A1/110 E1692)

**29**  6 April 1692. Bradford on Avon. The dwellinghouse of Frances Yerbury. [*Presbyterian*: VCH 3, 107]. Benjamin Flower. (WRO A1/110 E1692)

**30**  6 April 1692. Chippenham. The dwellinghouse of Benjamin Flower. [*Presbyterian*: VCH 3, 107]. Benjamin Flower. (WRO A1/110 E1692)

**31**  [1692]. Atworth in Bradford on Avon [*and elsewhere*]. The house of Anthony Widdowes of Atworth, the house of Robert Richards in Broughton Gifford (*Broaton*), the house of Edward Shipard in Melksham (*Millsom*). Baptist. Robert Rogers, William Shipard, William Earls. [*At foot*] 'William Earle of Shaw in parish of Melksham his dwelling house and barne are for religious worship of Anabaptists, Edward Shephard of the same his dwelling house for the same, William Shepherd of Atworth in the parish of Bradford the same.' (WRO A1/110 E1692)

**32**  [1692]. Atworth in Bradford on Avon, and Melksham. The house of James Clark of Atworth, the house of Israel Maishman in Melksham (*Millsom*) and the house of Mrs Floure, widow, in the same parish. Baptist. Richard Ettelie, Abraham Littell, Thomas Booklie. (WRO A1/110 E1692)

**33**  [1692]. Trowbridge. Certain rooms and places in and belonging to the now dwellinghouse of Thomas Tilson. [*Presbyterian*: Webb]. Baruch Nowell, William Broadribb, Edward Davis. (WRO A1/110 E1692)

**34**  [1692]. Trowbridge. Certain rooms and places in and belonging to the now dwellinghouse of Richard Shrapnell. [*Presbyterian*: Webb]. Baruch Nowell, Edward Davis, William Broadribb. (WRO A1/110 E1692)

**35**  4 Oct 1692. Trowbridge. Certain rooms and places in and belonging to the now dwellinghouse of Henry Crabb. [*Presbyterian*: Webb]. Baruch Nowell, James Gibbs, Edward Davis. (WRO A1/110 M1692)

**36**  25 April 1693. Mere. A house. John Buckler. (WRO A1/110 E1693)

**37**  25 April 1693. Westbury. The barn of James Reason alias Marshman in his close near the west end of the town. Thomas Whatly, Samuel Whereat. (WRO A1/110 E1693)

**38**  25 April 1693. Westbury Leigh (*Ligh*) in Westbury. The barn of William Selfe, clothier. [*Baptist*: Doel 93]. Roger Cater, John Belton, Jane Knight, William Withey, Jeffery Whitaker. (WRO A1/110 E1693)

**39**  3 Oct. 1693. Chisledon? (*Cheeslen*). My dwellinghouse. The mark of Henry Looker. (WRO A1/110 H1694)

**40** 9 Jan. 1694. Shalbourne. The house of John Backer. John Backer, Gille Pocock, George Backer, Robert Churn, Margaret Munday, Thomas Smith, Thomas Pocock. (WRO A1/110 H1694)

**41** 1 Oct. 1694. Lacock. The dwellinghouse of John Bond junior. [*Baptist*: see **31**]. Anthony Widdows, John Bond. (WRO A1/110 M1694)

**42** 6 Nov. 1694. Shrewton. The house of Nicholas Coker. Ephraim Mooer, James Hayter. (WRO A1/110 M1694)

**43** 3 April 1695. Steeple Ashton. The dwellinghouse of William Ball. Baptist. Thomas Axford, John George. (WRO A1/110 E1695)

**44** [*ca.* 1695? *undated, precedes* **47** *in the earliest bundle in* WRO A1/250, *but the order of this bundle has been disturbed.*]. Calne. The house of Samuel Stephens in Church Street. [*Presbyterian*: see **45**]. Samuel Stephens, James Bristowe, William Staples. (WRO A1/250)

**45** [*ca.* 1695? *undated, as* **44**]. 'Stockfields' in Calne. The house of several dissenters lately built (Mr Stephen James being minister). [*Presbyterian*: Gordon 125, 291]. Stephen James, James Bristowe, William Staples. (WRO A1/250)

**46** [*ca.* 1695?. *undated, as* **44**]. Calne. The dwellinghouse of Nicholas Ball. John Goddard, John Esex?. (WRO A1/250)

**47** 18 July 1695. Westport St Mary. The house or building called the meeting house adjoining the dwellinghouse of Robert Nichols. [*Baptist?*: Oliver 28]. Joseph Mathews, Robert Nickols, Thomas Mill . . . [*damaged*]. (WRO A1/250)

**48** 8 Oct. 1695. Bradford on Avon. The dwellinghouse of Thomas Bush. [*Presbyterian?*: VCH 7, 33]. Robert Butcher. (WRO A1/110 M1695)

**49** 8 Oct. 1695. Bradford on Avon. The dwellinghouse of Thomas Powell. [*Presbyterian?*: see **48**]. Robert Butcher. (WRO A1/110 M1695)

**50** 8 Oct. 1695. Colerne. The dwellinghouse of Samuel Ford. [*Presbyterian?*: see **48**]. Robert Butcher. (WRO A1/110 M1695)

**51** 8 Oct. 1695. Malmesbury. The dwellinghouse of Rebecca Baskervile, widow. [*Quaker?*: see **24, 118**]. William Hitchcock. (WRO A1/110 M1695)

**52** 8 Oct. 1695. Ogbourne St George. The dwellinghouse of John Arnald. [*Presbyterian?*: see **48**]. Robert Butcher. (WRO A1/110 M1695)

**53** 8 Oct. 1695. Shalbourne. The house of Robert Churn. [*Unsigned*]. (WRO A1/110 M1695)

**54** 8 Oct. 1695. Swindon. The dwellinghouse of Edmund Law. [*Presbyterian?*: see **48**]. Robert Butcher. (WRO A1/110 M1695)

**55** 14 Jan. 1696. Trowbridge. The house or building newly erected in a close of Mr Joseph Holton called the Conigar. [*Baptist*: Doel 102]. Edward Grant, Edward Mortymor. (WRO A1/110 H1696)

**56** 22 April 1696. South Marston in Highworth. My house. [*Baptist*: see **230**]. Thomas Hunt. (WRO A1/110 E1696)

**57** 22 April 1696. Stratton St Margaret. My house. Robert Panting (WRO A1/110 E1696)

**58** 2 June 1696. Hurdcott [*in Barford St Martin or Winterbourne Earls*]. The dwellinghouse of Ann Chandler. Samuel Cooper. (WRO A1/110 E1696)

**59** 13 Oct. 1696. Winterbourne Monkton. The dwellinghouse of Mary Abbott. Samuel Cooper. [*same document as* **60**]. (WRO A1/110 M1696)

**60** 15 Oct. 1696. Calne. The dwellinghouse of William Lamton, tanner. Richard Evans, James Thornley. [*same document as* **59**]. (WRO A1/110 M1696)

**61** [1697]. Shrewton. The dwellinghouse of Robert Manfield. Baptist. Nicholas Frowde, Richard King. (WRO A1/110 H1697)

**62** 6 Oct. 1697. Sunton in Collingbourne Kingston [*and elsewhere*]. The dwellinghouse of Thomas Crouch of Sunton, the dwellinghouse of Christian Long in Upavon, the dwellinghouse of Richard Wristbridg in Burbage. Thomas Crouch, Christian Long, Richard Wristbridg, John Steevens, Thomas Ollden, William Fribbens, William Dike, William Clark, Edward Marshall. (WRO A1/110 M1697)

**63** 12 Jan. 1698. Downton. The house of John Ashley in Downton. John Ashly, Humphrey Cotten. (WRO A1/110 H1698)

**64** 13 Jan. 1698. Donhead St Andrew. The house of John Gould. [*Presbyterian*: see **186**]. David Minty, George Blake. (WRO A1/110 H1698)

**65** 13 Jan. 1698. Donhead St Andrew. The house of Sarah Strong. [*Presbyterian*: see **186**]. David Minty, George Blake. (WRO A1/110 H1698)

**66** 13 Jan. 1698. South Newton. The house of George Blake. [*Presbyterian*: see **186**]. David Minty, George Blake. (WRO A1/110 H1698)

**67**  14 Jan. 1698. Downton, and Whaddon in Alderbury. The house of John Coles in Downton, the house of John Sanger in Whaddon in Alderbury. Baptist. John Sanger, Thomas Capon, Thomas Smith. (WRO A1/110 H1698)

**68**  3 May 1698. Horningsham. The now dwellinghouse of John Brown. [*Baptist?*: see **71** (Browne)]. John Browne, John Doner. (WRO A1/110 E1698)

**69**  3 May 1698. Lacock. The now dwellinghouse of George Fisher. [*Baptist*: see **41**]. John Bond, George Fisher. (WRO A1/110 E1698)

**70**  21 May 1698. Bratton [*in Westbury*]. The now dwellinghouse of Jeffery Whittaker. [*Baptist*: see **43**]. William Ball, Samuel Himons. (WRO A1/110 E1698)

**71**  21 May 1698. Mere. The dwellinghouse of Deborah Morris, widow. [*Baptist*: see **89**]. Isaac Knight, Samuel Williames, John Browne. (WRO A1/110 E1698)

**72**  12 July 1698. Erlestoke. A dwellinghouse now vacant of Mr Henry Axford. [*Baptist*: see **3, 43**]. John Axford, John Aldridge, William Ball. (WRO A1/110 T1698)

**73**  11 Jan. 1699. Fisherton Anger, and Kington St Michael. The dwellinghouse of Thomas Hayward of Fisherton Anger, the dwellinghouse of Charles Barrett in Kington St Michael. [*Quaker*: WNQ 2, 181]. Robert Shergold, . . .ewlett [*illegible*]. (WRO A1/110 H1699)

**74**  [1699]. Ford [*in Laverstock or North Wraxall*]. The dwellinghouse of John Andrews. [*Presbyterian*: see **75**]. James Bristowe, George Harris. (WRO A1/110 H1699)

**75**  [1699]. East Knoyle. The dwellinghouse of Mr Samuel Clifford senior. [*Presbyterian*: VCH 3, 106]. James Bristowe, George Harris. (WRO A1/110 H1699)

**76**  [1699]. Fisherton Anger. The dwellinghouse of James Bristowe. [*Presbyterian*: see **75**]. James Bristowe, George Harris. (WRO A1/110 H1699)

**77A**  16 March 1699. Trowbridge. The dwellinghouse of Adam Chivers. John Edwards, Walter [*perhaps* William] Reeves. (WRO A1/250)

**77B**  18 April 1699. Biddestone. The dwellinghouse of Mary Hulbert, widow. [*Baptist*: see **69**]. John Bond, George Fisher, Abel Sayne? [cf. Sabin, **153, 154**], William Sanbury, inhabitants of Biddestone [*all names are written in the same hand*]. (WRO A1/110 E1699)

**77C**  18 April 1699. Chippenham. The dwellinghouse of John Shepard alias

Morgan. John Plant, the mark of George A Nowill, inhabitants of Chippenham. (WRO A1/110 E1699)

**77D**　18 April 1699. Grittleton. The house called Mayes of John Sargent. Joseph Beames, Joseph Stancomb, inhabitants of Grittleton. (WRO A1/110 E1699)

**77E**　18 April 1699. Kingswood. The dwellinghouse of Nathaniel Coopye of Kingswood. William Griffin, Nathaniel Foord, Thomas Bence, Francis Foord. (WRO A1/110 E1699)

**77F**　18 April 1699. Ogbourne St George. The dwellinghouse of Jonathan Rashleigh. [*Presbyterian*: see **87**]. Jonathan Rashleigh, Edward Pierce, inhabitants of Ogbourne St George. (WRO A1/110 E1699)

**77G**　18 April 1699. Tockenham. The dwellinghouse of William Lawes. William Hulett, Richard Hulet. (WRO A1/110 E1699)

**77H**　18 April 1699. Tockenham. The house of Onisimus Tayler. William Hulett, inhabitant of Tockenham. (WRO A1/110 E1699)

**77J**　18 April 1699. Whitley in Melksham. The now dwellinghouse of John Draper. Joseph Marshman, William Moore. (WRO A1/110 E1699)

**78**　11 July 1699. Chapmanslade [*in Corsley or Westbury*]. The barn of Robert Hopkins. Robert Hopkins, William Holding? (WRO A1/250)

**79**　11 July 1699. Corsley. The dwellinghouse of Thomas Rogers. [*Baptist*: see **119**]. Jonathan Coombes, Samuel Adlam, inhabitants of Corsley. (WRO A1/110 T1699)

**80**　11 July 1699. Heytesbury. The dwellinghouse of John Button. William Lanham, Henry Lanham, inhabitants of Heytesbury. (WRO A1/110 T1699)

**81**　11 July 1699. Warminster. The dwellinghouse of Edward Haynes. James Elliott, James Slade, inhabitants of Warminster. (WRO A1/110 T1699)

**82**　11 July 1699. Westbury. The dwellinghouse of Daniel Tucker. Samuel Rimmen?, Stephen Millere, inhabitants of Westbury. (WRO A1/110 T1699)

**83**　[1699]. Marlborough. The house of Mr Joseph Lews. Richard Coleman, Henry Coleman, William Gibbons, William Page, John Laburn, Joseph Lewis. (WRO A1/110 T1699)

**84**　25 Sept. 1699. Bradford on Avon. The new erected house of Mr Anthony Methuen. [*Presbyterian*: Murch 64]. William Dangerfield. (WRO A1/250)

**85** 3 Oct. 1699. Biddestone. The now dwellinghouse of Benjamin Bond. Benjamin Bond, Andrew Daniel, inhabitants of Biddestone. (WRO A1/250)

**86** 3 Oct. 1699. Biddestone. The now dwellinghouse of John Fifield. Benjamin Bond, Andrew Daniel, inhabitants of Biddestone. (WRO A1/250)

**87** 3 Oct. 1699. Coate in Liddington [*recte* Swindon *or* Chisledon?]. The now dwellinghouse of John Warman. [*Presbyterian*: Gordon 337]. Jonathan Rashleigh, Edward Sharbury. (WRO A1/250)

**88** 3 Oct. 1699. West Kington. The now dwellinghouse of John Dark. Benjamin Bond, Andrew Daniel, inhabitants of West Kington [*but see* **85** *and* **86**]. (WRO A1/250)

**89** 31 March 1700. Corsley (*Corsly Magna*). The now dwellinghouse and barn near adjoining of Jonathan Coombs. [*Baptist*: VCH 3, 111]. Isaac Knight, Samuel Adlam. (WRO A1/250)

**90** 9 April 1700. Cherhill. The dwellinghouse of Richard Bradfill. Michael Celott, Richard Hawkins. (WRO A1/250)

**91** 9 April 1700. Horningsham. The now dwellinghouse of Abigail Pobjah, widow. [*Independent*: see **101**, *but cf* **68** *and* **71**, *where Brown(e) appears to sign as a Baptist*]. John Brown, William Carr, Benet Singer. (WRO A1/250)

**92** 9 April 1700. Langley Burrell. The house of Michael Billett. Michael Celott, Richard Hawkins. (WRO A1/250)

**93** 9 April 1700. Notton in Lacock. The now dwellinghouse of the widow Colborne. John Church, John Britin, James Westfield. (WRO A1/250)

**94** [1700? *MS undated, but found between* **92** *and* **95**]. Westport St Mary. The house of Thomas Estmead. John Gingell, William Hanks. (WRO A1/250)

**95** 1 June 1700. Figheldean. The house of Mr Charles Read. William Sheppard, Thomas George, Daniel Dyke. (WRO A1/250)

**96** 15 July 1700. Southwick in North Bradley. The dwellinghouse of Stephen Jones. [*Quaker*: see **109**]. Stephen Jones, John Hodges. (WRO A1/250)

**97** 16 July 1700. Codford St Mary *or* St Peter. The house of Tristram Flower. Thomas Collins, John Smith. (WRO A1/250)

**98** 16 July 1700. Sedgehill. The house of Mr Edward Froud. [*Baptist*: VCH 3, 112]. John Guyre, Enoch Williames, John Williames. (WRO A1/250)

**99**   16 July 1700. Stockton. The house of Richard King. [*Baptist?*: see **61** (King)]. Richard King, Thomas Collins, John Smith. (WRO A1/250)

**100**   16 July 1700. Westbury. The house of John Oatbridge. [*Unsigned*]. (WRO A1/250)

**101**   8 Oct. 1700. Horningsham. A new erected building standing on a close of pasture or garden ground in possession of George French. [*Independent: the Independent Chapel minute book records a licence granted at Marlborough in 1700* (Banton 17). *This certificate was presented at Marlborough sessions*]. Bennett Sangar, William Carr. (WRO A1/250)

**102**   15 Oct. 1700. West Kington. The barn of Joan Bennett, widow. [*Quaker*: see **24, 118**]. William Hitchcock, Daniel Webb. (WRO A1/250)

**103**   6 Dec. 1700. Sutton Mandeville. The dwellinghouse of William Verrett. [*Presbyterian*: see **15**]. Samuel Welis?, Joseph Buckler. (WRO A1/250)

**104**   20 Dec. 1700. Heytesbury (*Heitsba.* .). The dwellinghouse of Robert Wickham. Robert Wickham, William Lansham?. (WRO A1/250)

**105**   10 Jan. 1701. Bradford on Avon. The dwellinghouse of John Clarke, chemist (*chymister*). Quaker. John Clark, Stephen Jones. (WRO A1/250)

**106**   10 Jan. 1701. Bradford on Avon. The dwellinghouse of Jonathan Tyler. Quaker. Jonathan Tyler, Stephen Jones. (WRO A1/250)

**107**   10 Jan. 1701. Calne. The dwellinghouse of John Cale? Quaker. John Cale, Stephen Jones. (WRO A1/250)

**108**   10 Jan. 1701. Warminster. The dwellinghouse of James Hodges. Quaker. James Hodges, Stephen . . . [*Jones*?]. (WRO A1/250)

**109**   12 April 1701. Bratton [*in Westbury*]. The barn or outhouse of James Hodges of Warminster. Quaker. James Hodges, John Hodges, Stephen Jones. (WRO A1/250)

**110**   26 April 1701. Mere. A meeting house within the town. Quaker. James Hodges, John Hodges, Stephen Jones. (WRO A1/250)

**111**   29 April 1701. Littleton ?Drew. The house of Walter Tanner. Robert Wastfeild, Matthew Light. (WRO A1/250)

**112**   29 April 1701. Kington St Michael. The house of Isaac Bowsheer. Robert Wastfeild, Matthew Light. (WRO A1/250)

**113**   29 April 1701. Melksham. The house of James Weeb and the barn of

John Weeb adjoining the said house. [*Baptist*: Cooper app.4] Samuel Cooke, Richard Crooke. (WRO A1/250)

**114** 29 April 1701. Nettleton. The house of John Tanner. Robert Wastfeild, Matthew Light. (WRO A1/250)

**115** 14 July 1701. Maiden Bradley. The dwellinghouse of George Awdry. William Shaw, John Perry, Richard Jubener?, Samuel Awdry, George Awdry. (WRO A1/250)

**116** 5 Oct. 1701. Chippenham. A certain building newly erected lying at the backside of the Bell Inn. Benjamin Scott, John Bedford, John Greenwood, inhabitants of Chippenham. (WRO A1/250)

**117** 7 Oct. 1701. ?Biddestone (*Bittlestone*?). The dwellinghouse of William Noyes. Richard Little, William Saintsbury. (WRO A1/250)

**118** 7 Oct. 1701. Castle Combe. The house of Sarah Young, widow. [*Quaker*: see **124**]. William Hitchcock, Edward Brown. (WRO A1/250)

**119** 7 Oct. 1701. Crockerton [*in Longbridge Deverill*]. The dwellinghouse of Christopher Adlam. [*Baptist*: VCH 3, 111]. John Whereat, Samuel Adlam. (WRO A1/250)

**120** 7 Oct. 1701. Kington St Michael. The dwellinghouse of Henry Milsum. William Edall, William Heath. (WRO A1/250)

**121** 14 Oct. 1701. Martin. The house of James Prince. Presbyterian. The mark of James Prince, Henry Prince, Simon Thaine, William Thaine, Henry Prince. (WRO A1/250)

**122** 10 Nov. 1701. Erlestoke. The dwellinghouse of Isaac Axford the younger. Quaker. Isaac Axford junior, Edward Gye, Thomas Beaven, Stephen Jones. (WRO A1/250)

**123** 31 Dec. 1701. Bratton [*in Westbury*]. The house of William Whittaker now in the occupation of Robert Bathe. [*Baptist*: see **70**]. William Whittaker, Jeffery Whitaker. (WRO A1/250)

**124** 10 April 1702. Bradford on Avon and Trowbridge. The dwellinghouses of James Willett, James Webb and Joseph Hall? in Bradford, and the dwellinghouse of Philip Long of Trowbridge. Quaker. Joseph Hall, James Webb, Stephen Jones, Philip Long. (WRO A1/250)

**125** 10 April 1702. Castle Combe and Box. The dwellinghouse of Sarah Young in Castle Combe, and the dwellinghouse of Elizabeth Rogers in Box. Quaker. Thomas Beaven, Sarah Young, Elizabeth Rogers. (WRO A1/250)

**126** 10 April 1702. Fovant and Dinton. The several dwellinghouses of Osmond Day, Elizabeth Dunne and James Abbot, all of Fovant, and the dwellinghouse of Sarah Shephard of Dinton. Quaker. Osmond Day, James Abbotts, Jonathan Tyler, Elizabeth Dunne. (WRO A1/250)

**127** 14 April 1702. Kingswood. A new built house in Kingswood (near adjoining the now dwellinghouse of Nathaniel Cooper). Nathaniel Ford, Daniel Ford, Nathaniel Cooper, John Furnell junior. (WRO A1/250)

**128** 14 April 1702. Seend [*in Melksham*]. The dwellinghouse of Rebecca Smith. [*Presbyterian*: Gordon 248]. Joseph Buckler, W. Dangerfield. (WRO A1/250)

**129** 10 July 1702. Devizes. The dwellinghouses of William Coole and Joseph Bartlett with the backsides and gardens thereunto belonging, also that new erected house lately built by the people called Quakers. Quaker. William Coole, Joseph Bartlett, Stephen Jones. (WRO A1/250)

**130** 14 July 1702. North Bradley. The house of William Willis. Joseph Harford, Henry Edwards?. (WRO A1/250)

**131** 14 July 1702. Westport St Mary. The house of Thomas Eastmead. John Gingell, William Hancks. (WRO A1/250)

**132** 15 July 1702. South Wraxall [*in Bradford on Avon*]. The dwellinghouse of William Pierce. William Pearce, John Underwood, Anthony Deverell, Humphrey Fernell. (WRO A1/250)

**133** 6 Oct. 1702. Highworth. The dwellinghouse of John Perrifield. John Cresby. (WRO A1/250)

**134** 29 March 1703. Hawkeridge in Westbury. The now dwellinghouse of William Green. Roger Hodges, Alexander Tapp. (WRO A1/250)

**135** 23 June 1703. Salisbury [*and elsewhere*]. The dwellinghouses of Robert Shergold and John Moore in Salisbury, the dwellinghouse of John Baker in East Harnham [*in Britford*], the dwellinghouse of Leonard Upjohn in Stapleford, and the dwellinghouse of Joseph Callowes in Newton. Quaker. Robert Shergold, John Moore, John Baker, Leonard Up . . . [*john?*], Joseph Callowes. (WRO A1/250)

**136** 10 July 1703. 'Mounton' [*perhaps Monkton Farleigh, Monkton in Broughton Gifford or Monkton Deverill*]. The dwellinghouse of Wiliam Peires. Quaker. John Neale, Robert Card. (WRO A1/250)

**137** 10 July 1703. Wootton Bassett. The dwellinghouse of William Norriss known by the name of the sign of the Bear. Quaker. Daniel Young, John Jafferes. (WRO A1/250)

**138** 15 July 1703. Trowbridge. The house or new erected building on the land of Abel Pierce. [*Presbyterian*: see **5**]. Abel Peerce, Edward Davis. (WRO A1/250)

**139** 2 Aug. 1703. South Wraxall [*in Bradford on Avon*]. The dwellinghouse of Joshua Swyer. The mark of Joshua Swyer, John Keeping. (WRO A1/250)

**140** 12 Jan. 1704. Burbage. The house of William Milsham. John Lane, John? Miller. (WRO A1/250)

**141** 26 Feb. 1704. Wilton and East Harnham [*in Britford*]. The dwellinghouse of William Merifild in Wilton, and of Richard Truman in East Harnham. Quaker. Richard Truman, William Merifild, Robert Shergold. (WRO A1/250)

**142** 1 April 1704. Crockerton [*in Longbridge Deverill*]. The messuage or house now in the occupation of Samuel Lewis which he holds by demise of his wife's father John Whereat. [*Baptist*: see **119**]. Richard Moody, Samuel Adlam. (WRO A1/250)

**143** 26 June 1704. Steeple Ashton. The dwellinghouse, barn and backside of James Smith. Quaker. James Smith, Thomas Truband, William Ballard. (WRO A1/250)

**144** 11 July 1704. Donhead St Mary. The dwellinghouse of John Haskell. [*Presbyterian*: Murch 93]. Compton South, John Haskell?. (WRO A1/250)

**145** 11 July 1704. Donhead St Mary. A certain house now or late in the occupation of Mr John Hastings. [*Presbyterian*: see **144**]. Compton . . . [*South?*]. (WRO A1/250)

**146** 29 Sept. 1704. Southwick in North Bradley. A new erected house in the lower side of the Common near the bridge. John Aldridge, Grace Greenhill. (WRO A1/250)

**147** 3 Oct. 1704. Calstone Wellington. The house of Edward Batton. David Downland, John James, Walter Chivers. (WRO A1/250)

**148** 10 Jan. 1705. Downton. The dwellinghouse of Richard Dawkins. [*Baptist*: VCH 3, 114]. James Edgell, William Turner, John Sanger, Benjamin Miller. (WRO A1/250)

**149** 26 March 1705. Warminster [*and elsewhere*]. The dwellinghouse of Henry Sanger in Warminster, the house of William Cooper in Bishopstone, the house of Robert Withers in [omitted], and the house lately built in Purton (called the Quakers meeting house). Quaker. Henry Sanger, John Hodges, Stephen Jones. (WRO A1/250)

**150**   28 July 1705. Limpley Stoke [in Bradford on Avon]. The now dwelling-house of Anthony Pyot. John Culverhouse, John Edwards. (WRO A1/250)

**151**   9 Jan. 1706. Downton. The dwellinghouse of Richard Dawkins. [Baptist: see **148**]. Benjamin Miller, James Coles. (WRO A1/250)

**152**   15 Jan. 1706. Broughton Gifford. The house of Joan Gore, widow. Thomas Stantiall, James Stantiall. (WRO A1/250)

**153**   2 April 1706. Allington in Chippenham. The dwellinghouse of William Lewis. Abel Sabin, John Mayer. (WRO A1/250)

**154**   2 April 1706. Corsham. The dwellinghouse of John Mair. Abel Sabin, William Chick. (WRO A1/250)

**155**   16 July 1706. Aldbourne. The barn or building of Mr Edward Witts formerly belonging to the widow Witts. William Lawrance, Joshua Wilde. (WRO A1/250)

**156**   8 Oct. 1706. Studley in Calne. The now dwellinghouse of William Ponting. Joseph Russell, William Browne. (WRO A1/250)

**157**   7 Jan. 1707. Christian Malford. The dwellinghouse of Walter Pryce and William Pryce, maltsters, also the dwellinghouse of John Silman, carpenter. Quaker. The mark of Walter Price, William Price, John Sellman, Richard Burges, the mark of John Sanders. (WRO A1/250)

**158**   7 Jan. 1707. West Kington. The dwellinghouses of William Marsh, yeoman, Roger Ballden, yeoman, and of John John [sic] Darke, sergemaker. Quaker. William Marsh, Roger Ballden, John Darke, Jonathan Tyler. (WRO A1/250)

**159**   31 March 1707. Avebury. The dwellinghouses of Samuel Morris and Richard Morris. [Presbyterian: VCH 3, 107]. John Griffin, Richard Baily, Thomas Cue, Edward Cue, Richard Morris. (WRO A1/250)

**160**   11 April 1707. Avebury. A new erected house lately built on part of the garden ground of and belonging to a tenement of Samuel Morris. [Presbyterian: see **159**]. John Griffin, Richard Morris, Edward Cue, Richard Baily, Thomas Cue. (WRO A1/250)

**161**   22 April 1707. Lacock. The dwellinghouse of Abel Seven. Abel Seven, William Saintsbury. (WRO A1/250)

**162**   22 April 1707. Langley Burrell. The dwellinghouse of Robert Westfeild. Robert Westfeild, John Coleman. (WRO A1/250)

**163**   4 July 1707. Bromham. The dwellinghouse and outhouses of William Smith senior of Bromham House. Quaker. William Smith senior, William Smith junior, John Hodges. (WRO A1/250)

**164**   14 July 1707. Melksham. The dwellinghouse of Walter Breach. Baptist. Walter Breach, John Atkins. (WRO A1/250)

**165**   10 Dec. 1707. Urchfont [*and elsewhere*]. Meeting houses in Urchfont, Easterton [*in Market Lavington*] and West Lavington. Quaker. Henry Sanger, Isaac Selfe junior, John Somner, Edward? Gye, Stephen Jones. (WRO A1/250)

**166**   26 Dec. 1707. Hilperton. The dwellinghouse of Edward Stevens, sergeweaver. Daniel Hawkins, John Green, John Bowles, Nathaniel Spencer. (WRO A1/250)

**167**   30 April 1708. Trowbridge. The houses of Edward Morttymour, . . . John Davisson, John Lawes and Andrew . . . [*Part of the certificate is missing*]. [*Baptist*: Doel 102]. . . . [*Several names missing*] Robert . . .ulton, John Smith [*A note from Edward Grant to Mr Edghill explaining that alterations to a meeting house require a new licence is appended. The document is endorsed to Mr James Edghill at Warminster*]. (WRO A1/250)

**168**   5 Oct. 1708. Calne. The dwellinghouse of Edward Hobbs in Hog Street. John Hosking, Stephen Orrell. (WRO A1/250)

**169**   20 April 1709. Hilperton. The dwellinghouse of John Boles. Francis Stevens, Jonathan Ritch, Nathaniel Spencer, Thomas Wooley, Francis Asphens. (WRO A1/250)

**170**   20 April 1709. Bewley in Lacock. The dwellinghouse of John Brinckworth. Robert Crew, Robert Bond, John Thorne, John Hibberd, Henry Chivers. (WRO A1/250)

**171**   25 June 1709. Warminster. The barn or shop of Richard Lot situate at the backside of his dwellinghouse. [*Presbyterian*: see **181**]. Robert Toogood, John Butler. (WRO A1/250)

**172**   12 July 1709. Keevil. The now dwellinghouse of Matthew Gunston. [*Baptist*?: see **70**]. William Ball, Robert Handcok. (WRO A1/250)

**173**   [1709? *MS undated, but found between* **172** *and* **174**]. Grittleton. The building newly erected on a close now in the occupation of Joseph Houlton, gentleman. [*Baptist*: VCH 3, 114]. Thomas Bristowe, Joseph Holton. (WRO A1/250)

**174** 4 Oct. 1709. Chippenham. The house of Charles Williams alias Tayler. Thomas Wort?, Charles Williams alias Taylor. (WRO A1/250)

**175** 4 Oct. 1709. Highworth. The dwellinghouse of Thomas Tichener called the Swan. John Cresby, Thomas Wort?. (WRO A1/250)

**176** 4 Oct. 1709. Stratton St Margaret. The dwellinghouse of John Herring. [*Unsigned*]. (WRO A1/250)

**177** 10 Dec. 1709. Corsham. A house lately erected on part of a close late in the possession of William Arnold. [*Quaker*: WNQ 5,550; 6,226; 6,230]. John Hand, William Jeffries, John Butler, Richard Gowen, Thomas Bayly, John Flower. (WRO A1/250)

**178** 23 Dec. 1709. North Bradley. A house lately erected on part of a close late in the possession of John Millerd. [*Baptist*: Doel 58]. Henry Usher, Richard Mathews, Joseph Miller, James Stanton, John Greene, William Bowles, Thomas Collier, John Harford. (WRO A1/250)

**179** 11 Jan. 1710. Coombe Bissett. The dwellinghouse of John Barber. [*Unsigned*]. (WRO A1/250)

**180** 11 Jan. 1710. Winterbourne ?Dauntsey (*Midle Winterborne*). The dwellinghouse of John Judd. [*Unsigned*]. (WRO A1/250)

**181** 25 March 1710. Warminster. The house or building newly erected and situate on certain land now in the occupation of John Butler, grocer, near the dwellinghouse of Lewis Cockey. [*Presbyterian*: Gunn 23–24]. Christopher Slade, Peter Lee. (WRO A1/250)

**182** 20 April 1710. Enford. The dwellinghouse or barn of John Willis. John Willis, John Neale. (WRO A1/250)

**183** 20 April 1710. Westport St Mary. The dwellinghouse of Joseph Mathews. [*Baptist*: Oliver 28]. Israel May, Nathaniel Mathews. (WRO A1/250)

**184** 11 July 1710. Chapmanslade [*in Corsley or Westbury*]. The dwellinghouse of Christopher Rymer. Edward Culverhouse, William Culverhouse. (WRO A1/250)

**185** 10 Aug. 1710. Upavon. The house of Jonathan Alexander. Richard Wristbridge, Nicholas Mills, Thomas Chrouch, John Rudell, Edward Marshall. (WRO A1/250)

**186** 10 Jan. 1711. Martin. The dwellinghouse of James Princc. [*Presbyterian*: see **121**]. Simon Thaine, David Minty. (WRO A1/250)

**187** 10 July 1711. Figheldean. A house. Samuel Dicks, Thomas Cooper. (WRO A1/250)

**188** 10 July 1711. South Wraxall [*in Bradford on Avon*]. Several rooms of the dwellinghouse of Joseph Smith. William Hancock, Thomas Pearce, Joseph Smith. (WRO A1/250)

**189** 3 Nov. 1711. Keevil. The hall, parlour and kitchen of the dwellinghouse of John Dalmer. [*Baptist*: see **70**]. William Ball, George Handcock. (WRO A1/250)

**190** 15 July 1712. Mere Park in Mere. The house of Deborah Morris, widow. [*Baptist*: see **71**]. Deborah Morris, John Claggett. (WRO A1/250)

**191** 1 Nov. 1712. Horningsham. The dwellinghouse of Martha Jenings. Robert Hill, Gilbert Brolip. (WRO A1/250)

**192** 14 Jan. 1713. Salisbury. A new built house in Gigant (*Gigging*) Street in St Martin's parish. [*Quaker*: see **135**]. Robert Shergold, James Lansdell, James Wilkens. (WRO A1/250)

**193** 1 Oct. 1713. Devizes. The dwellinghouse of Edward Pierce, gentleman. [*Presbyterian?*: VCH 10, 296]. Benjamin Stephens, Thomas Collins, Hugh Gough, George Willis, George Causway, Walter Willoughby. (WRO A1/250)

**194** 13 Jan. 1714. Chalford in Westbury. The dwellinghouse of Robert Browne. [*Baptist*: Doel 93]. William Wilkins. (WRO A1/250)

**195** 13 Jan 1714. Purton. The building lately erected for a meeting house. [*Quaker*: see **110**]. John Hodges, Thomas Aucland. (WRO A1/250)

**196** 13 Jan. 1714. Westbury. The dwellinghouse of Thomas Reynolds. [*Baptist*: Doel 93]. William Wilkins. (WRO A1/250)

**197** 6 April 1714. Marston in Potterne. The dwellinghouse of Daniel Smith. Daniel Smith, Samuel Yomens. (WRO A1/250)

**198** 8 July 1714. Melksham. A house lately erected on a piece of ground late in the possession of James Webb. [*Baptist*: Cooper app. 6]. Samuel Cooke, Joseph Heming, James Webb, Sibellen Marshman. (WRO A1/250)

**199** 5 Oct 1714. Bowden in Burbage. The dwellinghouse of William Fribbens. William Fribbens, Edward Marshile. (WRO A1/250)

**200** 19 Sept. 1715. Downton. The new erected meeting house of William Coles and John Barling. [*Baptist*: VCH 3, 114]. Benjamin Miller, minister,

William Coles, Thomas Hatcher, Joseph Chubb, John Barling, Charles Spring, Abraham Randoll. (WRO A1/250)

**201**  22 Sept. 1715. Whiteparish [*but dated from Hamptworth in Downton*]. The dwellinghouse of Christopher Biddlecom. [*Baptist*: VCH 3, 114]. Benjamin Miller, minister, Christopher Biddelcom, Stephen Winter, William Hayter, Charles Spring. (WRO A1/250)

**202**  18 Jan. 1716. Seend [*in Melksham*]. The dwellinghouse of Nicholas Twinny. [*Presbyterian*: see **256**]. William Sainsbury. (WRO A1/250)

**203**  18 Jan. 1716. Seend [*in Melksham*]. The dwellinghouse of Nicholas Twinny. [*Presbyterian*: see **256**]. [*Unsigned*]. (WRO A1/250)

**204**  1716. Pewsey. The house of Richard Wristbridge. William Dyke, Samuel Subdean, John Tyler, Richard Wristbridg, Thomas Compton, John Briant. (WRO A1/250)

**205**  30 March 1716. Melksham. A new erected house lately built on a piece of ground purchased of James Webb at the City. [*Baptist*: Cooper app. 7]. Samuel Cook, Francis Webb, James Hiscock, Zebulan Marshman. (WRO A1/250)

**206**  7 April 1716. Rushall (*Russell*). The house of John Tyler. [*Baptist?*: VCH 10, 146]. John Tyler. (WRO A1/250)

**207**  [1716? *MS undated, but found between* **206** *and* **208**]. Broughton Gifford. The dwellinghouse of Thomas Hickman. Baptist. Thomas Hickman, Samuel Mortimor, Walter Breach, members of the society. [*Endorsed and struck through*] 'To Mr Thos. Hickman att Shaw near Milksham.' (WRO A1/250)

**208**  10 April 1716. Nettleton. The late dwellinghouse of John Tanner. [*Quaker?*]. Richard Sargent, John Sargent, Francis Edwards. [*In another hand*] 'Quker'? (WRO A1/250)

**209**  10 April 1716. Ramsbury. A new erected edifice or building about thirty foot square (more or less) on ground late part of the backside, yard, close or garden of a messuage or tenement commonly called or known by the name or sign of the Sw. . .[*missing*]. [*Presbyterian*: VCH 12, 45]. Samuel Cox, Stephen Knackston, Stephen Smith, Thomas North, Edward Gatt?, Joseph Jennings, Thomas Jennings. (WRO A1/250)

**210**  [1716? *MS undated, but found between* **208** *and* **209**]. Whiteparish. The dwellinghouse of John Barling. John Barling, Christopher Biddelcombe, John Lane. (WRO A1/250)

**211**  [1716? *MS undated, but found between* **208** *and* **209**]. Wilton and

Quidhampton [*in Fugglestone St Peter*]. The dwellinghouses of Mary Brown of Wilton and John Thring of Quidhampton. George Thring. (WRO A1/250)

**212** 31 Dec. 1716. Market Lavington. A house lately erected called the Quakers' meeting house. Quaker. John Gye, Edward Gye, Isaac Selfe, William Miell. (WRO A1/250)

**213** 30 April 1717. Castle Combe. The dwellinghouse of Jane Davis, widow. John Fabian, John Tanner, William Gaye, Francis Edwards. (WRO A1/250)

**214** 30 April 1717. Castle Combe. The late dwellinghouse of Richard Sargent. John Cumner, Isaac Bowshear, William Gaise, Francis Edwards. (WRO A1/250)

**215** 5 Oct. 1717. Penleigh in Westbury. The barn of William Wereat. William Weratt, Christopher Phipps. (WRO A1/250)

**216** 8 Oct. 1717. Charlton near Malmesbury. The late dwellinghouse of Ann Webe, widow. Thomas Panting, William Hillier, Richard Sargent. (WRO A1/250)

**217** 3 July 1718. Heytesbury. The now dwellinghouse of Henry Lanham. Samuel Bowcher, Nicholas Dyat, Joseph White. (WRO A1/250)

**218** 2 Dec. 1718. Rowde. The dwellinghouse of Richard Watts. Thomas Lancaster, Richard Watts, the mark of James Dracke. (WRO A1/250)

**219** 10 March 1719. Groundwell in Blunsdon St Andrew. The dwelling-house of Edward Godwin. Edward Godwin, Thomas Fitchew, Edmund Waine. (WRO A1/250)

**220** 30 March 1719. Westport St Mary. The dwellinghouse of Moses Price. John Waite, Edward Yate, Thomas Hobbs, Nicholas Rumsy. (WRO A1/250)

**221** 7 April 1719. Chippenham. The dwellinghouse of James Alexander. Robert Wastfeild. (WRO A1/250)

**222** 7 April 1719. Colerne. The barn of Mary Jones now in the possession of Thomas Coleman. Robert Wastfeild. (WRO A1/250)

**223** 7 April 1719. Goatacre [*in Hilmarton*]. The dwellinghouse of Sybil Alderman. John Haskins. (WRO A1/250)

**224** 9 May 1719. Horningsham. The work house of Mr John Crey. [*Independent*: see **101**]. George French, Bennett Sanger. (WRO A1/250)

**225** 14 July 1719. Westbury. The dwellinghouse of George Withey. George Withey, Richard Flowers, Anthony Withey. (WRO A1/250)

**226** 26 Sept. 1719. Amesbury. The house of Thomas Cook. [*Quaker*: see **259, 260**]. John Hodges, Henry Sanger. (WRO A1/250)

**227** Oct. 1719. Trowbridge. The dwellinghouse of Walter Bignell, clothier. John Rider, Samuel Norman. (WRO A1/250)

**228** 6 Jan. 1720. Warminster. A new erected house in Common Close. [*Independent*: Gunn 35]. Peter Lee, William Bayly. (WRO A1/250)

**229** 26 March 1720. East Knoyle. The house now in the possession of Nicholas Williams. [*Baptist*; VCH 11, 96]. John Williams, John Williams. (WRO A1/250)

**230** 2 Oct. 1720. South Marston (*Mason*) in Highworth. A house in the possession of Robert Jefferies. [*Baptist*: see **263**]. Thomas Hunt, John Jordan. (WRO A1/250)

**231** 5 Oct. 1720. Trowbridge. The house of John Silverthorn. Anthony Read, John Silverthorn. (WRO A1/250)

**232** 3 Jan. 1721. Seend [*in Melksham*]. The house of Mr John Elliss in the lower Green. [*Presbyterian*: see **256**]. Nicholas Twinny, Aliff Wikins, Hugh Gough, Stephen Flower. (WRO A1/250)

**233** 3 May 1721. Marlborough. A building of Sarah Crabbs in a street called the Marsh Green, having the street on the east, a dwellinghouse now in the possession of Elizabeth Jones on the north, the dwellinghouse now in the possession of John Gaskoyn on the south, and a garden now in the possession of Mrs Wall on the west. [*Independent*: see **253**]. Thomas Seymour, Thomas Hancock, Joseph Hockly, Thomas Hunt, Richard Dangerfield. (WRO G22/1/122)

**234** 14 Jan. 1723. Birdbush in Donhead St Mary. The new erected meeting house. [*Presbyterian*: Stribling 25]. Thomas Hodding. (WRO A1/250)

**235** 1 April 1723. Avebury. The house called the meeting house. [*Independent*: Dunscombe 7]. Joseph Hayward, Thomas Griffin, George Arnold, Edward Cue, Thomas Robinson, Samuel Morris. (WRO A1/250)

**236** 29 July 1723. Westbury. The barn and dwellinghouse joining together of Sarah Mattock, widow. [*Baptist*: see **123**]. John Arnold, Robert Withy, William Whitaker. (WRO A1/250)

**237** 8 Oct. 1723. Trowbridge. The building newly erected called the

Presbyterian meeting house. Presbyterian. Abel Pearce, John Flower. (WRO A1/250)

**238** 4 Dec. 1723. Market Lavington. The dwellinghouse or malthouse of Thomas Lancaster, maltster. Thomas Lancaster, John Sloper junior. (WRO A1/250)

**239** 13 April 1724. Bromham. The dwellinghouse of Elizabeth Pead, widow. William Rose, Edward Goulding. (WRO A1/250)

**240** 10 Nov. 1724. Corsley. The dwellinghouse of John Meers. Robert Meares, Joshua Cuff. (WRO A1/250)

**241** 4 March 1725. Grittleton. The dwellinghouse of James Bristow, the dwellinghouse of Daniel Sargeant, and the dwellinghouse of Sarah Bristow, widow. [*Quaker*: see **259, 260**]. Henry Sanger, William Gardener. (WRO A1/250)

**242** [1725? *MS undated, but found between* **241** *and* **257**]. Middle Winterslow (*in Winterslow*]. The house of Henry Gibbons. [*Baptist*: see **305**]. John Rede, Henry Gibbons, Stephen Kent, Henry Steele, William Browning, Richard Mills, Samuel Leach. (WRO A1/250)

**243** 12 March 1725. Studley in Trowbridge. The now dwellinghouse of Sarah Elliot. [*Baptist?*: Doel 112]. Edward Barton, John Hurne, Thomas Hurne. [*This certificate has been written twice*]. (WRO A1/250)

**244** 6 April 1725. Langley Burrell. The dwellinghouse of Elizabeth Sabben. William Jones, Daniel Mundee, Robert Fisher. (WRO A1/250)

**245** 13 May 1725. Seend [*in Melksham*]. The dwellinghouse of Mr Stephen Flower. [*Presbyterian*: see **256**]. Nicholas Twinny, Hugh Gough, George Willy, Japhet Goodfellow. (WRO A1/250)

**246** 19 April 1726. Tisbury. The building newly erected on a close of William Furnel. [*Presbyterian*: Stribling 27]. William Randell, Andrew Alford. (WRO A1/250)

**247** 11 July 1726. Upton in East Knoyle. The dwellinghouse of John Williams. [*Baptist*: VCH 11, 96]. Samuel Williams, William Church. (WRO A1/250)

**248** 23 June 1727. Marlborough. The common hall called the Town Hall alias the Guildhall. [*Quaker*: see **259, 260**]. Henry Sanger, William Gardener. (WRO A1/250)

**249**   23 June 1727. Sutton Benger. The dwellinghouse of John Fry. [*Quaker*: VCH 3, 127]. Henry Sanger, William Gardener. (WRO A1/250)

**250**   24 June 1727. Sutton Benger. The dwellinghouse of William Price. [*Quaker*: see **249**]. Henry Sanger, William Gardener. (WRO A1/250)

**251**   12 July 1727. Bradford on Avon. The dwellinghouse of John Deverell. The mark of John Deverell, the mark of John Morris. (WRO A1/250)

**252**   11 Sept. 1727. Marlborough. A building situate on the north-west side of a messuage or tenement of Thomas Higham in High Street, parish of St Peter's, having the several backsides or gardens of Thomas Higham and John Batt on or towards the north-west, the stable or outhouse of Richard Munday on or towards the north-east, and the several messuages or tenements, backsides and gardens of Thomas Higham and Stephen Wild on or towards the south-east. Quaker. Isaac Farnell, Thomas Powell. (WRO G22/1/124)

**253**   30 Sept. 1727. Marlborough. A building now in the possession of Thomas Hancocke, gentleman, lately used as a brewhouse, lying in the High Ward, parish of St Peter and St Paul, the land of Nathaniel Merriman junior on or towards the north-east, the land of William Gough, gentleman, on or towards the south-west, the land of Thomas Hancocke on or towards the south-east, and a lane known as Back Lane or Blind Lane on or towards the north-west. [*Independent*: Stribling 20]. Thomas Hancock, Joseph Hockly, Benjamin Hockly, Thomas Hunt, Charles Hunt, Roger Neale. (WRO G22/1/123)

**254**   15 July 1728. Corsham. The house or building previously erected for a meeting house (but of late not so used). George Weeb, Robert Crew. (WRO A1/250)

**255**   16 April 1729. Corsham. The dwellinghouse of William Bull. Alwyn Hill, William Jones. (WRO A1/250)

**256**   6 April 1730. Seend [*in Melksham*]. The dwellinghouse of Nicholas Twinney. [*Presbyterian*: VCH 10, 296 (Chauncy)]. N. Chauncy, Hugh Gough, Stephen Bell. (WRO A1/250)

**257**   10 July 1732. East Knoyle. The dwellinghouse of Enoch Williams. Anabaptist. Robert Toogood, John Ponton, William Bowden. (WRO A1/250)

**258**   4 Oct. 1732. Ashton Keynes. The dwellinghouse or hired house of Thomas Taylor alias Corver. [*Quaker*: see **259, 260**]. Isaac Furnell, Robert Freman, Henry Seale. (WRO A1/250)

**259**   8 July 1734. Pickwick [*in Corsham*]. The dwellinghouse or hired house of

Thomas Bennett. [*Quaker*: see **266**]. Henry Sanger, John Neate junior, Henry Seale junior. (WRO A1/250)

**260** 8 July 1734. Westbury. The dwellinghouse or hired house of James Matravis. [*Quaker*: see **266**]. Henry Sanger, John Neate junior, Henry Seale junior. (WRO A1/250)

**261** 14 July 1734. Bratton [*in Westbury*]. The house now newly erected on a piece of ground commonly known by the name of Brown's Plot lying at the north-east corner of a ground called Brown's Berry. [*Baptist*: see **123**]. William Axford, John Aldridge Ballard, John Blatch, Henry Whitaker, Edward Frowd, Jeffery Whitaker, Philip Whitaker. (WRO A1/250)

**262** [1734? *MS undated, but found between* **259** *and* **264**]. Pickwick in Corsham. The dwellinghouse or hired house of Thomas Bennet. [*Quaker*: see **259**]. [*Unsigned*]. (WRO A1/250)

**263** [1735? *MS undated, but found between* **260** *and* **266**]. Stratton St Margaret. The dwellinghouse of Richard Jordan. Baptist. Richard Jordan, John Jordan, Richard Harvey, Jacob Panting. (WRO A1/250)

**264** 10 July 1735. Cleverton in Lea and Cleverton. The dwellinghouse of John Mills. Presbyterian. Francis Langly?, Henry Church. (WRO A1/250)

**265** 10 July 1735. Luckington. The hired house of Mary Burnley. Quaker. Giles Shurman?, William Fry. (WRO A1/250)

**266** 1 Oct. 1735. Luckington. The hired house of Sarah Burley. Quaker. John Jeffares, John Neate, Henry Seale junior, Andrew Sealy. (WRO A1/250)

**267** 6 Oct. 1735. Stratton St Margaret. The dwellinghouse of John Lea and Thomas Lea. Baptist. Nathaniel Merriman, Samuel Hawkes, Thomas Hancock. (WRO A1/250)

**268** 5 July 1737. Mere. The dwellinghouse or hired house of Joseph Gould. [*Quaker*: see **260**]. James Matravers, Joseph Hull, Paul Newman, John Moore. (WRO A1/250)

**269** 12 July 1737. Aldbourne. A new erected house in West Street. Presbyterian. Robert Whitheare, William Smith, Joshua Pizzie, Richard Witts. (WRO A1/250)

**270** 10 April 1738. Donhead St Mary. The house of John King. Presbyterian. John King, Gawain Little, Edmund Lush, Jacob Lush, the mark of Richard Lass, John Gray. (WRO A1/250)

**271** 21 June 1738. Ford in North Wraxall. The now dwellinghouse of John

Brewer. [*Baptist*: see **261, 276**]. John Edwards, John Watts, Henry Whitaker. (WRO A1/250)

**272**  11 July 1738. Corsley. The houses of John Batterel and Abraham Sanger. James Hopkins, John Mines, William Slade. (WRO A1/250)

**273**  10 Jan. 1739. Bradford on Avon. The dwellinghouse of John Pittman. [*Independent*: VCH 7, 33]. John Pitman, Ebenezer Earle, John Harvy, Nathaniel Pontin. (WRO A1/250)

**274**  [1739? *MS undated, but found between* **273** *and* **277**]. Broad Chalke. The dwellinghouse of Joseph Gould. [*Independent*: Haynes 2]. Joseph Gould, Robert Witt, Robert Crouch, Robert Newman, Benjamin Rabbets, James Bristowe. (WRO A1/250)

**275**  1 May 1739. Malmesbury. The house late in the possession of Thomas Hobbs in Abbey Row. William Hiller, John Hiller, James Hanks. (WRO A1/250)

**276**  9 July 1739. Keevil. The dwellinghouse of Mr Anthony Pyard. [*Baptist*: see **261**]. John Watts, Jeffery Whitaker, Anthony Piard. (WRO A1/250)

**277**  10 July 1739. Ridge in Chilmark. The dwellinghouse of Thomas Lampard. William Edwards, Thomas Lovett, Philip Moore. [*At foot, in another hand*] 'Mr John Halliday of Iford in the parish of Westwood near Bradford, Wilts.' (WRO A1/250)

**278**  17 April 1740. Easterton [*in Market Lavington*]. The dwellinghouse of Edward Draper. Anabaptist. James Collins, James Filkes, Samuel W. Webb. (WRO A1/250)

**279**  7 April 1741. Bradford on Avon. A house newly erected as a meeting house near St Margaret's Street, joining Morgans Hill. [*Independent*: VCH 3, 125]. Joshua Read, John Pitman, Francis Hislop, Jacob Norman. [*At foot*] 'We know not the form of words required by the act of Parliament'. (WRO A1/250)

**280**  3 Oct. 1741. Brinkworth. The new erected house on the lands of John Henly. [*Independent*: Antrobus 14]. John Weeks, Jeremiah Clifford. [*At foot*] 'Send this by the post to Israel May.' (WRO A1/250)

**281**  16 Nov. 1741. Castle Combe. The dwellinghouse of Benjamin Ladd. William Archard, Benjamin Ladd. (WRO A1/250)

**282**  17 Dec. 1741. Stratton St Margaret. The orchard, barn, barton, garden and . . . [*missing*], the dwelling (*houseing*) of John Lea and Thomas Lea lying contiguous. [*Baptist*: see **267**]. William Lawrence, Thomas Lea, Thomas Jordan. (WRO A1/250)

**283**  11 Jan. 1742. Westport St Mary. The dwellinghouse of Thomas Hobbes. Giles Pantin, Thomas Hobbs. (WRO A1/250)

**284**  23 Feb. 1742. Chippenham. The house of Joanna Eastridge. Quaker. Robert Rose, Andrew Rendoll junior, Joseph James, Richard Billett. (WRO D1/2/26)

**285**  31 March 1742. Alderton. The dwellinghouse and barn of Susannah Jaques, widow. Daniel Freem, Daniel Rogers, Daniel Watts. (WRO A1/250)

**286**  2 Oct. 1742. Brinkworth. The barn of Mr Robert Smith called 'Woulter' [*perhaps Water Hills*]. Robert Smith, John Henley, Thomas Aylife, John Henley junior. (WRO A1/250)

**287**  2 Oct. 1742. Kington Langley [*in Kington St Michael*]. The dwelling-house and barn of Richard Dovey. Richard Dovey, Philip Pearce, John Bright, John Salter. (WRO A1/250)

**288**  11 Jan. 1743. Monkton Farleigh. The dwellinghouse of Thomas Harris. Presbyterian. Thomas Harris, minister, Walter Grant, Benjamin Thearle? (WRO A1/250)

**289**  30 March 1743. Clack in Lyneham. The dwellinghouse of John Bryant. [*Independent?*: VCH 9, 103]. Matthew Heath, William Vines, Richard Smith. (WRO A1/250)

**290**  1 Oct. 1743. Brinkworth. The dwellinghouse of Francis Langley. [*Presbyterian*: see **264**]. Francis Langly, Henry Langly. (WRO A1/250)

**291**  4 April 1744. Hannington. The house, barn, stable, etc. of Diana Roberson. [*Baptist: wording similar to* **292**]. William York, William Bayley, John Daws, Samuel Day. (WRO A1/250)

**292**  4 April 1744. Stratton St Margaret. The house, barn, and stable of John Parsons, 'not having any worship of this kind lyeth att so great a distance that the inhabitance of the place above mentioned are not able to preform [*sic*] their duty.' [*Baptist*: see **263**]. William Day, Richard Jordan. (WRO A1/250)

**293**  July 1744. Langley Burrell. The dwellinghouse of Patience Knight, widow. Thomas Brown, the mark of William Jones. (WRO A1/250)

**294**  9 July 1744. Stanton St Quinton. The dwellinghouse of John Cockle. John Cockle, George Sandell. (WRO A1/250)

**295**　11 July 1744. Atworth (*Atford*) [*in Bradford on Avon*]. The dwellinghouse of Mr Henry Long. Henry Long, Robert Crew, Edward Crew. (WRO A1/250)

**296**　11 July 1744. Shurnhold (*Shirnal*) in Melksham. The messuage or tenement (now void) belonging to William Smith, gardener. William Smith, Charles Gerish, William Sawyer. (WRO A1/250)

**297**　9 Jan. 1745. Calne. The dwellinghouse of Simon Baker. Thomas Rawlings, Simon Backer. (WRO A1/250)

**298**　24 March 1745. Colerne. The dwellinghouse of John Tanner. Benjamin Ladd, John Tanner. (WRO A1/250)

**299**　15 April 1745. Foghamshire in Chippenham. The dwellinghouse of Joanna Cook, spinster. Robert Brien, William Mills. (WRO A1/250)

**300**　21 April 1745. Wilton. The dwellinghouse of Joseph Young. [*Presbyterian*: VCH 6, 32]. John Furz, John Chusens, Joseph Young, John Dolling, Thomas Blanford, John Smith, John Carpenter, John Kerby, Thomas Ward, Jonathan Turner senior, Jonathan Turner junior. (WRO A1/250)

**301**　[1745? *MS undated, but found between* **300** *and* **304**]. Luckington. A meeting or place for religious worship. [*Quaker*: see **265**]. William Fry, Richard Fry, Walter Price. (WRO A1/250)

**302**　22 April 1745. Broad Blunsdon [*in Highworth*]. The dwellinghouse of Jonathan Barnes. William Wiggins, Jonathan Garlick. (WRO A1/250)

**303**　22 April 1745. Swindon. The dwellinghouse of William Lang . . . [*missing*]. William Edwards, Richard Heath, the mark of Thomas Tibbell. (WRO A1/250)

**304**　25 April 1745. Urchfont. The house of John Manning newly built in the part commonly called the Upper Green. [*Anabaptist*: see **278**]. James Collins, Samuel Wright, esquire?, John Neaves, Thomas Weston. (WRO A1/250)

**305**　20 Dec. 1749 (17 Jan. 1750). Winterslow. The house of John Hooker. Baptist. William Steele, William Futcher, William Rogers, John Hooker, John Rede. (WRO D1/2/26)

**306**　7 Feb. 1751 (8 Feb. 1751). Salisbury. The house in Brown Street built for religious worship. Baptist. Richard Payne, John Rede, George Carter, Joseph Blake, Richard Holloway, Thomas Powell, Richard Spaggs. (WRO D1/2/26)

**307**　2 June 1754 (4 June 1754). Downton. 'On the account of some inconveniences attending the place of our meeting [we] have lately made another place convenient.' [*Particular Baptist*: see **344**]. Aaron Barling, John Weeks, Samuel Snelgar, William Weeks, Anthony Berryman, Thomas Eastman, Nathaniel Eastman, Thomas Weeks. (WRO D1/2/26)

**308**  15 June 1754 (18 June 1754). Winterslow. The dwellinghouse of John Sopp. [*Baptist*: see **305**]. William Steele, Thomas Etheredge, William Futcher, John Sopp, John Hooker. (WRO D1/2/26)

**309**  (13 July 1756). Bradford on Avon. A house or edifice lately erected adjoining the dwellinghouse of John Silby. Methodist. John Silby and others [*Only the licence, issued by Quarter Sessions, has been found*]. (WRO 1103/42)

**310**  9 Sept. 1756 (10 Sept. 1756). Salisbury. The house called Shoemakers Hall in Hog Lane. Independent. Henry Warne, John Shergold, Thomas Ward, James Begbie, William Warne, Joshua Sibly, John Stormont, Robert Newman, Benjamin Batchelor. (WRO D1/2/26)

**311**  30 July 1759 (6 Aug. 1759). Salisbury. A certain house lately erected in Church Street in St Edmund's parish. [*Methodist*: VCH 6, 159]. Thomas Johnson, John Warfield, William Simmonds, Thomas Mannings, William Mannings, Francis Jarrett. (WRO D1/2/26)

**312**  17 Nov. 1759 (27 Nov. 1759). Bewley in Lacock. The dwellinghouse and yard adjoining of Edward Barton. Independent. Christopher Mends, Edward Barton, Isaac Cottles, Robert Crew, George Nash, Walter Stevens, William Bockland. (WRO D1/2/27)

**313**  9 Dec. 1760 (25 Aug. 1761). Wilton and Salisbury. The houses of Oliver Hayhurst and Richard Ryley of Wilton, the houses of Martin Neave and Joseph Moore in Salisbury, and the house of James Moore in Castle Street, Salisbury (to be used occasionally). Quaker. Oliver Hayhurst, Richard Riley, Martin Neave, Sarah Croker, James Moore, Joseph? Moore. (WRO D1/2/27)

**314**  7 Sept. 1761 (9 Sept. 1761). Monk's in Corsham. The house of James Archar now occupied by Mary Tinson. Independent. George Stantial, Isaac Archar, Henry Banks, David Moody, John Davis, William Sawyer, William Adams, Baynard Bryant, Richard Silverthorne, Baynard Bryant junior, George Naish. (WRO D1/2/27)

**315**  21 Oct. 1765 (19 Nov. 1765). Westbury. The house which was some years since erected, at the south-west end of the town. [*Presbyterian*: HOOCCW 12–13]. J. Meylett, minister, Paul Phipps, Nicholas Phipps, William Phipps, Stephen Browne, William Ingram, Benjamin Peach, John Stillman, John Huntley. (WRO D25/6)

**316**  4 Dec. 1765 (5 Dec. 1765). Cholderton (*West Cholderton*). The dwellinghouse of Henry Blatch. Independent. James Blatch, Henry Blatch, John Hooker, Benjamin Blatch, William Blatch, David Andrews. (WRO D1/2/27)

**317**   2 Oct. 1766 (2 Oct. 1766). Ratfyn [*in Amesbury*]. Mr James Blatch has set apart a house. Independent. James Blatch, William Blatch, Henry Blatch, William Foorder, Thomas Wingrove, Thomas Powell. (WRO D1/2/27)

**318**   3 Jan. 1767 (12 Jan. 1767). East Town in Steeple Ashton. The house of John Baggs. Independent. John Baggs, Richard Watts, Daniel Hill, the mark of Robert Townsend, Thomas Turner, William Ferris. (D1/2/27)

**319**   4 June 1767 (4 June 1767). Salisbury. A new meeting house in Scots Lane, under the ministerial care of Mr John Wheeller. [*Independent*: see **310**]. John Wheeller, Henry Warne, John Stormont, Joseph Warne, George Randall, Abraham Newman, John Batchelor, William Banning. William Warne. (WRO D1/2/27)

**320**   (7 Jan. 1768). Damerham. The house of Mr James Dowding. James Dowding, Peter Bullin, John White, William Masters, Ann White, the mark of Sarah Baily. (WRO D1/2/27)

**321**   27 July 1768 (1 Aug. 1768). Maiden Bradley. The dwellinghouse of Henry Dyer, farmer. [*Methodist*: Hall 206]. Alexander Mather, Henry Dyer, John Marfield, William Skane. (WRO D1/2/27)

**322**   14 Dec. 1768 (4 Jan. 1769). Hilperton. The house of Sarah Webb. Independent. Sarah Webb, Mary Webb, Sarah Slade, William Ferris, Stephen Slade, John Cogswell. (WRO D1/2/27)

**323**   10 Sept. 1770 (17 Sept. 1770). Chippenham. A house or building lately erected to be used as a dissenters' meeting house. Richard Hall, James Andrews, Francis Edwards, Thomas Brooks, Henry Elliott, Walter Brooks. (WRO D1/2/27)

**324**   17 Aug. 1771 (28 Aug. 1771). Devizes. The dwellinghouse of Martha Phillips, widow, situated in the New Port, St John's parish. Edward Bayly, John Filkes, Thomas Neeves, housekeepers in Devizes. (WRO D1/2/27)

**325**   (24 Sept. 1771). Melksham. The dwellinghouse belonging to William Coleman of Melksham and John Jones of Devizes, in Melksham. Charles Collingborn, Thomas Hoase, John Bayly, housekeepers in Melksham. (WRO D1/2/27)

**326**   4 Jan. 1772 (8 Jan. 1772). Devizes. The messuage and dwellinghouse late in the possession of Mr John Ferris and now in the possession of Mr Richard Buck in St Mary's parish. Edward Bayly, Thomas Neeves, William Hopkins, housekeepers in Devizes. (WRO D1/2/27)

**327** 13 May 1772 (30 May 1772). 'Farely' [*Monkton Farleigh or Farley in Alderbury*]. The dwellinghouse of Margaret Hatcher. Methodist. John Batten, Ann Williams, the mark of Marion Lawrence?, Philip Carter Williams?, the mark of Jeremy Mills?. (WRO D1/2/27)

**328** 20 May 1772 (30 May 1772). Aldbourne. The house of Thomas Vokins. Methodist. John Smith, James Mudge, Stephen Mudge, Thomas Vokins. (WRO D1/2/27)

**329** 11 Sept. 1772 (15 Sept. 1772) Marlborough. The dwellinghouse of John Orchard opposite to Mr Jackson's, sackweaver, in the Marsh in St Mary's parish. Independent. Henry Turner, John Allen, Joseph Allen, housekeepers in Marlborough. (WRO D1/2/27)

**330** 24 Oct. 1772 (30 Oct. 1772). Cricklade. The dwellinghouse of Thomas Batt opposite to Mr Pledwell's?, gentleman, in St Sampson's parish. Independent. Thomas Batt, Jonathan Barns, Henry Smart, housekeepers in Cricklade St Sampson's. (WRO D1/2/27)

**331** 2 Jan. 1773 (5 Jan. 1773). Hilperton. The messuage or tenement and dwellinghouse now in the possession of Stephen Slade. Independent. Stephen Slade, James Slade, Joseph Cottle, George Holloway, Henry Slade, John Cogswill, William Gaiton, housekeepers in Hilperton. (WRO D1/2/27)

**332** 6 Jan. 1773 (15 Jan. 1773). Corsley. A meeting house belonging to John Tucker and George Rabbits at Corsley Lane End. Methodist. John Tucker, George Rabbitts, Thomas Adames, Thomas Holley, housekeepers in Corsley. (WRO D1/2/27)

**333** 6 Jan. 1773 (15 Jan. 1773). Warminster. The dwellinghouse of William Adlam in Back Lane. Methodist. Caleb Daniel, Nathaniel White, James Bond, Charles Dudden, housekeepers in Warminster. (WRO D1/2/27)

**334** 30 Jan. 1773 (6 Feb. 1773). Crudwell. A building belonging to Thomas Ludlow known by the name of a chandler's shop and opposite to Richard White's. Independent. Matthew Robertson, William Robertson, the mark of Richard White, housekeepers in Crudwell. (WRO D1/2/27)

**335** 15 March 1773 (17 March 1773). Trowbridge. The house late in the occupation of Mr Abraham Martain of Fore Street, but now belonging to John Spalding. [*Sandemanians*: Rogers 67]. Peter Rudman, minister, George Skane and David Stow, deacons, James Newman, John Morley, James Parffett. (WRO D1/2/27)

**336** 10 May 1773 (11 May 1773). Tollard Royal. The dwellinghouse of George Green. Methodist. George Green, John Sims, John Green, Elias Sibly, George Green junior. (WRO D1/2/27)

**337**   30 June 1773 (23 Sept. 1773). Lyneham. A dwelli
William Jacobs opposite to the Green. Independent. ᴅᵃⁿⁱᵉⁱ ᴵᵃᵒ, ᴶᵒ....
Reynolds, William Jacobs, William Ody, Jonathan Goff, Joseph Hatten,
Richard Bushell, James Taner, housekeepers in Lyneham. (WRO D1/2/27)

**338**   7 Aug. 1773 (11 Aug. 1773). Devizes. Part of the dwellinghouse of
William Swan, ironmonger, situated in the New Port, St John's parish.
Independent. Thomas Hood, Philip Phillips, John Slade, John Ashly, John
Sloper, Philip Caedby, housekeepers in Devizes. (WRO D1/2/27)

**339**   25 May 1774 (27 June 1774). North Bradley. The messuage or tenement
and dwellinghouse now in the possession of George Batchelor. Independent
[*recte* Baptist?: see **361** and Doel 187]. George Batchelor, John Dicks, John
Hussey, William Wilkens, John Butcher, John Silverthorn, John Wingrove,
John Gibbs, housekeepers in North Bradley. (WRO D1/2/27)

**340**   10 March 1775 (21 March 1775). Hankerton. A dwellinghouse belonging
to Henry Hill. Independent. Giles Ludlow, Charles How, Henry Hill,
housekeepers in Hankerton. (WRO D1/2/27)

**341**   27 March 1775 (27 March 1775). Seend [*in Melksham*]. We have built and
set apart a convenient house or room at the west end of Seend. Methodist.
Thomas Rutty, Daniel Flower, Thomas Twinny, housekeepers in Seend.
(WRO D1/2/27)

**342**   17 April 1775 (11 April 1775 [*sic*]). Potterne. A dwellinghouse belonging
to Thomas Hill. Independent. John Thomas, the mark of James Wicks, the
mark of Thomas Hill, Robert Burden. (WRO D1/2/27)

**343**   17 April 1775 (11 April 1775 [*sic*]). Urchfont. An outhouse and building
with the court or curtilage thereto belonging being the property of Mr Charles
Giddings. Independent. Robert Sloper, John Sloper, Thomas Hood, John
Slade, Thomas Jones. (WRO D1/2/27)

**344**   21 Oct. 1775 (21 Oct. 1775). Downton. A meeting house adjoining a
slaughterhouse belonging at present to Nathaniel Eastman lying near the road
leading from Salisbury to Ringwood. Particular Baptist. Samuel Evans,
Nathaniel Eastman, G. Guier, John Eastman, Nathaniel Eastman junior.
(WRO D1/2/27)

**345**   3 Jan. 1776 (9 Jan. 1776). Bodenham in Downton. The house of Mrs
Anna Attwaters, widow. Baptist. H. Philips, John Grose, Samuel Temple-
man, John Smith, Thomas Adlem, Edward Lanham, James Davis. (WRO
D1/2/27)

**346**   28 March 1776 (23 April 1776). Amesbury. The house of Adam

Alldridge. Independent. Adam Alldridge, Harry Alldridge, Joseph Bishop, George Williams, John Tinnims, Thomas Goddard. (WRO D1/2/27)

**347** 15 April 1776 (24 April 1776). Ashton Keynes. A dwellinghouse belonging to Richard Fry opposite to Home Common. Independent. Richard Fry, Robert Selby, Jeremiah Telling, Thomas Mathews, George Deneley, Hannah Taylor, Edward Telling, Thomas Jefferis, William Jefferis, Sarah Jefferis, housekeepers in Ashton Keynes. (WRO D1/2/27)

**348** 20 April 1776 (24 April 1776). Sherston. A house belonging to John Ball near to the Upper Cross. Independent. William Thompson, Thomas Newlands, Joseph Pinnell, John Goulden, Nathaniel Thompson, John Ind, housekeepers in Sherston. (WRO D1/2/27)

**349** 30 Sept. 1776 (8 Oct. 1776). Broad Chalke. The dwellinghouse of James Laws in South Street. Independent. David Whitmarsh, Josiah Gould, Robert Fox, James Lawes, David Lawes, Richard Follot. (WRO D1/2/27)

**350** 1 Jan. 1777 (17 Jan. 1777). Devizes. The house of Thomas Gibbs in St Mary's parish. Methodist. Thomas Gibbs, Samuel Wells, William Shill. (WRO D1/2/27)

**351** 4 Jan. 1777 (17 Jan. 1777). Kingston Deverill. The house of Priscilla Tudgey, widow. Methodist. The mark of Priscilla Tudgey, John Pressly, Joseph Raxworthy, inhabitants of Kingston Deverill. (WRO D1/2/27)

**352** 8 March 1777 (11 March 1777). Devizes. A certain building lately erected in St Mary's parish commonly called the Independent Chapel. Independent. John Filkes, Daniel Baker, John Slade, Thomas Hood, John Sloper, James Crook, housekeepers in Devizes. (WRO D1/2/27)

**353** 8 March 1777 (11 March 1777). Urchfont. The house of John Hadrill. Independent. John Hadrill, John Pierce, John Giddings, housekeepers in Urchfont. (WRO D1/2/27)

**354** 30 April 1777 (12 May 1777). Longbridge Deverill. A house or building now rented by William Jameson and the property of Richard Hayes. Independent. William Jameson, William Newman, Benjamin Adlam, William Slade, Thomas Lovett, Ralph Barker, James Moffat, John Curtis. (WRO D1/2/27)

**355** 29 Sept. 1777 (8 Oct. 1777). East Stowell in Wilcot. The house of John Absalom. Independent. John Absalom, John Bartholomew, Philip Pavey?, housekeepers at East Stowell. (WRO D1/2/27)

**356** 30 Oct. 1777 (7 Nov. 1777). South Newton. A house, the property of Joseph Horn. Independent. Joseph Horn, Benjamin Horn, James Wooldridge,

William Wingrove, William Fisher, John Jefferis, Thomas Davis, housekeepers in South Newton. (WRO D1/2/27)

**357** 6 June 1778 (8 June 1778). Castle Eaton. The dwellinghouse of James Matthews. Independent. Daniel Iles, James Mathews, John Smith, housekeepers in Castle Eaton. (WRO D1/2/27)

**358** 29 Oct. 1778 (30 Oct. 1778). Wilton. The dwellinghouse of John Sutton, baker. Methodist. John Sutton, Daniel Whitmarsh, Thomas Pierce, the mark of John Jannowy, the mark of Thomas Wingrove, the mark of William Chalk, housekeepers in Wilton. (WRO D1/2/27)

**359** 7 March 1779 (16 March 1779). Imber. A house or building in the possession of and property of William Aldridge Ballard. Independent. Thomas Scammell, William Jameson, William Slade, Thomas Lovett, Thomas Ubsdell, Ralph Barker, Harry Toogood, Robert Butt junior, Thomas Brown, James Aldridge. (WRO D1/2/28)

**360** 5 June 1779 (3 July 1779). Wootton Bassett. A dwellinghouse of William Arman. Independent. William Arman, Peter Skinner, Richard Skinner, William Rix, Bartholomew Horsell, William Jefferis, William Young, Edward Briant. (WRO D1/2/28)

**361** 15 April 1780 (1 May 1780). North Bradley. A new meeting house. Baptist. Robert Marshman, William Clift, George Batchelor, John Hussey, John Dicks, William Butcher, Joshua Keats, John Sargent, John Butcher, William Vincent. (WRO D1/2/28)

**362** 20 April 1780 (1 May 1780). Bodenham in Downton. The house of Mr Attwaters situated by the side of the road from Salisbury to Downton. Baptist. Henry Philips, Thomas Attwater, John Grove, James Adams, Samuel Templeman, John Smith, John Smith junior, John Merris, Cornelius Hackett, John Green. (WRO D1/2/28)

**363** 15 June 1780 (24 June 1780). Wilton. A house in Frog Lane late the property of Messrs Haws and Adcock. Methodist. James Hiscutt, Daniel Whitmarsh, John Sutton, James Bland, housekeepers in Wilton. (WRO D1/2/28)

**364** 16 Oct. 1780 (21 Oct. 1780). Stoke Farthing in Broad Chalk. The dwellinghouse of Thomas Haydon, labourer. Methodist. Thomas Day, Robert Fox junior, Thomas Haydon, John Burton, Stephen Barter, John Golden, housekeepers in Broad Chalk. (WRO D1/2/28)

**365** 8 Jan. 1781 (9 Jan. 1781). Bulford. The house of Mr Thomas Mold, papermaker, adjoining the paper mill as being one with the same. Methodist.

Thomas Mould, James Rattew, John Rattew, Thomas Lawrence, housekeepers in Bulford. (WRO D1/2/28)

**366**   20 June 1781 (1781). Tisbury. The messuage or tenement and dwellinghouse now in the possession of Thomas Turner. Independent. Thomas Turner, William Turner, John Targett, William Marsh, James Sydenham, housekeepers in Tisbury. (WRO D1/2/28)

**367**   28 July 1781 (18 Aug. 1781). Ebbesborne Wake. The messuage or tenement and dwellinghouse now in the possession of John West. Independent. The mark of John West, Peter Randell, William Gould, John Adams, Robert Harris, housekeepers in Ebbesborne Wake. (WRO D1/2/28)

**368**   9 Aug. 1781 (18 Aug. 1781). Limpley Stoke [*in Bradford on Avon*]. The messuage or tenement and dwellinghouse now in the possession of John Lasbury. Independent. John Lasbury, Thomas Lasbury, Thomas Kelson, Charles Giles, James Bull, John Wilkins, housekeepers in Limpley Stoke. (WRO D1/2/28)

**369**   7 Dec. 1781 (23 Jan. 1782). Clyffe Pypard. The dwellinghouse of Mr Abel Greeneway. Baptist. Abel Greenway, Susanna Greenaway, James Archer, Jacob Archer, William Chequer, Thomas Milsom, the mark of John Church, the mark of Richard Church, the mark of Charles Snow, the mark of Jacob Milsome, housekeepers in Clyffe Pypard. (WRO D1/2/28)

**370**   30 Dec. 1781 (18 Jan. 1782) Ebbesborne Wake. We have repaired a house now in the possession of John West to set it aside as a meeting house. Independent. The mark of John West, William Gould, John Adams, the mark of John Trobridg, housekeepers in Ebbesborne Wake. (WRO D1/2/28)

**371**   21 Jan. 1782 (23 Jan. 1782). Wroughton. Part of the dwellinghouse of Mr John Tanner. Baptist. John Tanner, Thomas Wallis, Thomas Suter, Amy Tanner, the mark of John James, the mark of Thomas Kimber, John Ody, Richard Tanner, housekeepers in Wroughton. (WRO D1/2/28)

**372**   26 March 1782 (27 March 1782). Trowbridge. The house in the possession of Mrs Mary Cook adjoining the dwellinghouse of Mr Thomas Martin. Methodist. Mary Cook, Joseph Porter, Benjamin Snelling, John Knapp, John Wibley, inhabitants and housekeepers of Trowbridge. (WRO D1/2/28)

**373**   11 Feb. 1783 (21 Feb. 1783). Bower Chalke. The messuage or tenement and dwellinghouse and premises now in the possession of Richard Gould. Independent. Richard Gould, John Gould, the mark of John Newman, William Gould, John Bennett, housekeepers in Bower Chalke. (WRO D1/2/28)

**374** (5 March 1783). Broad Chalke. The dwellinghouse of Robert Fox, labourer. Methodist. Robert Fox, John Golden, William Bridle, John Antram, housekeepers in Broad Chalke. (WRO D1/2/28)

**375** 2 July 1783 (2 Aug. 1783). Semington [*in Steeple Ashton*]. The messuage or tenement and dwellinghouse now in the occupation of William Beaven. Independent. Martin Drinkwater, William Beavan, John Wilshire, William Ferris, housekeepers in Semington. (WRO D1/2/28)

**376** 4 July 1783 (9 July 1783). Christian Malford. A house belonging to Daniel Bath. Independent. Daniel Bath, Richard Compton, Thomas Compton, Sarah Skuse, Richard Hull, inhabitants of Christian Malford. (WRO D1/2/28)

**377** 8 April 1784. Imber. The house of Thomas Gibbs. Baptist (*dissenters who scruple infant baptism*). J Collins, Peter Anstie, Benjamin Webb Anstie, John Cooper. [*At foot*] 'Mr Wm Whitchurch of Frome Sellwood in the co. of Somerset has taken the oaths as a protestant dissent.' (WRO A1/110 E1784)

**378** 20 April 1784. Melksham. A house purposely erected. Baptist (*dissenters who scruple infant baptism*). James Collins, John Ledyard, William Taylor (WRO A1/110 E1784)

**379** 17 May 1784 (24 Aug. 1784). Winterslow. The dwellinghouse of Mr Saney Collins. Independent. John Chalk, Thomas Bell, Charles Collins, John Sopp senior, John Sopp junior, William Collins, housekeepers in Winterslow. (WRO D1/2/28)

**380** 14 Sept. 1784 (21 Sept. 1784). Broughton Gifford. The messuage or tenement and dwellinghouse now in the occupation of Isaac Bull. Independent. William Goore, James Mortimr, Isaac Bull, John Harford, Jacob Keen, housekeepers in Broughton Gifford. (WRO D1/2/28)

**381** 5 Oct. 1784 (9 Oct. 1784). Wilcot. The dwellinghouse of Mr Richard Pavy. Independent. Cornelius Winter, Joseph Surman, Richard Pavey, John Bertholomew, William Geall, Daniel Thorngate, Adam Barber. (WRO D1/2/28)

**382** 24 Feb. 1785 (5 March 1785). Pewsey. The dwellinghouse of William Yeats. Independent. William Yeats, John Winter, William Munday, John Lydard, Gabriel Brine, David Sheppard, Thomas Whitebread. (WRO D1/2/28)

**383** 4 April 1785. Great Cheverell. The house of Sarah Light together with the courts adjoining. Independent. The mark of Sarah Light, the mark of Elizabeth Dowden, the mark of Anna Dowden, the mark of John Matthews, the mark of William Dowden, housekeepers in Great Cheverell, Thomas Wastfield. (WRO A1/110 E1785)

**384** 4 April 1785. Littleton Pannell in West Lavington. The house of William Chapman together with the courts adjoining. Independent. William Chapman, David Saunders, Thomas Goddard, housekeepers at Littleton. (WRO A1/110 E1785)

**385** [?April 1785]. Bromham. The house of John Herring. [*Note*] 'Original certificate not found.' (WRO A1/150/22)

**386** 23 May 1785. Avebury. The dwellinghouse of Mr Richard Thring. Independent. William Alexander senior, the mark of John Philpot, the mark of Robert Philpot, the mark of William Nurden, the mark of Michael Wiltshire, the mark of Thomas Cary, John Horsell, John Wiltshire, Joseph Blake, Thomas Wiltshire, William Russell, the mark of Thomas Alexander. (WRO D1/2/28)

**387** 26 Nov. 1785. Stratton St Margaret. The dwellinghouse of Susanna Fowler. Independent. Mary Day, John Jordan, William Day, Richard Woolford, William Hall, Susanna Fowler, housekeepers in Stratton St Margaret. (WRO D1/2/28)

**388** 1 April 1786 (11 April 1786). Tollard Royal. The house of George Green, farmer. Methodist. Simon Day, Elias Green, George Green, John Sims, Joseph Sims, John Green, housekeepers in Tollard Royal. (WRO D1/2/28)

**389** 19 May 1786 (25 May 1786). Wilcot. The dwellinghouse of Daniel Thorngate. Independent. Cornelius Winter, John Bartholomew, John Bartlet, Adam Barber, Philip Pavey, Daniel Thorngate. (WRO D1/2/28)

**390** 1 Sept. 1786 (7 Sept. 1786). Sutton Veny. A house now rented by James Foyle and the property of William Hinton. Independent. James Foyell, William Imber, Joseph Everett, William Cunnington, Ralph Barker, Harry Toogood. (WRO D1/2/28)

**391** [?Sept. 1786]. Highworth. The house of John Hedges in Swindon Street. Independent. [*Note*] 'Origl. cert not found.' (WRO A1/150/22)

**392** 9 Nov. 1786 (11 Nov. 1786). Fonthill Giffard. A building adjoining the dwellinghouse of Thomas Stephens. Independent. The mark of Thomas Stephens, the mark of Joseph Crouch, John Steevens, William Turner, Walter Hayward, Thomas Snow, housekeepers in Fonthill Giffard. (WRO D1/2/28)

**393** 9 Nov. 1786 (20 Nov. 1786). Fonthill Giffard. A building adjoining the dwellinghouse of Thomas Stephens. Independent. Thomas Stevens, the mark of Joseph Crouch, the mark of John Stevens, the mark of Walter Hayward,

Thomas Snow, William Clemons, housekeepers in Fonthill Giffard. (WRO D1/2/28)

**394** [?Jan. 1787]. Bulkington [*in Keevil*]. The house of John Wiltshire. Independent. [*Note*] 'Original certificate not found.' (WRO A1/150/22)

**395** 5 March 1787 (6 March 1787). Hindon. The dwellinghouse of William Wyer. Independent. James Burleigh, William Sandle, William Wyer, the mark of Joseph Scammell, William Clemons, John Gough, housekeepers in Hindon. (WRO D1/2/28)

**396** 6 May 1787 (22 Dec. 1787). Fonthill Giffard. A dwellinghouse called or known by the name of Fields. Independent. E Spencer, the mark of Joseph Crowch, the mark of John Stevens, James Nisbick, William Gattrell, Thomas Snow, housekeepers in Fonthill Giffard. (WRO D1/2/28)

**397** 27 July 1787 (30 July 1787). Salisbury. A large room in the house of William Fricker, gentleman, situate in Salt Lane in St Edmund's parish. Quaker. William Fricker, William Whitchart, Edward Humphreys, John Humphreys, of Salisbury. [*This certificate is addressed to*] 'Shute Barrington commonly call'd the Honble and Rt. Revd. Shute Lord Bishop of Sarum.' (WRO D1/2/28)

**398** 27 July 1787 (30 July 1787). Quidhampton in Fugglestone St Peter. A large room in the house of James Smith, clothier. Quaker. William Fricker, William Whitchart, Edward Humphreys, John Humphreys. (WRO D1/2/28)

**399** 24 Aug. 1787 (27 Aug. 1787). Stowell in Wilcot. The house together with the spaces or courts in the front and back part of the said house belonging to or in the occupation of John Bartlett. Baptist (*Protestant dissenters scrupling the baptizing of infants*). James Dyer, James Collins, Thomas Freeman, John Bartlett, Thomas Robince, Luke Thorngate. (WRO D1/2/28)

**400** 27 Aug. 1787 (8 Sept. 1787). Donhead St Mary. A building now occupied by Silas Harris, heel-maker. Independent. Silas Harris, Joseph Wiyett, the mark of John Harris, Joseph Jenkins, William Horder, housekeepers in Donhead St Mary. (WRO D1/2/28)

**401** 26 Sept. 1787 (27 Sept. 1787). Worton in Potterne. The house of George Biggs. Independent. Jonathan White, George Biggs, William Biggs, James Biggs, Robert Hampton, housekeepers in Worton. (WRO D1/2/28)

**402** 1 Oct. 1787 (31 Oct. 1787). Yatesbury. The dwellinghouse of Mr John Daish. Independent. William Bird, Thomas Colemen, William Willis, John Shurgal, Joseph Tuck, John Daish. (WRO D1/2/28)

**403** 2 Oct. 1787 (3 Oct. 1787). Downton. A meeting house built on land commonly called Gravel Pit. General Baptist. The mark of Samuel Bailey, the mark of Samuel Thorne, Henry Shergold, John Kellaway, William Green. (WRO D1/2/28)

**404** 24 Jan. 1788 (1788). Downton. The dwellinghouse of Samuel Baeley. General Baptist. Henry Shergold, the mark of Samuel Bailey, Samuel Thorn. (WRO D1/2/28)

**405** 31 Jan. 1788 (9 Feb. 1788). Imber. The two houses of Thomas Westfield junior inhabitated by Thomas Westfield junior together with the gardens adjoining. Baptist (*who scruple infant baptism*). John Clem, John Carter, Thomas Chambers, the mark of John Blagdon, housekeepers in Imber. (WRO D1/2/28)

**406** 31 Jan. 1788 (1788). Norton Bavant. The house of John Blagden. Independent. William Webb, Edward Moody, Thomas Chambers, the mark of John Blagdon, housekeepers in Norton Bavant. (WRO D1/2/28)

**407** 22 April 1788 (29 April 1788). Quidhampton [*in Fugglestone St Peter*]. The dwellinghouse of Benjamin Chiverton, yeoman. Methodist. Nicholas Pearce, William Tabor, Charles Tongs, housekeepers in Quidhampton. (WRO D1/2/28)

**408** 19 May 1788 (20 May 1788). Farley [*in Alderbury?*]. The house of John Batten with the garden thereunto belonging. Independent. The mark of Thomas Batten, Robert White, Edward Williams, James Parson, George Ballard, Matthew Noyes. (WRO D1/2/28)

**409** 16 June 1788 (30 June 1788). Highworth. A dwellinghouse converted for the sole purpose of the service and worship of Almighty God, situate in the High Street opposite to the Bull Inn. Independent. Thomas Collins, the mark of William Hagetts, William Sheppard, the mark of Thomas Anns, Philip Cook, Thomas Angel, Joseph Bailey, John Hedges, William Hiscocks, John Baughan, Edward Green, William Winning. [*Not registered in WRO D1/2/28, but the original certificate and licence are reproduced in facsimile in* Beck, 4].

**410** 30 June 1788 (5 July 1788). Winterslow. A large room in the house of John Bath, dealer in fish. Quaker. William Fricker, William Whitehart, Edward Humphreys, John Humphreys, of Salisbury. (WRO D1/2/28)

**411** (15 July 1788). Coate in Bishops Cannings. The house of Frederick Pinchin. (WRO A1/150/22, not on A1/110 T1788)

**412** (15 July 1788). Keevil. The house of James Bendy. (WRO A1/150/22, not on A1/110 T1788)

**413** 18 Aug. 1788 (25 Aug. 1788). Corsham. A house lately a malthouse the property of James Berry, yeoman, of the parish of 'Keinton', Wiltshire, situated in Corsham behind a dwellinghouse belonging to James Berry occupied by William Ballinger. Independent. Abraham Tanner, Alexander McLoud, Thomas Chubb, Betty Barton, Thomas Gay, Thomas Whiteker, Thomas Franklin, Michael Ford, residing in Corsham. (WRO D1/2/28)

**414**  21 Aug. 1788 (25 Aug. 1788). Lacock. A dwellinghouse the property of Thomas Dowswell formerly known by the name of the White Hart. Independent. Robert Stevens, James Naish, William Hitcens, John Angel junior, John Angel senior, James Smolkem, Joseph Angel, John Prichard, residing in Lacock. (WRO D1/2/28)

**415**  8 Oct. 1788 (10 Jan. 1789). Broughton Gifford. A house fitted up for the purpose. Baptist. Stephen Taylor, John Keen, Henry Keen, Isaac Bull, Stephen Weston, John Gwyer, John Sealy, John Down, William Davis, John Davis, George Cleverly, James Mayell. (WRO D1/2/28)

**416**  13 July 1789. East Knoyle. The dwellinghouse of James Lush. Independent. Emanuel Ewens, James Lush, John Lampard, the mark of William Inches, William Shephard, Luke Fletcher, housekeepers in East Knoyle. (WRO D1/2/28)

**417**  15 Dec. 1789 (15 Feb. 1790). Avebury. A dwellinghouse the property of Mr Richard Thring and Mr Robert Nalder. Independent. George Underwood, William Cullimore, the mark of Thomas Mortemore, John Wiltshire, Gabriel Chivers, Thomas New, Joseph Blake, Thomas Griffin, William Russell, Thomas Cary, the mark of William Hillier, John Merchant, William Roman. (WRO D1/2/28)

**418**  14 Jan 1790 (30 Jan. 1790). Atworth [*in Bradford on Avon*]. A dwellinghouse the property of William Webb. Baptist. James Blake, William Gay, James Webb, Stephen Taylor, John Barlow, James Hulbert, John Blatchley, housekeepers in Atworth. (WRO D1/2/28)

**419**  18 Feb. 1790 (18 Feb. 1790). Bradford on Avon. A house or building now rented by William Chapman and the property of Mary Barber of Trowbridge. Particular Baptist. Thomas Jotham, William Jotham, Richard Pollard, Isaac Dole, Thomas Hart, John Davis, Nathaniel Alexander, Grace Mathews, the mark of Edmund Biggs, Mary Chapman, Ann Alexander, William Chapman, Samuel Mathews, Sary Winfries, Mary Hart. (WRO D1/2/28)

**420**  18 Feb. 1790 (19 Feb. 1790). Farley [*in Alderbury*]. The house, yard and barn of Thomas Williams. Baptist. Thomas Williams, Henry Hatcher, George Ballard, Edward Williams, Robert Hatcher, Matthew Noyse, Abraham Prewett, William Bell. (WRO D1/2/28; WRO D26/3)

**421**  20 Feb. 1790 (24 Feb. 1790). Warminster. A building formerly occupied by John Whittlock deceased as a blacksmith's shop, but now in the tenure of James Ludlow situate in the West End of Warminster. [*Methodist*?: Gunn 62, VCH 8, 127]. William Jervis, James Ludlow, John Spicer, Benjamin Steedman, housekeepers in Warminster. (WRO D1/2/28)

**422**  28 March 1790 (31 March 1790). Winterslow in Idmiston (*Edminston*). The house and garden of William Collins. Independent. William Collins, Alexander Collins, the mark of John Stone, the mark of John Hutfield, James Collins. (WRO D1/2/28)

**423**  10 May 1790 (15 May 1790). Winterslow. The house and garden of John Stone on the Common. Independent. James Collins, the mark of Stephen Perrich, the mark of John Stone, the mark of John Hutfield, Alexander Collins, housekeepers in Winterslow. (WRO D1/2/28)

**424**  11 June 1790 (12 June 1790). Warminster. A house now rented by Thomas Ponton and the property of Samuel Lewis. Independent. Ralph Barker, B Everett, Robert West, Thomas Lock, James Moffat, John Moore. (WRO D1/2/28)

**425**  12 Aug. 1790 (13 Aug. 1790). Bradford on Avon. A house or building situate in a field commonly known or called by the name of Berefield, the property of Caleb Hodges and others. Independent. Caleb Hodges, John Batchelor, Edward Ricketts, James Alexander, Henry Wiltsher, James Daunton, Jonah Smith, James Bull. (WRO D1/2/28)

**426**  16 Aug. 1790 (29 Jan. 1791). Salisbury. We have lately altered our house in Scots Lane by enlarging and rendering it more eligible and convenient for the congregation assembling therein. Independent. John Adams, Joseph Warne, William Wheeler, William Banning?, James Crower, Thomas Mist Harrison, William Button, Thomas Luke, Abraham Newman, Thomas Blundell, John Franklin, William Bennett, housekeepers in Salisbury. (WRO D1/2/28)

**427**  31 Dec. 1790 (3 Jan. 1791). Donhead St Andrew. A building now occupied by James Kellaway, miller. Independent. James Kelleway, Sebastian Haskell, William Singleton, Thomas Gould, Silas Foot, housekeepers in Donhead St Andrew. (WRO D1/2/28)

**428**  17 Jan. 1791 (22 Jan. 1791). Tinhead in Edington. The house of James Oram. Independent. Richard Rice, James Coulrick, James Ford, Thomas Lad, Simon Haggard, James Oram, housekeepers in Edington. (WRO D1/2/28)

**429**  2 May 1791 (9 May 1791). Sutton Veny. A tenement now occupied by William Imber the proprietor of the premises. Independent. Thomas Gibbons,

William Imber, Edward Imber, William Long, John Barter, Thomas Imber, Ralph Barker, Thomas Lovett, Richard Pierce, R. Everett. (WRO D1/2/28)

**430** 25 June 1791 (28 June 1791). Staverton in Trowbridge. The messuage or tenement and dwellinghouse now in the possession of Peter Collier. Independent. William Linzey, William Axford, William Hudd, Peter Collier, housekeepers in Staverton. (WRO D1/2/28)

**431** 25 June 1791. Staverton in Trowbridge. The messuage or tenement and dwellinghouse now in the possession of Peter Collier. Independent. William Linzey, William Axford, William Hudd, Peter Collier, housekeepers in Staverton. (WRO A1/110 T1791)

**432** 10 Oct. 1791 (20 Oct. 1791). Fox Holes in Longbridge Deverill. A building newly erected. William Keene, Thomas Harrington, Benjamin Harrington, Robert Butcher, housekeepers in Longbridge Deverill. (WRO D1/2/29)

**433** 10 Jan. 1792. Bremhill. A building in the occupation of Ambrose Hayward. Independent. Ambrose Hayward, William Pullen, John Freem, Joseph Gale, Cooper Gale, Thomas Hull. (WRO A1/110 H1792)

**434** (25 Jan. 1792). Devizes. A new erected edifice or building with a court in which the chapel is built in the Old Port, St Mary's parish. [*Independent?*: see 506]. J.L. Fenner, minister, John Anstie, George Hillier, Richard Knight, William Williams. (PRO RG31/8 Devizes Borough)

**435** 15 Feb. 1792 (20 Feb. 1792). Pewsey. The dwellinghouse of William Flippens. Independent. William Griffin, James Noyes, John Lediard, Gabriel Brine, the mark of William Flippens, Daniel Thorngate, Thomas Thorngate. (WRO D1/2/29)

**436** 20 Feb. 1792 (15 March 1792). Malmesbury. A house now in the occupation of John Player, labourer. Independent. John Brown, minister, George Garlick, tanner, John Jefferies, grocer, Henry Jefferies, gentleman. (WRO D1/2/29)

**437** 23 April 1792 (2 May 1792). Upton Lovel *or* Upton Scudamore. A house now rented by Edward Barnes and the property of Daniel Pierce. Independent. Thomas Gaisford, Thomas Matravers, John Brunker, George Mansell, Edward Barnes, Joseph Barnes, housekeepers in Upton. (WRO D1/2/29)

**438** 14 June 1792 (16 June 1792). Brixton Deverill. Part of the dwellinghouse belonging to Richard Collins. Independent. Richard Collins, John Rudick, William Brunem, William Andres, Robert Nok, James Sheppard, housekeepers in Brixton Deverill. (WRO D1/2/29)

**439** 16 July 1792 (25 July 1792). Staverton in Trowbridge. The dwelling-house of William Hibbard. Independent. Joseph Deane, William Axford, the mark of William Sinzey [*recte Linzey*], the mark of Joseph Sinzey [*recte Linzey*], William Herbert, Job White. (WRO D1/2/29)

**440** 23 Aug. 1792 (27 Aug. 1792). Bradford on Avon. A house built for public worship situated upon Says Green. Particular Baptist. John Lloyd, minister, Thomas Jotham and John Davies, deacons, Thomas Aland, all of Bradford on Avon. (WRO D1/2/29)

**441** 24 Sept. 1792 (13 Nov. 1792). Holt [*in Bradford on Avon*]. The messuage or tenement and dwellinghouse now in the occupation of Samuel Mortimer. Independent. The mark of Samuel Martimer, the mark of Samuel Ken, the mark of William Archard, the mark of Richard Harford, housekeepers in Holt. (WRO D1/2/29)

**442** 17 Oct. 1792 (18 Oct. 1792). Marlborough. A house late a workshop belonging to John Simmonds in St Peter's parish. Independent. John Simmons, Richard Howell, Thomas Frankling, Robert Biffin, John Mortimer, Robert Stone. (WRO D1/2/29)

**443** 8 Nov. 1792 (28 Nov. 1792). Barford St Martin. The dwellinghouse of James Musselwhite, carrier. Methodist. Jonathan Lampard, Thomas Lampard, John Hibberd, housekeepers in Barford St Martin. (WRO D1/2/29)

**444** 24 Dec. 1792 (7 Jan. 1793). Whiteparish. We have set apart and appointed a house nearly opposite the sign of the Kings Head, now in the occupation of William Butler. Methodist. John Thistlethwayte, Elizabeth Alford, William Mannings, Sarah Russell, William Buttler, Isaac Prince, William Brown. (WRO D1/2/29)

**445** 7 Jan. 1793 (21 Jan. 1793). Bradford on Avon. A house called the Grove meeting house. [*Presbyterian*: Murch 65]. James Baker, Robert Bryant, John Moggridge, John William Yerbury, Robert Hooper, Edward Williams, John H Moggridge, housekeepers in Bradford on Avon. (WRO D1/2/29)

**446** 11 Nov. 1793 (23 Nov. 1793). Porton in Idmiston. The dwellinghouse and yard of William Cook. Baptist. The mark of William Cook, Richard Frith, the mark of William Smith, the mark of William Brown, the mark of Thomas Smith. (WRO D1/2/29)

**447** 1793 (25 Nov. 1793). Sutton Veny. A house newly erected. Independent. James Hayward, John White, William Imber, Jonas Dutch, housekeepers in Sutton Veny. (WRO D1/2/29)

**448** 28 Nov. 1793 (17 Dec. 1793). Rowde. The house standing in the courtyard of the premises now in the possession of James Dyer. Baptist. The mark of Charles Jones, the mark of F. Southernwood, B. Winterson, Martha Helps, John Jefferies, Rachel Jefferies, David Helps, householders in Rowde. (WRO D1/2/29)

**449** 10 Dec. 1793 (17 Dec. 1793). Downton. South Lane Chapel. Particular Baptist. Joseph Jellyman, John Bain, Benjamin Eastman, Mary Eastman, Esther Eastman, Jacob Taunton, Betty Taunton, Sarah Eastman, Elizabeth Stainer, John Budden, Grace Budden, Esther Kelleway, Nathaniel Eastman, Samuel Taunton, Moses Barling, John Barling, Christopher Guyer, William Guyer, Richard Dove, Mary Whittle, Mary Feltham, James Feltham, housekeepers in Downton. (WRO D1/2/29)

**450** 18 Dec. 1793 (27 Dec. 1793). Aldbourne. The house of John Bridgman. Independent. John Bridgeman, James Presey, William Cumner, William Salt, John Lawrence, William Cruse, James Mudge, housekeepers in Aldbourne. (WRO D1/2/29)

**451** 17 Jan. 1794 (28 Jan. 1794) Warminster. A house in the possession of William Jervis, carpenter. H. Moore, William Jervis, John Spicer, Benjamin Guy, Thomas King, John Odlam. (WRO D1/2/29)

**452** 28 Feb. 1794 (8 March 1794). Pewsey. The dwellinghouse of James Noyes. Independent. James Noyes, Philip Naish, George Benger, William Flipence, Thomas Popjoy, Henry Brayer. (WRO D1/2/29)

**453** 6 March 1794 (8 March 1794). Bradford on Avon. A house or building on Morgans Hill. Independent. Thomas Hart, Ann Cadby, William Dunn, William Taylor, Elizabeth Cadby, Mary Hart, Robert Cadby, James Palmer, Dorothy Langly, William Taylor, housekeepers in Bradford on Avon. (WRO D1/2/29)

**454** 24 March 1794 (28 March 1794). Wilton. The dwellinghouse of James Targett, carpenter. Methodist. The mark of William Jieffery, the mark of John Downton, Henry Downton, Samuel Downton, John Crabb junior, James Targett, housekeepers in Wilton. (WRO D1/2/29)

**455** 26 March 1794 (31 March 1794). Chilton Foliat. A house in the possession of Thomas Ashton. Methodist. William Perritt, Thomas Ashton, the mark of John Duck, Sarah Duck. (WRO D1/2/29)

**456** 4 June 1794 (25 June 1794). Tinhead in Edington. The house of Harry Price junior, formerly a malthouse. [*Independent*: see **428**]. Richard Price, James Oram, Simon Haggard, Harry Price, Edward Price, James Coulrick, housekeepers in Edington. (WRO D1/2/29)

**457** 29 June 1794 (July 1794). Ford in Laverstock. The dwellinghouse and garden of James Harder. Methodist. James Hodder, William Callaway, the mark of Elizabeth Hodder, the mark of Susan Marshall, Elizabeth Sanders. (WRO D1/2/29)

**458**  [?July 1794]. Maiden Bradley. The dwellinghouse of John Dolman. Methodist. [*Note*] 'Original certificate not found.' (WRO A1/150/22)

**459**  31 Oct. 1794 (4 Nov. 1794). Market Lavington. The house of William Smith. [*Independent*: Attley 24]. Samuel Hobbs, John Gauntlett, William Moore, George Gauntlett, the mark of William Smith, inhabitants of Market Lavington. (WRO D1/2/29)

**460**  4 March 1795 (4 March 1795). Fisherton Anger. A house in the possession of Thomas Smith. Methodist. Thomas Smith, John Perren, Ann Jefferys, John Bath, George Stephenson. (WRO D1/2/29)

**461**  6 March 1795 (6 March 1795). Winterbourne Earls. A house in the possession of George Marshall. Methodist. George Marshall, Edmund Joles, John Mundy, Michael Marshall. (WRO D1/2/29)

**462**  21 March 1795 (25 March 1795). Shrewton. The house and premises of William Hewett. [*Baptist*: see **479**]. William Hewett, Thomas Kellow, the mark of Guy Coombs, the mark of Isaac Dogget, William Weare, William Blake, the mark of Thomas Shergold, John Beast, inhabitants of Shrewton. (WRO D1/2/29)

**463**  2 May 1795 (14 May 1795). Trowbridge. We have built a chapel. Methodist. James Pond, James Silcock, Richard Amer, John Whatley, George Gray, Thomas Billet. (WRO D1/2/29)

**464**  18 May 1795 (20 May 1795). Amesbury. The dwellinghouse of George Harrison. Independent. Henry Blatch, George Harrison, Philip Eyres, Robert Eyres, John Aisher, John Whitmarsh. (WRO D1/2/29)

**465**  6 June 1795 (27 Jan. 1797). Laverstock. A house in the possession of Elizabeth Ratey. Methodist. The mark of Elizabeth Rattey, the mark of George Rattey, the mark of John Cundick, the mark of Elizabeth Cundick, Francis Hall, James Oder, John Parsons, George Hacker, George Higton. (WRO D1/2/29)

**466**  20 June 1795 (16 Jan. 1796). Winterbourne Stoke. The house and premises now rented and occupied by Richard Holmes. Independent. Richard Holmes, the mark of William Kellow, John Pearse, the mark of Jane Pearce, the mark of Robert Lodg, the mark of William Weet, inhabitants of Winterbourne Stoke. (WRO D1/2/29)

**467**  [?July 1795]. Mere. A building erecting in Dark Lane. Independent. [*Note*] 'Original certificate not found.' (WRO A1/150/22)

**468**   25 Oct. 1795 (7 Dec. 1795). Fovant. The dwellinghouse of Thomas Scamel. Independent. The mark of Thomas Scamel, John Day, the mark of William Day, the mark of Ann Day, the mark of Ann, Scamel. (WRO D1/2/29)

**469**   7 Dec. 1795 (19 Feb. 1796). Alderbury. The dwellinghouse of Mark Wentworth. Independent. John Adams, John Hunt, the mark of John Cook, Susannah Wentworth, Mark Wentworth, the mark of Mary Wentworth, John Griffin. (WRO D26/3)

**470**   10 Dec. 1795 (12 Feb. 1796). Kington St Michael. The dwellinghouse of Solomon Wallop. Independent. William Pullin, John Knight, Edward Langley, Thomas Cole, Thomas Cole junior, William Wilmott. (WRO D1/2/29)

**471**   4 Jan. 1796 (5 Jan. 1796). Redlynch in Downton. The house of John Bundy. [*Baptist*: see **472**]. John Bain, Mary Bain, Randal Bampton, Richard Dove, Jacob Taunton, Joseph Dredge, Nathaniel Eastman, Esther Kelleway, Benjamin Eastman, housekeepers and inhabitants in Downton. (WRO D1/2/29)

**472**   8 Jan. 1796 (12 Jan. 1796). Redlynch in Downton. The house of John Reeves. Baptist. John Reeves, Joseph Jellyman, Jacob Taunton, Joseph Dredge, Nathaniel Eastman, Esther Kelleway, Benjamin Eastman, Thomas Taunton, John Bain, Mary Bain, Randal Bampton, housekeepers and inhabitants in Downton. (WRO D1/2/29)

**473**   19 Jan. 1796 (30 Jan. 1796). Berwick St James. The house of Mr Henry Giles. [*Baptist*: see **479**]. Henry Giles, Mary Giles, Henry Dyer, Betty Garrett, Thomas Kellow, William Hewett. (WRO D1/2/29)

**474**   22 Feb. 1796 (23 Feb. 1796). Lower Charlton in Downton. The house of Philip Whittle. Baptist. The mark of Philip Whittle, John Bain, Joseph Jellyman, William Wornell, Samuel Taunton, Jacob Taunton, Nathaniel Eastman, Joseph Dredge, Esther Eastman, Esther Kelloway, Benjamin Eastman, housekeepers in Downton. (WRO D1/2/29)

**475A**   26 Feb. 1796 (26 Nov. 1796). Milford [*in Laverstock*]. The dwellinghouse of Thomas Pottle. Independent. Thomas Pottle, George Offer, Elizabeth Pine, Sarah Geffery, Jane Lamberd, Jane Decket, William Sainsbury, William Butlr. (WRO D1/2/29)

**475B**   12 April 1796 (16 April 1796). Pitton [*in Alderbury*]. The house of Mr Stephen Philips. Baptist. The mark of Stephen Philips, George Bishop, the mark of Mary Hatcher, Stephen Collins. (WRO D26/3)

**476**   3 June 1796 (20 June 1796). Chilton Foliat. A chapel in the possession of John Hogsflesh and other trustees for that purpose appointed is now newly erected. Methodist. William Perritt, John Hogsflesh, John Martin. (WRO D1/2/29)

**477**  30 July 1796 (26 Nov. 1796). South Burcombe (*Burcomb*). The dwelling-house of Henry Blandford. Independent. James Thring, the mark of Robert Church, Henry Blandford, George Hiberd, George Whitmarsh, Alexander Witt, John Hunt. (WRO D1/2/29)

**478**  19 Aug. 1796 (26 Nov. 1796). Hullavington. The dwellinghouse of Mrs Mary Marsh. Independent. Simon Pitt, minister of the gospel, William Jacques, Aaron Marsh, George Stephens, Giles Crisp, John Dalmer, Aaron Pinnell. (WRO D1/2/29)

**479**  9 Dec. 1796 (16 March 1797). Shrewton. The meeting house newly erected. Baptist. Thomas Kellow, William Weare, Joseph Weare, the mark of Isaac Dogget. (WRO D1/2/29)

**480**  22 March 1797 (25 April 1797). Wootton Bassett. A meeting house, late in the occupation of George Tegle, gardener. Independent. John Bartholomew, minister, Thomas Smith, Thomas Ayliffe, Daniel Wigmore, the mark of John Gleard, George Blake, John Sutton. (WRO D1/2/29)

**481**  1 April 1797 (24 June 1797). Malmesbury. A house situated in Back Street. Independent. William Wooles, minister, Simon Pitt, George Garlick, Henry Jefferis, Henry Pockeridge, Nathaniel Godwin, Abram Ponting. (WRO D1/2/29)

**482**  13 April 1797 (25 April 1797). Maiden Bradley. The dwellinghouse of William Newbury junior. Independent. Richard Beard, John Miles, James Rutley, James Dole, Samuel Young, Margaret Beard. (WRO D1/2/29)

**483**  19 April 1797 (29 April 1797). Westbury Leigh in Westbury. A new meeting house and a yard adjoining. Baptist. Robert Marshman, James Edwards, Samuel Barnes, John Marshman, John Edwards, Edmund Eyers, William Wilkins, Richard Holloway, Richard During. (WRO D25/6)

**484A**  22 April 1797 (24 April 1797). Urchfont. A house in the occupation of Mrs Sarah Giddings. Independent. Christopher Garrett, minister, the mark of Sarah Giddings, John Giddings, William Gilbert. (WRO D1/2/29)

**484B**  30 April 1797 (30 May 1797). Pitton [*in Alderbury*]. The house of Mr Edward Windsor with the barn or outhouse adjoining. Baptist. E. Windsor, John Morris, Sarah Stone. (WRO D26/3)

**485**  16 May 1797 (29 May 1797). Great Hinton in Steeple Ashton. The house and court in front of the house now inhabited by John Kemp. Methodist. James Blake, churchwarden, James Bartlett, overseer, Henry Crook, Richard

Watts, the mark of Edward Jefferies, John Kemp, householders in Hinton. (WRO D1/2/29)

**486**  17 May 1797 (29 May 1797). Semington [*in Steeple Ashton*]. The house, court and garden of the said house inhabited by David Marks. Methodist. David Marks, William Watts, the mark of William Beaven, Thomas Hinwood, James Watts, householders in Semington. (WRO D1/2/29)

**487**  27 May 1797 (9 June 1797). Rodbourne in Malmesbury. The dwellinghouse of Mr William Marsh. Independent. Simon Pitt, minister of the gospel, William Lane, James Nichols, Richard Lidinton, William Pullin, William Marsh, Samuel Hawkins. (WRO D1/2/29)

**488**  8 July 1797 (12 Aug. 1797). All Cannings. A house. Independent. William Barrett, Stephen Durnford, James Witchell, Joseph Maslen. (WRO D1/2/29)

**489**  9 July 1797 (12 Aug. 1797). Alton [*Barnes?: Alton Priors was not a parish*]. The dwellinghouse of William Page in the parish of Alton. Independent. William Page, William Price, Daniel Thorngate, William Barrett. (WRO D1/2/29)

**490**  17 July 1797 (7 Aug. 1797). Enford. The house and premises thereunto belonging of Ann Carter. Independent. The mark of Ann Carter, the mark of John Bond, the mark of Mary Hale, the mark of Elizabeth Hillier, the mark of Jane Wissen, the mark of Thomas Hale, of Enford. (WRO D1/2/29)

**491**  18 July 1797 (10 Aug. 1797). Porton in Idmiston. The house of Mr. John Hibberd. Baptist. William Allen, Elizabeth Allen, Joseph Callaway, John Hibberd. (WRO D1/2/29)

**492**  6 Aug. 1797 (7 Aug. 1797). Great Wishford. The house of Mr George Abree. George Abree, Mary Scamell, Sarah Shergold, Ann Swain, James Shergold, James Cannos, the mark of William Lily, the mark of Mary Lily, the mark of John Tofen. (WRO D1/2/29)

**493**  7 Aug. 1797 (10 Aug. 1797). Colerne. A barn, the property of Mary Knight, situated at the south side of the town. Independent. William Rawlings, Mary Sumsion, Elizabeth Elkington, Ann Ford, Henry Burgess, Mary Knight, Thomas Aust, housekeepers residing in Colerne. (WRO D1/2/29)

**494**  14 Aug. 1797 (4 Sept. 1797). Westbury. A house now rented by William Hague and the property of Joseph Hague. Independent. Joseph Clift, John Millard, Christopher Pearce, Samuel Bourne, Thomas Gaisford, John Dyer, John Hill, John Callaway, George Mantell, housekeepers in Westbury. (WRO D25/6)

**495**   14 Aug. 1797 (4 Sept. 1797). Westbury. A house now rented by William Blewett and the property of Mr James Singer. Independent. Samuel Bourne, George Mantell, John Bourne, Samuel Greenhill, Thomas Licke, Miech . . . [*illegible*], James Phipps, James Holloway, Stephen Brunker, James Randall, housekeepers in Westbury. (WRO D25/6)

**496**   (17 Aug. 1797). Holt [*in Bradford on Avon*]. The house of Mr Thomas Butler. Thomas Beaven, Thomas Butler, Samuel May, Thomas Collingbourn, james Cooper, housekeepers in Holt. (WRO D1/2/29)

**497**   (17 Aug. 1797). South Wraxall [*in Bradford on Avon*]. The house of Elizabeth Morris. Philip Gisford, the mark of James Mison, Walter Morris, the mark of William Huntley, the mark of Benjamin More, Francis Little, Robert Bush, Robert Bush, Robert Barton, housekeepers in South Wraxall. (WRO D1/2/29)

**498**   28 Aug. 1797 (4 Sept. 1797). Hilcott in North Newnton. The house of John Clift as now inhabited by Thomas Beth, with the garden and all things thereunto belonging. Independent. The mark of Thomas Beth, William Kent, of Hilcott. (WRO D1/2/29)

**499**   28 Aug. 1797 (4 Sept. 1797). Fifield in Enford. The house of Thomas Hillier, together with the garden, courts and all things thereunto belonging. Independent. The mark of Thomas Hale, the mark of Edward Ragbourne, the mark of Thomas Hillier, the mark of John Tarrent, the mark of Mary Hale, the mark of Betty Hillier, the mark of Ann Dike, of Fifield. (WRO D1/2/29)

**500**   2 Sept. 1797 (4 Sept. 1797). Quidhampton in Bemerton [*recte Fugglestone St Peter*]. The dwellinghouse of Alexander Goodfellow. Independent. James Edwards, John Malyn Wells, Joseph Williams, Alexander Goodfellow, James Hayter, John Jeffery. (WRO D1/2/29)

**501**   3 Sept. 1797 (16 Sept. 1797). East Knoyle. The dwellinghouse of Benjamin Case, shepherd with the court adjoining. Independent. Edward Lampard, John King, William Shephard, William Dewy, Ann Lampard, Ann Small, housekeepers in East Knoyle. (WRO D1/2/29)

**502**   11 Sept. 1797 (20 Sept. 1797). Wedhampton in Urchfont. The house of Robert Deane as inhabited by James Deane together with the garden, outhouses and all things thereunto belonging. Independent. John Giddings, Robert Giddings, John Morriss Hadrill, of Urchfont. (WRO D1/2/29)

**503**   4 Nov. 1797 (4 Nov. 1797). Wilton. A house in the possession of John Milman. [*Independent*: see **524**]. James Crabb, William Howell, John Crabb, William Crabb, Emanuel Richmond, the mark of J. Milman. (WRO D1/2/29)

**504**   11 Nov. 1797 (9 Mar. 1798). Startley in Great Somerford. The dwellinghouse of Jacob Hand. Independent. Simon Pitt, minister, Thomas Sealy, George Richmond, Thomas Barnes, Henry Barnet, Charles Tanner, Robert Reynolds. (WRO D1/2/29)

**505** 20 Nov. 1797 (9 Mar. 1798). Lea [*in Lea and Cleverton?*]. The dwelling-house of Richard Reeve. Independent. William Wilmot, minister, John Reeve, William Woodard, Henry Reeve, John Reeve senior, Richard Reeve, Robert Wilmot. (WRO D1/2/29)

**506** 2 Dec. 1797 (20 Jan. 1798). Stanton St Bernard. A house. Independent. William Barrett, William Williams, William Rabbetts, John Pope, Thomas Mills, A. Jackson. (WRO D1/2/29)

**507A** 20 Dec. 1797 (6 Jan. 1798). Stratford sub Castle. A dwellinghouse the property of Thomas Ogden inhabited by Thomas Lampard. Independent. Roger Alexander, Thomas Lamppard, George Lamppard, John Price, the mark of William Tutt, the mark of William Smith. (WRO D1/2/29)

**507B** 21 Dec. 1797 (20 Jan. 1798). Figheldean. A dwellinghouse, the property of Robert Sloper and others, inhabited by George Holmes. Independent. Thomas Whitmarsh, James Keel, William Kinger, George Peck, Elizabeth Holms, George Holms. (WRO D1/2/29)

**508** 9 Jan. 1798 (20 Jan. 1798). Whiteparish. The now dwellinghouse of Joseph West near the church and known by the name of the Parsonage House. Methodist. Joseph Alford, Joseph West, Elizabeth Brown, Henry Alford, John Roberts, William Mannings, Sarah Rusell, James Chalk. (WRO D1/2/29)

**509** 25 Jan. 1798 (25 Jan. 1798). East Harnham in Britford. A house in the possession of James Maine. Methodist. David Jeanes, James Maine, Mark Wentworth, William Targett, Richard Wooff, Richard Curtis, William Lamborn, Thomas Smith, Thomas Biddlecombe senior, Thomas Biddlecombe junior. (WRO D24/7)

**510** 8 Feb. 1798 (9 March 1798). All Cannings. A house occupied by James Witchal. Independent. William Barritt, William Lewis, James Witchell, Thomas Maton. (WRO D1/2/29)

**511** 15 Feb. 1798 (9 Mar. 1798). Allington in All Cannings. A house. Independent. William Cook, William Barrett, Daniel Parry. (WRO D1/2/29)

**512** 5 March 1798 (13 March 1798). Hilperton. The house of Susannah Slade together with the garden and court adjoining. Baptist. Henry Slade, Robert Gilbert, William Linzey, housekeepers in Hilperton. (WRO D1/2/29)

**513** 5 March 1798 (24 March 1798). West Ashton in Steeple Ashton. The house of William Boulter together with the garden and court adjoining. Joseph

Maslen, Jacob Maslen, the mark of William Boulter, the mark of Thomas Mitchel, housekeepers at West Ashton. (WRO D1/2/29)

**514** 6 March 1798 (14 March 1798). Compton in Enford. The house and garden of William Hussey, esquire, of Salisbury as inhabited by John Adams. Independent. Charles Eyles, John Adams, Richard Whitmarsh. (WRO D1/2/29)

**515** 10 March 1798 (18 May 1798). Sherston. A room in the possession of Mr George Garlick. Independent. Simon Pitt, minister, John Goulden, David Rice, Thomas Evans, Robert Rice, Jonathan Tanner, Robert Pinnell. (WRO D1/2/29)

**516** 22 March 1798 (7 April 1798). East Knoyle. The dwellinghouse of Benjamin Case with the court adjoining. Independent. Benjamin Case, William Sheppard, John King, Edward Lear, William Dewey, Edward Lampard. (WRO D1/2/29)

**517** (23 April 1798). Bradford on Avon. We have erected a meeting house situate on Morgans Hill. Baptist. John Hinton, Francis England, William Taylor, Thomas Nicholls, housekeepers in Bradford on Avon. (WRO D1/2/29)

**518** 27 April 1798 (18 May 1798). Worton (*Workton*) in Potterne. The house of Thomas Few. Independent. Jonathan White, Thomas Brien, Robert Hampton, Thomas Few, the mark of James Holloway, the mark of John Compton, housekeepers in Worton. (WRO D1/2/29)

**519** 25 May 1798 (26 May 1798). Etchilhampton. A house in the occupation of Robert Dean. Independent. William Barrett, James Sainsbury, Robert Dean, William Maslen, Samuel Beaven. (WRO D1/2/29)

**520** 21 June 1798 (27 June 1798). Aldbourne. The house of Ann Parris. Methodist. Ann Parris, William Salt, Benjamin Laurence, John Bridgeman, Rachel Salt, Sarah Laurence, Thomas Goddard, housekeepers in Aldbourne. (WRO D1/2/29)

**521** 26 June 1798 (25 July 1798). Melksham. The workshop and the avenue thereto which was the property and occupied by the late Mr John Grey and since his decease by his son Mr Arthur Grey. [*Methodist*: VCH 3, 130]. Joseph Hook, Abraham Shewring, William Shill, John Pope, James Ovens, Job Coleman, Joseph Gregory, Thomas Buckland, Harry Smart, William Day, Thomas Holly, householders in Melksham. (WRO D1/2/29)

**522** 28 June 1798 (9 July 1798). Hodson in Chisledon. A dwellinghouse now in the occupation of William Walker. Independent. William Walker, Charles

Walker, Thomas Wheeler, Henry Looker, Joseph Looker, Robert Mouden. (WRO D1/2/29)

**523**  11 July 1798. West Knoyle. Two rooms, the parlour and milkhouse, in my late dwellinghouse, and which I now rent of my brother and is in my own occupation, and the other part of which house is in the occupation of Mills as tenant to me. Independent. John Ridgley, Robert Butt, William Keens, S. Way, U. Brodribb. (WRO A1/110 T1798)

**524**  14 July 1798 (14 July 1798). Wilton. A house in the possession of James Crabb. [*Independent*: see **549**]. John Rebbeck, James Crabb, John Crabb, William Larkam, W. Howell, N. Young. (WRO D1/2/29)

**525**  1 Aug. 1798 (11 Aug. 1798). Whiteparish. A house in Whiteparish Street in the occupation of Joseph West. Methodist. Joseph West, Sarah Russell, Elizabeth Alford, Henry Alford, James Chalk, William Mannings. (WRO D1/2/29)

**526**  23 Aug. 1798 (3 Sept. 1798). Monkton Deverill. My present dwelling-house with the brewhouse adjoining and communicating therewith and the adjoining courtyard. Independent. Edward Presley. (WRO D1/2/29)

**527**  27 Aug. 1798 (4 Sept. 1798). Melksham Forest in Melksham. The house occupied by Edward Shadwell. Baptist (*Protestant dissenters scrupling the baptizing of infants*). James Powell, Samuel Picker, William Perfect, William Huntly, Thomas Cook, householders in Melksham. (WRO D1/2/29)

**528**  27 Aug. 1798 (4 Sept. 1798). Whitley Common in Melksham. The house occupied by Sarah Bryant, widow. Baptist (*Protestant dissenters scrupling the baptizing of infants*). John Davis, Thomas Ward, Robert Manning, James Cannings, Thomas Small, householders in Melksham. (WRO D1/2/29)

**529**  15 Sept. 1798 (22 Sept. 1798). Studley in Chippenham [*recte Calne?*]. A house occupied by Ann Brittain. Independent. William Burgess, the mark of Jonathan Brittain, the mark of Ann Brittain, Ann Holley, Jane Brittain, inhabitants of Studley. (WRO D1/2/29)

**530**  15 Sept. 1798 (22 Sept. 1798). Derry Hill in Pewsham. A house occupied by Thomas Scott at the bottom of Derry Hill. Independent. Hezekiah Wilshire, the mark of Sarah Wiltshire, the mark of Stephen Cole, John Cole, Enoch Fortune, inhabitants at the bottom of Derry Hill. (WRO D1/2/29)

**531**  21 Sept. 1798 (21 Sept. 1798). Stapleford. A house in the possession of George Liversuch. The mark of George Leversuch, William Hiscocks, Thomas Baker, Benjamin Inggs. (WRO D1/2/29)

**532**  27 Sept. 1798 (16 Oct. 1798). Bowerhill in Melksham. A certain building, the property of .... john ....rris of Melksham. Independent or Congregational. J. Honywill, Thomas Hoare, John Smith, Ann Budgin, all of Melksham. (WRO D1/2/29)

**533** 29 Sept. 1798 (2 Oct. 1798). Little Hinton. The dwellinghouse of James Edwards. Independent. James Edwards, Thomas Adams, William Adams, Samuel Jones, Sarah Edwards. (WRO D1/2/29)

**534** 29 Sept. 1798 (2 Oct. 1798). Wanborough. The dwellinghouse of Mary Smith. Methodist. Mary Smith, John Smith, Charles Kent, Charles Maslen. (WRO D1/2/29)

**535** 30 Sept. 1798 (1 Feb. 1799). Hullavington. The dwellinghouse of Mr John Marsh. Independent. William Pullin, minister, William Jacques, John Dalmer, John Wilcks, Giles Crisp, Aaron Pinnell, Aaron Marsh. (WRO D1/2/29)

**536** 1 Oct. 1798 (18 Oct. 1798). Grittenham in Brinkworth. The lower part of a house in the occupation of John Sutton, farmer, called Bonds Farm. Independent, John Bartholomew, minister, John Bushell, James Goodwin, John Barnes, Thomas Henly, William Hendon, William Godwin. (WRO D1/2/29)

**537** 1 Oct. 1798 (18 Oct. 1798). Lyneham. A lower room in the house of Richard Bushel, blacksmith. Independent. John Bartholomew, minister, John Sutton, David Sutton, Jacob Sutton, James Bushell, Cornelius Aires, John Barnes. (WRO D1/2/29)

**538** 5 Oct. 1798 (18 Oct. 1798). Dauntsey. A lower room in the house of Peter Haward, labourer. Independent. The mark of John Hayward, the mark of Joseph Wekfield, the mark of John Wekfield, John Kaw, the mark of Joseph Wackfield senior, Thomas Skull, John Bartholomew, minister. (WRO D1/2/ 29)

**539** 19 Oct. 1798 (2 Nov. 1798). Spirthill (*Shirtle*) in Bremhill. A house occupied by William Hadrill. William Hadrell, J. Lewis, Philip Hadrell, the mark of James Cook, the mark of Judith Hadril, inhabitants of Spirthill. (WRO D1/2/29)

**540** 21 Oct. 1798 (23 Oct. 1798). Upton Scudamore. A house now inhabited by Robert Rymell and his own property. Baptist. John Turner, William Pearce, Robert Rymell, Robert Turner, John Townsend, John Townsend junior, John Brunker, Thomas Whatley, William Wilkins, Paul Cockel, Daniel Pearce, William Cross, housekeepers in Upton Scudamore. (WRO D1/2/29)

**541** 24 Oct. 1798 (1 Feb. 1799). Norton. The dwellinghouse of John Watts.

Independent. Simon Pitt, minister, John Bennett, John Buckland, John Benjamin, William Kilmister, Thomas Brume, the mark of John Watts. (WRO D1/2/29)

**542**  25 Oct. 1798 (16 Nov. 1798). Hilcott in North Newnton. A building newly erected with a plot of ground adjoining 100 feet by 50 feet. Independent. John Moore, John Matthews, John Keepence, Ann Matthews, William Barrett, Daniel Parry. (WRO D1/2/29)

**543**  26 Oct. 1798 (1 Feb. 1799). Rodbourne in Malmesbury. A house in the possession of William Field. Independent. Simon Pitt, minister, William Godwin, William Field, James Nichols, William Pullin, Richard Lidinton, John Chambers, Robert Tanner. (WRO D1/2/29)

**544**  28 Oct. 1798 (29 Oct. 1798). Winterbourne Stoke. The house of Mr John Pearce. Baptist. John Pearce, George Grant, Charles Toomer, James Kellow, John Oxford, Thomas Kellow, Ann Long, Thomas Harper, Robert Williams, Joseph Wear, housekeepers within Winterbourne Stoke, Shrewton and Maddington. (WRO D1/2/29)

**545A**  30 Oct. 1798 (3 Nov. 1798). Hodson in Chisledon. A newly erected house in the possession of Thomas Wheeler and other trustees. Methodist. Thomas Wheeler, Robert Moulding, Henry Looker, Joseph Looker, Charles Walker, William Walker. (WRO D1/2/29)

**545B**  (8 Nov. 1798). West Wellow. A building of James Bishop. The mark of James Bishop of West Wellow [*and two others, not named in the return*]. (PRO RG31/5 Winchester diocese)

**546**  17 Nov. 1798. South Newton. A house in the possession of Susan Randall. The mark of Mary Randall, the mark of Susan Randall, the mark of Grace Blake, the mark of Hannah Shergold, the mark of Elizabeth Weston. (WRO D1/2/29)

**547**  19 Nov. 1798 (1 Dec. 1798). Studley Green in Bremhill [*recte Calne?*]. The house now in the possession of John Dark. Baptist. J. Taylor, George Noble, James Burgess, Thomas Smith, Isaac Taylor. (WRO D1/2/29)

**548A**  27 Nov. 1798 (4 Dec. 1798). Woodsend in Aldbourne. A house now in the possession of John Kemp. Methodist. John Kemp, John Bridgeman, Edward Bridgeman, Andrew Toll, Joseph Wechcum, Luke Anmlin, Thomas Goddard. (WRO D1/2/29)

**548B**  (12 Dec. 1798). Kingswood. A dwellinghouse. Robert Gainer of Kingswood [*and others, not named in the return*]. (PRO RG31/2 Gloucester diocese)

**548C** (12 Dec. 1798). Kingwood. A workshop. Robert Gainer of Kingswood [*and others, not named in the return*]. (PRO RG31/2 Gloucester diocese)

**549** 17 Dec. 1798 (29 Dec. 1798). Codford St Peter. A house. Independent. Richard Lewis, Benjmain Rebbeck, William Lacy, John Rebbeck. (WRO D1/2/29)

**550** 15 Jan. 1799 (25 Jan. 1799). Wanborough. A house and premises in the possession of Mary Smith. Methodist. Mary Smith, Richard Cooke, Thomas Wheeler, Thomas Smith, William Walker (WRO D1/2/29)

**551** 30 Jan. 1799 (23 Feb. 1799). Crockerton in Longbridge Deverill. A house in the possession of Daniel Pain. Daniel Pain, Robert Pain, the mark of John Whatley, the mark of Samuel Ball, Thomas King, John Gregory, William Palmer. (WRO D1/2/29)

**552** 21 March 1799 (23 April 1799). Fyfield. A house in the occupation of William Smith. Independent. The mark of William Smith, Charles Maslen, Josiah Brine, William Hillier. (WRO D1/2/29)

**553** 25 March 1799 (29 March 1799). Shaw Hill in Melksham. The dwelling-house of James Weakly. [*Baptist*: see **415, 527**]. Samuel Nicker, John Yearsley, John Davis, James Powell, Stephen Taylor. (WRO D1/2/29)

**554** 12 April 1799 (25 April 1799). Colerne. The house of Thomas Bethel. Independent. Thomas Aust, James Tanner, Mary Knight, housekeepers in Colerne. (WRO D1/2/29)

**555** 15 April 1799 (23 April 1799). Upavon. A house in the occupation of Roger Bavidge. Independent. William Barrett, James Hague, Edward Wells, the mark of Roger Bavidge, John Workman. (WRO D1/2/29)

**556** 14 May 1799. Winterbourne Dauntsey. We have lately erected a house, our property. Independent. John Adams, John Gausby, John Hunt, John Smith, William Wheeler, Alexander Wills, Henry Blatch, Henry Blatch junior, James Blatch, Joseph Vidler, George Smith. (WRO D7/2)

**557** 28 May 1799 (1 June 1799). Enford. The house of William Knight junior, together with the garden and all the premises thereunto belonging. Baptist. T. Wastfield, the mark of John Biffin, William Attwood, Charles Offer. (WRO D1/2/29)

**558** 28 May 1799 (28 May 1799). Swallowfield. The meeting house of William Scriven. William Scriven, William Cordery, Thomas Ludlow, Thomas Lyford. (WRO D1/2/29)

**559** 11 June 1799 (10 July 1799). Fisherton Delamere. A house now rented by

John Turner and the property of Benjamin Rebbeck. Independent. William Fowles, William Abery, Thomas Doughty, housekeepers in Fisherton Delamere. (WRO D1/2/29)

**560**   12 June 1799 (15 June 1799). Bromham. A newly erected building. [*Methodist*: Jones 100]. William Horner, Thomas Atwood, John Akerman, Robert Truman. (WRO D1/2/29)

**561**   4 July 1799 (11 July 1799). Chilmark. The dwellinghouse of Charity Humphrey. Independent. The mark of Charity Humphrey, Priscilla Goodfellow, Martha Wyer, William Sainsbury, John Hunt. (WRO D1/2/29)

**562**   8 July 1799 (7 Aug. 1799). Wanborough. A house and premises the property of Charles Kent. Methodist. Charles Kent, Thomas Smith, John Smith, William Perritt. (WRO D1/2/29)

**563**   12 July 1799 (20 Sept. 1799). Cricklade. A meeting house, and 44 square feet of ground adjoining for a burying place, in Calcutt Lane, St Sampson's parish. Independent. John Tinson, Thomas Batt, John Smith, William Sealey, Richard Day, John Franklin, John Bartholomew, minister, dwelling in Cricklade. (WRO D1/2/29)

**564**   29 July 1799 (13 Aug. 1799). Atworth [*in Bradford on Avon*]. A house built as a meeting house. Independent. John Barton, Thomas Hulbert, James Hulbert, James Tanner, John Chiffins, housekeepers in Atworth. (WRO D1/2/29)

**565**   15 Aug. 1799 (20 Sept. 1799). Patney. The house of Thomas Wells. Independent. William Barrett, William Akerman, Thomas Wells. (WRO D1/2/29)

**566**   20 Aug. 1799 (20 Sept. 1799). Foxley. A room in the possession of Richard Thompson. Independent. Simon Pitt, minister, Richard Thompson, John Bennett, the mark of Alice Matthews, the mark of Thomas Broom, the mark of Thomas Gale, the mark of John Watts. (WRO D1/2/29)

**567**   21 Aug. 1799 (20 Sept. 1799). Little Somerford. A room in the possession of Daniel Greeman. Independent. Simon Pitt, minister, the mark of William Greeman, Richard Reeve, the mark of William Bridgman, the mark of Daniel Greeman, John Heath, John Reeve. (WRO D1/2/29)

**568**   16 Sept. 1799 (5 Oct. 1799). Melksham. A warehouse lately in the possession of James Rawlings. [*Methodist*: see **521**]. J. Powell, M. Hook, Joseph Hook, Joseph Gregory, Henry Greogory. (WRO D1/2/29)

**569**   7 Oct. 1799 (4 Nov. 1799). All Cannings. A house in the occupation of Thomas Masslen. Independent. William Barrett, Joseph Maslen, William

Lewis, Thomas Maten, John Beake, Thomas Rivers, Stephen Durnford, Thomas Neate. (WRO D1/2/29)

**570** 14 Nov. 1799 (27 Nov. 1799). Pickwick in Corsham. The house of Seth Witts. [*Independent*: see **852**]. Oliver Manly, Thomas Lawrence Whitaker, Matthew Aland Shepherd. (WRO D1/2/29)

**571** 26 Nov. 1799 (14 June 1800). Potterne. A house being made convenient for worship. Independent. Jacob Gale, Richard Fielding, Robert Burden, the mark of James Blackman. (WRO D1/2/29)

**572** 20 Dec. 1799 (21 Dec. 1799). Warminster. The register or licence of our meeting house, called the Old Meeting House in Meeting House Lane, erected in or about the year 1704, which was taken out by and granted to our predecessors about that time, is mislaid or lost. Presbyterian. Thomas Hinton, George Wansey, William Wansey, P. Warren, Edmund Halliday, housekeepers in Warminster. (WRO D1/2/29)

**573** 7 Feb. 1800 (8 Feb. 1800). Donhead St Mary. The dwellinghouse of George West commonly called Holm Farm [*Methodist*: see **727**]. George West, James Whitmarsh, Rachel West. (WRO D1/2/29)

**574** 24 Feb. 1800 (5 March 1800). Alvediston. A house in the possession of Francis Smith. Francis Smith, Peter Randell, James King. (WRO D1/2/29)

**575** 3 March 1800 (4 March 1800). Market Lavington. A meeting house and burial ground late in the possession of the people called Quakers. Independent. Christopher Garrett, minister, John Gauntlett, Richard Ward, Benjamin Crook, Joseph Ward. (WRO D1/2/29)

**576** 20 April 1800 (26 April 1800). Chapmanslade in Westbury. A new meeting house and a yard adjoining. Baptist. John Parsons, Richard Parsons, Thomas Scammell, William Clift, Samuel Tucker, John Dymott, John Fowles, John Watts, William Baber, William Alldridge, James Baber, Richard Drury. (WRO D25/6)

**577** 9 May 1800 (14 June 1800). Crudwell. A dwellinghouse belonging to Mr George Garlick. Independent. Simon Pitt, minister, William Wall, Richard Harding, Jonathan Cole, George White, William White, Edward Poole. (WRO D1/2/29)

**578** 9 May 1800 (14 June 1800). Hankerton. The dwellinghouse of Charles Hoare. Independent. George Garlick, minister, John Beale, James Ratcliffe, William Harding, William Godwin, George Skuss, Charles Hore. (WRO D1/2/29)

**579** 26 May 1800 (14 June 1800). Littleton Drew. A dwellinghouse now in the occupation of Samuel Chappell, yeoman. Independent. William Wilmot, minister, Samuel Chappell, Samuel Chappell junior, Charles Pinnell, James Pinnell junior, William Rouls, John Ferriss. (WRO D1/2/29)

**580**   27 May 1800 (5 Dec. 1800). Tinhead in Edington. A house belonging to William Potter. [*Methodist*: Jones 127–128, VCH 8, 249]. Robert Lyne, William Taylor, John Smart, Isaac Morgan, John White. (WRO D1/2/29)

**581**   7 June 1800 (23 July 1800). Charlton [*near Malmesbury*]. The dwelling-house of Bradford Hughs. Independent. Simon Pitt, minister, Samuel Andrews, Robert Lea, Joseph Hughe, Henry Telling, Bradford Hughs, George Law. (WRO D1/2/29)

**582**   4 July 1800 (23 July 1800). Hullavington. The dwellinghouse of Mr Jacob Milsom. Independent. Simon Pitt, minister, William Jacques, Aaron Marsh, William Brooks, John Dalmer, William Gane, Aaron Pinnell. (WRO D1/2/29)

**583**   30 Sept. 1800 (1 Oct. 1800). Fisherton Anger. The house of George Moody. Baptist. George Moody, Prudence Moody, Joseph Churchill, Jane Churchell, housekeepers in Fisherton Anger. (WRO D1/2/29)

**584**   8 Nov. 1800 (1 Dec. 1800). Overton. A house in the occupation of Daniel Cullimore. Independent. Thomas Lawes, Daniel Cullimore, James Fowler. (WRO D1/2/29)

**585**   22 Dec. 1800 (22 Dec. 1800). Enford. The house of Thomas Wastfield together with the garden and premises belonging to the said house. [*Baptist*: see **557**]. Thomas Wastfield, Henry Tinnams. (WRO D1/2/29)

**586**   29 Dec. 1800 (30 Dec. 1800). Fovant. The dwellinghouse of Samuel Goodfellow. Independent. Robert Futcher, Alexander Gould, John Skot?, Samuel Goodfellow. (WRO D1/2/29)

**587**   9 Jan. 1801 (13 Jan. 1801). Tilshead. A house in the possession of William Lawes. Independent. Christopher Garrett, minister, Ann Slade, William Compton, James Payne, William Lawes. (WRO D1/2/29)

**588**   22 Feb. 1801 (24 Feb. 1801). Orcheston St Mary. The house of Christopher Weston. Baptist. Christopher Weston, Matthew Hutchins, Thomas Harper, Thomas Kellow, Joseph Weare, the mark of William Cannings, James William Kellow, housekeepers in Orcheston St Mary, Maddington and Shrewton. (WRO D1/2/29)

**589**   21 April 1801 (5 May 1801). Westbury. A house now occupied by Mary Coombs and her own property. Independent. George Mantell, William

Hooper, John Dyer, Samuel Self, John Callaway, Samuel Bourne, John Crosby, Elizabeth Crosby, housekeepers in Westbury. (WRO D25/6)

**590** 21 April 1801 (5 May 1801). Westbury. A house now occupied by John Watts, and of which he is the proprietor. Independent. Robert Milgrove, James Phipps, Jeremiah Hewett, John Hopkins, Richard During, John Watts, housekeepers in Westbury. (WRO D25/6)

**591** 13 June 1801 (20 June 1801). Chippenham. A house in the occupation of Mr James Lee situated on the Causeway. [*Methodist*: Hall 37]. Thomas Stanton, Thomas Gee, William Pickersgill, John Collar, John Dole, William Smith. (WRO D1/2/29)

**592** 29 July 1801 (2 Sept. 1801). Warminster Common in Warminster. A house and 12 lugs of ground adjoining in the occupation of John Adlam, clothworker. Methodist. John Adlam, Francis Weller, Thomas Dodimead, Benjamin Price, William Steedman, William Daniell. (WRO D1/2/29)

**593** 23 Nov. 1801 (25 Nov. 1801). Chitterne St Mary. The house, gardens and all things thereunto belonging being the property of George Grant of Winterbourne Stoke, now occupied by his son, John Grant. Baptist. Thomas Wastfield, John Park, Mary Allright. (WRO D1/2/29)

**594** 28 Jan. 1802 (3 Feb. 1802). Aldbourne. The house of William Cruse. Methodist. Thomas Stanley, John Lawrence, Elizabeth Cousins, Ephraim Coplin, Elizabeth Goddard. (WRO D1/2/29)

**595** 1 Feb. 1802 (25 Feb. 1802). Broad Chalke. A house belonging to Josiah Gould. Independent. Josiah Gould, Cornelius Gould, Thomas Read, James Hart, John Bennett, James Lawes, Samuel Parrett, Thomas Maton, John Gould, John Powell, Joseph Thick. (WRO D1/2/29)

**596** 3 March 1802 (10 April 1802). Maiden Bradley. The dwellinghouse lately occupied by William Carr junior, now bought and to be fitted up. Independent. Richard Beard, William Brimson, John Miles, William Newberry, William Hoskince, John Gould. (WRO D1/2/29)

**597** 7 March 1802 (16 March 1802). Broughton Gifford. A room, called the club room, in the dwellinghouse of Elizabeth Clack, widow. Elizabeth Clack, Stephen Taylor, William Long, James Mortimer, John Harford, James Goore, Jacob Keen. (WRO D1/2/29)

**598** 20 March 1802 (26 March 1802). Wroughton. A house in the possession of William Austin. Methodist. William Austin, Joseph Matthews, John Tanner, John Austin, William Pickett, William Mills, Thomas Fry. (WRO D1/2/29)

**599** 28 March 1802 (14 June 1802). Oaksey. A room in the possession of Joseph Brown. Independent. William Taylor, Joseph Taylor, James Ratcliff, Isaac Paine, Joseph Robertson, Henry Telling. (WRO D1/2/29)

**600** 11 April 1802 (11 April 1802). Chilmark. A house belonging to Thomas Rowden and in the occupation of John Adams, Joseph Vidler and others. Independent. Thomas Rowden, John James Stuckey, John Adams, Joseph Vidler, Thomas Luke, John Griffin, Joseph Pothecary, John Lanham, James Franklin. (WRO D1/2/29)

**601** 15 April 1802 (15 April 1802). Westbury. The dwellinghouse of Robert Abraham. Methodist. Robert Abraham, Thomas Mist Harrison, William Aver. (WRO D25/6)

**602** 18 April 1802 (23 April 1802). Alderbury. The dwellinghouse of John Cook. Methodist. John Cook, Edward Williams, Thomas Mist Harrison. (WRO D26/3)

**603** 26 April 1802 (14 June 1802). Lea [*in Lea and Cleverton*?]. The dwelling-house of Daniel Bidmead. Independent. John Reeve, William Woodward, Robert Matthews, Henry Reeve, Richard Reeve, Olife Richmond, Daniel Bidmead, minister. (WRO D1/2/29)

**604** 21 June 1802 (22 June 1802). Warminster. The house, garden, court and premises thereunto belonging, the property of Philip Scammell of Edington and James Scammell of Imber, now inhabited by Ann Scammell, widow. Baptist. T. Wastfield, M. Allright, S. Wastfield. (WRO D1/2/29)

**605** 15 July 1802. Winterbourne Dauntsey. The dwellinghouse of William Pitt. Methodist. William Pitt, Thomas Mist Harrison. (WRO D7/2)

**606** 23 August 1802 (3 Sept. 1802). Middlehill in Box. A certain building belonging to Jacob Ford. James Tanner, John Smith, John Tanner. (WRO D1/2/29)

**607** 6 Sept. 1802 (6 Sept. 1802). Shripple in Idmiston. The dwellinghouse of James Collins. Methodist. James Collins, the mark of John Stone, Stephen Collins, Thomas Mist Harrison. (WRO D1/2/29)

**608** 11 Oct. 1802 (12 Oct. 1802). Westbury. A large room belonging to Mrs Elizabeth Gibbs. Methodist. William Gerish, Caleb Butt, George Hatterrley, Robert Abraham, Samuel Beaven, William Hooper. (WRO D25/6)

**609** 20 Dec. 1802 (25 Dec. 1802). Market Lavington. A house in the occupation of Mr Thomas Ubsdale. Independent. Christopher Garrett, minister, Thomas Ubsdale, John Crook, William Maynard. (WRO D1/2/29)

**610** 20 Dec. 1802 (25 Dec. 1802). West Lavington. A house in the occupation of Richard Beaven. Independent. Christopher Garrett, minister, Richard Beavin, James Beaven. (WRO D1/2/29)

**611** 23 March 1803 (23 April 1803). Gastard in Corsham. A large room now in the occupation of and belonging to Thomas Osbourne, labourer. Methodist. Benjamin Bishop, John Moore, James Marrett, Matthew A. Shepherd, Thomas Marrett, James Roadway. (WRO D1/2/29)

**612** 16 Aug. 1803 (3 Sept. 1803). Bishopstone. The dwellinghouse of John Ford. Baptist and Independent. Thomas Cool, John Ford, John Kellow, George Lee, John Saffery, Sarah Hewett, Joseph Thick, Thomas Read, Thomas Norris, John Chalk, William Roberts. (WRO D1/2/29)

**613** 5 Nov. 1803 (27 Dec. 1803). Corston in Malmesbury. The dwellinghouse of Joseph Millard. Independent. Simon Pitt, minister, William Weaver, William Field, William Gay, Somerset Robins, James Nichols, Joseph Millarr. (WRO D1/2/29)

**614** 13 Dec. 1803 (17 Dec. 1803). Aldbourne. A dwellinghouse belonging to and in the occupation of Ephraim Coplin. [*Methodist* see **594**], Ephraim Coplin, Benjamin Lawrence, Sarah Lawrence, John Lawrence, William Salt, William Vipond. (WRO D1/2/29)

**615** 19 Dec. 1803 (27 Dec. 1803). Hullavington. The dwellinghouse of William Giles. Independent. Simon Pitt, minister, William Gane, John Dalmer, John Sargent, William Godwin, John Marsh, William Brooks. (WRO D1/2/29)

**616** 12 Jan. 1804 (12 Jan. 1804). Swindon. A new erected house or chapel. Independent. James Strange, George Mantell, Joshua Reynolds, John Iles, Richard Strange, James Pearcy, housekeepers in Swindon. (WRO D1/2/29)

**617** 22 May 1804 (22 May 1804). Upton Lovell. A house. Methodist. James Smith, George Oliver, John Poor, Thomas Wills Andrews, the mark of Christopher Oak, housekeepers in Upton Lovell. (WRO D1/2/29)

**618** (2 June 1804). Chippenham. A certain building situated in St Mary's Street. Baptist. John Paul Porter, minister, Joseph Bagnell, John Salway, Richard Alexander, William Spackman, Ann Colbourn, George Edgecomb. (WRO D1/2/29)

**619** 9 June 1804 (12 June 1804). Aldbourne. A house in the possession of Thomas Gwyn. Charles Holmes, Richard Witts, Thomas Goddard. (WRO D1/2/29)

**620** 18 June 1804 (2 July 1804). Melksham. A building. Methodist. Charles

Maggs, John Weeks, Samuel Rutty, Job Coleman, William Shell, William Day, James Ovens, Abraham Shewring. (WRO D1/2/29)

**621**  8 July 1804 (28 July 1804). Broughton Gifford. A new-built room adjoining and being part of the dwellinghouse of Elizabeth Clack, widow. Samuel Tucker, Robert Weakley, James Goore, William Long, Isaac Bull. (WRO D1/2/29)

**622**  10 July 1804 (28 July 1804). Warminster. A new-built chapel situated in Chain Street. Methodist. Thomas King, James Ludlow, John Gregory, William Jervis. (WRO D1/2/29)

**623**  26 Nov. 1804 (1 Nov. 1804 [sic]). Tidpit in Martin. The house of Mrs Sarah Moody. Independent and Baptist. Sarah Moody senior, Sarah Moody junior, William Roberts, James Butler, John Moss. (WRO D1/2/29)

**624**  11 Jan. 1805 (12 March 1805). Market Lavington. A house. Independent. Christopher Garrett, minister, Thomas Ubsdale, Thomas Webb, William Scane. (WRO D1/2/29)

**625**  15 Feb. 1805 (8 March 1805). Bourton in Bishops Cannings. A house in the occupation of Mary Neat. Independent. Stephen Watts, Thomas Hood, John Amber, housekeepers in Bishops Cannings. (WRO D24/2)

**626**  17 March 1805 (20 March 1805). Bulford. The newly-erected house (the property of Mr James Rose), now rented and to be fitted up for worship. Independent. Henry Blatch, James Rose, William Sturges, Matthew Devenish, James Chalk, George Harrison. (WRO D1/2/29)

**627**  28 March 1805 (18 May 1805). Bishopstone. A house newly erected in a pasture ground called Pontons. Independent. John Hewett, Sarah Hewitt, Catherine Dudman, Martha Undrell, George Lee, Thomas Cool, Elizabeth Barter, John Kellow, John Ford, Thomas Clark, Thomas Norris, John Read, Thomas Read. (WRO D1/2/29)

**628**  28 April 1805 (27 Feb. 1808). Bushton in Clyffe Pypard. A room in the possession of John Twine. Independent. William Wilmot, minister, Roger Little, Thomas Milsom, Thomas Mathews, James Archer senior, Jacob Archer junior, Thomas Sayer, dwelling in Bushton. (WRO D1/9/2/4)

**629**  (20 May 1805). Wroughton. A building lately erected and known by the name of the Methodist Chapel. Methodist. Thomas Wheeler, Joseph Matthews, John Austin, John Tanner. (WRO D1/2/29)

**630**  24 May 1805 (24 May 1805). Corton in Boyton. A house. Methodist. Thomas Wills Andrews, James Smith, the mark of James Wheller, Gregory Rebbeck, Joshua Rebbeck. (WRO D1/2/29)

**631**  14 June 1805 (29 July 1805). Wroughton. We have erected and set apart a building. Independent. William Pickett, Thomas Carpenter, Henry Cook, W. Ossboorn, John Wheeler, J. Major, S. Mead. (WRO D1/2/29)

**632**  6 July 1805 (8 July 1805). Shrewton. The house of William Weare. Baptist. Matthew Hutchins, the mark of William Cannings, Joseph Weare senior, Joseph Weare, John Pearse, housekeepers in Shrewton, Maddington, Winterbourne Stoke and Orcheston St Mary. (WRO D1/2/29)

**633**  19 July 1805 (29 July 1805). Bulford. The dwellinghouse occupied by Samuel Mould. Independent. Henry Blatch, Matthew Devenish, George Harrison, Samuel Mould, James Chalk, Robert Gale, minister. (WRO D1/2/29)

**634**  31 July 1805 (1 Oct. 1805). Oare in Wilcot. A house, garden and other contiguous premises now in the occupation of John Weeks. Independent. Samuel Clift, Daniel Thorngate, John Eyls, William Strong, James Thorngate, James Oram. (WRO D1/2/29)

**635**  11 Oct. 1805 (12 Oct. 1805). Stanton St Bernard. A house in the occupation of William Ettwell, labourer, to be occasionally used. Methodist. William Ettwell, William Holmes, William Waroman, Charles Hayter. (WRO D1/2/29)

**636**  30 Nov. 1805 (5 Dec. 1805). East Knoyle. A part of the dwellinghouse of William Sheppard with the court adjoining. Independent. William Sheppard, William Dewey, John Gough, Ann Small, James Burleigh, William Sandell. (WRO D1/2/29)

**637**  14 Jan. 1806 (14 Jan. 1806). Amesbury. The dwelling or premises of Joseph Edwards. Methodist. Joseph Edwards, Stephen Harding, Joseph Truckle, William Bishop, Robert Harding, Robert Crowther. (WRO D1/2/29)

**638**  13 Feb. 1806 (6 March 1806). Shaw Hill in Melksham. The dwelling-house of Mary Buckly. [*Baptist*: see **528**]. James Cannings, Harry Pocock, John Davis. (WRO D1/2/29)

**639**  19 March 1806 (21 March 1806). Eastcott in Urchfont. The house of Hannah Ellis, inhabited by herself in one part and William Sainsbury in the other, together with the premises thereunto belonging. Baptist. T. Wastfield, John Clem, the mark of Martha Clem. (WRO D1/2/29)

**640**  12 April 1806 (15 April 1806). Stratford Tony (*Stratford Saint Anthony*). The dwellinghouse and appurtenances of Samuel Short. Independent and Baptist. Samuel Short, Sarah Hewett, Benjamin Kent, Catherine Dudman, James Chamberlain, Martha Undrell. (WRO D1/2/29)

**641** 29 May 1806 (21 June 1806). Hilperton. We have erected a house for worship. Baptist. John Edwards, Samuel Diplock, James Miles, Richard Little, living in Hilperton. (WRO D1/2/29)

**642** 30 June 1806 (15 July 1806). Bulford. The newly erected meeting house (the joint property of Matthew Devenish of Bulford and Henry Blatch of Ratfyn), and also a room adjoining thereto intended to be used as a vestry. Independent. Henry Blatch, Matthew Devenish, William Sturges, James Chalk, Thomas Sturges, F.W. Dury, protestant dissenting minister, Bulford. (WRO D1/2/29)

**643** 29 Aug. 1806 (24 Sept. 1806). Wanborough. A new erected house, or chapel. Independent. Joseph Peirce, Edward Darten, Charles Kent, Thomas Smith, John Sweeper, housekeepers in Wanborough. (WRO D1/9/2/1)

**644** 15 Dec. 1806 (2 Jan. 1807). Ludgershall. The dwellinghouse and premises of Mr George Dobbs. Baptist and Independent. William Roberts, W. Mersham, Joshua Wheeler, William Cook, George Muspratt. (WRO D1/2/29)

**645** 20 Jan. 1807 (14 Feb. 1807). Quidhampton in Fugglestone St Peter (*Foulstone*). The dwellinghouse of Job Saunders. Methodist. The mark of Samuel Borrough, George Harwood, Abraham Axton, housekeepers in Quidhampton. (WRO D1/2/29)

**646** 23 Jan. 1807 (2 Feb. 1807). Holt in Bradford on Avon. The dwelling-house of Thomas Pretty. Methodist. Thomas Tattershall, minister, Thomas Pretty, John Rison, Robert Slugg, William Maynard, Samuel Chapman, Ambrose Cooper, John Tucker. (WRO D1/2/29)

**647** 26 Jan. 1807 (14 Feb. 1807). Whiteparish. A house in Whiteparish Street, in the occupation of James Chalk. Methodist. James Chalk, Charles Hayter, Hannah Hayter, James Rose, Ann Rose, William Butler. (WRO D1/2/29)

**648** 2 Feb. 1807 (3 Feb. 1807). Salisbury. A room in the house occupied by John Lawrence on the Canal in St Thomas's parish, in the possession of John Cooke. [*Independent*: see **690**]. James Sabine, minister, John Cooke, S. Devenish, Richard Cooke, Samuel Everett. (WRO D1/2/29)

**649** 14 Feb. 1807 (17 Feb. 1807). Marlborough. A house in Kingsbury Street, St Mary's parish. Peculiar Calvinist. Thomas Hancock, John Page, Robert Biffin, James Hancock junior, Thomas D. Rose, George Brown, James Looker, Joseph Jennings, owners of the house. (WRO D1/2/29)

**650** 5 March 1807 (27 March 1807). South Newton. The dwellinghouse of William Lawrence. Methodist. Edward Jeffrey, the mark of William Ganger, the mark of John Sampson, housekeepers in South Newton. (WRO D1/9/2/1)

**651** 7 March 1807 (18 March 1807). Idmiston. The dwellinghouse of James Thomas. Methodist. John Shears, John Gilbert, Joseph Edwards, William Harding. (WRO D1/9/2/1)

**652** 10 March 1807 (21 March 1807). Chisledon. A house belonging to William Choules. Methodist. William Choules, Thomas Wheeler, Henry Looker, Charles Walker. (WRO D1/2/29)

**653** 18 March 1807 (26 Jan. 1808). Britford. The dwelling or premises of George Mitchell. Methodist. Daniel Harding, George Michell, William Harding, Peter Dredge. (WRO D24/2)

**654** April 1807 (10 April 1807). Whaddon [*in Alderbury?: described as a peculiar jurisdiction*]. The house or premises of Richard Penton. Richard Penten, the mark of Jonathan Southwell, the mark of John Smith, Susannah Haiter, the mark of Rebecca Williams. (WRO D1/9/2/1)

**655** 10 April 1807 (21 April 1807). Salisbury. A room on the premises occupied by John Batchelor in St Thomas's parish. [*Independent*: see **690**]. John Batchelor, Samuel Davenish, Samuel Everett, John Perren, David Winzar. (WRO D1/2/29)

**656** 22 June 1807 (23 June 1807). Ebbesborne Wake. We have prepared a house now in our possession as a meeting house. Independent. William Gould, Mark Kerly, George Thick, John Gould, housekeepers in Ebbesborne Wake. (WRO D1/9/2/1)

**657** 21 Sept. 1807 (16 Dec. 1807). Devizes. A certain building in St Mary's parish. Methodist. John Martin, minister, George Blake, Elizabeth Hamlin, the mark of Samuel Hamblin, James Blake, Stephen Berrett, Thomas Jeffery. (WRO D1/9/2/4)

**658** 30 Oct. 1807 (27 Feb. 1808). Foxham in Bremhill. The dwellinghouse of David Hull. Independent. Joseph Gale, Thomas Savage, Elias Ferris, James Freeth, William James. (WRO D1/9/2/4)

**659** 30 Oct. 1807 (27 Feb. 1808). Winterbourne. The dwellinghouse of William Hillier. Independent. Daniel Bidmead, minister, Henry Sawyer, John Chequer, Jacob Skuce, John? Waite, William Church. (WRO D1/9/2/4)

**660** 23 Feb. 1808 (29 Feb. 1808). Aldbourne. The lately erected building. [*Methodist*: see **646**]. Thomas Tattershall, minister, John Atkins, Robert Wheeler, Joseph Moss, John Hall, James Bailey. (WRO D1/9/2/4)

**661** 1 April 1808 (25 June 1808). Christian Malford. The dwellinghouse of Zechariah Dickson. Independent. Thomas Savage, Elias Ferris, William

Williams, Adam Stumphousen, Solomon Wallop, Robert Ferris, housekeepers in Christian Malford. (WRO D1/9/2/4)

**662**   23 April 1808 (25 April 1808). West Coulston in Edington. The house of Richard Perritt, now inhabited by John Perritt. Baptist (*dissenters who scruple infant baptism*). T. Wastfield, John Elem. (WRO D1/9/2/4)

**663**   23 May 1808 (4 June 1808). Lacock. A house lately built by subscription on a piece of ground bought for that purpose from Timothy Phelps of Lacock, smith. Independent or Congregational. Joseph Baker, Robert Stephens, John Angel, John End, John Dolman, housekeepers of Lacock. (WRO D1/9/2/4)

**664**   3 June 1808 (6 June 1808). Westbury. A house built for protestant dissent, the property of Samuel Beven, Thomas Lucas, James Watts and other trustees. Methodist. James Watts, Thomas Lucas, Samuel Beven, Robert Abraham, Mark Daniel. (WRO D25/6)

**665**   26 June 1808 (29 July 1808). All Cannings. The house of Robert Carpenter. Methodist. John Martin, minister, the mark of Robert Carpenter, Elizabeth Hamlen, Stephen Barrett, the mark of Martha Carpenter, William Wawman, John Clark. (WRO D1/9/2/4)

**666**   18 July 1808 (31 Aug. 1808). Lea [*in Lea and Cleverton?*]. A place known by the appellation of Zion Chapel. Calvinistic Methodist. Daniel Bidmead, minister, William Reeve, John Reeve, Olliffe Richmond, William Elford, Henry Reeve. (WRO D1/9/2/4)

**667**   10 Oct. 1808 (28 Nov. 1808). Monkton Farleigh. The dwellinghouse belonging to John Little. Methodist. John Little, William Penny, Charles Penny, Mary Penny, Joshua Tuttle. (WRO D1/9/2/4)

**668**   9 Nov. 1808 (28 Nov. 1808). Shaw Hill in Melksham. The dwelling-house of William Hedges. [*Baptist*: see **528**]. James Cannings, Harry Pocock, Abraham Little. (WRO D1/9/2/1)

**669**   13 Jan. 1809 (18 Jan. 1809). Devizes. The house of John Cheater. Arminian Methodist. William Homer? [*Horner?*], minister, Thomas Hazeland, John Clarke, Thomas Obern. (WRO D1/9/2/4)

**670**   14 March 1809 (25 March 1809). Hankerton. A building and ground in the occupation of James Ratcliff. Calvinistic Methodist. Richard Emery, minister, William White, James Ratcliff, William Wait, Jonathan Cole, George Skuse. (WRO D1/9/2/4)

**671**   3 June 1809 (28 June 1809). Marlborough. A house and garden in St Mary's parish, now occupied by Samuel Clift. Independent. Samuel Clift,

William Strugnell, John Shaylor, Henry Knight, the mark of William Smith, Frances Bridgman. (WRO D1/9/2/4)

**672** 6 June 1809 (12 June 1809). Broughton Gifford. A newly erected meeting house. James Mortimer, James Goor, Isaac Mortime, Robert Weakely. (WRO D1/9/2/4)

**673** 9 June 1809 (12 June 1809). Damerham. The dwellinghouse or premises of Henry Shepperd. Methodist. John Willis, Peter Bulling, Daniel Harding, William Harding. (WRO D1/9/2/4)

**674** 18 Oct. 1809 (27 Oct. 1809). Urchfont. The house of Alice Witchel to be used for occasional worship. [*Methodist*: Jones 100]. William Blewett, Robert Abraham, James Akerman, Margaret Butt, Lay Mower. (WRO D1/9/2/4)

**675** 20 Oct. 1809 (27 Oct. 1809). Idmiston. The dwellinghouse of Stephen Zellwood. Methodist. Joseph Edwards, Stephen Harding, Thomas Clarke, Jacob Smith. (WRO D1/9/2/4)

**676** 17 Nov. 1809 (2 Dec. 1809). Winterbourne Gunner. The dwellinghouse of Thomas Tutton. Methodist. Joseph Edwards, William Davies, William Palmer, Job Sutton, Ambrose Banning, Thomas Sutton. (WRO D1/9/2/4)

**677** 27 Nov. 1809 (26 Dec. 1809). Bishopstone. The dwellinghouse and premises of William Norris. Methodist. William Norris, Thomas Newbery, John Pope, Thomas Povey, Thomas Baili, Henry Woodward, Henry Roberts. (WRO D1/9/2/4)

**678** 12 Feb. 1810 (10 March 1810). Chisledon. The dwellinghouse of John Romains. Methodist. The mark of John Romains of Chisledon, John Harwood, John Wait, Thomas Wheeler, Henry Looker. (WRO D1/9/2/4)

**679** 15 Feb. 1810 (17 Feb. 1810). Winterslow. The house of James Collings. [*Independent*?: see **379**]. James Collings, Elizabeth Chalk, Thomas Bell, Alexander Collins, William Shears. (WRO D1/9/2/4)

**680** 25 Feb. 1810 (10 March 1810). Woodfalls, (*Woodfields*) Hill in Downton. The dwellinghouse or premises of Jolliffe Quinton. Methodist. Stephen Newman, Thomas Clark, John Cale, William Harding, Elijah Parsons. (WRO D1/9/2/4)

**681** 22 March 1810 (21 April 1810). Bradford on Avon. A meeting house erected in Bradford. Baptist. James Barnett, Francis Everett, John Hinton, John Edmonds, G. Head, T. Hart, William Taylor, Jeremiah Batchelor. (WRO D1/9/2/4)

**682** 16 April 1810 (27 April 1810). Ludgershall. A building newly erected in

Cox's Lane near the dwellinghouse of Mr George Dobbs. Independent and Baptist. Lewis Winchester, Joshua Wheeler, George Muspratt, Henry Reeves. (WRO D1/9/2/4)

**683**   23 April 1810 (1 May 1810). Warminster Common in Warminster. A house and ten luggs of ground adjoining now occupied by Mary Elliott, widow. Methodist. William Daniell, Joseph Adlam, Thomas King, William Jervis. (WRO D1/9/2/4)

**684**   12 May 1810 (19 May 1810). Pitton [*in Alderbury*]. A house and premises occupied by Thomas Whitlock. Methodist. Thomas Whitlock, Elizabeth Whitlock, John Read, Mary Read, John Stone. (WRO D26/3)

**685**   5 June 1810 (7 June 1810). Marlborough. A certain house in the possession of John Purdue. Methodist. John Purdue, Henry Roberts, Thomas Balley, Thomas May, Anthony Edwards. (WRO D1/9/2/4)

**686**   18 June 1810 (25 Sept. 1810). Fisherton Anger. The dwellinghouse of John Sutton. Methodist. John Sutton, Amos Bevan, Stephen Bell, John Newman, Daniel Harding. (WRO D1/9/2/4)

**687**   18 June 1810 (22 June 1810). Shripple in Idmiston. A chapel. Methodist. Thomas Bell junior, Stephen Bell, Daniel Harding, John Sutton, William Sanger junior. (WRO D1/9/2/4)

**688**   10 July 1810 (25 July 1810). Semley. The house and premises adjoining of John Gray. Methodist. John Gray, Isaac Denness, James Brockway, John Sanger, Morgan Wilmot, Edward Lear, James Burt, James Sydserff. (WRO D1/9/2/4)

**689**   20 July 1810 (20 July 1810). Penknap between Westbury Leigh and Dilton Marsh in Westbury. A house built as a place of meeting. Particular Baptist. George Phillips, minister, James Hopkins, Felix Hall, Abraham Dew, William Ball, John Hopkins, Isaac Hillman, Samuel Tucker, John Harris, Thomas Curtis, Joel Hague. (WRO D25/6)

**690**   21 July 1810 (21 July 1810). Salisbury. The new meeting house erected in Endless Street in St Edmund's parish. Independent. Samuel Everett, Samuel Devenish, John Perren, John Cooke, John Batchelor, Alexander Wills, George Barrett, R. Jones. (WRO D1/9/2/4)

**691**   13 Sept. 1810 (17 Sept. 1810). Holt in Bradford on Avon. A meeting house. [*Baptist*: see **681**]. James Barnett, John Hinton, Thomas Stratton, Thomas Beaven, James Beaven, William Sparks, William Sparks senior, Charles Daniel, Charles Cadby, housekeepers in Holt. (WRO D1/9/2/4)

**692**   25 Sept. 1810 (1 Oct. 1810). Chisledon. A certain building now in the possession of William Chouls of Chisledon. Methodist. William Chouls, Thomas Wheeler, John Hall, Joseph Tanner. (WRO D1/9/2/4)

**693**  15 Oct. 1810 (3 Nov. 1810). Salisbury. A building called the school room and the premises adjoining the property of William Sanger junior situated in Gigant Street. Methodist. William Sanger junior, William Sanger senior, Joshua Cobden, Charlotte Hallett, William Smith, Richard Barnes, William Yeatman, Stephen Bell, Sarah Hallott, Joseph Sanger, George Gilbert. (WRO D1/9/2/4)

**694**  10 Nov. 1810 (17 Nov. 1810). Redlynch in Downton. A dwellinghouse and premises in the occupation of Charles Witt. Methodist. John Cole, Stephen Newman, the mark of Charles Witt, Daniel Harding. (WRO D1/9/2/4)

**695**  26 Nov. 1810 (1 Dec. 1810). Warminster. A house and premises thereunto belonging in Meeting House Lane. Baptist. William Jutson, William Hinton, Thomas Hardish, William Cottle, William Scammell, James Hinton. (WRO D1/9/2/4)

**696**  (1 Dec. 1810). Chippenham. A certain building erected in a lane leading into High Street. Baptist. John Paul Porter, minister, William Spackman, George Edwards, Joseph Lewis, Richard Alexander, George Edgecumbe, Thomas Every, John Gay. (WRO D1/9/2/4)

**697**  (1 Dec. 1810). Hilmarton. A certain dwellinghouse. Baptist. John Dymott, minister, Walter Chivers, Isaac Hart, Elisha Lawrence, James Hunt, Charles Wilkins, the mark of Lydia Hart. (WRO D1/9/2/4)

**698**  1 Feb. 1811 (9 Feb. 1811). Bewley Common in Lacock. The dwellinghouse and premises of Mr Benjamin Barton. Trinitarian Baptist. Daniel Cole senior, Robert Stephens, John Reeves, John End, George Hill, Christopher Stantial, Thomas Knee, householders in Lacock. (WRO D1/9/2/4)

**699**  2 Feb. 1811 (5 Feb. 1811). Berwick St John. A building now occupied by Thomas Scammel junior, labourer. Independent. The mark of William Horder, George Gray, Thomas Scammel, the mark of Abner Abbot, Thomas Scammel, housekeepers in Berwick St John. (WRO D1/9/2/4)

**700**  9 March 1811 (23 March 1811). Salisbury. A house in Greencroft Street in the occupation of Sarah Cook. Methodist. Sarah Cook, William Sanger senior, Joseph Barnett, Benjamin Hoare, Robert Hallett. (WRO D1/9/2/4)

**701**  24 March 1811 (20 April 1811). Marston in Potterne. The house, the property of Mr James Biggs, now inhabited by James Beard and Betty Robins. Joseph Hook, the mark of James Holloway, the mark of Richard Coleman,

David Naish, Thomas Stow, Benjamin Stow, Stephen Stow. (WRO D1/9/2/4)

**702** 17 April 1811 (27 April 1811). West Grimstead. The house, the property of Mr Henry Rumbold, now inhabited by Alice Cable. Methodist. C. Compton, M. Compton, H. Cooke, N. Cooke, P. Cooke, housekeepers. (WRO D1/9/2/4)

**703** 12 June 1811 (22 June 1811). Salisbury. A newly erected chapel and premises in Church Street. Methodist. William Sanger senior, William Sanger junior, Arthur Williams, William Smith, Stephen Bell. (WRO D1/9/2/4)

**704** 7 July 1811 (8 July 1811). Winterbourne Stoke. A house, the property of Mr George Grant. Baptist. William Withers, Thomas Kellow, George Grant, James Kellow, William Grant, James Grant, Henry Dyer, living in Winterbourne Stoke and Shrewton. (WRO D1/9/2/4)

**705** 20 July 1811 (7 Sept. 1811). Homington. A house in the occupation of Stephen Rose. Methodist. Thomas Hewlett, Stephen Rose, James Rose, John Sutton, Charles Bishop, Amos Beven. (WRO D1/9/2/4)

**706** 22 July 1811 (17 Aug. 1811). Little Hinton. The dwellinghouse and premises belonging to William Norris and now in his occupation. [*Methodist*: see **677**]. The mark of William Norris, tenant, Michael Edwards, William Arnell, Edward Edwards, John Ford, John Anger, Charles Edwards, the mark of Walter Hayward. (WRO D1/9/2/4)

**707** 6 Aug. 1811 (17 Aug. 1811). Stratford sub Castle *or* Tony. The house of John Whatley. Baptist. The mark of John Whalley, James Butler, William Penny, S. Lambert, John Penny, William Sworn, John James. (WRO D1/9/2/4)

**708** (17 Aug. 1811). Codford St Peter. A new meeting house. [*Independent*: see **549**]. Benjamin Rebbeck, Samuel Doughty, James Alford, Christopher Alford, John Bendall, Christopher Hinwood. (WRO D1/9/2/4)

**709** 2 Sept. 1811 (7 Sept. 1811). Corsley. A house or building. Baptist. William Clift, John Eyres, Isaac Watts, Jerm. Adams. (WRO D1/9/2/4)

**710** 5 Sept. 1811 (14 Sept. 1811). West Knoyle. The dwellinghouse of John Sanger. Methodist. John Sanger, Isaac Denness, John Riddick, William Coward, Jonathan Smith, William Sheppard, dwelling in West Knoyle. (WRO D1/9/2/4)

**711** 9 Sept. 1811 (14 Sept. 1811). Wanborough. The dwellinghouse of John Sweeper. Methodist. John Sweeper of Wanborough, John Moulding, William

Long, Thomas Edwards, David Naish, Edward Honeybone. (WRO D1/9/2/4)

**712** 11 Oct. 1811 (16 Oct. 1811). Chippenham. A house. Methodist. J. Sandy, T. Lewis, T. Vennell, M. Sandy, William Pearson. (WRO D1/9/2/4)

**713** 12 Oct. 1811 (23 Oct. 1811). Damerham. A chapel is erected. Methodist. William Sanger junior, William Sanger senior, John Sutton, Stephen Bell, trustees of the chapel. (WRO D1/9/2/4)

**714** 21 Oct. 1811 (23 Oct. 1811). Marlborough. A chapel, the property of George Pocock, in Oxford Street. Methodist. George Pocock, William Strugnell, William Merewether, Richard Barnes, R. Rees, Henry Roberts, William Reason, William Screen, Charles Dobson, John Page, Thomas Turner, G.G. McTier. (WRO D1/9/2/4)

**715** 23 Oct. 1811 (30 Oct. 1811). Crudwell. The dwellinghouse of Sarah Cole. [*Methodist*: see **753**]. John Rogers, the mark of George Moorhouse, William Hall, William Hall senior, George Simmonds. (WRO D1/9/2/4)

**716** 26 Oct. 1811 (30 Oct. 1811). Boreham in Warminster. A house now in the occupation of John Parham. [*Methodist*: see **392, 622, 683**]. E. Hawkins, John Gunning, Thomas King, James Bush, Charles King, John Adlam, John Harper. (WRO D1/9/2/4)

**717** 28 Oct. 1811 (6 Nov. 1811). Poulton. The dwellinghouse of Robert Whelers. [*Methodist*: see **753**]. John Allen, George Moorhouse, John Rogers, Robert Wheeler, Thomas Norris. (WRO D1/9/2/4)

**718** 1 Nov. 1811 (6 Nov. 1811). Uffcott in Broad Hinton. A building. [*Methodist*: Hall 112]. Peter Hadrill, John Maskline, George Martin, Thomas Newton, James Scholefield. (WRO D1/9/2/4)

**719** 4 Nov. 1811 (9 Jan. 1812). Winsley in Bradford on Avon. A building recently erected. [*Methodist?*: Hall 37 (George Dermott)]. George Domott, John Goold, Thomas Dicke, Charles Greenly, Cornelius Byfield, Thomas Warren. (WRO D1/9/2/4)

**720** 5 Nov. 1811 (7 Dec. 1811). Ashton Keynes. The dwellinghouse of Augustus Savoury Jenkins. [*Methodist*: see **753**]. George Moorhouse, James Vines, John Rogers, A.S. Jenkins. (WRO D1/9/2/4)

**721** 11 Nov. 1811 (7 Dec. 1811). Donhead St Andrew. The dwellinghouse of John Sanger. Methodist. Jacob Richards, John Sanger, Edward Lear, Thomas Brochway, Silas Hiskens, James Bush. (WRO D1/9/2/4)

**722** 11 Nov. 1811 (26 Nov. 1811). Norton Bavant. A dwellinghouse occupied by William Ransom. Independent. Henry Perrott, John Butcher, William Ball, William Ransom. (WRO D1/9/2/4)

**723**   14 Nov. 1811 (7 Dec. 1811). Overton. A house in the possession of William Joyce. Methodist. William Joyce, George Cook, Henry Roberts, Richard Barnes, Rees Rees, William White, William Screen, John Day. (WRO D1/9/2/4)

**724**   29 Nov. 1811 (10 Feb. 1812). Bushton in Clyffe Pypard. A room in the possession of Ann Marrat. Independent. William Church, Roger Little, Paul Church, James Bushell, David Sutton, James Sutton, dwelling in Bushton. (WRO D1/9/2/4)

**725**   25 Dec. 1811 (28 Feb. 1812). North Wraxall. A house erected. Independent. William Collins, minister, Abraham Billett, Samuel Chappell, William Billett, Stephen Beazer, Daniel Taylor, Hillarius Schneider, John Schneider, James Drew. (WRO D1/9/2/4)

**726**   10 Jan. 1812 (11 July 1812). Keevil. A building. Methodist. William Pearson, Charles Colwell, minister, James Pullen, Samuel Curnick, James Nelson. (WRO D1/9/2/4)

**727**   4 Feb. 1812 (10 Feb. 1812). Donhead St Mary. The dwellinghouse of Thomas Young. Methodist. Thomas Young, George Trowbridge, John West, George West, Edward Williams, dwelling in Donhead St Mary. (WRO D1/9/2/4)

**728**   15 Feb. 1812 (19 Feb. 1812). West Grimstead. A house in the occupation of Joseph Compton. Methodist. N. Cooke, Henry Cook, Charlotte Compton, Martha Compton, Joseph Compton. (WRO D1/9/2/4)

**729**   13 March 1812 (12 May 1812). Oaksey. The dwellinghouse of John Earl. [*Methodist*: see **753**]. George Moorhouse, James Vines, John Earle, A.S. Fenkins [*recte* Jenkins: see **720**]. (WRO D1/9/2/4)

**730**   (26 March 1812). Minety. A dwellinghouse. [*Methodist*: see **753**]. George Moorhouse of Minety [*and others, not named in the return*]. (PRO RG31/2 Gloucester diocese)

**731**   10 April 1812 (11 July 1812). Studley in Bremhill. A building. Methodist. J. Sandey, minister, William Henly, Henry Witts, William Russ, Selina Pontin, Betty Seage, Hannah Holly, the mark of James Holley, the mark of Isaac Britain, the mark of John Holley. (WRO D1/9/2/4)

**732**   10 April 1812 (20 April 1812). Swallowfield. A house belonging to Thomas Simonds in the occupation of Richard Taylor. Thomas Norman, Robert Watts, Richard Taylor, John Paice, Richard Sutton, William Clements,

George Searle, Thomas Simmonds, George Jennings, Sander Willson, John Allright, James Hopkins. (WRO D1/9/2/4)

**733**   13 April 1812 (5 May 1812). Fovant. The dwellinghouse belonging to Thomas Best junior now in the occupation of Lucy Foot. [*Independent*: Wiltshire Register 1827]. Thomas Best junior, Daniel Harding, Robert Harding, Thomas Jay junior, the mark of Lucy Foot. (WRO D1/9/2/4)

**734**   7 May 1812 (9 May 1812). Redlynch Common in Downton. A room in the occupation of John Dixon. Methodist. Richard Robarts, minister, John Dixon, William Snelgrove, Abraham Batt, Richard Jennings. (WRO D1/9/2/4)

**735**   5 July 1812 (21 Aug. 1812). Teffont Magna. A room in the occupation of Edward Mole. Methodist. Edward Larkam, Samuel Blake, James Domeny, Edward Mole, Daniel Clement, John Crowter. (WRO D1/9/2/4)

**736**   6 July 1812 (1 Aug. 1812). Collingbourne? Ducis (*Lower Collingbourn*). A building, the property of William S. Wakeford esquire of Andover, Hants., at present inhabited by John Hilliar, near the shop of James Bennen, blacksmith, and near the dwellinghouse of farmer Black. Independent and Baptist. Lewis Winchister, George Musprall, John Linsly, Henry Reeves. (WRO D1/9/2/4)

**737**   2 Sept. 1812 (12 Sept. 1812). Hamptworth [*in Downton*]. A house in the occupation of Elizabeth Rawlins. Methodist. William Arney, Henry Newman, John Rice. (WRO D1/9/2/1)

**738**   7 Sept. 1812 (18 Sept. 1812). Teffont Magna. A house in the occupation of James Goodfellow. Methodist. John Fuller, Henry Cool, James Goodfellow, Jesse Mullins, Thomas Mayne. (WRO D1/9/2/1)

**739**   9 Sept. 1812 (22 Sept. 1812). Edington. A cottage with its appurtenances now or lately in the occupation of Elizabeth White, widow. [*Baptist*: see **662**]. Thomas Wastfield of Imber, schoolmaster. (WRO D1/9/2/1)

**740**   26 Sept. 1812 (30 Sept. 1812). Netton in Durnford. A new chapel. Methodist. Robert Dear, William Hall, John Yeats, George Sillwood?, Henry Alexander?, Susanna Davis, William Tucker, James Saunders, John Davy. (WRO D1/9/2/1)

**741**   16 Oct. 1812 (24 Oct. 1812). South Newton. A new chapel. Methodist. William Larkam, Thomas Jeffery, John Young, Reuben Read. (WRO D1/9/2/ 1)

**742**   2 Nov. 1812 (4 Nov. 1812). Homington. A house in the occupation of John Blake. Methodist. Thomas Tueeffen, Thomas Hulet, William Street, Thomas Harris. (WRO D1/9/2/1)

**743**    16 Nov. 1812 (30 Nov. 1812). Stockton. A messuage or tenement now in the occupation of Keziah Occulstone. [*Independent*: see **690**]. Samuel Devenish of Codford St Peter, dissenting minister, Joseph Gibbs. (WRO D1/9/2/1)

**744**    12 Dec. 1812 (23 Dec. 1812). Redlynch in Downton. A house belonging to John Chalk. Methodist. Charles Witt, William Snelgrove, William Arney. (WRO D1/9/2/1)

**745**    28 Dec. 1812 (29 Dec. 1812). Trowbridge. A building near the bridge, at present occupied by Mr Robert Marshman, the owner of which is Thomas Timbrell esquire. [*Baptist*: see **846**]. William Eacott of Trowbridge, clothworker, William Marshman, John Way, Samuel Hurd. (WRO D1/9/2/1)

**746**    1 Jan. 1813 (14 Jan. 1813). Froxfield. A building or messuage or tenement in the occupation of Edward Hobbs and the property of William Meariweather. [*Independent*: see **778**]. Joseph Faulknor of Hungerford, auctioneer, J. Neeves, Richard Lope?, Robert Lye. (WRO D1/9/2/1)

**747**    1 Jan. 1813 (23 Jan. 1813). Poulshot. A building. Methodist. George Blake, minister, William Hicks, Joseph Blake, Francis Earl, Betty Earl, Isaac Beale, Thomas Godwin, Thomas Panton?. (WRO D1/9/2/1)

**748**    27 Jan. 1813 (25 March 1813). Potterne. The chapel and dwellinghouse of Jacob Gale. Baptist. James Gale, James Shipman, Samuel Fielding, James Bigwood, Jacob Gale, Philip Burden. (WRO D1/9/2/1)

**749**    2 Feb. 1813 (24 Feb. 1813). Bratton in Westbury. A dwellinghouse now in the occupation of John Stiles, labourer. Methodist. John Bedford of Warminster, Methodist minister. (WRO D1/9/2/1)

**750**    8 Feb. 1813 (13 Feb. 1813). West Grimstead. A house and premises belonging to Thomas Mussel. Methodist. Henry Cook, N. Cook, M. Comton, C. Compton, Joseph Compton. (WRO D1/9/2/1)

**751**    14 Feb. 1813 (24 Feb. 1813). Whiteparish. The dwellinghouse of Thomas Kener. William Loopman? [*Cookman?*], Isaac Loopman? [*Cookman?*], Ann Mashment, Ann Harford, George Prince, the mark of T Kener, William Early, Elizabeth Brown, Jane Brown, William Maggs, Mary Maggs. (WRO D1/9/2/1)

**752**    2 April 1813 (17 April 1813). Bapton [*in Fisherton Delamere*]. A dwellinghouse in the occupation of James Titford. [*Methodist*: Hall 206]. John Dean of Salisbury, minister, D. . .[*illegible*] Gardner, James Titford. (WRO D1/9/2/1)

**753**    13 April 1813 (5 May 1813). Ashton Keynes. The dwellinghouse of

James Vines. [*Methodist*★]. George Moorhouse, James Vines. [*At foot*] 'W. Sanger 5th May 1813.' (WRO D1/9/2/1)

**754** 20 April 1813 (21 April 1813). Quidhampton in Fugglestone St Peter. A dwellinghouse, the property of James Hayter, and in the occupation of William Crouch. Independent. Joseph Williams, Nehemiah Broadway, Alexander Goodfellow, housekeepers in Quidhampton. (WRO D1/9/2/1)

**755** 6 May 1813 (1 June 1813). Shaw Hill in Melksham. A messuage or tenement occupied by William Hedges, belonging to James Marshman. [*Baptist*★]. Thomas Ward of Melksham, dissenting minister. [*Pencilled at foot*] 'Revd. Mr. Saffree 1st June 1813.' [*same document as* **756**]. (WRO D1/9/2/1)

**756** 6 May 1813 (1 June 1813). Whitley in Melksham. A messuage or tenement occupied by Isaac Cannings, belonging to Elizabeth Nash and Rebecca Scott. [*Baptist*: see **755**]. John Davis of Melksham, bookkeeper. [*same document as* **755**]. (WRO D1/9/2/1)

**757** 29 May 1813 (1 July 1813). Horningsham. A house belonging to Thomas Ridgley, labourer. Methodist. John Bedford of Warminster, Methodist preacher. [*at foot*] 'Mr Gregory – Eagle I.' (WRO D1/9/2/1)

**758** 1 June 1813 (1 July 1813). Wylye. A building lately occupied by John Perior as a malthouse, being the property of Christopher Brandiss. [*Independent*: see **690**]. Samuel Devenish of Codford St Peter, dissenting minister. (WRO D1/9/2/1)

**759** 9 July 1813 (31 July 1813). Yatton Keynell. A house and premises in the possession of Thomas Freke. [*Methodist*: Hall 112]. James Odgers of Hungerford. (WRO D1/9/2/1)

**760** 8 Sept. 1813 (14 Sept. 1813). Marlborough. A building, part of the Kings Arms public house, Kingsbury Street, let to George Goatley, consisting of a school room, a play room and a small sleeping room, this his dwelling also, in St Mary's parish, now in the occupation of John Weston, tenant of Mr John Bunsden, Marlborough, saddler, brewer, etc.; belonging to Arnold Copeland of Uxbridge, Middlesex. George Goatley of Marlborough, schoolmaster, John Simmons, Charles Dobson, William Screen, Henry Turner. (WRO D1/9/2/1)

**761** 29 Sept. 1813 (2 Oct. 1813). Chitterne All Saints. The dwellinghouse and premises of William Richards. Baptist and Independent. William Roberts, John Blake, William Richords, Thomas Gibbs. (WRO D1/9/2/1)

**762** 11 Oct. 1813 (19 Nov. 1813). Studley in Bremhill. A house occupied by Richard Panting. Baptist. Richard Panting, Jane Panting, Mary Wiltshire, William Wiltshire, Martha Wiltshire, inhabitants of Studley. (WRO D1/9/2/1)

**763** 13 Oct. 1813 (20 Oct. 1813). Cholderton. A dwellinghouse, the property of W.S. Blatch. Methodist. William S. Blatch, George Sillwood. (WRO D1/9/2/1)

**764** 14 Oct. 1813 (22 Oct.). Limpley Stoke in Bradford on Avon. A tenement occupied by James Richards. Baptist. James Bernard, John Bull, Isaac Batten, Elimelech Edmonds, Joseph Stapleton, James Hart, Francis Everett, Thomas Nicholls, John Edmonds, John Hinton. (WRO D1/9/2/1)

**765** 21 Oct. 1813 (5 Nov. 1813). Hurst. A house now in the occupation of Francis Payne. The mark of Francis Payne, Robert Rhodes, Joseph Bathe, Richard Aldridge, James Colbourne, James Leach. (WRO D1/9/2/1)

**766** 8 Nov. 1813 (19 Nov. 1813). Swindon. A house now in the possession of William Noad. Methodist. Dennis Hale?, John Noad, Leonard Hill, James Page, William Noad, Nathaniel May. [*Pencilled at foot*] 'Mr Gellard 18 Nov. 1813.' (WRO D1/9/2/1)

**767** 12 Nov. 1813 (26 Nov. 1813). Market Lavington. A house, called a meeting house. Independent. A.E. Saunders, John Ward, Richard Ward, John Gauntlett, William Moore, Benjamin Ward, Alexander Cannings. (WRO D1/9/2/1)

**768** 7 Jan. 1814. Poole Keynes. The dwellinghouse of Matthew James. [*Independent*: see **905**]. Matthew James, labourer, John Reynolds, Henry Reynolds. (WRO A1/250)

**769** 16 April 1814 (19 April 1814). Ford in Laverstock. A dwellinghouse in the occupation of Sarah Davis. [*Methodist★*]. George Gillard, of St Edmund's parish, Salisbury. (WRO D1/9/2/1)

**770** 21 May 1814 (2 July 1814). Sherston. A house now in the occupation of William Merchant. Independent. Simon Pitt, minister, George Garlick, William Merchant, Thomas Deverell, Thomas Bull, John Ball, Joseph Clarke. [*At foot*] 'For Smith newsman.' (WRO D1/9/2/1)

**771** 9 June 1814 (18 June 1814). Wanborough. A house and premises in the occupation of Thomas Williams, labourer [*Methodist*: VCH 9, 185]. George Spicer, Thomas Williams, Thomas Smith, residing in Wanborough. (WRO D1/9/2/1)

**772** 14 Sept. 1814 (23 Sept. 1814). Shalbourne. The house of Thomas Strange. Methodist. William Fowler of Hungerford. [*Endorsed*] 'Revd. G. Gillard, Methodist Chapel, Salisbury.' (WRO D1/9/2/1)

**773** 19 Sept. 1814 (23 Sept. 1814). Downton. A chapel at Lode Hill (*Loodhill*). [*Methodist★*]. George Gillard of Salisbury. (WRO D1/9/2/1)

**774** 29 Sept. 1814 (5 Oct. 1814). Westwood. A house occupied by John Godwin. [Methodist*]. George Gillard of Salisbury. (WRO D1/9/2/1)

**775** 17 Oct. 1814 (18 Oct. 1814). Great Hinton in Steeple Ashton. Part of a messuage at Fore Street, belonging to me. [Methodist?: VCH 8, 216]. Charles Milsom, farmer of Steeple Ashton. (WRO A1/250)

**776** 7 Nov. 1814 (28 Jan. 1815). Stratton St Margaret. The dwellinghouse and premises belonging to Daniel Hall and now in his occupation. [Independent?: see 387]. Daniel Hall, Joshua Hyde, Thomas Garrett, John Garrett, Mary Day, William Day, William Adams, Thomas Day. (WRO D1/9/2/1)

**777** 29 Nov. 1814 (28 Jan. 1815). Studley in Calne. A new built chapel. Baptist. William Wiltshire, Martha Wiltshire, Jane Panting, Mary Wiltshire, Thomas Wiltshire, inhabitants of Studley. [At foot] 'Draper, newsman.' (WRO D1/9/2/1)

**778** 4 Dec. 1814 (22 Dec. 1814). Shalbourne. A building belonging to Silvanus Bevan, esquire, of Fosbury and occupied by him. [Independent: see 921]. Richard Bevan, William Wakeford, Silvanus Bevan, James Martin, Robert Lye, Moses Douce?, J. Faulknor. [Note] 'Mr. Barrett – Shoemaker.' [Endorsed] 'Mr Barrett, Catherine St.' (WRO D1/9/2/1)

**779** 26 Jan. 1815 (28 Jan. 1815). Broad Town in Broad Hinton or Clyffe Pypard. The house of Isaac Lowder. [Methodist: see 836]. William Fowler of Hungerford. (WRO D1/9/2/1)

**780** 26 Jan. 1815 (28 Jan. 1815). Rodbourne Cheney. The house of George Greenaway. [Methodist: see 836]. William Fowler of Hungerford. (WRO D1/9/2/1)

**781** 26 Jan. 1815 (28 Jan. 1815). Wootton Bassett. The house of Joseph Dash. [Methodist*]. William Fowler of Hungerford. [Endorsed] 'Revd. G. Gillard, Methodist Chapel, Salisbury.' (WRO D1/9/2/1)

**782** 1 May 1815 (3 May 1815). Woodstock in Box. A house in the possession of Samuel Rowe. [Methodist*]. George Gillard of Salisbury. (WRO D1/9/2/1)

**783** 28 June 1815 (31 June 1815). Bishopstone. A house in the occupation of Richard Toomer. Methodist. William Sanger junior, John Moore. (WRO D1/9/2/1)

**784** 31 July 1815 (29 Aug. 1815). Pinkney in Sherston. A dwellinghouse in the occupation of Thomas Ball. Independent. G. Garlick, minister, Thomas Ball, Joseph Clarke, Thomas Deverell, Edward Purnell, John Ball, William Merchant, dwelling in Pinkney. [Endorsed in pencil] 'Mr. Burrell.' (WRO D1/9/2/1)

**785**  5 Aug. 1815 (10 Aug. 1815). Charlton in Downton. The house and premises belonging to James Noyce. [*Methodist*★]. Thomas Newton of Salisbury, minister of the gospel. [*Pencilled at foot*] 'Mr. Sanger.''(WRO D1/9/2/1)

**786**  5 Aug. 1815 (10 Aug. 1815). Warminster Green in Downton. The house and premises belonging to Daniel Wilkins. [*Methodist*★]. Thomas Newton of Salisbury, minister of the gospel. [*Pencilled at foot*] 'Mr. Sanger.' (WRO D1/9/2/1)

**787**  12 Sept. 1815 (23 Sept. 1815). Easton Grey. The dwellinghouse of Thomas Woodward. Baptist. T. Martin, minister, James Dancey, Joseph Thompson, Thomas Woodard, John Carter, Israel Saginton, Nathaniel Hanks, Matthew Hanks, in Easton Grey. (WRO D1/9/2/1)

**788**  25 Sept. 1815 (27 Sept. 1815). Coate in Bishops Cannings. A dwellinghouse and premises in the occupation of Grace Hiscock, widow. [*Independent*: see **1275**]. George Elgar Sloper, Mary Anne Sloper, Richard Elliott, Jane Giddings, Joseph Crooksey. (WRO D1/9/2/1)

**789**  2 Oct. 1815 (4 Oct. 1815). Maddington. The house of John Baker. Independent. Thomas Davis, John Baker, Henry Prior, James Windsor, Francis Windsor, William Weare, housekeepers in Shrewton and Maddington. (WRO D1/9/2/1)

**790**  7 Oct. 1815 (7 Oct. 1815). Berwick St James. A house now in the occupation of John Morrant. [*Independent*: see **789**]. George Shergold of Great Wishford, the mark of John Morrant of Berwick St James, John Grant of Winterbourne Stoke, Thomas Davis of Shrewton. (WRO D1/9/2/1)

**791**  7 Oct. 1815 (28 Oct. 1815). West Ashton in Steeple Ashton. A house in the occupation of William Little. [*Independent*★]. Benjamin Kent, R. Long, Elias Burbidge, Henry Sever, William Little, Eliza Little. [*At foot*] 'Mr. Thring, Wilton.' (WRO D1/9/2/1)

**792**  17 Oct. 1815 (19 Oct. 1815). West Amesbury in Amesbury. A house called Little Amesbury House in the occupation of Edmund Grange. [*Independent*: see **789**]. Edmund Grange, occupier, Solomon Trew of West Amesbury, Thomas Davis of Shrewton, R.J. Grange of West Amesbury. (WRO D1/9/2/1)

**793**  20 Oct. 1815 (23 Oct. 1815). Brokenborough. The dwellinghouse of Abraham Smith. [*Independent*: see **818**]. Abram Smith, John Shipton, Joseph White, William Jefferis, George Pike, William Mills, Thomas Martin. (WRO D1/9/2/1)

**794**  30 Oct. 1815 (2 Nov. 1815). Collingbourne ?Kingston (*Upper Collingbourn*). The house of Joseph Cornish. [*Methodist*★]. William Fowler of Hungerford. [*Endorsed*] 'Revd. G. Gillard, Methodist Chapel, Salisbury.' (WRO D1/9/2/1)

**795**  7 Nov. 1815 (7 Nov. 1815). Alderbury. A house in the occupation of Joseph Pearce. Methodist. William Sanger junior, Joseph Bennett, Henry Cook. [*Pencilled at foot*] 'Mr. Sanger.' (WRO D1/9/2/1)

**796**  8 Nov. 1815 (30 Jan. 1816). Martin. The dwellinghouse of Bernard Harris. Independent. Michael Saunders, Lares Loden?, Bernard Saunders, Thomas Ely, Bernard Harris, James Jenkins, Thomas Flemington, Robert Bailey. [*Pencilled at foot*] 'Mr. Thring, Wilton, 30th Jany. 1816.' (WRO D1/9/2/1)

**797**  18 Nov. 1815 (18 Nov. 1815). Barford St Martin. A house in the occupation of John Goode. [*Methodist★*]. William Sanger junior, Joseph Trapnell, Joseph Harding. (WRO D1/9/2/1)

**798**  18 Nov. 1815 (22 Nov. 1815). Chittoe in Bishops Cannings. A house occupied by Thomas Hunt. Baptist. The mark of Thomas Hunt, the mark of Stephen Gee, James Hunt, John Martimer, the mark of Thomas Gray, the mark of James Hunt, inhabitants of Chittoe. (WRO D1/9/2/1)

**799**  26 Dec. 1815 (6 Jan. 1816). Littleton Drew. A house lately erected. Independent. Samuel Chappell, Charles Pinnell, James Ayliffe, William Isaac, William Buckwell, George Arthurs. [*Endorsed*] 'Mr. Safferee.' [*who was, however, a Baptist minister*]. (WRO D1/9/2/1)

**800**  4 Jan. 1816 (24 Feb. 1816). Bushton in Clyffe Pypard. The house of Edward Stratton, labourer. [*Independent*: see **724, 978**]. The mark of Edward Stratton, John Panting, Joshua Hyde, William Church, John Bedford. (WRO D1/9/2/1)

**801**  6 Jan. 1816 (10 Jan. 1816). Whiteparish Common in Whiteparish. A house in the occupation of Charles Noble. Methodist. William Sanger junior, Richard Oats. (WRO D1/9/2/1)

**802**  7 Jan. 1816. Malmesbury. The dwellinghouse of Simon Weaver. Simon Weaver, labourer, of Malmesbury, John Fullaway, Henry Reeves, Matthew Hanks, William Bracher?. (WRO A1/250)

**803**  10 Jan. 1816 (20 Jan. 1816). Great Hinton in Steeple Ashton. A building in the occupation of Mary Sims and Jane Shapman. Independent. B. Kent, William Little junior, Oliver Manly, the mark of Mary Sims, the mark of Jane Shapman. [*Endorsed*] 'Rev Mr Turner [*deleted*] Salisbury.' (WRO D1/9/2/1)

**804**  10 Jan. 1816 (16 Jan. 1816). Westport St Mary. A building lately erected on the Abbey Row in the town of Malmesbury. [*Baptist*: see **787**]. Thomas

Martin, minister, George Pike, Joseph Thompson, John Carter, Moses Jones, Israel Saginton. (WRO D1/9/2/1)

**805**  10 Feb. 1816 (13 Feb. 1816). Stratford sub Castle. A house in the occupation of Jonathan Viney. [*Methodist*★]. William Sanger junior, of Salisbury. (WRO D1/9/2/1)

**806**  12 Feb. 1816 (5 March 1816). Chute. A house in the occupation of William Cox. Joseph Norris, James Batchelor, Joseph Shipway, Thomas Hopgood, Charles Cook. (WRO D1/9/2/1)

**807**  13 Feb. 1816 (14 Feb. 1816). Warminster Green in Downton. The house of William Blake. [*Methodist*★]. William Sanger junior. (WRO D1/9/2/1)

**808**  14 Feb. 1816 (23 Feb. 1816). Southwick in North Bradley. A meeting house lately erected. Baptist. William Norress, Enoch Bennett, Absalom Bennett, David Stillman. (WRO D1/9/2/1)

**809**  18 Feb. 1816 (24 Feb. 1816). Goatacre (*Godaker*) in Hilmarton. The house of Mary Grinaway. Robert Henly, Jacob Henly, Cornelius Edwards, Joseph Rivers senior, Joseph Rivers junior, John Rivers. (WRO D1/9/2/1)

**810**  28 Feb. 1816 (21 March 1816). Dauntsey. A house now in the occupation of Thomas Scull, shoemaker. Independent. John Fowler, minister, Thomas Skull, David Greenman, yeoman, Peter Hayward, labourer, John Morse, watchmaker, Richard Hull, labourer, John Merriett, yeoman, Adam Hollidge, carpenter. (WRO D1/9/2/1)

**811**  2 March 1816 (21 March 1816). Rowde. A dwellinghouse belonging to the executors of Simon Noad deceased. Baptist. Jeremiah Helps, Stephen Webb, William Holloway, John Smart, William Wootton, the mark of David Helps. (WRO D1/9/2/1)

**812**  5 March 1816 (13 April 1816). Earldoms [*extra-parochial place*]. A house belonging to and in the occupation of William Rawlins. Methodist. William Sanger junior. (WRO D1/9/2/1)

**813**  5 March 1816 (13 April 1816). Newton Tony. A house belonging to and in the occupation of Sarah Elton. Methodist. William Sanger junior. (WRO D1/9/2/1)

**814**  17 March 1816 (30 March 1816). Tidcombe [*in Tidcombe and Fosbury*]. A house in the occupation of John Kimber. [*Independent?*: see **921, 949**]. James Smart, Edward Gosling. [*Pencilled at foot*] 'Mr. Wm Rumsey, Andover.' [*Identical format to* **815, 817**]. (WRO D1/9/2/1)

**815**  18 March 1816 (30 March 1816). Great Bedwyn. A house in the occupation of Mr James Gregory. [*Independent*?: see **814**]. William Bartlett, surgeon, Stephen Pullin of Great Bedwyn, John Smallbones, James Dowling. [*Identical format to* **814, 817**]. (WRO D1/9/2/1)

**816**  18 March 1816 (29 March 1816). Great Cheverell. The house of James Potter, as now inhabited by Mark Sawyer, together with the garden and premises thereunto belonging. Independent. Mark Sawyer, John Price, of Great Cheverell. (WRO D1/9/2/1)

**817**  19 March 1816 (30 March 1816). Fosbury in Tidcombe and Fosbury. A house in the occupation of Thomas Lovelock. [*Independent*?: see **814**]. James Leader, John Hoare. [*Identical format to* **814, 815**]. (WRO D1/9/2/1)

**818**  26 April 1816 (29 April 1816). Brokenborough. The dwellinghouse of William Mills. [*Independent*: see **613, 615**]. William Tranter, Thomas Martin, William Mills, Simon Pitt, John Hawkins, in Brokenborough. (WRO D1/9/2/1)

**819**  27 April 1816 (13 May 1816). Wilton in Great Bedwyn. A house in the occupation of George Stagg. Edward Elkins, John Dows. (WRO D1/9/2/1)

**820**  4 May 1816 (18 May 1816). Nettleton. The dwellinghouse and premises of Henry West. Independent. Daniel Taylor, Henry West, James Drew, Samuel Chappel. (WRO D1/9/2/1)

**821**  7 May 1816 (10 Sept. 1816). Barford St Martin. A dwellinghouse in the occupation of Daniel Hibberd. Independent. George Jakes, Daniel Dawkins, William Snelgrove. [*At foot*] 'Mr Thring – Wilton – 10th Sept. 1816 pd for.' (WRO D1/9/2/1)

**822**  14 May 1816 (18 May 1816). Poulshot. The dwellinghouse in the possession of William Cozens, for the instruction of children and for worship. William Cozens, James Banks, Eliza Banks, Henry Lewis, Marianne Lewis. (WRO D1/9/2/1)

**823**  15 May 1816 (18 May 1816). Calne. The house now in possession of Isaac Porch in Castle Street. Baptist. John Compton. H. Chivers, John Chivers, Thomas Blake, Walter Chivers, Henry Lane, S. Ponting. (WRO D1/9/2/1)

**824**  17 May 1816 (18 May 1816). Barford St Martin. A building now in erection. [*Methodist*★]. William Sanger junior, of High Street, Salisbury, gentleman. (WRO D1/9/2/1)

**825**  27 May 1816 (11 June 1816). Great Bedwyn. A house in the occupation of Mary Beck. William Bartlett, surgeon, James Gregory. [*Pencilled at foot*] '7th June 1816 Mr Barrett.' (WRO D1/9/2/1)

**826**  3 June 1816 (3 June 1816). Amesbury. A house and premises the property and in the occupation of Thomas Truckle. [*Methodist*★]. William Sanger junior, of Salisbury, gentleman. (WRO D1/9/2/1)

**827**  3 June 1816 (3 June 1816). No Man's Land [*extra-parochial place*]. A house and field the property and in the occupation of James Winter. [*Methodist*★]. William Sanger junior, of Salisbury, gentleman. (WRO D1/9/2/1)

**828**  10 June 1816 (11 June 1816). Southwick in North Bradley. A house occupied by Edward Sainsbury. [*Methodist*★]. George Gillard of St Edmund's parish, Salisbury. (WRO D1/9/2/1)

**829**  20 June 1816 (22 June 1816). Shrewton. The chapel of George Baring. Baptist. George Baring, Joseph Weare, William Weare, William Windsor, Thomas Dewey, housekeepers in Shrewton. (WRO D1/9/2/1)

**830**  29 June 1816 (29 June 1816). Tilshead. A house now in the occupation of Thomas Ford. [*Independent?*: see **587**]. Thomas Ford, Leonard Lawes, James Payne, William Lawes. [*Pencilled at foot*] 'Mr Beeby, Saturday.' (WRO D1/9/2/1)

**831**  1 July 1816 (2 July 1816). Berwick St James. The house of Ann Gilbert. Baptist. Henry Cornish, Stapleford, Thomas Godwin, William Godwin, William Thyte, Thomas Blanchard, the mark of Elizabeth Blanchard, James Blanchard, the mark of Phoebe Morrant, the mark of Sarah Young, John White, the mark of John Gilbert, the mark of Ann Gilbert, Mary Godwin, Mary Kellow, the mark of Ann Gilbert, the mark of George Marshall, the mark of Jane Marshall, the mark of Issachon Blanchard, the mark of George Day, the mark of Hester Stanmer, the mark of Mary Pirty, the mark of John Morron, the mark of William Gilbert, housekeepers in Berwick St James and Stapleford. (WRO D1/9/2/1)

**832**  10 July 1816 (20 July 1816). Charlton in Downton. A house in the occupation of Mary Wheeler. [*Methodist*★]. William Sanger junior, of Salisbury. (WRO D1/9/2/1)

**833**  10 July 1816 (20 July 1816). Landford. A house, the property of Samuel Moody. [*Methodist*★]. William Sanger junior, of Salisbury. (WRO D1/9/2/1)

**834**  11 July 1816 (20 July 1816). Amesbury. A Methodist chapel. Methodist. William Sanger junior, of Salisbury. [*Endorsed*] 'Mr Sanger to bear date 20th July.' (WRO D1/9/2/1)

**835**  16 July 1816 (31 July 1816). Horningsham. The dwellinghouse of Henry Garrett. [*Methodist*★]. Alexander Weir of Warminster, minister of the gospel. [*At foot*] 'Mr Sanger.' (WRO D1/9/2/1)

**836** 23 July 1816 (29 July 1816). Swindon. The Methodist chapel. Methodist. William Fowler of Hungerford. [*Endorsed*] 'Revd. G. Gillard, Methodist Chapel, Salisbury.' (WRO D1/9/2/1)

**837** 2 Aug. 1816 (5 Oct. 1816). North Tidworth. A house in the occupation of John Blackmor. Methodist. William Sanger junior, of Salisbury, Methodist minister. (WRO D1/9/2/1)

**838** 21 Aug. 1816 (24 Aug. 1816). Hamptworth in Downton. The dwelling-house of James Harris. [*Baptist*?: see **853**]. The mark of James Harris, George B. Poynton, Henry Barter, Emmanuel Darke. (WRO D1/9/2/1)

**839** 14 Oct. 1816 (18 Oct. 1816). Donhead St Mary. The house and premises of William Brothers, in the occupation of Silas Williams. [*Methodist*: Hall 210]. Mark Daniell of Shaftesbury, minister of the gospel, the mark of Silas Williams, John Gillingham, W. Morgan. (WRO D1/9/2/1)

**840** 22 Oct. 1816 (29 Oct. 1816). Ansty. A house and premises occupied by James Butt. William Hopkins of Tisbury, dissenting minister, James Butt, John Butt, Samuel Hibberd. (WRO D1/9/2/1)

**841** 24 Oct. 1816 (31 Oct. 1816). Salisbury. A house in Salt Lane in the occupation of Mark Rogers Enery. Methodist. Mark Rogers Enery, Joseph Harding, Henry Trew, William Sanger junior. (WRO D1/9/2/1)

**842** 28 Oct. 1816 (29 Oct. 1816). Ridge (*Rudge*) in Chilmark. A house and premises occupied by James Lane. William Hopkins of Tisbury, dissenting minister, James Lane, Thomas Bevis, James Bevis. (WRO D1/9/2/1)

**843** 29 Oct. 1816 (3 Nov. 1816). Netheravon. A house and premises lately in the occupation of Robert Poole. Baptist. Henry Parsons of Shrewton, maltster. (WRO D1/9/2/1)

**844** 30 Oct. 1816 (31 Oct. 1816). Amesbury. A house in Marlbrough Street in the occupation of Joseph Truckle. Methodist. Joseph Truckle, Thomas Truckle, Stephen Harding. (WRO D1/9/2/1)

**845** 14 Jan. 1817 (18 Jan. 1817). Coombe Bissett. A house in the occupation of William Street. Methodist. William Street, Henry Street, John Marshall. [*Pencilled at foot*] 'Sanger.' (WRO D1/9/2/1)

**846** 23 Jan. 1817 [*An earlier certificate, of 6 Nov. 1816, was drafted irregularly, and no licence was issued*] (24 Jan. 1817). Trowbridge. A chapel called Zion Chapel, lately erected. Baptist. Samuel Hurd, William Eacott, James Hayward, Thomas Ball, James Summers. [*At foot*] 'By Gatehouse, Jany 24. 1817.' (WRO D1/9/2/1)

**847** 1 Feb. 1817 (10 Feb. 1817). Westwood. Some part of a house belonging to and in the occupation of William Fisher. Baptist. William Fisher, Francis England, George Manders?, Edward Edge, Joseph England. [*Pencilled at foot*] 'Revd. J. Saffery, 10 Feby 1817.' (WRO D1/9/2/1)

**848** 16 Feb. 1817 (25 Feb. 1817). Great Wishford. A dwellinghouse the property of William Scamels. Independent. George Shergold, Francis Shergold, Emanuel Shergold, Thomas Shergold, James Canens, John Scamell, George Scamill. [*At foot*] 'Mr. Thring, Wilton recd. 2/6.' (WRO D1/9/2/1)

**849** 17 Feb. 1817 (25 Feb. 1817). Market Lavington. We do intend occasionally to use a house called the school-rooms in the centre of Market Lavington, consisting of two large rooms. Independent. A.E. Saunders, R. Willitts, Alexander Cannings, Benjamin Ward, John Gauntlett, Richard Ward, householders in Market Lavington. (WRO D1/9/2/1)

**850** 27 Feb. 1817 (12 March 1817). Startley in Great Somerford. The dwellinghouse of Ralph Punter. Independent. Simon Pitt, minister, the mark of William Field, the mark of Jacob Comley, James Nichols, Simon Hows, Jacob Hand, the mark of Ralph Punter. [*Endorsed*] 'Mr. Hanks.' (WRO D1/9/2/1)

**851** 3 March 1817 (12 March 1817). Dauntsey. A house now in the occupation of John Merrot, labourer. Independent. John Fowler, minister, Richard Hull, Joseph Ferris, John Morse, David Greenman, John Merret, Peter Hayward. [*Endorsed*] 'Mr Hanks constable of Hd Marby [*hundred of Malmesbury*].' (WRO D1/9/2/1)

**852** 17 March 1817 (7 April 1817). Steeple Ashton. A building in the possession or occupation of Oliver Manly. Independent. Benjamin Kent, minister, Oliver Manley, Thomas Lawrence Whitaker. (WRO D1/9/2/1)

**853** 7 April 1817 (7 April 1817). Salisbury. A house in George Court, High Street, St Thomas's parish, now in the possession of Samuel Beeby. [*Baptist?*: see **868**]. Samuel Beeby, James Turquand, George Bracher, Henry Wright, Benjamin Blake, Joseph Lucas, G.B. Poynton. (WRO D1/9/2/1)

**854** 18 April 1817 (25 April 1817). Eden Vale in Westbury. I intend opening my dwellinghouse on Sunday next, 20 April 1817, for worship. [*New Lights*: VCH 8, 185]. Henry Hayter. (WRO D1/9/2/1)

**855** 28 April 1817 (15 May 1817). Cricklade. A house inhabited by Richard Gardner in St Mary's parish. William Edwards, Thomas Haskings, John Smith, Thomas Garner, Richard Fry, John Miles. [*Pencilled at foot*] '15th May 1817, for Mr. Thos. Page, Redland Brickyard, Blunsdon near Cricklade. To be left at Mr. Roses Grocer, Marlboro'h. By G.Geo.' (WRO D1/9/2/1)

**856**  29 April 1817 (10 May 1817). Ogbourne St George. A house and premises, the property and in the occupation of John Gosling of Marlborough. [*Methodist*★]. William Sanger junior, of Salisbury, gentleman. [*At foot*] 'Mr. Sanger pd for.' (WRO D1/9/2/1)

**857**  14 May 1817 (17 May 1817). Lockeridge in Fyfield [*recte Overton*]. A house and premises in the occupation of Charles Quelch. Wesleyan Methodist. William Sanger junior, of Salisbury, gentleman. [*Endorsed*] 'Mr. Sanger, New Street, Salisbury, paid.' (WRO D1/9/2/1)

**858**  22 May 1817 (14 Feb. 1818). Calne. A building. Baptist. John Sidford, auctioneer, Thomas Ford, James Hale. [*Pencilled at foot*] 'Mr. Saffery, 14th Feby 1818.' (WRO D1/9/2/1)

**859**  9 June 1817 (14 June 1817). Lockeridge in Overton. A house and premises in the occupation of Charles Quelch. Methodist. William Sanger junior, of Salisbury, gentleman. (WRO D1/9/2/1)

**860**  9 June 1817 (11 June 1817). Manton in Preshute. A house in the occupation of James Kimmer. Methodist. William Sanger junior, of Salisbury, gentleman. (WRO D1/9/2/1)

**861**  9 June 1817 (14 June 1817). Ogbourne St Andrew. A house and premises, the property and in the occupation of Joseph Waldin. Methodist. William Sanger junior, of Salisbury, gentleman. (WRO D1/9/2/1)

**862**  15 July 1817 (24 July 1817). Lockeridge in Overton. A house and premises, the property and in the occupation of Charles Huntley. Wesleyan Methodist. William Sanger junior, of Salisbury, gentleman. [*Endorsed*] 'Mr. Sanger will be obliged to Mr. Lush to let him have this in a day or two.' (WRO D1/9/2/1)

**863**  1 Aug. 1817 (16 Aug. 1817). Marlborough. Buildings in St Mary's parish in the possession and occupation of Thomas Hall. Independent. Thomas Hall, John Gosling, Thomas Allen, Thomas Bredby, John Day, John Trueman. [*Endorsed in pencil*] 'pd for Rd to be calld for Saturday Augt 16th 1817.' (WRO D1/9/2/1)

**864**  12 Aug. 1817 (22 Aug. 1817). Corsley. A Methodist chapel in Forge Lane End. Methodist. Frederick Snelgrove of Corsley. (WRO D1/9/2/1)

**865**  5 Sept. 1817 (13 Sept. 1817). Wroughton. An outhouse belonging to Mr Thomas Pickett of Wroughton. [*Methodist*: Hall 112]. John Radford of Swindon. (WRO D1/9/2/1)

**866**  13 Sept. 1817 (1 Nov. 1817). Cricklade. A building in St Sampson's parish. Thomas Page, John Smith, Thomas Smith, Thomas Hopkins, Richard Gardener, William Edwards, Thomas Constable. (WRO D1/9/2/1)

**867**　13 Oct. 1817 (25 Oct. 1817). Damerham. A house now in the occupation of William Beach. William Beach, Stephen Beach, John Beach, William Shearing, George Evans, Joshua Harris. [*At foot*] 'Mr. Wills.' (WRO D1/9/2/1)

**868**　30 Oct. 1817 (31 Oct. 1817). Redlynch in Downton. A house now in the possession of James Shelley. [*Baptist*: see **1063**]. Samuel Beeby, Samuel Wort, James Perrin, James Shelley. (WRO D1/9/2/1)

**869**　10 Nov. 1817 (11 Nov. 1817). Eastcott in Urchfont. A house in the occupation of Jane West. Independent. Richard Ward, minister, George Slade, minister, John Gauntlett, John Axford?, John Eeles, Sarah Cumins. [*At foot*] 'Mr. Sainsbury to call next Friday 18th.' (WRO D1/9/2/1)

**870**　22 Dec. 1817 (27 Dec. 1817). Urchfont. A new built meeting house. Independent. Christopher Garrett, minister, C Garrett junior, Thomas Webb, James Garrett, H Carter. (WRO D1/9/2/1)

**871**　(3 Jan. 1818). Knook. The house now occupied by Rawlence Shergold. Independent. James Fowles, overseer, John Orchard, John Andrews, John Sims, the mark of Rawlence Shergold. (WRO D1/9/2/1)

**872**　15 Jan. 1818 (14 Feb. 1818). Alderbury. A house in the occupation of Sarah Cook. [*Methodist*★]. William Sanger junior, of Salisbury. (WRO D1/9/2/1)

**873**　15 Jan. 1818 (14 Feb. 1818). Charlton. A house, the property and in the occupation of Joseph Chubb. [*Methodist*★]. William Sanger junior, of Salisbury. (WRO D1/9/2/1)

**874**　19 Jan. 1818 (10 Feb. 1818). Westbury. I intend to open a room on my premises on Sunday next, 25 Jan. 1818. Thomas Orchard. [*At foot*] 'Sent pr post 13th Feby 1818.' (WRO D1/9/2/1)

**875**　1 Feb. 1818 (6 Feb. 1818). Staverton in Trowbridge. A house now in the occupation of James Bull. Wesleyan Methodist. William Dalmour, Samuel Marks, John Marks, James Ricketts, Thomas Richards, Stephen Gay, George Rison, James Pullin. (WRO D1/9/2/1)

**876**　19 Feb. 1818 (23 Feb. 1818). Ford [*in Laverstock*]. A house, the property of Samuel Whitchurch, esquire, and in the occupation of Charles Percy. [*Methodist: in same hand as* **877**]. The mark of Charles Percy of Ford, labourer. (WRO D1/9/2/1)

**877**  19 Feb. 1818 (23 Feb. 1818). Winterbourne Earls. A house, the property of Mr Henry Mundy and in the occupation of Richard Walker. [*Methodist*: see **881**]. Job Sutton of Winterbourne Gunner, miller. (WRO D1/9/2/1)

**878**  16 March 1818 (17 March 1818). Ludgershall. An inhabited tenement or messuage in the possession of William Edwards. John Walcot of Ludgershall, protestant dissenting minister, William Edwards. (WRO D1/9/2/1)

**879**  21 March 1818 (1 March 1818 [*sic*]). Steeple Ashton. A room belonging to Eleanor Berrett of Steeple Ashton. Samuel Beaven of Littleton in Steeple Ashton. (WRO D1/9/2/1)

**880**  25 March 1818 (26 May 1818). Rockley in Ogbourne St Andrew. A cottage or dwellinghouse now in the occupation of John Peck. [*Methodist:* Hall 112]. James Etchells of Hungerford. (WRO D1/9/2/1)

**881**  9 April 1818 (4 May 1818). Winterbourne Gunner. A chapel building and school room adjoining, all under one roof, the property of Elizabeth Sutton [*Methodist*: see **887**]. Job Sutton of Winterbourne Gunner. (WRO D1/9/2/1)

**882**  21 April 1818 (4 May 1818). Melksham. The house of Richard Cannings in Folly Lane. Baptist. J Spackman, John Buckland, Richard Cannings, Robert Chadwick, Mark Organ. (WRO D1/9/2/1)

**883**  2 May 1818 (26 May 1818). Hilperton. A house now in the occupation of James Hooper. Wesleyan Methodist. James Blake, Stephen Blake, G Gray, James Hooper. (WRO D1/9/2/1)

**884**  15 May 1818 (11 June 1818). Tisbury. The dwellinghouse of William Rawkins. [*Methodist*: Hall 210]. John Wright of Shaftesbury, minister, William Rawkins. [*Pencilled at foot*] '9th June 1818, for Mr. Williams, to be done by to morow.' (WRO D1/9/2/1)

**885**  27 May 1818 (27 May 1818). Salisbury. A building in St Thomas's parish in the possession of Robert Elmer. Robert Elmer, Joseph Lucas, Sarah Lake, Jonah Pipe, John Berley, Sarah Blake. (WRO D1/9/2/1)

**886**  3 June 1818 (9 June 1818). Lockeridge in Overton. Premises, the property of John Gosling, esquire, consisting of three tenements and gardens adjoining. [*Methodist*★]. William Sanger junior, of Salisbury, gentleman. [*At foot*] 'Mr. Lush will have the goodness to let Mr. Sanger have these tomorrow *without* fail, June 3rd 1818.' (WRO D1/9/2/1)

**887**  3 June 1818 (16 June 1818). Winterbourne Gunner. A chapel and school room adjoining, the property of Elizabeth Sutton [*Methodist*★]. William Sanger junior, of Salisbury, gentleman. (WRO D1/9/2/1)

**888**   12 June 1818 (16 June 1818). Preshute. A field or close, the property of and in the occupation of John Gosling, esquire, of Marlborough, containing by estimation three acres. Methodist. John Pyer, John Hall, Paul More. (WRO D1/9/2/1)

**889**   26 June 1818 (11 July 1818). Fonthill Giffard. A dwellinghouse now occupied by John Stevens, labourer. Independent. Thomas Sims, John Abbott, Thomas Bennett Sims. (WRO D1/9/2/1)

**890**   13 July 1818 (23 Oct. 1818). Hurdcott in Winterbourne Earls. A house now in the occupation of James Jeffrey. James Jeffery, William Smith, William Beavis, Philip Pearcey, John Hayter, Urias Smith. [Pencilled at foot] 'Mr. Wills.' (WRO D1/9/2/1)

**891**   14 July 1818 (25 July 1818). Collingbourne Kingston. A dwellinghouse in the occupation of James Durman. [Methodist★]. William Sanger junior, of Salisbury, gentleman. (WRO D1/9/2/1)

**892**   14 July 1818 (25 July 1818). Woodborough. A dwellinghouse in the occupation of William Shipman. [Methodist★]. William Sanger junior, of Salisbury, gentleman. (WRO D1/9/2/1)

**893**   27 July 1818 (8 Aug. 1818). Tilshead. A cottage. [Independent?: see **587**]. Thomas Maffey, minister, James Payne, proprietor of the house, John Munday, occupier. [Accompanying letter] 'July 27th 1818. Sir, I have sent the adress to you and hope it might be sufficiently expressive according to your directions given me on Friday last. I will thank you not to fail in sending me the Licence by the Medium of the Sarum post, Directed to Thos. Maffey at Shrewton, and just mention what your expence is and I will send you the money by the Sarum Carrier next week. PS I think of preaching at the cottage next Sabbath. And am your obdn servn. Thos Maffey.' (WRO D1/9/2/1)

**894**   1 Sept. 1818 (8 Sept. 1818). Salisbury. The Baptist meeting house, Brown Street. Baptist. John Saffery, William Long, George Buckland, James Butler, John Morris, John Jones, William Butler, Samuel Lamppard, William Targett, James Chism, resident in Salisbury. (WRO D1/9/2/1)

**895**   18 Sept. 1818 (20 Oct. 1818). Fonthill Giffard. A dwellinghouse now occupied by John Stevens, labourer. Independent. Thomas Sims, John Abbott, Robert Doughty. (WRO D1/9/2/1)

**896**   28 Sept. 1818 (29 Sept. 1818). North Tidworth. A house belonging to John Miles and in the occupation of James Annetts. [Methodist: see **945**]. James Annetts, occupier, I Habberfied?, Harriet Habberfied, John P Sweetapple, inhabitants. (WRO D1/9/2/1)

**897**   12 Oct. 1818 (27 Oct. 1818). Mere. A house, the property of and inhabited by Thomas Mills, labourer. Thomas Denny, Francis Webb. (WRO D1/9/2/1)

**898** 16 Oct. 1818 (14 Nov. 1818). Crudwell. A meeting house. Independent. William Weaver, minister, William Hays, Crudwell, Thomas Steele, William Wall, William Elyard?, Henry Hays, Robert Poole, Thomas Freeth. (WRO D1/9/2/1)

**899** 20 Oct. 1818 (10 Nov. 1818). Bradford on Avon. A newly erected building or chapel. Wesleyan Methodist. Daniel Campbell, minister, John Pretty, James Kendall, Lewis Williams, Charles Cooper, William Bullock, David Jones, William Sargent, inhabitants of Bradford. [*Endorsed in pencil*] 'These 4 certificates with one for Chute sent a few days since Mr. Sanger will be obliged to Mr. Lush to let him have on Wednesday Novr. 11th without fail.' (WRO D1/9/2/1)

**900** 26 Oct. 1818 (29 Oct. 1818). Chute Hatchett in Chute. A house in the occupation of John Arnold. Methodist. Harry Noyes of Thruxton, Hampshire. [*Endorsed*] 'Mr. Lush will let Mr. Sanger have this in a day or two.' (WRO D1/9/2/1)

**901** 6 Nov. 1818 (10 Nov. 1818). Devizes. A new Methodist chapel in Back Street. Methodist. John Smith of Salisbury. (WRO D1/9/2/1)

**902** 6 Nov. 1818 (10 Nov. 1818). Durnford. A house in the occupation of Richard Conduit. [*Methodist*★]. William Sanger junior, of Salisbury. (WRO D1/9/2/1)

**903** (10 Nov. 1818). Wanborough. A newly erected building or chapel. Wesleyan Methodist. James Spicer, the present proprietor of the chapel. (WRO D1/9/2/1)

**904** 21 Nov. 1818 (1 Dec. 1818). Ogbourne St George. A dwellinghouse and garden in the occupation of James Wilmot of Ogbourne St George. [*Independent*: see **1030**]. The mark of James Wilmot, James Saunders, preacher of the gospel. (WRO D1/9/2/1)

**905** 1 Dec. 1818 (10 Feb. 1818). Poole Keynes. A house now in the occupation of William Brook. Independent. Abraham Palmer, minister, Henry Reynolds, John Reynolds, Thomas Strange, George Freeth, William Brook, Joseph Poole. [*Pencilled at foot*] 'Gatehouse paid 4d.' (WRO D1/9/2/1)

**906** 4 Dec. 1818 (5 Dec. 1818). Axford in Ramsbury. A house and premises in the occupation of Mary Hannetts, widow. [*Methodist*★]. William Sanger junior, of Salisbury. (WRO D1/9/2/1)

**907** 31 Dec. 1818 (3 Feb. 1819). Trowbridge. The house of Isaac Purnall at

White Row. Baptist. Isaac Purnell, Thomas Morris, Isaac Watts, James Bull, John Long, Thomas Ball. [*Endorsed in pencil*] 'Gatehouse.' (WRO D1/9/2/1)

**908**   7 Jan. 1819 (22 Jan. 1819). Heddington. The dwellinghouse of Judith Filpott. Baptist. John King, Christianna King, Mary Reeves, James Reeves, James Hand, James Caudle, Henry Norman, Samuel Norman, of Heddington. [*Pencilled at foot*] 'Mr. Beeby.' (WRO D1/9/2/1)

**909**   3 Feb. 1819 (5 Feb. 1819). Chitterne St Mary. A house lately fitted up. Baptist. James Wheeler, Thomas Small, Elijah Feltham, William Richards, Thomas Gibbs, William Compton. (WRO D1/9/2/1)

**910**   12 Feb. 1819 (18 Feb. 1819). Manningford Bohun [*in Wilsford*]. The house in the occupation of William Rudman. [*Methodist*: Hall 206.]. John Smith of Salisbury. (WRO D1/9/2/1)

**911**   12 Feb. 1819 (15 Feb. 1819). Overton. The house of James Lewis. [*Methodist*: Hall 206]. John Smith of Salisbury. (WRO D1/9/2/1)

**912**   12 Feb. 1819 (18 Feb 1819). Woodborough. The house in the occupation of William Shipman. [*Methodist*: see **892**]. John Smith of Salisbury. (WRO D1/9/2/1)

**913**   4 March 1819 (6 March 1819). Overton. A house in the occupation of Daniel Hiscocks, Wesleyan Methodist. William Sanger junior. [*At foot*] 'Mr Lush will let WS have this on Saturday.' (WRO D1/9/2/1)

**914**   4 March 1819 (12 March 1819). Shalbourne. A dwellinghouse and barn in the occupation of Thomas Butcher. [*Independent*: see **949**]. Charles Cannon, John Cannon. [*Endorsed*] 'Mr. Robt. Tasker, Mach. maker Abbots Ann near Andover.' (WRO D1/9/2/1)

**915**   17 March 1819 (1 May 1819). Boreham in Warminster. The house of Stephen Whatley. Baptist. Joshua Mitchell, dissenting minister, John Fleming, William Allen, James Skinner, Thomas Slade. (WRO D1/9/2/1)

**916**   3 April 1819 (7 April 1819). Fonthill Bishops. A house and premises, owned and inhabited by John Moore, in Bishops Hold. The mark of John Moore, William Hopkins, dissenting minister, John Moore junior, James Uphill. [*Pencilled at foot*] 'Mr. Cook.' (WRO D1/9/2/1)

**917**   7 April 1819 (10 April 1819). North Bradley. A building called a Wesleyan chapel in Lamberts Marsh by the side of the lane leading from the turnpike road to Pauls Hole. Wesleyan Methodist. Samuel Lear of Trowbridge, Methodist minister. (WRO D1/9/2/1)

**918**   19 April 1819 (22 April 1819). Turleigh (*Turlyn*) in Bradford on Avon. A building belonging to Ann Atwood near her dwellinghouse and open to the street. Ann Atwood at Turleigh, widow. [*Pencilled at foot*] 'Mr. Luxford.' (WRO D1/9/2/1)

**919** 20 April 1819 (27 April 1819). Semington [*in Steeple Ashton*]. A newly erected building or chapel. [*Wesleyan Methodist*: see **899**]. Daniel Campbell of Bradford on Avon, minister. (WRO D1/9/2/1)

**920** 4 May 1819 (7 May 1819). South Wraxall in Bradford on Avon. A building, hitherto used for the purpose of a dwellinghouse, of which John Barton is tenant. (*Independent:* Stribling 46]. James Hamlyn of Holt [*in Bradford on Avon*], dissenting minister, John Barton. (WRO D1/9/2/1)

**921** 23 May 1819 (25 May 1819). Shalbourne. A house in the occupation of Mr Charles Cannon. [*Independent*: see **949**]. Richard Bevan of Fosbury House, Shalbourne [*recte Tidcombe and Fosbury*], James Smart, S Bevan, J Walcott. [*At foot*] 'Mr. Richd Bevan, Fosbury House, Shalbourn.' (WRO D1/9/2/1)

**922** 29 May 1819 (4 June 1819). Amesbury. A barn in the occupation of Mary Cove. Wesleyan Methodist. William Sanger junior, of Salisbury. (WRO D1/9/2/1)

**923** (8 June 1819). 'East Stoke' in Erlestoke. The house of William Godwin. Baptist. Robert Edminson, John Price, the mark of John Godwin. [*Pencilled at foot*] 'To Wm Kellow of Winterborne Stoke.' (WRO D1/9/2/1)

**924** 17 June 1819 (3 July 1819). Hilperton. A new building called a Wesleyan Methodist chapel by the side of the road leading to Hilperton Marsh. Wesleyan Methodist. Samuel Lear of Trowbridge, Methodist minister. (WRO D1/9/2/1)

**925** 21 June 1819 (3 July 1819). Horton in Bishops Cannings. A house now in the occupation of Daniel Stevens. Methodist. Daniel Stevens, John Ogilvie, Joshua Lisk. (WRO D1/9/2/1)

**926** 30 June 1819 (2 July 1819). Corsley. The dwellinghouse in the occupation of William Cook. [*Wesleyan Methodist*: Hall 88]. Thomas Rogers of Frome, Somerset, minister. [*At foot*] 'Mr. Garner.' (WRO D1/9/2/1)

**927** 27 Aug. 1819 (22 Sept. 1819). Chirton. A house belonging to and in the occupation of John Wells. Wesleyan Methodist. John Wells, John Ogilvie, Joshua Lisk. (WRO D1/9/2/1)

**928** 13 Sept. 1819 (30 Sept. 1819). Corton in Boyton [*but dated from Warminster*]. The house of Sarah Carter. Sarah Carter, William Goddard, John Randal, John Willet?. (WRO D1/9/2/1)

**929** 8 Nov. 1819 (12 Nov. 1819). Corsley. The shop occupied by John Gutch junior. Independent. John Gutch junior, John Watts, John Gutch, James Gutch, James Down, Robert Mines, John Everett Good. [*At foot*] 'Mr. Barrett, Cath. Street, pd.' (WRO D1/9/2/1)

**930** 22 Dec. 1819 (30 Dec. 1819). Berwick Bassett. A room on the ground floor in a house belonging to John Nalden, esquire, and occupied by William Hacker, labourer. [*Independent*: see **1003**]. William Cornwall of Avebury, protestant dissenting minister, Stephen Crook. [*Pencilled at foot*] 'Mr. Thring.' (WRO D1/9/2/1)

**931** 27 Dec. 1819 (15 Jan. 1820). Charlton [*near Malmesbury: endorsed postmark* 'Malmsbury']. The dwellinghouse of Jacob Boobyar. [*Baptist\**]. Richard Baker, Thomas Martin, Jacob Boobyer, Thomas Cary, Charles Curtis, Robert Taylor, in Charlton. [*Endorsed*] 'The Revd Mr. Saffery, Baptist Minister, Salisbury, Wilts.' (WRO D1/9/2/1)

**932** 27 Jan. 1820 (1 Feb. 1820). Whitley in Melksham. A house now occupied by Matthew Bigwood. Wesleyan Methodist. Charles Maggs of Melksham, coal merchant. (WRO D1/9/2/1)

**933** 28 March 1820 (3 April 1820). Ogbourne St Andrew. A building in the possession or occupation of John Sims. Independent. Thomas Smelt? of Marlborough, Independent minister, the mark of Benjamin Smith, the mark of Robert Dear, the mark of John Jennings. (WRO D1/9/2/1)

**934** 30 March 1820 (8 April 1820). Grafton in Great Bedwyn. A house and premises in the occupation of William Jackman. Methodist. William Sanger junior, of Salisbury, gentleman. (WRO D1/9/2/1)

**935** 11 April 1820 (1 June 1820). Malmesbury. A house now in the occupation of Moriah Rugg, widow. Independent. John Fowler, minister, John Fullaway, Richard Emery, John Morse, Thomas Fullaway. [*Endorsed in pencil*] 'Mr Harris.' (WRO D1/9/2/1)

**936** 12 April 1820 (15 April 1820). 'Newtown' in Ramsbury. A dwellinghouse and premises in the occupation of Elizabeth Day. Methodist. William Sanger of Salisbury, gentleman. [*Endorsed*] 'Mr. Sanger hopes Mr. Lush will let him have this Saturday.' (WRO D1/9/2/1)

**937** 17 April 1820 (5 June 1820). Box. The dwellinghouse of Samuel Roe. [*Wesleyan Methodist*: see **899**]. Daniel Campbell of Bradford on Avon, minister. [*At foot*] 'Revd Mr. Smith, Hog Lane.' (WRO D1/9/2/1)

**938** (20 April 1820). Donhead St Mary. The dwellinghouse of William Candy, belonging to Joseph Sims of Wimborne [*Dorset*]. [*Methodist?*: Jones

101]. William Candy of Donhead St Mary, farmer, George Button, George West, John Candy, James Candy. (WRO D1/9/2/1)

**939** 28 April 1820 (29 April 1820) Stapleford. A dwellinghouse, malthouse and premises occupied by Henry Cornish. [*Baptist*: see **831**]. Henry Cornish of Stapleford. (WRO D1/9/2/1)

**940** 10 June 1820 (30 June 1820). Marlborough. A house and premises belonging to John Gosling, esquire. Methodist. William Sanger junior, of Salisbury, gentleman (WRO D1/9/2/1)

**941** 10 June 1820 (30 June 1820). Marlborough. A house and premises in the occupation of Joseph Phelps. Methodist. William Sanger junior, of Salisbury, gentleman. (WRO D1/9/2/1)

**942** 14 June 1820 (20 June 1820). Chirton. Part of a dwellinghouse now in the occupation of William King of Chirton. [*Wesleyan Methodist*: see **932**]. Charles Maggs of Melksham, coal merchant. [*At foot*] 'Mr. Smith, Hog Lane.' (WRO D1/9/2/1)

**943** 22 June 1820 (30 June 1820). Little Hinton. A house and premises the property and in the occupation of Mr Charles Wilson of Little Hinton. Methodist. William Sanger junior, of Salisbury, gentleman. [*Same document as* **945**]. [WRO D1/9/2/1)

**944** 26 June 1820 (4 July 1820). Donhead St Andrew. A building now occupied by John Handsford, labourer. Independent. James Kelleway, Jesse Abbot, Henry Gold, Joseph Haskell, the mark of John Handsford, housekeepers in Donhead St Andrew. (WRO D1/9/2/1)

**945** 27 June 1820 (30 June 1820). Netheravon. A new Methodist chapel, the property of Mr John Sweetapple. Methodist. William Sanger junior, of Salisbury, gentleman. [*Same document as* **943**]. [WRO D1/9/2/1)

**946** 4 July 1820 (4 July 1820). Longbridge Deverill. The dwellinghouse of Sarah Snelgrove. [*Wesleyan Methodist*: Hall 241]. James Sydserff of Warminster. [*At foot*] 'Mr. Harrison.' (WRO D1/9/2/1)

**947** 20 July 1820 (5 Aug. 1820). Fonthill Giffard. A dwellinghouse and court now occupied by James Still, licensed hawker ['labourer' *deleted*]. Independent. Thomas Bt Sims, Thomas Sims. [*Endorsed in pencil*] 'Mr. Windsor.' (WRO D1/9/2/1)

**948** 24 Aug. 1820 (3 Nov. 1820). Chilton Foliat. A courtyard, the property and in the occupation of Mr John Martin. Methodist. William Sanger of St Edmund's parish, Salisbury. (WRO D1/9/2/1)

**949** 9 Sept. 1820 (7 Nov. 1820). Great Bedwyn [*but dated from Shalbourne*]. A dwellinghouse in the occupation of Thomas Knock. Independent. Charles Cannon, Thomas Butcher. [*Note on attached sheet*] 'For Mr Tasker, Abbotts Ann.' (WRO D1/9/2/1)

**950** 2 Oct. 1820 (5 Oct. 1820). Idmiston. A building, the property of Israel Sillwood, farmer, of Idmiston. Methodist. William Gilpin of Salisbury, Methodist minister. (WRO D1/9/2/1)

**951** 2 Oct. 1820 (5 Oct. 1820). Woodborough. A building, the property of Thomas Shipman, baker, of Woodborough. Methodist. William Gilpin of Salisbury, Methodist minister. (WRO D1/9/2/1)

**952** 13 Oct. 1820 (1 Nov. 1820). Nettleton. The house and garden in the occupation of Micaiah West. [*Baptist**]. Joseph Rodway of Grittleton, John Marsh. [*Endorsed in pencil*] 'Mr. Saffree.' (WRO D1/9/2/1)

**953** 20 Oct. 1820 (30 Oct. 1820). East Grimstead *or* West Grimstead. A building, the property of Henry Cooke, John Sutton and others. Methodist. William Gilpin of Salisbury, Methodist minister. (WRO D1/9/2/1)

**954** 2 Nov. 1820 (2 Nov. 1820). Alvediston. The dwellinghouse occupied by William Green. R? Emery of Salisbury. (WRO D1/9/2/1)

**955** 13 Nov. 1820 (21 Nov. 1820). Fovant. A meeting house erected on a part of the land lately belonging to William Rowden of Bishopstone, known by the name of Nightingales Orchard, but now invested in the hands of trustees. [*Independent*: Wiltshire Register 1827]. Thomas Best, Thomas Jay, John Combes. (WRO D1/9/2/1)

**956** 21 Dec. 1820 (21 Dec. 1820). Salisbury. The dwellinghouse now in the occupation of Sarah Poole in Winchester Street. Sarah Poole. [*Endorsed in pencil*] 'Mr. Hy Street.' (WRO D1/9/2/1)

**957** 3 Jan. 1821 (13 Jan. 1821). Marlborough. A chapel and premises adjoining, in the occupation of John Gosling esquire, in St Peter's parish. Independent Methodist. William Sanger of Salisbury, gentleman. (WRO D1/9/2//1

**958** 11 Jan. 1821 (25 Jan. 1821). Clevancy in Hilmarton. A house occupied by Isaac Clifford. Baptist. Isaac Clifford and Ann Clifford of Clevancy, Lydia Hart, Martha Barrington, Isaac Hart and Samuel Cripps of Hilmarton. (WRO D1/9/2/1)

**959** 12 Jan. 1821 (15 Feb. 1821). Swallowfield. A meeting house. Sander Willson of Swallowfield, gentleman, John Willson. (WRO D1/9/2/1)

**960** 18 Jan. 1821 (27 Jan. 1821). Bowden Hill in Lacock. A building in the occupation of James Hillier, clothworker. Methodist. William Gilpin of Salisbury, Methodist minister. (WRO D1/9/2/1)

**961** (20 Jan. 1821). Fonthill Giffard. A house in the possession of Francis Harding, the property of Samuel Wheeler. Charles Crickmay of Fonthill Giffard, John Perratt, Henry Biddiscomb. (WRO D1/9/2/1)

**962** 15 March 1821 (15 March 1821). Spirthill in Bremhill. The house of George Thrush. Particular Baptist. John Andrews, James Thrush, George Thrush, Hannah Thrush, William Willis, Dinah Sommers, inhabitants of Bremhill. (WRO D1/9/2/1)

**963** 26 March 1821 (2 April 1821). Milton ?Lilborne. A house and premises in the occupation of John Tarrant. Methodist. William Sanger of Salisbury. [*Pencilled at foot*] 'To be made out by Monday Night.' (WRO D1/9/2/1)

**964** 3 April 1821 (6 April 1821). Fyfield. A house, the property of Richard Somerbee, in the occupation of William Hillier. Independent Methodist. William Sanger of Salisbury. (WRO D1/9/2/1)

**965** 10 April 1821 (18 April 1821). Melksham. The house of John Curnick in the City. Baptist. Thomas Cleverley, John Tuff, John Tayler senior, John Taylor junior, Abraham Little, John Buckland. [*Endorsed*] 'By Ireland [*deleted*] Pd 4d.' (WRO D1/9/2/1)

**966** 23 April 1821 (28 April 1821). Trowbridge. The house of Mr Richard Harris at White Row. Baptist. Joseph Stephen Dunn, Samuel Webly, Henry Cuznie. (WRO D1/9/2/1)

**967** 7 June 1821 (25 July 1821). Upavon. A house and garden, the property and in the occupation of Roger Fleet, butcher. Independent Methodist. William Sanger of Church Street, Salisbury, gentleman. (WRO D1/9/2/1)

**968** 29 June 1821 (16 July 1821). Oaksey. A dwellinghouse belonging to Mr Thomas Wilton. Independent. Thomas Freeman, minister, Thomas Wilton, William Elford, William Hays, Henry Hays, William Wall, Isaac Grayell. (WRO D1/9/2/1)

**969** 21 July 1821 (24 Sept. 1821). Sherston. The tenement now occupied by Benedict Webber. [*Independent*?: see **770**, **784**]. Benedict Webber, Thomas Deverell, John Stamp, William Morris, William Marchent. (WRO D1/9/2/1)

**970** (25 July 1821). Minety. The dwellinghouse of Robert Taylor. [*Baptist*★]. Robert Taylor, William Morse, Robert Timbrill, Jacob Boobyer, Thomas Hays, in the parish of Minety. [*Pencilled at foot*] 'Mr. Saffree.' (WRO D1/9/2/1)

**971**　2 Aug. 1821 (18 Aug. 1821). Wootton Rivers. A house and premises in the occupation of Henry Barnett. Independent Methodist. William Sanger of Salisbury, gentleman. (WRO D1/9/2/1)

**972**　3 Aug. 1821 (18 Aug. 1821). East Knoyle (*Bishops Knoyle*). A schoolroom belonging to George Thick. Baptist. Edmund Kiddle, J L Turner, William Dewey. [*At foot*] 'Note – Sent to Mr. Mitchell, Dissenting Minister, Warminster, 21st Augt 1821.' [*Pencilled at foot*] '3/6 for writing the above, Certificate 2/6 for Registering the same, which you'll send by Mr. Smith, Salisbury Newsman.' (WRO D1/9/2/1)

**973**　13 Aug. 1821 (18 Aug. 1821). Alderton. The house and garden in the occupation of John Woodman. [*Baptist*: Oliver 72]. Joseph Rodway of Grittleton, John Tilly. (WRO D1/9/2/1)

**974**　13 Aug. 1821 (18 Aug. 1821). Hullavington. A chapel lately erected together with the land thereunto adjoining, vested in the hands of Joseph Rodway, John Mash and others. [*Baptist*: Oliver 72]. Joseph Rodway of Grittleton, John Tilly. (WRO D1/9/2/1)

**975**　30 Aug. 1821 (24 Sept. 1821). Wedhampton in Urchfont. A tenement now in the occupation of Sarah Stone. [*Methodist*: Hall 160]. Seth Morris. (WRO D1/9/2/1)

**976**　17 Sept. 1821 (21 Nov. 1821). Lydiard Millicent (*North Lyddiard Millicent*). A house now in the occupation of Rev Walter Lowrie. [*Independent*: see **1031, 1032**]. James Walter Lowrie, William Haines, Richard? Woollford. (WRO D1/9/2/1)

**977**　29 Sept. 1821 (29 Sept. 1821). Chisenbury [*in Enford*]. A new chapel, the property of John Pearce Sweetapple. Independent Methodist. William Sanger of Salisbury, gentleman. [*At foot*] 'Note – Wm. Sanger's respects to Mr. Lush will thank him to enter this to day as the Chapel is to be opened on Monday Oct. 1st. Church Street, Sept. 29th 1821.' (WRO D1/9/2/1)

**978**　24 Oct. 1821 (30 Oct. 1821). Clyffe Pypard. A house in the occupation of John Panting. Independent. Joseph Estcourt, minister, John Panting, John Bedford, William Church. (WRO D1/9/2/1)

**979**　3 Nov. 1821 (6 Nov. 1821). Westbury. A building erected upon the burial ground of the Old Meeting. [*Independent**]. William Stern Palmer, protestant dissenting minister, William Gaisford, William James, William Smith, John Allworth, Samuel Chubb, James Hampton, James Brunker, [*Endorsed in pencil*] 'Revd Mr. Good.' (WRO D1/9/2/1)

**980**　20 Nov. 1821 (20 Nov. 1821). Fisherton Anger. A dwellinghouse, the property of John Holmes of Fisherton Anger. (*Wesleyan Methodist*★). William Gilpin of Salisbury. (WRO D1/9/2/1)

**981** (21 Nov. 1821). South Marston [*in Highworth*]. A house now in the occupation of James Shorter. [*Independent*★]. James Shorter, George Fisher, Henry Grubb. [*Pencilled at foot*] 'Revd. Mr. Good.' (WRO D1/9/2/1)

**982** 26 Nov. 1821 (11 Dec. 1821). Biddestone [*but dated from Corsham*]. A house in the possession of G J Archer of Corsham. Independent. G Slade, G J Archer, M Barton. [*Pencilled at head*] 'Revd. Mr. Good, to be dated 6 Dec.' (WRO D1/9/2/1)

**983** 28 Nov. 1821 (28 Nov. 1821). Ram Alley in Burbage [*recte Savernake Park extra-parochial place*]. A house and premises in the occupation of William Dash. Independent Methodist. William Sanger of Church Street, Salisbury, gentleman. [*At foot*] 'Mr. Lush will let the Certificate bear date this day.' (WRO D1/9/2/1)

**984** 6 Dec. 1821 (15 Dec. 1821). Trowbridge. A building known by the name of the Barracks, the property of John Taylor. Methodist. William Sanger of Church Street, Salisbury, gentleman. (WRO D1/9/2/1)

**985** 7 Dec. 1821 (5 Jan. 1822). Gastard in Corsham. A building in the occupation of George Frankling. Thomas Gay, James Dunsdon, John Moore. (WRO D1/9/2/1)

**986** 12 Dec. 1821 (15 Dec. 1821). Little Cheverell. A dwellinghouse in the occupation of Samuel Phillips junior. [*Wesleyan Methodist*★]. William Gilpin of Salisbury. (WRO D1/9/2/1)

**987** 21 Dec. 1821 (22 Dec. 1821). Durrington. A dwellinghouse, the property of Isabella Collier and now in the occupation of Thomas Farley, tailor. [*Independent*?: see **626, 633, 642**]. Thomas Farley, Henry Blatch, Christopher Ingram, Edward White, James Angear, Jonathan Sawyer, Samuel Sturges. [*Endorsed*] 'Mr. Slea.' (WRO D1/9/2/1)

**988** 4 Jan. 1822. Trowbridge. A building in the occupation of Mrs Dunn. Baptist. P McFarlane, Peter Anstie, Mr Stephen Dunn?. (WRO A1/250)

**989** 31 Jan. 1822 (2 Feb. 1822). Bradford on Avon. The now dwellinghouse of Jeremiah Batchelor of Newtown. [*Methodist*: see **991**]. James M Byron of Bradford on Avon, minister. (WRO D1/9/2/1)

**990** 31 Jan. 1822 (2 Feb. 1822). Leigh in Bradford on Avon. The now dwellinghouse of James Hibberd. [*Methodist*: see **991**]. James M Byron of Bradford on Avon, minister. (WRO D1/9/2/1)

**991**   31 Jan. 1822 (2 Feb. 1822). Upper Bearfield in Bradford on Avon. The now dwellinghouse of John Wells. Methodist. James M Byron of Bradford on Avon, minister, [*Endorsed*] 'Rev. Joshua Fielden, Methodist Chapel, Salisbury. 31 January, Post paid double. NB Mr. Fielding will please to present this to the Court and I will send the expence without delay, J.M. Byron, 31 Jan. 1822.' (WRO D1/9/2/1)

**992**   2 Feb. 1822 (4 Feb. 1822). Farley (*Faireley*) [*in Alderbury*]. A dwellinghouse in the occupation of James Hawkins, labourer. [*Wesleyan Methodist*★]. William Gilpin of Salisbury. [*At foot*] 'not pd.' (WRO D1/9/2/1)

**993**   12 Feb. 1822 (20 Feb. 1822). Broad Hinton [*but dated from Wootton Bassett*]. A house in the occupation of Robert Comely. [*Independent*: see **978**]. Joseph Estcourt, minister, Robert Comely. [*Endorsed*] 'Mr. Good.' (WRO D1/9/2/1)

**994**   4 March 1822 (8 March 1822). Corsham. A building in the occupation of William Tylee. Uriah Goold, William Trinder?, Thomas Halbert. (WRO D1/9/2/1)

**995**   4 March 1822 (11 March 1822). Warminster. A house in the occupation of Mary Gunning of Pound Street. [*Wesleyan Methodist*★]. Henry Young Cheverton of Warminster, William Gilpin. (WRO D1/9/2/1)

**996**   12 March 1822 (11 March 1822 [*sic*]). Britford. A dwellinghouse in the occupation of James Penny. [*Wesleyan Methodist*★]. William Gilpin of Salisbury. (WRO D1/9/2/1)

**997**   13 March 1822 (17 April 1822). Oaksey. A house now in the occupation of Rev J W Lowrie. [*Independent*★]. J W Lowrie, Thomas Jones, Henry Telling. [*Endorsed*] 'Rev. Mr. Good, Salisbury, Wilts. paid.' (WRO D1/9/2/1)

**998**   15 March 1822 (18 March 1822). Baydon. A dwellinghouse and premises now in the occupation of John Alder, carpenter. Methodist. William Griffith, Methodist minister of Hungerford. [*Pencilled at foot*] 'William Gilpin.' (WRO D1/9/2/1)

**999A**   17 April 1822 (20 April 1822). Bradford on Avon. A room adjoining a factory belonging to Mr England, in Wind Street. [*Independent*: VCH 7, 33, 34]. William Coombs, William Thorn. (WRO D1/9/2/1)

**999B**   (19 April 1822). Minety. A dwellinghouse. [*Independent*: see **997**]. J W Lowrie of Minety. (PRO RG31/2 Gloucester diocese)

**1000**   17 May 1822 (15 June 1822). Hook in Lydiard Tregoze. A house in the occupation of John Ferris. [*Independent*★]. Joseph Estcourt, minister, John Rumming, Thomas Heale, Thomas Tuck, William Rumming. [*At foot*] 'To be forewarded by favr of Revd. Mr. Good.' [*same document as* **1001**]. (WRO D1/9/2/1)

**1001** 17 May 1822 (15 June 1822). Lyneham. Two adjoining houses and court belonging thereunto in the parish of Lyneham near the village of Tockenham, in the occupation of David Sutton and John Littel. [*Independent*★]. Joseph Estcourt, minister, John Sutton, John Bryand, Joseph Millar, John Littel. [*Endorsed*] 'Revd. J E Good, Salisbury.' [*same document as* **1000**]. (WRO D1/9/2/1)

**1002** 22 May 1822 (15 June 1822). Ludgershall. A dwellinghouse and premises belonging to, and occupied by, James Baiden. James Baiden of Ludgershall. [*Pencilled at foot*] 'Mr Harding, sadlr.' (WRO D1/9/2/1)

**1003** 22 May 1822 (15 June 1822). Winterbourne Monkton. A house or building in the possession of Robert New. Independent. William Cornwall, Stephen Crook, James Fowler. [*At foot*] 'Mr Lush's compliments to Mr Thring and informs him that this certificate cannot be registered until it is stated whether the parish is Monkton Farley or Monkton Deverill.' [Winterbourne has been inserted before Monkton]. [WRO D1/9/2/1]

**1004** (27 Aug. 1822). Urchfont. A chapel belonging to me. [*Independent Methodist*: see **977**]. John Pearse Sweetapple of Chisenbury. [*At foot*] 'To call at ½ past 12.' [*Pencilled at foot*] 'Greenly, Act? of R?.' (WRO D1/9/2/1)

**1005** 31 Aug. 1822 (7 Sept. 1822). Oare in Huish [*recte Wilcot?*]. A house and premises in the occupation of Ambrose Fislock. Independent Methodist. William Sanger of Church Street, Salisbury. (WRO D1/9/2/1)

**1006** 18 Sept. 1822 (18 Sept. 1822). Winterbourne Gunner. A new erection called the Wesleyan Methodist chapel. Wesleyan Methodist. William Gilpin of Salisbury. (WRO D1/9/2/1)

**1007** 20 Sept. 1822 (5 Oct. 1822). Oare in Wilcot. A house and premises in the occupation of Ambrose Fishlake. Independent Methodist. William Sanger of Church Street, Salisbury, gentleman. (WRO D1/9/2/1)

**1008** 7 Oct. 1822 (8 Oct. 1822). Alton Barnes. The dwellinghouse of James Powel. [*Wesleyan Methodist*★]. William Gilpin of Salisbury. (WRO D1/9/2/1)

**1009** 19 Oct. 1822 (23 Oct. 1822). Warminster. The dwellinghouse of Richard Haynes. [*Wesleyan Methodist*★]. William Gilpin of Salisbury. (WRO D1/9/2/1)

**1010** 22 Oct. 1822 (23 Oct. 1822). Burbage. A new erection called the Wesleyan chapel. Wesleyan Methodist. William Gilpin of Salisbury. (WRO D1/9/2/1)

**1011**   3 Nov. 1822 (5 Nov. 1822). Hilperton Marsh in Hilperton. A messuage or tenement in the occupation of John Moor, weaver. [*Baptist or Unitarian*: Doel 110]. Richard Wright of Trowbridge, dissenting minister, James Haden, S Price. [*Endorsed*] 'Jas Applegate fm Chough Inn.' (WRO D1/9/2/1)

**1012**   4 Nov. 1822 (5 Nov. 1822). Potterne. A dwellinghouse, the property of Sarah Prieters?. [*Wesleyan Methodist★*]. William Gilpin of Salisbury. (WRO D1/9/2/1)

**1013**   12 Nov. 1822 (16 Nov. 1822). Westbury. I intend opening a room occupied by Mr Henry Railton, the property of Mr Stephen Hunt, on 17 Nov. 1822. John Neat of Westbury. [*At foot*] 'Silcox, Goat, Dr 2/6.' (WRO D1/9/2/1)

**1014**   16 Nov. 1822 (27 Nov. 1822). Coate in Liddington. A building in the possession of Thomas Bessant. Independent. The mark of Thomas Bessant, Sarah Freeman, Lawrence Lawrence, George Mantell. [*Pencilled at foot*] 'Revd. Mr. Good.' (WRO D1/9/2/1)

**1015**   20 Nov. 1822 (20 Dec. 1822). Stratton St Margaret. A house now in the occupation of Richard Kerby. Independent. The mark of Richard Kerby, John Jones, John Ellison, of Stratton St Margaret. (WRO D1/9/2/1)

**1016**   23 Nov. 1822 (27 Nov. 1822). Melksham. The house of William Trowbridge. [*Wesleyan Methodist★*]. William Gilpin of Salisbury. (WRO D1/9/2/1)

**1017**   3 Dec. 1822 (9 Dec. 1822). Yatesbury. The dwellinghouse of Charles Coleman. Baptist. Charles Coleman, John Coles, George Penny, John Russ, dwelling in Yatesbury. (WRO D1/9/2/1)

**1018**   10 Dec. 1822 (20 Dec. 1822). Longbridge Deverill. The dwellinghouse of John Wheeler, labourer. Wesleyan Methodist. Joseph Bowes of Warminster, Wesleyan Methodist minister. (*Pencilled at foot*] 'Mr. Galpin.' (WRO D1/9/2/1)

**1019**   16 Dec. 1822 (18 Dec. 1822). Christian Malford. The house of Charles Hodgson. [*Wesleyan Methodist★*]. William Gilpin of Salisbury. (WRO D1/9/2/1)

**1020**   Dec. 1822 (21 Dec. 1822). Bradford on Avon. The house of John Milsom in Newtown. Baptist. John Milsom, James Kelson, James Batchlor, Jeremiah Batchlor, Jeremiah May, John Mathews. [*At foot*] 'Mr Silcox.' (WRO D1/9/2/1)

**1021**   16 Dec. 1822 (21 Dec. 1822). Hilmarton. The dwellinghouse of Isaac Hart. Baptist. William Milford, Jacob Hervey, Jasper Locke, John Andrews,

Thomas Fell, Isaac Hart, Samuel Crispe. [At foot] 'Gatehouse.' (WRO D1/9/2/1)

**1022** 23 Dec. 1822 (3 Jan. 1823). Woodborough. A building or chapel, the property of John Clarke. [*Wesleyan Methodist*★]. William Gilpin of Salisbury. (WRO D1/9/2/1)

**1023** 30 Dec 1822 (6 Jan. 1823). Eastcott (*Hiscott*) in Swindon. A tenement now in the occupation of William Sharps. [*Wesleyan Methodist*★]. Daniel Osborne, William Sand. [*At foot*] 'Mr. Galpin pd for.' (WRO D1/9/2/1)

**1024** 31 Dec. 1822 (31 Dec. 1822). Maiden Bradley. A building recently erected. Independent. Joseph Miles, William Brimson, William Newbuary, Christopher Williams, William Waters, Michael Doman, inhabitants of Maiden Bradley. (WRO D1/9/2/1)

**1025** (3 Jan. 1823). Highworth. A dwellinghouse in the south-west part of the town, called the Horse Fair, belonging to John Painter now the owner and occupier thereof. [*Baptist*: see **1151**]. John Painter, Luke Bowels, Edmund Hedges, W Weldon, minister, Jabez Hedges, John Hedges, Richard Clack, Samuel Flaister. (WRO D1/9/2/1)

**1026** 18 Jan. 1823 (22 Jan. 1823). Turleigh in Bradford on Avon. The house of John Smith. Baptist. John Smith, Thomas Smith, Jacob Chapman, John Sims, John Mathews, John Morris. [*Pencilled at foot*] 'Silcox.' (WRO D1/9/2/1)

**1027** 27 Jan. 1823 (29 Jan. 1823). Cherhill. The house in the occupation of Sarah Jones. Independent Methodist. William Sanger of Church Street, Salisbury. (WRO D1/9/2/1)

**1028** 26 March 1823 (27 March 1823). Compton Bassett. A house in the occupation of Henry Butler. Independent Methodist. William Sanger of Salisbury. (WRO D1/9/2/1)

**1029** 1 April 1823 (14 April 1823). Zeals in Mere. A dwellinghouse in the occupation of John Mansfield. Independent. Robert Cross, Francis Webb, Thomas Toogood, James Ford, James Landers, Samuel Little, of Mere. (WRO D1/9/2/1)

**1030** 30 April 1823 (2 May 1823). Ogbourne St George. A building in the possession and occupation of William Bayly. Independent. John Thomas Low, Robert Goddard, James Willmot. (WRO D1/9/2/1)

**1031** 1 May 1823 (7 May 1823). Ashton Keynes. A house or building in the occupation of Richard Bartlett. Independent. J W Lowrie, minister, Richard Bartlett, Timothy Cove, William Browning. (WRO D1/9/2/1)

**1032**  1 May 1823 (7 May 1823). Leigh [*in Ashton Keynes?*]. A house. Independent. J W Lowrie, minister, the mark of Thomas Habgood, Timothy Cove. [*Endorsed*] 'Revd. H. Larter, Highworth, Wilts.' [*Endorsed postmark Malmsbury*]. (WRO D1/9/2/1)

**1033**  2 May 1823 (2 May 1823). Kington St Michael. A house in the occupation of James Miles. Independent. J E Good, James Cottle. [WRO D1/9/2/1)

**1034**  11 May 1823 (9 June 1823). Marlborough. A place for public worship in Herd Street, fronting the west on the east side, erected new and called Ebenezer Chapel 1823, in St Mary's parish, [*Baptist?*: VCH 12, 226]. Robert Rose, grocer, Charles Dobson, tailor, Reuben Edmonds, fellmonger, Richard Price, carpenter, Thomas D Rose, grocer, Thomas Sly, carpenter, W Weldon, minister. [*Endorsed*] 'For Geo.Geo.' (WRO D1/9/2/1)

**1035**  12 July 1823 (14 July 1823). Baydon. A newly erected building, known by the name of the Wesleyan chapel. Wesleyan Methodist. William Gilpin of Salisbury. (WRO D1/9/2/1)

**1036**  16 July 1823 (19 July 1823). Marlborough [*recte* Preshute]. A new chapel in St Margaret's parish. Independent Methodist. William Sanger of Church Street, Salisbury. (WRO D1/9/2/1)

**1037**  16 July 1823 (19 July 1823). Wilsford. A new chapel, the property of Richard Wise. Independent Methodist. William Sanger of Church Street, Salisbury. [*Endorsed in pencil*] 'Mr. Lush will be so good to let Mr. Sanger have these in a day or two.' (WRO D1/9/2/1)

**1038**  25 July 1823 (18 Aug. 1823). Enford. A house in the occupation of John Rawlins. Independent Methodist. William Sanger of Church Street, Salisbury (WRO D1/9/2/1)

**1039**  1 Aug. 1823 (16 Aug. 1823). Stratford sub Castle. The house of George Dibden. Baptist. John Saffery of Salisbury. (WRO D1/9/2/1)

**1040**  14 Aug. 1823 (18 Aug. 1823). East Harnham in Britford. An orchard in the occupation of Samuel Naish, containing one acre. Independent or Tent Methodist. William Sanger of Church Street, Salisbury. (WRO D1/9/2/1)

**1041**  4 Sept. 1823 (4 Sept. 1823). Fisherton Anger. A garden and premises, the property and in the occupation of Joseph Sanger of Salisbury. Independent Methodist. William Sanger of Church Street, Salisbury, gentleman. [*Endorsed*] 'Mr Lush will have the goodness to date this Sepr. 4th, Wm Sanger.' (WRO D1/9/2/1)

**1042**  13 Sept. 1823 (13 Sept. 1823). East Harnham in Britford. Part of a house in the occupation of William Drew. Independent or Tent Methodist. William Sanger of Church Street, Salisbury. (WRO D1/9/2/1)

**1043**   (15 Sept. 1823). Rushall. An inhabited tenement in the possession of William White. W White, John Oram, Thomas Daniel. (WRO D1/9/2/1)

**1044**   20 Sept. 1823 (20 Sept. 1823). Milford [*in Laverstock*]. A field called the Horse Pits containing six acres, in my own occupation. Independent Methodist. William Sanger of Church Street, Salisbury, gentleman. (WRO D1/9/2/1)

**1045**   8 Oct. 1823 (23 Dec. 1823). Chute. The house of George Bishop. [*Wesleyan Methodist*: Hall 11]. Hugh Carter of Andover, Hants. [*Pencilled at foot*] '23rd Decr. 1823. Carrier will call.' (WRO D1/9/2/1)

**1046**   10 Oct. 1823 (17 Oct. 1823). Kington Langley (*Tangley*) in Kington St Michael. The dwellinghouse of John Gough, labourer. [*Wesleyan Methodist*: see **1097**]. William Griffith of Melksham, minister of the gospel. (WRO D1/9/2/1)

**1047**   11 Oct. 1823 (11 Oct. 1823). Salisbury. A large room and entrance hall in the occupation of Samuel Collins in New Canal. Independent or Tent Methodist. William Sanger of Church Street, Salisbury gentleman. (WRO D1/9/2/1)

**1048**   11 Oct. 1823 (22 Oct. 1823). Wroughton [*but dated from Swindon*]. A newly erected building called the Wesleyan Methodist chapel. Wesleyan Methodist. Daniel Osborne, William Sand. (WRO D1/9/2/1)

**1049**   15 Nov. 1823 (15 Nov. 1823). Dinton. A dwellinghouse now in the occupation of Susannah Marks. [*Wesleyan Methodist*: Hall 206]. Alexander Weir. (WRO D1/9/2/1)

**1050**   8 Dec. 1823 (13 Dec. 1823). Great Cheverell. A building in the possession or occupation of George Giddings, labourer. Independent. The mark of George Giddings, William Farmer, John Guard. [*Pencilled at foot*] 'Revd. Mr Good, 12 Decr/23.' (WRO D1/9/2/1)

**1051**   15 Dec. 1823 (29 Dec. 1823). Monkton Deverill. The dwellinghouse belonging to Joseph Norres. James Rogers, Isaac Collins. [*Endorsed*] 'Please direct to James Rogers, George Street, Warminster, Wilts.' [*Endorsed in pencil*] 'Mr. Bell, Mill.' (WRO D1/9/2/1)

**1052**   22 Dec. 1823 (29 Dec. 1823). Longbridge Deverill. The dwellinghouse belonging to Luke Ball. James Rogers, George Rogers. [*Endorsed in pencil*] 'Mr Bell, Mill.' (WRO D1/9/2/1)

**1053**   22 Dec. 1823 (23 Dec. 1823). Salisbury. A room called or known by the name of the Freemasons Hall in the George Yard, High Street, the property of James Troubridge senior, and in my occupation. Tent Methodist. William Sanger of Church Street, Salisbury, gentleman. (WRO D1/9/2/1)

**1054**    23 Dec. 1823 (22 Jan. 1824). Ditchampton in Burcombe. A house, the property and in the occupation of Daniel Moore. Tent Methodist. William Sanger of Church Street, Salisbury, gentleman. (WRO D1/9/2/1)

**1055**    27 Dec. 1823 (15 Jan. 1824). Eastcott in Swindon. A dwellinghouse in the occupation of George Snow. Independent. L Lawrence, William Reynolds, Richard Page, George Snow, the mark of James Prosser, housekeepers in Swindon. (WRO D1/9/2/1)

**1056**    9 Jan. 1824 (27 Jan. 1824). Melksham. The house of James Watson. Baptist. Thomas Small, John Tuff, John Buckland, Abraham Little, Thomas Cleverly, John Taylor. [*Pencilled at foot*] 'Jan 27th 1824 from Thos Small, Melksham, by Silcox.' (WRO D1/9/2/1)

**1057**    24 Jan. 1824 (10 Feb. 1824). Hilcott in North Newnton. The house and premises now in the occupation of Jonathan Kneepence, bricklayer. [*Wesleyan Methodist*: see **1097**]. William Griffith of Melksham. [*Pencilled in margin*] 'Weare Feb 9.' (WRO D1/9/2/1)

**1058**    6 Feb. 1824 (10 Feb. 1824). Everleigh. A house now occupied by A Jay. [*Wesleyan Methodist*: Hall 11]. Hugh Carter of Andover. [*At foot*] 'Revd. Mr. Wear, Salt Lane.' (WRO D1/9/2/1)

**1059**    7 Feb. 1824 (10 Feb. 1824). Broughton Gifford. A building. [*Wesleyan Methodist*?: see **1058**]. John Rison of Woolley in Bradford on Avon [*Pencilled at foot*] 'Weare, Feb. 9.' (WRO D1/9/2/1)

**1060**    10 Feb. 1824 (10 Feb. 1824). Bower Chalke. A house in my possession. Henry Gould of Bower Chalke, shopkeeper. [*At foot*] 'Henry Gould pd.' (WRO D1/9/2/1)

**1061**    23 Feb. 1824 (2 March 1824). Tollard Royal. A house in my possession. Joseph Green of Tollard Royal, labourer. [*At foot*] 'Rd White Handley will call Tuesday 2nd March.' (WRO D1/9/2/1)

**1062**    27 Feb. 1824 (8 March 1824). Purton. A house now in the occupation of William Greenaway. William Greenaway, William Neale, Isaac Wheeler, of Purton. (WRO D1/9/2/1)

**1063**    2 March 1824 (2 March 1824). Redlynch in Downton. A new erected chapel belonging to Samuel Wort. Baptist. Samuel Wort, J L Alford. (WRO D1/9/2/1)

**1064**   5 March 1824 (31 March 1824). Badbury in Chisledon. A tenement now in the occupation of John Cox. [*Wesleyan Methodist*: see **1048**]. Daniel Osborne, William Sand senior. (WRO D1/9/2/1)

**1065**   5 March 1824 (31 March 1824). Wootton Bassett [*but dated from Swindon*]. A tenement now in the occupation of George Tremnell. [*Wesleyan Methodist*: see **1048**]. Daniel Osborne, William Sand senior. (WRO D1/9/2/1)

**1066**   6 March 1824 (31 March 1824). Winterbourne Bassett. [*but dated from Swindon*]. A tenement now in the occupation of Jane Barnes. [*Wesleyan Methodist*: see **1048**]. Daniel Osborne, William Sand senior. (WRO D1/9/2/1)

**1067**   8 March 1824 (13 March 1824). South Marston in Highworth. A building now in the occupation of William Pineger. [*Independent★*]. William Pineger, John Shorter, James Hughes, of South Marston. [*Pencilled at foot*] 'Revd Mr Good.' (WRO D1/9/2/1)

**1068**   31 March 1824 (31 March 1824). Winterbourne Earls. A dwellinghouse now in the occupation of John Sainsbury. [*Wesleyan Methodist*: Hall 206]. Alexander Weir. (WRO D1/9/2/1)

**1069**   12 April 1824 (25 May 1824). Clyffe Pypard. The house in which William Church resides. [*Independent*: see **1326**]. William Church of Bushton, wheelwright, John Panting, William Brown. [*Pencilled at foot*] 'to be signed by William Church,' (WRO D1/9/2/1)

**1070**   28 April 1824 (30 June 1824). Bradford on Avon. A large room, part of a certain dwellinghouse in the occupation of James Mead, basketmaker, near the Market Place, is used and occupied on Sundays by persons protestant and not dissenting from the established church, assembling for the purposes of religious prayer and exhortation. Joseph Harvey, William Harvey, Richard Grist, John Bubb, Daniel Wilshire, William Merrick, James Grist, inhabitants of Bradford on Avon. (WRO D1/9/2/1)

**1071**   30 April 1824 (9 June 1824). Warminster. The dwellinghouse of James Pike. James Pike, George Rogers, John Tabor, Levi Larrance. [*At foot*] 'Mr Bell.' (WRO D1/9/2/1)

**1072**   (10 May 1824). Bradford on Avon. A chapel on a parcel of ground called the Conigre, Newtown. [*Independent★*]. William Coombs, James Earle, of Bradford on Avon. [*Endorsed in pencil*] 'for Mr. Good.' (WRO D1/9/2/1)

**1073**   19 May 1824 (24 May 1824). Trowbridge. The brewery belonging to Thomas Timbrell, esquire. John Gibbens of Trowbridge. [*Endorsed*] 'The Trowbridge carier will call for the certificate on Tuesday next.' [*Identical format to* **1074**]. (WRO D1/9/2/1)

**1074** 19 May 1824 (24 May 1824). Wingfield. My dwellinghouse. William Webb of Wingfield. [*Endorsed*] 'The Trowbridge carrier will call for the certificate on Tuesday next.' [*Identical format to* **1073**]. (WRO D1/9/2/1)

**1075** 28 May 1824 (5 June 1824). Bratton in Westbury. A building late a malthouse, the property of Edward Froud Seagrim M.D. Methodist. Joseph Bowes of Warminster, Methodist minister. (WRO D1/9/2/1)

**1076** 31 May 1824 (5 June 1824). Wingfield. A building in the possession or occupation of James Dark. Baptist. Joseph Stephen Dunn, Peter McFarlane, Peter Anstie. [*Pencilled at foot*] 'Deacon Butler.' (WRO D1/9/2/1)

**1077** 3 June 1824 (20 Oct. 1824). Warminster. A dwellinghouse and premises now in the holding and occupation of James Ball. [*Methodist*: see **1092**]. James Ball of Warminster. (WRO D1/9/2/1)

**1078** 5 June 1824 (8 June 1824). Trowle Common in Bradford on Avon. A part of my premises. James Harding of Trowle Common. [*Endorsed*] 'The Carrier will call for the Certificate on Tuesday next. By Silcox.' (WRO D1/9/2/1)

**1079** 18 June 1824 (10 Aug. 1824). Dauntsey. A house. Independent. John Morse, minister, Joseph Barnes, Richard Hull, Thomas Hopkins, David Greenman, David Skull, Peter Hayward, Joseph Ferris?. [*Pencilled at foot*] 'Mr Mark Hanks, Malmesbury, 10 Augt 1824.' (WRO D1/9/2/1)

**1080** 21 June 1824 (17 July 1824). Avebury. A house in the occupation of William Hillier on the west side of the village. [*Baptist*: see **1227**]. Thomas D Rose, John Clements, Thomas Cary, John Ponting, the mark of William Hillier. (WRO D1/9/2/1)

**1081** 2 July 1824 (7 July 1824). Oare in Wilcot. A house and premises in the occupation of Mathew Baiden. Independent Methodist. William Sanger of Church Street, Salisbury. (WRO D1/9/2/1)

**1082** 15 July 1824 (30 July 1824). Kingston Deverill. The house and premises now in the holding and occupation of John Long. John Long of Kingston Deverill, John Andrews, the mark of George Glart?. (WRO D1/9/2/1)

**1083** 19 July 1824 (30 July 1824). Semley. A stone building. Particular Baptist. George Shell, Stephen Mullins, James Coward, Stephen Burden, John Pike, John Barratt, [*Pencilled at foot*] 'By Goold.' (WRO D1/9/2/1)

**1084** 3 Aug. 1824 (9 Aug. 1824). Corsham. A newly erected house and land adjoining, enclosed around with a stone wall, in Stumps Lane, leading from Corsham to Pickwick. Uriah Goold of Corsham, Henry Spackman. (WRO D1/9/2/1)

**1085**  24 Aug. 1824 (25 Aug. 1824). Durrington. The newly erected meeting house, the property of Sarah Blatch of Ratfyn. [*Independent*: see **987**]. Henry Cozens, John May, Thomas Farley, James Toomer, James Giddings, James Angear. [*Pencilled at foot*] 'Augt 25 to be called for.' (WRO D1/9/2/1)

**1086**  24 Aug. 1824 (4 Sept. 1824). Goatacre in Hilmarton [*but dated from Salisbury*]. A building or chapel. Independent. J E Good, M Murch. (WRO D1/9/2/1)

**1087**  26 Aug. 1824 (6 Sept. 1824). Colerne. A building which has been recently built. Independent. Thomas Aust, Charles Butler. [*At foot*] 'Bath? Aug 29 1824.' (WRO D1/9/2/1)

**1088**  27 Aug. 1824 (6 Sept. 1824). Kington St Michael [*but dated from Salisbury*]. The house of Arthur Twiner. [*Independent*: see **1086**]. J E Good, M Murch. [*Endorsed*] 'Rev Mr Good, Salisbury.' (WRO D1/9/2/1)

**1089**  30 Aug. 1824 (4 Sept. 1824). Kington St Michael [*but dated from Salisbury*]. The house of Jacob Isaac. Independent. J E Good, M Murch. [*Endorsed*] 'Rev. J. E. Good, Salisbury, Wilts, paid by Mr. Burchill.' (WRO D1/9/2/1)

**1090**  13 Sept. 1824 (20 Oct. 1824). Warminster Common [*in Warminster*]. The house and premises now in the possession of Edward Tucker. Methodist. Edward Tucker, George Grant. (WRO D1/9/2/1)

**1091**  22 Sept. 1824 (24 Sept. 1824). Westbury. A building or meeting house at Cooks Stile. [*Baptist*: Doel 196]. Richard Durand of Westbury, bookkeeper, Nathaniel Overbury, Samuel Chubb, William Taylor. (WRO D1/9/2/1)

**1092**  12 Oct. 1824 (20 Oct. 1824). Longbridge Deverill. The house and premises now in possession of James Ball. Methodist. James Ball, Henry Pitman. (WRO D1/9/2/1)

**1093**  (16 Oct. 1824). Corsham. A house in the occupation of James Davis. Independent. J E Good, Thomas Harris. [*Pencilled at foot*] 'Mr. Good.' (WRO D1/9/2/1)

**1094**  (25 Oct. 1824). Damerham. A room in the occupation of Hubert Chubb. Independent. Hubert Chubb, Mary Brine, William Kittin?. [*Pencilled at foot*] 'Mr. Good.' (WRO D1/9/2/1)

**1095**  30 Oct. 1824 (15 Nov. 1824). Mere. The house and premises now in the holding and occupation of William Coward. William Coward of Mere, Thomas Green, Thomas Grady, Thomas Light, William Duncan. Henry Trap . . . [*illegible*], T. . .[*illegible*] Coward. [*Endorsed*] 'This will be Pead for when call for by the Bann.'? (WRO D1/9/2/1)

**1096**   1 Nov. 1824 (10 Nov. 1824). Stapleford. A building on the Knapp, in the occupation of George Blake, to be used for a meeting house and a school for teaching of children and adults. Methodist. The mark of William Mabbett, George Blake, Enos Shergold, the mark of Abraham Osgood. (WRO D1/9/2/1)

**1097**   20 Nov. 1824 (11 Dec. 1824). Whitley in Melksham. A newly erected building, known by the name of the Wesleyan chapel. Wesleyan Methodist. William Griffith of Melksham, Methodist minister. (WRO D1/9/2/1)

**1098**   21 Nov. 1824 (23 Nov. 1824). Dilton Marsh in Westbury. A dwellinghouse and orchard occupied by John Grant. John Ford of Trowbridge. (WRO D1/9/2/1)

**1099**   8 Dec. 1824 (14 Dec. 1824). Boreham in Warminster. A dwellinghouse occupied by me. Robert Turner of Boreham. (WRO D1/9/2/1)

**1100**   15 Dec. 1824 (8 Jan. 1825). Purton. A barn now in the occupation of Job Lewis. [*Independent**]. Job Lewis, Charles Templer, M Slater, of Purton. [*Pencilled in margin*] 'Rev. Mr. Good.' ([WRO D1/9/2/1)

**1101**   24 Jan. 1825 (24 Jan. 1825). Netherhampton. A dwellinghouse now in my occupation. [*Wesleyan Methodist**]. Walter Hutchings. [*Pencilled at foot*] 'Jan 24/25 Mr Bradnack.' (WRO D1/9/2/1)

**1102**   28 Jan. 1825 (29 Jan. 1825). Alderbury. A new chapel. [*Wesleyan Methodist**]. Isaac Bradnack of Salisbury, minister of the gospel. (WRO D1/9/2/1)

**1103**   28 Jan. 1825 (14 Feb. 1825). Teffont Magna. A new chapel now erected. [*Wesleyan Methodist**]. Isaac Bradnack of Salisbury, minister of the gospel. (WRO D1/9/2/1)

**1104**   28 Jan. 1825 (29 Jan. 1825). Warminster Green in Downton. A new chapel. [*Wesleyan Methodist**]. Isaac Bradnack of Salisbury, minister of the gospel. (WRO D1/9/2/1

**1105**   7 Feb. 1825 (18 Feb. 1825). Calne. A warehouse now in the occupation of William Chivers. Baptist. William Chivers, John Chivers, John Motimer, William Butcher, Edward Weston, dwelling in Calne. (WRO D1/9/2/1)

**1106**   15 Feb. 1825 (23 Feb. 1825). Upper Stoke in Bradford on Avon. A building. [*Wesleyan Methodist*: Hall 37]. James Heaton of Bradford on Avon. (WRO D1/9/2/1)

**1107**   21 Feb. 1825 (5 March 1825). Biddestone. A building late in the occupation of Jonathan Powell. [*Independent*★]. Henry Wibley of Corsham, George Pulling. [*Pencilled at foot*] 'Revd. Mr. Good.' (WRO D1/9/2/1)

**1108** 14 March 1825 (14 March 1825). Preshute. A chapel, the property of John Gosling, esquire, in the village of St Margaretts, parish of Preshute. Independent Methodist. William Sanger of Church Street, Salisbury. (WRO D1/9/2/1)

**1109** 19 March 1825 (26 March 1825). Farleigh Wick in Monkton Farleigh. A building. John Davis of Bradford on Avon. (WRO D1/9/2/1)

**1110** 23 March 1825 (26 March 1825). Everleigh. The house of A Jee. [*Wesleyan Methodist*★]. Hugh Carter of Andover, Hants. [*Endorsed*] 'The Revd I Bradnack, Methodist Chapel, Salisbury.' (WRO D1/9/2/1)

**1111** 9 April 1825 (22 April 1825). Highworth. A house now in the occupation of Joseph Kirby. [*Independent*★]. Joseph Kirby, Henry Larter, Samuel Brown, of Highworth. [*Endorsed in pencil*] Mr. Good's compls.' (WRO D1/9/2/1)

**1112** 12 April 1825. Trowbridge. A newly erected building in the Courts, called Bethesda Chapel. Baptist. P McFarlane, Joseph Stephen Dunn, Stephen B Clift. (WRO A1/110 E1825)

**1113** 6 May 1825 (1 Aug. 1825). Overton. A building in the possession or occupation of William Drew. Independent. William Drew, William Waite, Thomas James. [*Pencilled at foot*] 'Mr Good.' (WRO D1/9/2/1)

**1114** 10 May 1825 (23 July 1825). West Dean. A dwellinghouse in my occupation. John Griffin of West Dean. (WRO D1/9/2/1)

**1115** 16 May 1825 (1 Aug. 1825). Urchfont. A building now in the possession of James Staples, and used by him as a school-room. Independent. James Staples, John Guard, Samuel Taylor. (WRO D1/9/2/1)

**1116** 17 May 1825 (27 July 1825). Wootton Bassett. A barn now in the occupation of Mr Joseph Clark. [*Independent:* see **1135**]. M Slater, Joseph Short, of Wootton Bassett. [*Pencilled at foot*] 'Wanted to Morrow.' (WRO D1/9/2/1)

**1117** 27 May 1825 (25 July 1825). Chute Hatchett in Chute. The dwellinghouse or tenement now in the occupation of George Dobbs. Baptist. George Dobbs, John Walcot, Baptist minister at Ludgershall. [*Pencilled at foot*] 'Beams, Ludgarshall Carr.' (WRO D1/9/2/1)

**1118** 1 June 1825. West Knoyle. A house and premises in the occupation of William Riddick. William Riddick, John Riddick. (WRO A1/250)

**1119** 7 June 1825 (1 Aug. 1825). Box. A building, the property of Mr James Rawlings. [*Independent*: see **1107**]. Henry Wibley, dissenting minister of Corsham. (WRO D1/9/2/1)

**1120** 8 June 1825 (23 July 1825). Bulkington in Keevil. A building known by the name of the Wesleyan Methodist Chapel. Wesleyan Methodist. William Griffith of Melksham. (WRO D1/9/2/1)

**1121** 2 Aug. 1825 (1 Aug. 1825 [*sic*]). Steeple Ashton. A building in the possession or occupation of Robert Grant. Baptist. Peter Anstie, John Smith, Robert Grant. [*Endorsed in pencil*] 'Mr Balles, Canal.' (WRO D1/9/2/1)

**1122** 22 Aug. 1825 (27 Aug. 1825). Hilperton Marsh in Hilperton. A dwellinghouse now in the occupation of Joseph Bartlett. Joseph Bartlett of Hilperton. (WRO D1/9/2/1)

**1123** 12 Sept. 1825 (13 Sept. 1825). West Knoyle. A dwellinghouse now in the occupation of Charles Riddick. Charles Riddick, William Riddick. [*Pencilled at foot*] 'Mr Gould Carrier.' (WRO D1/9/2/1)

**1124** 9 Sept. 1825 (24 Sept. 1825). Brinkworth. The house and premises of Walter Matthews, now in the holding and occupation of Robert Mathews, cordwainer. Walter Matthews of Brinkworth. [*In margin*] 'Mr Davis, I have received the 2/6 for the Licence I believe as correct, H.G. Hanks.' (WRO D1/9/2/1)

**1125** 19 Sept. 1825 (3 Oct. 1825). West Ashton [*in Steeple Ashton*]. A building in the possession or occupation of George Wicks. Baptist. William Wicks, William Linzay, Abraham Richmond, Martin Conlen, William Trapnell, Samuel Wibley, Edward Jefferies. [*Endorsed*] 'Mr Long, Grocer.' (WRO D1/9/2/1)

**1126** 21 Sept. 1825 (24 Sept. 1825). Lea [*in Lea and Cleverton?*]. A house and premises in the holding and occupation of Isaac Woodward. Isaac Woodward of Lea. [*In same hand as* **1127**]. (WRO D1/9/2/1)

**1127** 21 Sept. 1825 (24 Sept. 1825). Malmesbury. A house and premises in the holding and occupation of Emanuel Greyl. Emanuel Greyl of Malmesbury. [*In same hand as* **1126**]. [WRO D1/9/2/1)

**1128** 24 Sept. 1825 (26 Sept. 1825). East Knoyle. A house and premises now in the occupation of Henry Elliott. [*Independent?*: see **1191**]. Henry Elliott of East Knoyle, John Maidment, James Elliott. (WRO D1/9/2/1)

**1129** 1 Oct. 1825 (4 Oct. 1825). Highworth. A new chapel called Zion Chapel. Independent. Henry J Larter, Samuel Brown, William Saunders, of Highworth. [*Pencilled at foot*] 'Mr Good.' (WRO D1/9/2/1)

**1130** 6 Oct. 1825 (20 Oct. 1825). Bedwyn Common in Great Bedwyn. A house and premises, the property and in the occupation of William Dobson. Independent Methodist. William Sanger of Salisbury. (WRO D1/9/2/1)

**1131** 15 Oct. 1825 (28 Oct. 1825). Sherston. The new building erected in Back Street as a meeting house, with the vestry, which has the street on the west, premises in the possession of Samuel Manning on the north, premises in the possession of Thomas Collingborne on the east, and premises in the possession of William Wicks on the south. [*Independent?*: see **969**]. Thomas Deverell of Sherston, gentleman, Thomas William Deverell, tiler, Roger Gantlett, shopkeeper, David Berry, carpenter, John Hunt, cooper, Francis Rice, plasterer, William Morris, shopkeeper. [*Identical format to* **1132**]. (WRO D1/9/2/1)

**1132** 17 Oct. 1825 (28 Oct. 1825). Sopworth. The message or tenement lately in the occupation of Mr Daniel Young, having the road or street on the east and land belonging to the Duke of Badminton [*sic, recte* Beaufort?] on the south, west and north. [*Independent?*: see **1131**]. Daniel Young of Sopworth, smith, John Bressington, labourer, John Jenkings, labourer. [*Identical format to* **1131**]. (WRO D1/9/2/1)

**1133** 17 Oct. 1825 (25 Oct. 1825). Worton in Potterne. A newly erected building known by the name of the Methodist chapel. Wesleyan Methodist. Joseph Bowes of Devizes, Wesleyan Methodist minister. [*Endorsed in pencil*] 'Mr. Bradnack, Mr. Bowes.' (WRO D1/9/2/1)

**1134** 25 Oct. 1825 (2 Nov. 1825). Goatacre in Hilmarton. A house now in the occupation of Frederic Tyler. Primitive Methodist. Benjamin Shimwell, Frederic Tyler. [*Pencilled at foot*] 'Mr Hanks, 2nd Novr.' (WRO D1/9/2/1)

**1135** (25 Oct. 1825). Wootton Bassett. A new chapel called Hephzibah is to be opened. Independent. Martin Slater, Thomas Harris, of Wootton Bassett. [*Pencilled at foot*] 'Revd Mr Good, 25th Octr. 1825.' (WRO D1/9/2/1)

**1136** 26 Oct. 1825 (29 Oct. 1825). Bradford on Avon. A building in Bradford on Avon now in the occupation of William Brown. Primitive Methodist. John Challinor, William Brown. [*Endorsed postmark Malmsbury*]. (WRO D1/9/2/1)

**1137** 29 Oct. 1825 (2 Nov. 1825). Corston in Malmesbury. A house now in the occupation of Christopher May. Primitive Methodist. Thomas Williams, Christopher May. [*Pencilled at foot*] 'Mr Hanks, 2d Nov.' (WRO D1/9/2/1)

**1138** 4 Nov. 1825 (26 Dec. 1825). Broad Blunsdon *or* Bury Blunsdon in Highworth. A house now in the occupation of Richard Coleman. Primitive Methodist. Thomas Williams, Richard Coleman. [*Pencilled at foot*] 'By Geo. Geo.' (WRO D1/9/2/1)

**1139** 4 Nov. 1825 (26 Dec. 1825). Stratton St Margaret. A building in the occupation of John Habgood. Primitive Methodist. John Hapgood, Thomas Williams. (WRO D1/9/2/1)

**1140** 7 Nov. 1825 (19 Nov. 1825). Swallowcliffe. A dwellinghouse in the occupation of Joseph Coombs. Joseph Coombs, Henry Wright. [*Pencilled at foot*] 'Gould, Don [*Donhead*] Carrier.' (WRO D1/9/2/1)

**1141** 9 Nov. 1825 (24 Dec. 1825). Brinkworth. A building and premises now in the occupation of John Burchell. Primitive Methodist. John Burchell, inhabitant, Samuel Heath, minister, [*At foot*] 'Mr Hanks.' (WRO D1/9/2/1)

**1142** 18 Nov. 1825 (19 Nov. 1825). Milton Lilborne. A newly erected chapel, the property of John Gosling, esquire. Independent Methodist. William Sanger of Salisbury, gentleman. (WRO D1/9/2/1)

**1143** 2 Dec. 1825 (31 Dec. 1825). Seagry. A chapel newly erected by the Primitive Methodists. Primitive Methodist. Samuel Heath, Benjamin Shimwell. [*Pencilled at foot*] 'Hanks's.' (WRO D1/9/2/1)

**1144** 3 Dec. 1825 (31 Dec. 1825). Cricklade. A house in St Sampson's parish now in the occupation of Richard Simmons. Primitive Methodist. Samuel Heath, Richard Simmons. [*Pencilled at foot*] 'Hanks's.' (WRO D1/9/2/1)

**1145** 24 Dec. 1825 (24 Dec. 1825). Salisbury. A room called and known by the name of the Freemasons Hall in the George Yard, High Street. The New Church signified by the New Jerusalem in the Revelations. John Harbin of Shirley, Hants., minister of the gospel, William Sanger. (WRO D1/9/2/1)

**1146** 28 Dec. 1825 (30 Dec. 1825). Mere. A house and premises now in the occupation of John Coward. John Coward of Mere, Robert Shepard, William Love. [*Pencilled*] 'To be sent to John Coward, Mere. To be dated 30th Decr 1825.' (WRO D1/9/2/1)

**1147** 13 Jan. 1826 (25 Feb. 1826). Upper Stratton in Stratton St Margaret. A house now in the occupation of Thomas Townsend. [*Independent\**]. Thomas Townsend, Daniel Hall, Joshua Hyde, of Upper Stratton. [*Pencilled at foot*] 'Revd. Mr. Good.' (WRO D1/9/2/1)

**1148** 25 Feb. 1826 (1 March 1826). Knowl Common in Mere. A house now occupied by Thomas Grey. [*Independent\**]. J E Good. (WRO D1/9/2/1)

**1149** 25 Feb. 1826 (1 March 1826). Salisbury. A building in Gigant Street in St Martin's parish heretofore used as a place of worship by Quakers. Independent. J E Good. (WRO D1/9/2/1)

**1150** 4 March 1826 (18 March 1826). Whitley in Melksham. The house of

William Taylor. Baptist. William Taylor, Thomas Ball, John Taylor, Samuel Hurd, William Chapman. (WRO D1/9/2/1)

**1151**   22 March 1826 (18 April 1826). Highworth. The dwellinghouse and premises of George Peaple. Baptist. George Peapell, Edmund Hedges, Richard Clack, Thompson Pator, Thomas Lawrence, William Pope. [*Pencilled*] 'Little Highworth drover.' (WRO D1/9/2/1)

**1152**   1 May 1826 (15 Jan. 1827). Hilmarton. A house now in the occupation of William Godwin. [*Independent★*]. John Lawrence, George Mead, Cornelius Edwards, of Hilmarton. [*Pencilled*] 'Mr. Good.' (WRO D1/9/2/1)

**1153**   1 May 1826 (15 Jan. 1827). Lyneham. A house now in the occupation of Job Simkins. [*Independent★*]. Job Simkins, Silas Simkins, Thomas Prior, of Lyneham. [*Pencilled*] 'Mr. Good.' (WRO D1/9/2/1)

**1154**   1 May 1826 (15 Jan. 1827). Preston in Lyneham. A house now in the occupation of James Ingram. [*Independent★*]. James Vines, William Simpkins, James Bushell, of Lyneham. [*Pencilled*] 'Mr. Good.' (WRO D1/9/2/1)

**1155**   7 May 1826 (16 May 1826). Eastrop in Highworth. A house on the premises of Randle Pedley. Randle Pedley, Thomas Lee, Thomas? Painter, John Burdett, Luke Dowles. [*At foot*] 'G. Geo.' (WRO D1/9/2/1)

**1156**   6 June 1826 (17 June 1826). Preshute. A building in the possession or occupation of Fanny Pearce, widow. Independent. William Stone, the mark of William Pinton, the mark of Isaac Steel, the mark of Charles Stag. [*Pencilled at foot*] 'Mr Good.' (WRO D1/9/2/1

**1157**   8 July 1826 (10 July 1826). Dilton Marsh in Westbury. A dwellinghouse, the property of Joseph Barnes, late in the occupation of Lazarus Waters. [*Baptist*: Doel 181]. Robert Marshman, weaver, Samuel Scott, carpenter, Joseph Barnes, baker. [*Pencilled at foot*] 'Will be called for this evening, Monday.' (WRO D1/9/2/1)

**1158**   24 July 1826 (25 July 1826). Ansty. A new building. Particular Baptist. James Cadley, John Butt, John James? Halloway, William Lever. [*Pencilled*] 'Wanted on Thursday next.' [*At foot*] 'Gould – Donhd.' (WRO D1/9/2/1)

**1159**   24 July 1826 (1 Aug. 1826). Berwick St John. A building. Particular Baptist. John Lush, Thomas Scammell, Robert Pickford, James Humby, Jesse Bugden. [*Pencilled at foot*] 'For Gould, 27 July.' (WRO D1/9/2/1)

**1160**   18 Aug. 1826 (22 Aug. 1826). Trowbridge. A house and premises now occupied by me. Philip Harman of Trowbridge. [*Pencilled at foot*] 'Silcox Aug 22nd.' (WRO D1/9/2/1)

**1161** 21 Aug. 1826 (21 Aug. 1826). Broad Town in Clyffe Pypard. A house and premises now in the holding and occupation of Mr Cornelius Trotman. Cornelius Trotman of Broad Town. (WRO D1/9/2/1)

**1162** 2 Oct. 1826 (2 Oct. 1826). Kingston Deverill. A building lately erected, and settled as a chapel belonging to the Wesleyan Methodists. Wesleyan Methodists. Henry Vyvyan Olver of Warminster, minister. (WRO D1/9/2/1)

**1163** 6 Oct. 1826. Melksham. A dwellinghouse in the occupation of Isaac Bolwell of Semington Lane. [*Wesleyan Methodist*: Jones 102]. William Worth of Melksham, preacher of the gospel. [*Endorsed*] 'The Rev Benjamin Andrews, Methodist Chapel, Salisbury.' [*same document as* **1164**]. (WRO D1/9/2/1)

**1164** 6 Oct. 1826 (10 Oct. 1826). Studley in Calne. A dwellinghouse in the occupation of James Godwin. [*Wesleyan Methodist*: Jones 102]. William Worth of Melksham, preacher of the gospel. [*same document as* **1163**]. (WRO D1/9/2/1)

**1165** 14 Oct. 1826 (16 Oct. 1826). Lacock. A dwellinghouse in the occupation of Richard Matthews. [*Wesleyan Methodist*: Jones 102]. William Worth, preacher of the gospel. (WRO D1/9/2/1)

**1166** 18 Oct. 1826 (19 Oct. 1826). East Knoyle. A house and premises in the occupation of George Elliott. [*Independent*?: see **1191**]. George Elliott of East Knoyle, John Maidment, yeoman, John Hoopper, labourer. [*Endorsed*] 'For Geo. Elliott at John Maidments, Milton Street, Bp's Knoile.' (WRO D1/9/2/1)

**1167** 23 Oct. 1826 (30 Oct. 1826). Semley. A house occupied by John Smith at Huglers Hole. John Smith of Huglers Hole, Benjamin Baverstock, James Hopewell, minister. [*Pencilled at foot*] 'For Lanning of Shaston.' (WRO D1/9/2/1)

**1168** 23 Oct. 1826 (23 Oct. 1826). Whiteparish. A building lately erected, and settled as a chapel belonging to the Wesleyan Methodists. Wesleyan Methodist. John Baker of Salisbury, minister. (WRO D1/9/2/1)

**1169** 31 Oct. 1826 (15 Jan. 1827). Preshute. A building in the occupation of William Witts. Independent. William Smith, John Dance, Timothy Brownjohn. [*Pencilled*] 'Mr Good.' (WRO D1/9/2/1)

**1170** 22 Nov. 1826 (4 Dec. 1826). Manningford Bohun [*in Wilsford*]. An uninhabited tenement, the property of John Oram. John Oram, Stephen Waight, John Simper. [*Pencilled at foot*] '4th Decr. 1826, Joseph Burden, pd fore.' (WRO D1/9/2/1)

**1171** 7 Dec. 1826 (8 Dec. 1826). Haxton in Fittleton. A room in the dwellinghouse of Roger Hitchcock, lately used as a schoolroom. Particular Baptist. Stephen Offer of Littlecott in Enford, miller. (WRO D1/9/2/1)

**1172**  2 Jan. 1827 (17 Jan. 1827). Garsdon. A house now in the holding and occupation of Thomas Stoneham. Thomas Stoneham of Garsdon. [*At foot*] 'Mr. Hanks – Masby [*Malmesbury*].' [*Certificate written twice*]. (WRO D1/9/2/1)

**1173**  5 Jan. 1827 (17 Jan. 1827). Dauntsey. A house now in the holding and occupation of John Wakfield. [*Primitive Methodist:* see **1141**]. The mark of John Wakfield of Dauntsey, Samuel Heath, minister. [*At foot*] 'Mr. Hanks, Masbury.' (WRO D1/9/2/1)

**1174**  27 Jan. 1827 (29 Jan. 1827). Calstone Wellington. A dwellinghouse in the occupation of Anthony Edwards. [*Wesleyan Methodist:* Jones 102]. William Worth of Melksham, preacher of the gospel. [*Endorsed*] 'The Rev. B. Andrews, Salt Lane Methodist Chapel, Salisbury, Wilts.' (WRO D1/9/2/1)

**1175**  30 Jan. 1827 (21 March 1827). Little Somerford. A house and premises in the occupation of Robert Lawes. Calvinistic Methodist. Daniel Bidmead, minister, Isaac Matthews, William Heath, Isaac Paine, M Reeve junior, dwelling in or near the parish of Lea. [*At foot*] 'Mr Hanks.' (WRO D1/9/2/1)

**1176**  5 Feb. 1827 (20 Feb. 1827). Brinkworth. A house and premises now in the holding and occupation of Mr John Hathrill. John Hathrill of Brinkworth. [*At foot*] 'Mr. Hanks.' [*Certificate written twice*]. (WRO D1/9/2/1)

**1177**  8 Feb. 1827 (20 Feb. 1827). Wootton Bassett. A room now in the holding and occupation of William Ind. [*Primitive Methodist:* see **1141**]. William Ind of Wootton Bassett, Samuel Heath. [*At foot*] 'Mr Hanks.' [*Certificate written twice*]. (WRO D1/9/2/1)

**1178**  15 Feb. 1827 (17 Feb. 1827). East Harnham in Britford. A building, a tenement in the occupation of Elizabeth Anne Biddlecombe, spinster. [*Independent:* see **1493**]. Samuel Sleigh, minister of the gospel at the meeting house in Scots Lane, Salisbury. [*At foot*] 'S Sleigh, resident at Mr Knight's, auctioneer in High Street.' (WRO D1/9/2/1)

**1179**  16 Feb. 1827 (19 March 1827). Hullavington. A house and premises now in the holding and occupation of Sarah Greenman. Sarah Greenman of Hullavington. (WRO D1/9/2/1)

**1180**  19 Feb. 1827 (20 Feb. 1827). Seend [*in Melksham*]. My dwellinghouse and premises. James Rutty, in Seend. (WRO D1/9/2/1)

**1181**  23 Feb. 1827 (19 March 1827). Bishopstone [*north Wiltshire?: George George was the Marlborough carrier*]. The dwellinghouse and premises of James

Painter. Baptist. James Painter of Bishopstone, William Pope, William Norris, Samuel Ford, John Holdway. [*Pencilled at foot*] 'Geo Geo.' (WRO D1/9/2/1)

**1182**   24 Feb. 1827 (2 March 1827). Great Somerford. A house in the occupation of Worthy Porter. Independent. Revd Samuel Raban, minister, Robert Cove Lloyd, Worthy Porter, John Reeve junior, John Reynolds, James Bidmead, Daniel Bidmead, minister. [*At foot*] 'Jno C Wheeler Esqr.' (WRO D1/9/2/1)

**1183**   10 March 1827 (12 March 1827). Bishopstone [*north Wiltshire?*: see **1181**]. The dwellinghouse and premises of William Pope. Baptist. William Pope of Bishopstone, James Painter, Samuel Ford, George Povey. [*Pencilled at foot*] 'Man will call this evening.' (WRO D1/9/2/1)

**1184**   19 March 1827 (22 March 1827). Braydon in Cricklade. A room now in the occupation of Mr Nosworthy. [*Independent\**]. M Slater, C Trimnell, A Connibee, of Wootton Bassett. [*Pencilled*] 'Revd Mr Good, 22nd March 1827'. (WRO D1/9/2/1)

**1185**   3 April 1827 (April 1827). Avon in Christian Malford. A dwellinghouse in the occupation of John Cole. Wesleyan Methodist. William Worth of Melksham, preacher of the gospel. [*Endorsed*] 'The Rev John Baker, Wesleyan Minister, Chh Street, Salisbury.' (WRO D1/9/2/1)

**1186**   7 April 1827 (24 April 1827). Clyffe Pypard. A chapel and premises at Broad Town Lane, now in the holding and occupation of Samuel Heath. [*Primitive Methodist*: see **1141**]. Samuel Heath, minister, George Holloway, minister. (WRO D1/9/2/1)

**1187**   7 April 1827 (20 April 1827). Malmesbury. A house and premises now in the holding and occupation of Adam Williams. Adam Willims of Malmesbury. [*Pencilled at foot*] 'Mr Hanks.' (WRO D1/9/2/1)

**1188**   10 April 1827 (20 April 1827). Stonehill in Charlton [*near Malmesbury*]. A house and premises now in the holding and occupation of James Hughes. James Hughes of Stonehill. [*Pencilled at foot*] 'Mr Hanks.' (WRO D1/9/2/1)

**1189**   20 April 1827 (28 April 1827). Easton Grey. The dwellinghouse of Thomas Shipton. Thomas Shipton, James Hart, Simon House, in Easton Grey. [*At foot*] 'recd 2/6, Mark Hanks, Constable, Masbury.' (WRO D1/9/2/1)

**1190**   10 May 1827 (19 May 1827). Broughton Gifford. A chapel newly erected. [*Wesleyan Methodist*: Jones 102]. William Worth of Melksham, preacher of the gospel. [*Endorsed*] 'Revd B Andrews, Salt Lane.' (WRO D1/9/2/1)

**1191** 14 May 1827 (22 May 1827). East Knoyle. A house and premises now in the occupation of Charles Jukes. [*Independent*?: VCH 11, 96]. Charles Jukes of East Knoyle, John Maidment, William Jukes. (WRO D1/9/2/1)

**1192** 16 June 1827 (30 June 1827). Plaitford (*Plightford*). A house in the possession of Margaret Cook. William Gibbs of Portsea, Hants., minister of the gospel, N Billing, the mark of Margaret Cook. (WRO D1/9/2/1)

**1193** (19 June 1827). Little Somerford. A house in the occupation of Thomas Thrush. [*Calvinistic Methodist*: see **1175**]. Isaac Paine, minister, William Heath, Francis Day, Charles Carey, inhabitants of Little Somerford. [*At foot*] 'For Mr Hanks, Masbury.' (WRO D1/9/2/1)

**1194** 21 June 1827 (6 Aug. 1827). Stratton St Margaret [*but dated from Highworth*]. A room in the house of Robert Gilman. [*Baptist*?: see **1289**]. Robert Gilman in Stratton St Margaret, William Adams, Richard Woolford. [*At foot*] 'Geo. Geo. 6th Aug 1827.' (WRO D1/9/2/1)

**1195** 24 June 1827 (3 July 1827). White Cross in Mere. A house and premises now in the holding and occupation of Paul Green. [*Primitive Methodist*: see **1200**]. Paul Green of White Cross, William Smart, Charles Parfit, Thomas Baynton. [*Pencilled at foot*] 'To be called for next Tuesday the 10th ins.' [*Certificate written twice*]. (WRO D1/9/2/1)

**1196** 9 July 1827 (13 July 1827). Hook in Lydiard Tregoze. The house and premises of Richard Wolford. Richard Wolford of Hook, William Wolford, James Horner. (WRO D1/9/2/1)

**1197** 17 July 1827 (17 July 1827). Barker's Street in Semley. A house and premises. Robert Fowler of Barker's Street, Frederick Fowler. [*Pencilled*] 'To be called for 31st July.' [*At foot*] '2 Gould.' (WRO D1/9/2/1)

**1198** 31 Aug. 1827 (3 Sept. 1827). West Overton [*in Overton*]. A building in the possession of Elizah Cope and John Pye. Independent. The mark of Joseph Webb, Elizah Cope, William Stone. [*Pencilled*] '3rd Septr 1827 Mr Good.' (WRO D1/9/2/1)

**1199** 3 Sept. 1827 (11 Sept. 1827). Hilperton Marsh in Hilperton. A dwellinghouse now in the occupation of James Selfe. James Selfe of Hilperton. [*At head*] 'Geo Geo 4 Sept [*deleted in pencil*].' [*Pencilled at head*] 'Applegate.' (WRO D1/9/2/1)

**1200** 5 Sept. 1827 (5 Sept. 1827). Salisbury. A room belonging to Mr Wing in New Street, St Thomas's parish. Primitive Methodist. Thomas Baynton of Salisbury. (WRO D1/9/2/1)

**1201** 10 Sept. 1827 (11 Sept. 1827 [*deleted*]). Salisbury. The yard and premises of Henry Wite in St Edmund's parish, now in the holding and occupation of Nathaniel North and others. The mark of Nathaniel North, the mark of William Truisler, Daniel Parsons, William Oakford, the mark of George Pike, John Sheppard. (WRO D1/9/2/1)

**1202**   9 Nov. 1827 (27 Nov. 1827). Bromham. Part of a dwellinghouse or building in the possession or occupation of George Perren. [*Baptist*: Davis 158]. George Perren, occupier, Charles Cawston, attendant. (WRO D1/9/2/1)

**1203**   10 Nov. 1827 (27 Nov. 1827). Bishops Cannings. A building in the possession or occupation of James Burton. [*Independent*: see **1493**]. James Burton, occupier, John Gaul?, attendant. [*Endorsed*] 'The certificate to be sent to the Rev. S. Sleigh at W. Knight's High St. or will be called for at any specified time.' [*Identical format to* **1202**]. (WRO D1/9/2/1)

**1204**   10 Dec. 1827 (18 Dec. 1827). Turleigh in Bradford on Avon. The house of John Morris senior. Baptist. John Morris senior, John Milsom, John Morris junior, Benjamin Banister, James Helson. [*At foot*] 'Silcox 18th Decr. 1827.' (WRO D1/9/2/1)

**1205**   14 Dec. 1827 (15 Jan. 1828). Wadswick in Box. A dwellinghouse, the property of Peter Doorey. Independent. Peter Doorey, Henry Aust, James Day, Thomas Shell, Moses Mizen, Nathaniel Webb, Joseph Doorey, housekeepers in Box. (WRO D1/9/2/1)

**1206**   24 Dec. 1827 (29 Dec. 1827). Warminster Common in Warminster. A new building called a Methodist chapel, with the court adjoining, near Bread Street. Methodist. W Daniell, Stephen Payne, J Provis, trustees. [*Pencilled at foot*] 'Revd Mr Slay.' (WRO D1/9/2/1)

**1207**   3 Jan. 1828 (25 Feb. 1828). Broad Town in Clyffe Pypard. A work shop in the possession of William Church. [*Independent*: see **1326**]. William Church of Bushton in Clyffe Pypard, carpenter, John Bedford, John Panting. [*Endorsed in pencil*] 'decided at Westm [*inster*] Sesions that the . . . [*illegible*] sect sho'd be set in Certate.' (WRO D1/9/2/1)

**1208**   9 Jan. 1828 (12 Jan. 1828). Downton. A dwellinghouse now in my occupation. General Baptist. The mark of Charles Thorn of Downton. (WRO D1/9/2/1)

**1209**   14 Jan. 1828 (18 Jan. 1828). Newtown in Tisbury. A house and premises now in the holding and occupation of Solomon Sanger. [*Primitive Methodist*: see **1200**]. Thomas Baynton, Solomon Sanger. (WRO D1/9/2/1)

**1210**   19 Jan. 1828 (15 Jan. 1828 [*sic*]). Chippenham. A building called the Tabernacle in the possession or occupation of the undersigned and others. Independent. Benjamin Rees, minister, John Cullis. (WRO A1/250)

**1211**  25 Jan. 1828 (29 Jan. 1828). Trowbridge. The dwellinghouse of James Bull. James Brown of Trowbridge. [*Endorsed in pencil*] 'Silcox Jany 29th 1828.' (WRO D1/9/2/1)

**1212**  13 Feb. 1828 (20 Feb. 1828). Bremhill. A dwellinghouse and premises now in the holding and occupation of William Hatherill. The mark of William Hatherill of Bremhill, John Guy, Thomas Summers. (WRO D1/9/2/1)

**1213**  13 Feb. 1828 (20 Feb. 1828). East Tytherton (*Tytherington*) in Bremhill. The dwellinghouse now in the holding and occupation of Thomas Smith. Jacob Guy of Bremhill, the mark of Thomas Smith, Robert Tipplle?, John Hatherel. (WRO D1/9/2/1)

**1214**  19 Feb. 1828 (15 March 1828). Bishopstone. A house now in the occupation of James Skinner. [*Independent★*]. James Skinner, Thomas Cue, William Norris. [*Pencilled at foot*] 'Revd Mr Good.' (WRO D1/9/2/1)

**1215**  28 Feb. 1828 (15 March 1828). Marlborough. A building in St Mary's parish in the occupation of William Anstridge?. Independent. Jerome Clapp, Robert Tozer, Joseph Towlson. [*Endorsed*] 'Revd Mr Good, Salisbury, Wilts.' (WRO D1/9/2/1)

**1216**  6 March 1828 (19 March 1828) Donhead St Mary. A dwellinghouse now in the occupation of William Henry Loxdale Eden. Wesleyan Methodist. James Dunbar of Shaftesbury, Dorset, Wesleyan minister. [*Pencilled at foot*] 'Mr Harding.' (WRO D1/9/2/1)

**1217**  11 April 1828 (15 April 1828). Chisbury in Little Bedwyn. A dwellinghouse now in the occupation of Thomas Hopgood. Wesleyan Methodist. Henry Vyvyan Olver of Hungerford, Wesleyan minister. (WRO D1/9/2/1)

**1218**  12 May 1828 (20 May 1828). Highway. A house in the occupation of Jasper Taylor. [*Wesleyan Methodist*: see **1217**]. Henry V Olver of Hungerford. [*Endorsed*] 'Mr George.' (WRO D1/9/2/1)

**1219**  13 May 1828 (13 May 1828). Rowberry (*Ruberry*) Cross in Donhead St Andrew. A dwellinghouse and premises now in the occupation of George Lush junior. [*Methodist*: see **1373**]. John Gillingham of Shaftesbury. [*Certificate written twice*] (WRO D1/9/2/1)

**1220**  14 May 1828 (16 May 1828). Collingbourne Ducis. A messuage or tenement now in the occupation of Joseph Lansley. Wesleyan Methodist. John Overton of Winton Street, Andover, Wesleyan minister. [*Certificate written twice*]. (WRO D1/9/2/1)

**1221**  19 May 1828 (19 May 1828). Salisbury. A newly erected chapel in

Crane Street. New Jerusalem Church. John Harbin, minister. (WRO D1/9/2/1)

**1222**   25 May 1828 (4 May 1828 [sic]). Braydon in St Sampson's parish, Cricklade. A new chapel. [Independent*]. John Richins, George Freeth, John Reynolds, William Reynalds, of Braydon. [Endorsed in pencil] 'For Mr Good 4th May 1828.' (WRO D1/9/2/1)

**1223**   7 June 1828 (10 June 1828) Bromham. A building in the possession or occupation of Thomas Burton. [Baptist: Davis 158]. Thomas Burton, occupier, George Perren, dissenting minister, William Attwood, William Perett. [Endorsed] 'Mr Knight, High Street.' (WRO D1/9/2/1)

**1224**   7 June 1828 (9 Aug. 1828). Steeple Ashton. A building in the possession or occupation of Samuel Wicks. Baptist. William Wicks, James Hart, William Hart, Alexander Richmond, John Millard, W Saffrey. (WRO D1/9/2/1)

**1225**   16 June 1828 (16 June 1828). Hilperton Marsh in Hilperton. A certain house now in the occupation of Joseph Bartlett etc. Joseph Bartlett. [Pencilled] 'Silcox, June 16/28.' [At foot] 'Applegate.' (WRO D1/9/2/1)

**1226**   23 June 1828 (28 June 1828). Trowbridge. My dwellinghouse and premises. [Baptist: Doel 154]. Zechariah Dyer of Trowbridge. [At foot] 'Applegate − 2.' (WRO D1/9/2/1)

**1227**   27 July 1828 (10 Oct. 1828). Avebury. A building in the possession or occupation of John Clements, George Smith, Samuel Fowler, William Mortimer, Aaron Jennings, John Pontin, Stephen Dark, William Chivers senior, William Chivers junior, George Randall, Thomas Carter, Robert Dredge, Joseph Parry junior. [Baptist: Oliver 18–19]. John Panting, Isaac Tuck, John Giddings, Thomas Carey, Jonathan Russell, William Hillier. (WRO D1/9/2/1)

**1228**   4 Aug. 1828 (9 Aug. 1828). Poulshot. A dwellinghouse in the occupation of William Davies. Wesleyan Methodist. Thomas Twiddy of Melksham. [Endorsed in pencil] 'Mr Andrews, Salt Lane, Wesleyan minister, Salt Lane.' [Endorsed] 'No signature, Inquire of Mr Andrews.' (WRO D1/9/2/1)

**1229**   6 Aug. 1828 (9 Aug. 1828). Poulshot. A dwellinghouse now in the occupation of William Davies. Wesleyan Methodist. William Sanger of Salisbury, gentleman. [Pencilled] 'Very much wanted.' (WRO D1/9/2/1)

**1230**   10 Aug. 1828 (9 Aug. 1828 [sic]). Tidcombe [in Tidcombe and Fosbury]. A dwellinghouse belonging to James Smart. Independent. James Smart, Benjamin Baverstock, John Walcot, dissenting minister, Ludgershall. [Endorsed] 'Beams − Ludgarshall carr. 12th Augt 1828.' (WRO D1/9/2/1)

**1231** 6 Sept. 1828 (20 Sept. 1828). Coate in Bishops Cannings. My house. The mark of Richard King of Coate. [*Endorsed in pencil*] 'Not paid, for Mr Sainsbury, Newsman, by next Saturday.' (WRO D1/9/2/1)

**1232** 1 Oct. 1828 (10 Oct. 1828). Bromham. A building in the possession or in the occupation of Charles Causton, Stephen Burton, Daniel Powell, Robert Dunkerton, William Perrit, George Perrin, John Stacy Bunn, Benjamin Anstie. Paul Anstie, James Overbury Christie, Charles Cadby, Richard Biggs, George Washington Anstie. [*Baptist*: Davis 158]. George Perren, Isaac Hilps, Charles Cawston. (WRO D1/9/2/1)

**1233** 3 Oct. 1828 (3 Oct. 1828). Damerham. A dwellinghouse now in the occupation of William Linton, baker. [*Wesleyan Methodist*: see **1216**]. James Dunbar of Salisbury, minister. [*Pencilled*] 'Mr Dunbar, Wesleyan minister, Church St.' (WRO D1/9/2/1)

**1234** 6 Oct. 1828 (4 Nov. 1828). Badbury in Chisledon. A building in the occupation of William Cox. Primitive Methodist. The mark of William Cox, John Habgood. (WRO D1/9/2/1)

**1235** 9 Oct. 1828 (31 Oct. 1828). Kingston Deverill. A house now in the holding and occupation of James Bramble. [*Primitive Methodist*: see **1248**]. William Paddison, William Ranger, John Briant, Frederick Pike. (WRO D1/9/2/1)

**1236** 16 Oct. 1828 (18 Oct. 1828). Rowde [*but dated from Devizes*]. My house. The mark of Paul Perret of Rowde. [*Pencilled*] 'Sainsbury 18 Oct 1828.' (WRO D1/9/2/1)

**1237** 22 Oct. 1828 (24 Oct. 1828). All Cannings. A building in the possession or occupation of Robert Woodroffe. [*Strict Baptist*: see **1264**]. Robert Woodroff, Joseph Parry, Richard Bullock, Richard Dowse. [*Pencilled at foot*] 'Devizes Coachman.' (WRO D1/9/2/1)

**1238** 30 Oct. 1828 (15 Nov. 1828). Allington in Chippenham. A building in the occupation of William Law. John Butter, James Muscale, William Law, Henry Law. [*Pencilled at foot*] 'Mr. Barratt.' [WRO D1/9/2/1]

**1239** 30 Oct. 1828 (4 Nov. 1828). Coate in Chisledon [*recte Liddington or Swindon?*]. A building in the occupation of Joseph Smith, Primitive Methodist. The mark of Joseph Smith, John Habgood. [*Pencilled at foot*] 'these are for George the Marlboro carrier Nov 3rd.' (WRO D1/9/2/1)

**1240** 3 Nov. 1828 (3 Nov. 1828). Alderbury. A dwellinghouse now in the occupation of Peter Jolin. [*Wesleyan Methodist*: see **1233**]. James Dunbar of Salisbury, minister. (WRO D1/9/2/1)

**1241**  11 Nov. 1828 (9 Dec                    Purton. The house and premises now in the holding anu occupation of John Hunt. [*Primitive Methodist*: see **1325**]. John Hunt, Uriah Watts. (WRO D1/9/2/1)

**1242**  13 Nov. 1828 (15 Nov. 1828). Tinhead [*in Edington*]. The building lately erected. [*Wesleyan Methodist*: see **1257**]. Thomas Twiddy of Melksham. [*Pencilled at foot*] 'Mr Dunbar Novr 15/28.' (WRO D1/9/2/1)

**1243**  18 Nov. 1828 (9 Dec. 1828). Clack in Lyneham. A Primitive Methodist chapel and premises, now in the holding and occupation of the Primitive Methodist Society and James Hitchcock, James Sutton and Francis Ferries their trustees. Primitive Methodist. Joseph Priddy of Clack, John Ride. (WRO D1/9/2/1)

**1244**  19 Nov. 1828 (9 Dec. 1828). Brinkworth. A Primitive Methodist chapel and premises, now in the holding and occupation of the Primitive Methodist Society and William Ind, Edward Walker, John Whale, etc. their trustees. Primitive Methodist. Robert Matthews of Brinkworth, John Petty. (WRO D1/9/2/1)

**1245**  19 Nov. 1828 (9 Dec. 1828). Cleverton in Lea and Cleverton. A house and premises now in the holding and occupation of James Whale. [*Primitive Methodist*: see **1244**]. James Whale of Cleverton, John Petty. (WRO D1/9/2/1)

**1246**  23 Nov. 1828 (27 Nov. 1828). Warminster Common in Warminster. A house now in the holding and occupation of James Bigwood. [*Primitive Methodist*: see **1141**]. James Bigwood of Warminster Common, Samuel Heath. [*Pencilled*] 'To be sent to Mr Provis's Waggon Office, Brown Street tomorrow [*'tomorrow' underlined twice*].' (WRO D1/9/2/1)

**1247**  24 Nov. 1828 (25 Nov. 1828). Winterslow. A meeting house standing on a piece or plot of garden ground lately occupied by Stephen Collins of Winterslow, the same having been demised and leased to him by the Right Honourable Henry Richard Vassall, Lord Holland. Baptist. Hugh Russell of Broughton, Hants., Baptist minister. [*Pencilled at foot*] 'Mr Saffry also one for Steple Ashton.' (WRO D1/9/2/1)

**1248**  30 Nov. 1828 (6 Dec. 1828). Martin. A dwellinghouse in the occupation of Ann Hersey [*deleted*] and William Flimington. Primitive Methodist. William Flemington, Cornelius Flemington, William Harries, George Burges, James Janes, John Hort, William Paddison, William Hughes, John Randell, William Ranger, inhabitants of Martin. (WRO D1/9/2/1)

**1249**  4 Dec. 1828 (9 Dec. 1828). Dauntsey. A house and premises now in the holding and occupation of James Potter. [*Primitive Methodist*: Tonks 91]. James Potter, John Ride. (WRO D1/9/2/1)

**1250**   4 Dec. 1828 (9 Dec. 1828). Kington St Michael. A house and premises now in the holding and occupation of James Hawkins. [*Primitive Methodist*: Tonks 91]. James Hawkins, John Ride. [*Pencilled*] 'To be called for Saturday the 6th Decr 1828. To be dated 6th Decr. not paid.' (WRO D1/9/2/1)

**1251**   4 Dec. 1828 (9 Dec. 1828). Purton. A house and premises now in the holding and occupation of Uria Moall. [*Primitive Methodist*: Tonks 91]. Uria Moall, John Ride. (WRO D1/9/2/1)

**1252**   23 Dec. 1828 (30 Dec. 1828). Wanborough. A building is erected. Independent. Charles Cannon, Robert Lye, Richard Lye. [*Pencilled at foot*] 'Revd Mr Good, 30 Decr.' (WRO D1/9/2/1)

**1253**   5 Jan. 1829 (22 Jan. 1829). Broad Blunsdon (*Broad Blunsdon St Lenords*) in Highworth. A building in the occupation of Elizabeth Newton. Primitive Methodist. Elizabeth Newton. (WRO D1/9/2/1)

**1254**   23 Jan. 1829 (3 Feb. 1829). Preshute. A building in the possession of William Davis. Independent. James Druet, George Greenaway, John Pope. [*Pencilled at foot*] 'Mr Good.' (WRO D1/9/2/1)

**1255**   27 Jan. 1829 (27 Jan. 1829). Tollard Royal. A dwellinghouse now in the occupation of John Rapson. Wesleyan Methodist. James Dunbar of Salisbury, Wesleyan minister. (WRO D1/9/2/1)

**1256**   2 Feb. 1829 (3 Feb. 1829). Trowbridge. The new built chapel called Bethel in the Upper Court. Baptist. Samuel Hurd, James Young, Job Payne, James Chapman, Job Rawlings, Jonah Purnell. [*At foot*] 'ps Direct Saml Hurd Back St Trowbridge pr Silcocks. Silcocks 3rd Feb 29.' (WRO D1/9/2/1)

**1257**   7 March 1829 (16 March 1829). Spirthill in Bremhill. A newly erected chapel known by the name of the Wesleyan chapel. Wesleyan Methodist. Thomas Twiddy of Melksham. [*At foot*] 'Mr Simmonds, Salt Lane.' (WRO D1/9/2/1)

**1258**   16 March 1829 (24 March 1829). Great Somerford. The dwellinghouse of Robert Ailiff. Robert Ayliffe, John Comley, Jacob Teagle, John Greenaway, in Great Somerford. (WRO D1/9/2/1)

**1259**   17 March 1829 (21 March 1829). Milford [*in Laverstock*]. A building in the occupation of Sarah Holloway. Sarah Holloway, John Cubitt, Henry Bowman, George Barrett. (WRO D1/9/2/1)

**1260**   24 March 1829 (1 April 1829). Coate in Bishops Cannings. A building in the possession or occupation of Richard Hiscock. Independent. Richard Hiscock, occupier, James Neeves, Richard Elliott. [*Pencilled at foot*] 'Mr Good April 1. 1829, not paid.' (WRO D1/9/2/1)

**1261**   27 March 1829 (1 April 1829). Donhead St Andrew. My house. [*Wesleyan Methodist*: see **1255**]. Alexander Barratt of Donhead St Andrew. [*Pencilled at foot*] 'Mr Dunbar first April 1829, paid.' (WRO D1/9/2/1)

**1262**   27 March 1829 (27 March 1829). Salisbury. Two rooms lately occupied by the Jerusalemists in the George Yard in St Thomas's parish. Primitive Methodist. James Parham, occupier, Nathaniel Watkins, minister, of Salisbury. (WRO D1/9/2/1)

**1263**   30 March 1829 (7 April 1829). Chisledon. A building and premises in the occupation of William King. Primitive Methodist. William King. (WRO D1/9/2/1)

**1264**   9 May 1829 (12 May 1829). Allington [*in All Cannings*]. A building in the possession or occupation of Joseph Parry. [*Strict Baptist*: VCH 3, 139]. Joseph Parry, Richard Bullock, Richard Douse, Lewis Tarant, John White, Robert Woodroffe. [*Pencilled at foot*] 'Wanted on Wednesday – Devizes Guard May 11. 29.' [*Identical format to* **1265**]. (WRO D1/9/2/1)

**1265**   9 May 1829 (12 May 1829). Bishops Cannings. A building in the possession or occupation of Mary Smith. [*Strict Baptist?*: see **1264**]. John Wiltshire, William Waite, John Minty, William Rose, Thomas Bailey, [*Pencilled at foot*] 'Wanted on Wednesday, Devizes Guard May 12 1829.' [*Identical format to* **1264**]. (WRO D1/9/2/1)

**1266**   14 May 1829 (19 May 1829). Wroughton. A small room in the possession of William Pickett. [*Calvinist in 1851*: VCH 11, 251]. William Pickett of Wroughton, carrier, Joel Hunt, John Hibberd, George Butler, William Millere. (WRO D1/9/2/1)

**1267**   27 May 1829 (29 May 1829). Salisbury. A room commonly called a vestry contiguous to the Baptist Chapel in Brown Street, for holding occasional worship. Baptist. P J Saffery, minister. (WRO D1/9/2/1)

**1268**   13 June 1829 (20 June 1829). Mere. Our silk house in Church Street. Independent. Charles Jupe, James Toogood, Robert Cross, James Lanan, James Little. [*Endorsed*] 'Mr Good – paid 2/6 at the delivery.' (WRO D1/9/2/1)

**1269**   17 June 1829 (17 June 1829). Hanging Langford [*in Steeple Langford*]. A house called or known by the name of Bennitts about thirty yards from Hanging Langford gate facing the public road from Wylye to Wishford. [*certificate continues*] 'by so doing you will confer a blessing as well as a favour on the whole village.' Baptist. James Ford, John Dew, the mark of Thomas Hinwood, Elizabeth Tucker, the mark of Jean Tucker. [*Pencilled at foot*] 'To be called for on Saturday next – June 17th 1829 – paid 2/6d.' (WRO D1/9/2/1)

**1270**   29 June 1829 (30 June 1829). Plaitford. A dwellinghouse occupied by

William Stright. [*Primitive Methodist*: see **1262**]. Nathaniel Watkins of Salisbury, minister, William Stright, occupier. [*Endorsed*] 'Mr Lea for Mr Watkins.' (WRO D1/9/2/1)

**1271** 13 July 1829 (14 July 1829). Bishopstone. The house and premises in the holding and occupation of James Tarant. James Tarant of Bishopstone. [*At foot*] 'Mr Lea, Winchester St. 14th July.' (WRO D1/9/2/1)

**1272** 14 July 1829 (15 July 1829). Purton. A new chapel. [*Independent★*]. M. Slater, Job Lewis, Charles Templar. [*pencilled at foot*] 'to be ready by Friday.' [*Endorsed*] 'Mr Good pd 2/6 July 15 1829.' (WRO D1/9/2/1)

**1273** 10 Aug. 1829 (17 Aug. 1829). Ramsbury. A house in the occupation of Robert Reason and William Greenwood. [*Independent*: see **1290**]. William Greenwood, Richard Frost, Ambrose Lanfear. (WRO D1/9/2/1).

**1274** 17 Aug. 1829 (24 Aug. 1829). Wanborough. The dwellinghouse of Thomas Smith (late Cuthbert). Methodist. Thomas Smith, Richard Jukes, John May. [*Endorsed*] 'For George George, Marlborough Carrier, Augt. 24th 1829, not paid.' (WRO D1/9/2/1)

**1275** 23 Sept. 1829 (3 Oct. 1829). Nursteed [*in Bishops Cannings*]. A building in the possession or occupation of William Bailey. Independent. William Baily, occupier, James Neeves, Richard Elliott, minister. [*Endorsed in pencil*] 'Mr Good.' (WRO D1/9/2/1)

**1276** 1 Oct. 1829 (28 Oct. 1829). Donhead St Mary. A house and premises now in the holding and occupation of John Taylor. John Taylor of Ludwell Lane in Donhead St Mary, Charles Matthews. (WRO D1/9/2/1)

**1277** 12 Oct. 1829 (12 Oct. 1829). Fisherton Anger. A chapel. New Jerusalem Church. John Harbin, minister. (WRO D1/9/2/1)

**1278** 15 Oct. 1829 (17 Oct. 1829). Damerham. A dwellinghouse in the occupation of William Hayter. Wesleyan Methodist. James Dunbar of St Edmund's parish, Salisbury, Wesleyan minister. [*Pencilled at foot*] 'Octr 17 1829, Harding, Fisherton.' (WRO D1/9/2/1)

**1279** 23 Oct. 1829 (28 Oct. 1829). East Hinton in Little Hinton. The house and premises now in the holding and occupation of Sarah Jones. [*Primitive Methodist*: Tonks 91]. Sarah Jones of East Hinton, John Woodley, Thomas Russell. [*Pencilled at foot*] 'Oct 28th 1829, to call at 4 o clock – Rantors.' (WRO D1/9/2/1)

**1280** 23 Oct. 1829 (27 Oct. 1829). Trowbridge. The dwellinghouse now occupied by me. James Brown of Trowbridge. [*At foot*] 'Silcox.' (WRO D1/9/2/1)

**1281**   26 Oct. 1829 (27 Oct. 1829). Bishops Cannings. A building in the possession or occupation of William King. William King, John Wiltshire, William Rose, William Waight. [*Pencilled at foot*] 'Devizes Coachmn 27th Oct paid.' (WRO D1/9/2/1)

**1282**   26 Oct. 1829 (28 Oct. 1829). Charlton in Donhead St Mary. A house and premises now in the possession of James Mullins. James Mullins of Donhead St Mary, Charles Mathews. [*Pencilled at foot*] 'Oct. 28. 1829 wanted 31st Oct.' (WRO D1/9/2/1)

**1283**   2 Nov. 1829 (9 Oct. 1829 [*sic*]). Aldbourne. A house, barn and other premises now in the holding and occupation of John Woodley. [*Primitive Methodist*: see **1279**]. John Woodley of Aldbourne, John Farmer, William Farmer. [*Pencilled at foot*] '9th Octr 1829, Geo. Geo.' (WRO D1/9/2/1)

**1284**   21 Nov. 1829 (21 Nov. 1829). Salisbury. A newly erected chapel in Brown Street. Baptist. P.J. Saffery, minister, William Long. [*On separate sheet*] 'W. Longs respects to Mr Lush and will thank him for the within certificate as early as possible, B.B. Row 21 Nov. 1829.' (WRO D1/9/2/1)

**1285**   27 Nov. 1829 (28 Nov. 1829). Tollard Royal. The houses and premises belonging to Samuel Sims, carpenter, of Tollard Royal. Wesleyan Methodist. James Dunbar of Salisbury, Wesleyan minister. (WRO D1/9/2/1)

**1286**   4 Dec. 1829 (9 Dec. 1829). Chittoe [*in Bishops Cannings*]. ['Chittoe' *is in a different hand, and seems to have been altered to* 'Chitton.' *The document is endorsed* 'Chilton.' *That Chittoe is the correct reading is confirmed by* WRO 1046/4, *Bromham marriage register, whch records the marriage of Abel Gee of Chittoe on 5 Nov. 1806.*]. A building in the possession or occupation of Abel Gee. George Morton, the mark of Abel Gee. [*Pencilled*] 'Devizes Coachman 9 Dec.' (WRO D1/9/2/1)

**1287**   18 Dec. 1829 (30 Dec. 1829). Great Somerford. The dwellinghouse of Robert Ayliffe. John Comby, the mark of John Greenaway, the mark of William Miles, in Great Somerford. [*Pencilled in margin*] '30 Dec 1829, Mr Hanks.' (WRO D1/9/2/1)

**1288**   21 Dec. 1829 (22 Dec. 1829). Berwick St John. A chapel has lately been erected. Baptist. John Lush junior, Thomas Scammell, Robert Pickford, James Humby, inhabitants of Berwick St John. [*Pencilled at foot*] 'Paid Dec. 22nd 1829 for Gould, Donhead Carr.' (WRO D1/9/2/1)

**1289**   22 Jan. 1830 (23 Feb. 1830). Stratton St Margaret. The house and premises now occupied by Adams. [*Baptist?*: see **1296**]. Ralph Day, William Kirby, Richard Fisher, Thomas Garratt, Richard Woolford, John Adams, William Adams. [*Pencilled at foot*] 'Geo Geo not pd. Feby 22nd 1830, pd 2d for Porterage.' (WRO D1/9/2/1)

**1290** 29 Jan. 1830 (1 Feb. 1830). Ramsbury. A building in the possession of William Lewington junior. Independent. Robert Tozer, William Greenwood, Jerome Clapp. [*Pencilled at foot*] 'pd Mr Good 1st Feb. 30.' (WRO D1/9/2/1)

**1291** 5 March 1830 (12 March 1830). Boreham in Warminster. A dwelling-house in the occupation of John Payne. [*Wesleyan Methodist*: Hall 241]. Evan Parry of Warminster, minister of the gospel. [*Pencilled at foot*] 'Mr. Bear, Warm: Dissr Warmin. pd.' (WRO D1/9/2/1)

**1292** 18 June 1830 (20 June 1830). Patney. A building in the possession or occupation of Thomas Wells. [*Baptist*: Doel 223]. J.S. Bunce, minister, Thomas Wells. [*Pencilled at foot*] 'Devizes Coachman wanted on Monday next · not pd.' (WRO D1/9/2/1)

**1293** 29 June 1830 (5 July 1830). Stratton St Margaret. A chapel and premises now in the holding and occupation of the Primitive Methodists. Primitive Methodist. John Habgood of Stratton St Margaret. [*At foot*] 'Paid Mr Strongman.' (WRO D1/9/2/1)

**1294** 8 July 1830 (8 July 1830). Charlton in Downton. The dwellinghouse of Henry Noble, shepherd. [*Wesleyan Methodist*: Hall 206]. John Simmons of Salisbury, minister. [*Pencilled at foot*] 'Simmonds, Salt Lane, July 8/30 not pd.' (WRO D1/9/2/1)

**1295** 9 Aug. 1830 (10 Aug. 1830). Westbury. A building occupied as a school room in Edward Street, of which I am the present tenant. [*Baptist*: Doel 197–198]. John Wilkins of Westbury, grocer and draper. (WRO D1/9/2/1)

**1296** 12 Aug. 1830 (16 Aug. 1830). Stratton St Margaret. The coach house and premises now occupied by Susanna Barrett. [*Baptist?*: Oliver 18, 19]. Stephen Barrett, Ralph Day, James Shorter, William Kirby, Richard Fisher. [*Endorsed*] 'Geo Geo to enter.' (WRO D1/9/2/1)

**1297** 4 Sept. 1830 (4 Sept. 1830). Hurdcott (*Hurkett*) in Winterbourne Earls. The dwellinghouse and premises in the possession of Philip Pearcy. Primitive Methodist. William Strongman of Salisbury, minister. (WRO D1/9/2/1)

**1298** 11 Sept. 1830 (11 Sept. 1830). Wilton. A house belonging to William Harding. [*Wesleyan Methodist*: Hall 206]. John Simmons of Salisbury, minister. (WRO D1/9/2/1)

**1299** 23 Sept. 1830 (31 Jan. 1831). Eastrop in Highworth. A dwellinghouse now in the occupation of Thomas Barnes. [*Independent★*]. The mark of Thomas Barnes, William Mathew?, Henry Larter, residing in Eastrop. [*Pencilled at foot*] 'From Mr Good pd 2/6 Delivered.' [*Identical format to* **1300**]. (WRO D1/9/2/1)

**1300** 12 Oct. 1830 (31 Jan. 1831). Hannington. A dwellinghouse now in the occupation of William Willavize. [*Independent★*]. The mark of William Willavize, Joseph Jarvis, Thomas Hanslow, residing in Hannington. [*Pencilled at foot*] 'Mr Good pd 2/6 delivered.' [*Identical format to* **1299**]. (WRO D1/9/2/1)

**1301** 23 Oct. 1830 (1 Nov. 1830). Ramsbury. A house and premises now in the holding and occupation of John Alexander. [*Primitive Methodist*: Tonks 91]. John Alexander of Ramsbury, John Ride. [*Pencilled at foot*] 'Mr Strongman Not pd.' (WRO D1/9/2/1)

**1302** 25 Oct. 1830 (15 Nov. 1830). Enford. An inhabited tenement occupied by William Hurcot. Baptist. George Knight, Stephen Offer. [*Pencilled at foot*] 'Smith, Hanch of Venison.' (WRO D1/9/2/1)

**1303** 26 Oct. 1830 (1 Nov. 1830). Bishopstone. A house and premises now in the holding and occupation of Jane Belcher. [*Primitive Methodist*: Tonks 91]. Jane Belcher of Bishopstone, John Ride. [*Pencilled at foot*] 'Mr Strongman Not pd.' [*Endorsed*] 'Nov. 1. 1830 Bishopstone North Wilts.' (WRO D1/9/2/1)

**1304** 29 Oct. 1830 (30 Oct. 1830). Fisherton Anger. A school room in my occupation. James Dredge of Fisherton Anger, schoolmaster. (WRO D1/9/2/1)

**1305** 29 Nov. 1830 (11 Dec. 1830). Thickwood in Colerne. A building in the occupation of John May. [*Independent?*: see **1087**]. Charles Butler, Daniel Aurt?, John Woodward. (WRO D1/9/2/1)

**1306** 18 Dec. 1830 (20 Dec. 1830). Cherhill in Compton [*recte Cherhill?*]. The house occupied by John Jordan. [*Primitive Methodist*: see **1440**]. John Harding of Marlborough. [*Pencilled at foot*] 'Geo Geo.' (WRO D1/9/2/1)

**1307** 7 Jan. 1831 (29 Jan. 1831). Maiden Bradley. A house and premises now in the holding and occupation of Richard White. Richard White of Maiden Bradley, John Smith, Daniel Miles. (WRO D1/9/2/1)

**1308** 10 Jan. 1831 (10 Jan. 1831). Barford St Martin. A meeting house and premises in the possession of the Primitive Methodists. Primitive Methodist. William Strongman. (WRO D1/9/2/1)

**1309** 10 Jan. 1831 (26 Feb. 1831). Hankerton. The dwellinghouse of Henry Gleed. Henry Gleed, William Wait, the mark of John Painter, the mark of Solomon Painter, John Beake?, William Beale, the mark of Francis Wallis, Thomas Poole, John Woodward, living in Hankerton. (WRO D1/9/2/1)

**1310** 25 Jan. 1831 (31 Jan. 1831). Bromham. A building in the possession or occupation of Esther Jones. The mark of Esther Jones, George Morton. [*Pencilled at foot*] 'Devizes Coachman.' (WRO D1/9/2/1)

**1311** 1 Feb. 1831 (1 Feb. 1831). Bromham. A building in the possession or occupation of John Steevens. John Stephens, Charles Cawston, Robert Carpenter?, the mark of David Mitchell, William Weston. (WRO D1/9/2/1)

**1312** 9 Feb. 1831 (11 Feb. 1831). Stert. A building in the possession or occupation of Charles Mower. Charles Mower, James O? Anstie, James Neeves, protestant dissenting minister. [*Pencilled at foot*] 'Devizes Coachman pd.' (WRO D1/9/2/1)

**1313** 10 March 1831 (14 March 1831). Damerham. A dwellinghouse and premises. [*Primitive Methodist*: see **1248**]. The mark of William Hayter, William Flemington. [*Pencilled at foot*] 'to be done by Saturday.' (WRO D1/9/2/1)

**1314** 4 April 1831 (19 April 1831). Semley. A dwellinghouse in the occupation of George Ings. Particular Baptist. George Ings, Thomas Foot, Isaac Ings, William Fowler. [*At foot*] 'Gould, Carr, pd.' (WRO D1/9/2/1)

**1315** 11 April 1831 (16 April 1831). North Tidworth. An inhabited tenement occupied by John Miles. Baptist. John Walcot, Baptist minister, Ludgershall, John Miles, North Tidworth. [*Pencilled at foot*] 'Beams, Carrier pd 2s/6d Mr L. recd.' (WRO D1/9/2/1)

**1316** 15 April 1831 (18 April 1831). Stert. A building in the possession or occupation of Charles Wiltshire. [*Baptist*: Doel 223]. J.S. Bunce, minister, the mark of Charles Wiltshire. (WRO D1/9/2/1)

**1317** 30 April 1831 (2 May 1831). Bradford on Avon. The house of William Slugg in Tory, as a protestant meeting house. Joseph Everitt, William Dimsdon?, James Holbrook, William Slugg, householders in Bradford on Avon. (WRO D1/9/2/1)

**1318** 31 May 1831 (14 June 1831). Chirton. A building in the possession or occupation of the Devizes Itinerant Society, [*Baptist*: Doel 223]. James O Anstie, secretary, J.S. Bunce, minister. [*Pencilled in margin*] 'Devizes Coachman June 14– 1831 paid for Porterage 2d.' (WRO D1/9/2/1)

**1319** 7 June 1831 (14 June 1831). Trowbridge. A building now in the occupation of John Spragg. Baptist. John Spragg, William Wicks, Zechariah Dyer, George Elliott, the mark of Thomas Nash, the mark of Samuel Barnard?, the mark of Richard Brewer, the mark of Stephen Doel. [*Endorsed*] 'June 14th 1831 For Silcox'. (WRO D1/9/2/1)

**1320** 22 June 1831 (22 June 1831). Wilton. A building denominated a Methodist chapel. Methodist. John Simmons of Salisbury, minister. (WRO D1/9/2/1)

**1321** 14 July 1831 (18 July 1831). Woolley in Bradford on Avon. A part of a dwellinghouse on White Hill. Shadrack Byefield of Bradford on Avon. [*Endorsed*] 'Address, Shadrack Byefield, Woolly near Bradford, Wilts.' (WRO D1/9/2/1)

**1322**  23 Aug. 1831 (8 Nov. 1831). East Knoyle. The dwellinghouse and premises now in my occupation. [*Wesleyan Methodist*: see **1364**]. William Harris of East Knoyle. (WRO D1/9/2/1)

**1323**  30 Sept. 1831 (6 Oct. 1831). Oxenwood in Shalbourne. A house and premises now in the holding and occupation of William Witbread. [*Primitive Methodist*: Tonks 91]. William Witbread of Oxenwood, Thomas Russell, John Ride. (WRO D1/9/2/1)

**1324**  1 Oct. 1831 (4 Oct. 1831). Trowbridge. A building in the occupation of Wicks. Baptist. William Wicks, Jacob Wicks, John England, John Baskorn?, James Norris, Job Purnell, John White, George Hibbert, John Axford, John Randell, John Simes. (WRO D1/9/2/1)

**1325**  3 Oct. 1831 (6 Oct. 1831). Wootton Bassett. A chapel and premises belonging to the Primitive Methodist connexion now in the holding and occupation of a certain number of trustees, of whom William Ind is the leading trustee. Primitive Methodist. William Ind of Wootton Bassett, Samuel West, Uriah Watts, James Hurd, Richard Jukes. (WRO D1/9/2/1)

**1326**  24 Oct. 1831 (3 April 1832). Wootton Bassett. A building in the occupation of Charles Hunt. Independent. Charles Hunt, John Chambers, William Brown, William Horton, William Church. [*Endorsed in pencil*] 'Geo Geo not pd.' (WRO D1/9/2/1)

**1327**  16 Nov. 1831 (16 Nov. 1831). Quidhampton in Fugglestone St Peter. The house and premises of James Bulling. [*Primitive Methodist*: WRO 1150/ 286]. James Bulling of Quidhampton, Richard Jukes, William Larkham. (WRO D1/9/2/1)

**1328**  12 Dec. 1831 (7 Jan. 1832). Cricklade. A large room and premises in St Sampson's parish, now in the holding and occupation of Richard Palmer. [*Primitive Methodist*: Tonks 88]. William Ferister of Cricklade, Richard Palmer, Isaac Brush, Isaac Mathews, John Williams, Samuel West, John Page [*all names are written in the same hand*]. (WRO D1/9/2/1)

**1329**  17 Dec. 1831 (5 March 1832). Horton in Bishops Cannings. A building recently erected. [*Wesleyan Methodist*: VCH 7, 194]. William Wilson of Devizes. [*Pencilled at foot*] 'Mr Shipman of Woodbro' pd 2/6.' (WRO D1/9/2/1)

**1330**  3 Jan. 1832 (7 Jan. 1832). Downton. The house and premises now in the holding and occupation of William Read. [*Primitive Methodist*: WRO 1150/ 286]. William Read of Downton, R. Jukes. (WRO D1/9/2/1)

**1331** 3 Jan. 1832 (7 Jan. 1832). Shalbourne. The house and premises in the holding and occupation of Thomas White. [*Primitive Methodist*: Tonks 91]. Thomas White of Shalbourne, Thomas Russell. (WRO D1/9/2/1)

**1332** 5 Jan. 1832 (7 Jan. 1832). Hannington. The house and premises now in the holding and occupation of John Drew. [*Primitive Methodist*: Tonks 88]. Jonathan Yates of Hannington, John Drew, Samuel West. (WRO D1/9/2/1)

**1333** 19 Jan. 1832 (23 Jan. 1832). Chilton Foliat. A house belonging to Fulwar Craven, esquire and in the occupation of Thomas Duck. [*Independent*: see **1252, 1273**]. Richard Frost, Ambrose Lanfear, Richard Lye, Joseph Parsons. (WRO D1/9/2/1)

**1334** 31 March 1832 (17 April 1832). Aldbourne. The house and premises now in the holding and occupation of Alexander Sherman. [*Primitive Methodist*: see **1283**]. Alexander Sherman of Aldbourne, William Farmer. [*Pencilled at foot*] 'Mr Jukes.' (WRO D1/9/2/1)

**1335** 31 March 1832 (17 April 1832). Ewin's Hill in Aldbourne. The house and premises now in the holding and occupation of John Davies. [*Primitive Methodist*: Tonks 91]. John Davies, Thomas Russell. [*Pencilled at foot*] 'Mr Jukes.' (WRO D1/9/2/1)

**1336** 1 April 1832 (3 April 1832). Donhead St Mary. A house occupied by John Wyatt. John Wyatt of Donhead St Mary. Benjamin Baverstock. (WRO D1/9/2/1)

**1337** 1 April 1832 (3 April 1832). Tisbury. A house occupied by Frederick Fowler. Frederick Fowler of Tisbury, Benjamin Baverstock. [*Pencilled at foot*] 'For John Wyatt.' (WRO D1/9/2/1)

**1338** 16 April 1832 (17 April 1832). Norton Bavant. A building or dwelling-house. Independent. James Everley, William Hiskett, William Bridle, resident in Norton Bavant. [*Endorsed*] 'PS As no post comes to Norton Bavant direct – We request the favor of your Lordship to direct the licence when forwarded to Mr W.M. Scammell, Close, Warminster, who will convey it to us.' (WRO D1/9/2/1)

**1339** 20 April 1832 (21 April 1832). Whiteparish. A dwellinghouse now in the occupation of John Wilson. Independent. Henry Abbott, John Wilsan. [*Endorsed in pencil*] 'Mr Wilson Whiteph, By Noyce, Spreadeagle.' (WRO D1/9/2/1)

**1340** 25 April 1832 (24 May 1832). Cleverton in Lea and Cleverton. A chapel and premises now in the holding and occupation of Francis Day. [*Primitive Methodist*: Tonks 88]. Francis Day of Little Somerford, Samuel West. [*Pencilled at foot*] 'Mr Jukes.' (WRO D1/9/2/1)

**1341** 25 April 1832 (9 May 1832). Moredon in Rodbourne Cheney. The house and premises now in the holding and occupation of Joseph Lester. [*Primitive Methodist*: Tonks 88]. Joseph Lester of Moredon, Samuel West. (WRO D1/9/2/1)

**1342** 25 April 1832 (9 May 1832). Purton Stoke in Purton. A chapel and premises now in the holding and occupation of Thomas Tuck. [*Primitive Methodist*: Tonks 88]. Thomas Tuck of Purton Stoke, Samuel West. (WRO D1/9/2/1)

**1343** 27 April 1832 (28 April 1832). Broad Town in Clyffe Pypard. A dwellinghouse now in the occupation of Richard Tuckey, labourer. Wesleyan Methodist. John Radford of Salisbury, Wesleyan minister. (WRO D1/9/2/1)

**1344** (30 May 1832). Swallowfield. A house now in the occupation of Henry Clark. [*Baptist★*]. Henry Clark, John Carter, Edward Webb. [*Pencilled at foot*] 'Mr Saffery not pd.' (WRO D1/9/2/1)

**1345** 27 June 1832 (30 June 1832). Kingston Deverill. A chapel. [*Wesleyan Methodist*: Hall 241]. Thomas Brothwood of Warminster. (WRO D1/9/2/1)

**1346** 29 Aug. 1832 (29 Oct. 1832). Homington. A house now in the holding and occupancy of William Case. [*Primitive Methodist*: WRO 1150/286]. Joseph Preston of Salisbury. (WRO D1/9/2/1)

**1347** 6 Sept. 1832 (10 Sept. 1832). Stratton St Margaret. The barn and premises now occupied by William Large. William Large, William Kirby, Richard Fisher. (WRO D1/9/2/1)

**1348** 6 Oct. 1832 (6 Oct. 1832). Cobb's Mill in Great Wishford. A house in the occupation of Benjamin Shurgold. [*Primitive Methodist*: WRO 1150/286]. Joseph Preston of Salisbury. (WRO D1/9/2/1)

**1349** 26 Oct. 1832 (3 Nov. 1832). Kingston Deverill. A dwellinghouse and premises now in the holding and occupation of George Garrett. George Garrett of Kingston Deverill, Richard Davies, George Ridgley. (WRO D1/9/2/1)

**1350** 27 Oct. 1832 (7 Nov. 1832). Pewsey. A detached building belonging to me. Thomas Godden of Pewsey. [*At foot*] 'paid 2/6 RG, pd carter 4d.' (WRO D1/9/2/1)

**1351** 31 Oct. 1832 (1 Nov. 1832). Crockerton [*in Longbridge Deverill*]. A chapel. [*Wesleyan Methodist*: Hall 241]. Thomas Brothwood of Warminster. (WRO D1/9/2/1)

**1352**  31 Oct. 1832 (1 Nov. 1832). Heytesbury. A house occupied by Henry Stepney. [*Wesleyan Methodist*: Hall 241]. Thomas Brothwood of Warminster. (WRO D1/9/2/1)

**1353**  6 Nov. 1832 (16 Jan. 1833). Bagshot in Shalbourne. The house and premises now in the holding and occupation of John Wells. [*Primitive Methodist*: see **1243**]. John Wells of Bagshot, John Phelps, John Ride. (WRO D1/9/2/1)

**1354**  20 Nov. 1832 (20 Dec. 1832). Quidhampton [*in Fugglestone St Peter*]. A house now in the holding and occupance of John Francis. [*Primitive Methodist*: WRO 1150/286]. Joseph Preston of Salisbury. (WRO D1/9/2/1)

**1355**  21 Dec. 1832 (4 April 1833). Poulton. A building in the occupation of James Byrne. Independent. William Adams, James Byrne, Thomas Herbert. (WRO D1/9/2/1)

**1356**  26 Dec. 1832 (27 Dec. 1832). Quidhampton in Fugglestone St Peter. A building in the possession or occupation of John Chown. Baptist. John Freeman, James Butler. (WRO D1/9/2/1)

**1357**  31 Dec. 1832 (9 Feb. 1833). Calne. A house and premises now in the holding and occupation of Thomas Embrey. [*Primitive Methodist*: Tonks 88]. James Baker of Chippenham, Samuel West, Samuel Turner. [*Endorsed*] 'Licences forms – For Mr Preston to take to the Bishop's office, For S. West, and to bring them with him to Bath when he comes to the Missionary Meeting there.' (WRO D1/9/2/1)

**1358**  31 Dec. 1832 (9 Feb. 1833). Heddington. A house and premises now in the holding and occupation of David Dandefield. [*Primitive Methodist*: Tonks 88]. Samuel West of Brinkworth, James Baker. (WRO D1/9/2/1)

**1359**  31 Dec. 1832 (9 Feb. 1833). Highworth. The house and premises now in the holding and occupation of Asher Gibbs. [*Primitive Methodist*: Tonks 88]. Asher Gibbs of Highworth, Samuel Gibbs, Samuel West. (WRO D1/9/2/1)

**1360**  31 Dec. 1832 (9 Feb. 1833). Hook in Lydiard Tregoze. A chapel and premises now in the holding and occupation of William Ind. [*Primitive Methodist*: Tonks 88]. William Ind of Wootton Bassett, Samuel West, Thomas Ferriss. (WRO D1/9/2/1)

**1361**  31 Dec. 1832 (9 Feb. 1833). Wroughton. The house and premises now in the holding and occupation of Frederick Newport. [*Primitive Methodist*:

Tonks 88]. Frederick Newport of Wroughton, Samuel West, Jonas Clark. (WRO D1/9/2/1)

**1362**   5 Jan. 1833 (5 Jan. 1833). Fisherton Anger. A building in Church Street. Wesleyan Methodist. John Radford of Salisbury, Wesleyan minister. (WRO D1/9/2/1)

**1363**   13 Jan. 1833 (9 Feb. 1833). Purton. The house and premises now in the holding and occupation of William Maul. [*Primitive Methodist*: Tonks 88]. William Maul of Purton, Samuel West, Jonas Clark, Charles Robins. (WRO D1/9/2/1)

**1364**   26 Jan. 1833 (29 Jan. 1833). East Knoyle *or* West Knoyle. A schoolroom occupied by William Harris, schoolmaster. Wesleyan Methodist. James Catts of Shaftesbury, Wesleyan minister. (WRO D1/9/2/1)

**1365**   1 Feb. 1833 (2 Feb. 1833). Woodford. A house now in the holding and occupation of George Smith. [*Primitive Methodist*: WRO 1150/286]. Joseph Preston of Salisbury, George Smith. (WRO D1/9/2/1)

**1366**   20 Feb. 1833 (25 Feb. 1833). Shaw in Lydiard Millicent. A building and premises now in the occupation of Benjamin Hollick. The mark of Benjamin Hollick of Shaw, H.E. Freeman of Swindon, farmer. (WRO D1/9/2/1)

**1367**   30 March 1833 (19 April 1833). 'Charlton.' A building in the possession or occupation of George Davis. The mark of George Davis, William White, James William Shellan?. (WRO D1/9/2/1)

**1368**   5 April 1833 (13 April 1833). Zeals in Mere. A dwellinghouse and premises now in the holding and occupation of William Smart. [*Primitive Methodist*?: see **1195**]. Richard Davies of Enmore Green in Motcombe, Dorset, George Cox, Benjamin Parfett. (WRO D1/9/2/1)

**1369**   8 April 1833 (10 April 1833). Chippenham. A house and premises now in the holding and occupation of John Boulton. [*Primitive Methodist*: Tonks 88]. James Baker of Chippenham, John Coxhead, Samuel West. (WRO D1/9/2/1)

**1370**   8 April 1833 (9 April 1833). Colerne. A room on my premises and now in my own occupation. John James of Colerne. (WRO D1/9/2/1)

**1371**   8 April 1833 (10 April 1833). Preston in Lyneham. A house and premises now in the holding and occupation of James Vines. [*Primitive Methodist*: Tonks 88]. Samuel West of Brinkworth, James Baker, John Coxhead. [*Endorsed*] 'House Licences to be signed at the Bishop's office.' (WRO D1/9/2/1)

**1372** 22 April 1833 (24 April 1833). Bishopstone [*north Wiltshire?*: see **1181**]. A house and premises now occupied by Samuel Ford senior. [*Baptist*: see **1181**]. Henry Tayler, the mark of William Norriss, the mark of Thomas Hancock, the mark of Robert Lambourn. (WRO D1/9/2/1)

**1373** 19 June 1833 (27 July 1833). Donhead St Andrew. A dwellinghouse occupied by Thomas Ford. Methodist. George Lush, Thomas Ford, George Fricker, George Lush senior. (WRO D1/9/2/1)

**1374** 7 July 1833 (16 July 1833). Hankerton. The dwellinghouse of Solomon Painter. The mark of Solomon Painter, the mark of Thomas Painter, the mark of Francis Wallis, the mark of John Painter, John Baker, William Wait, William Beale, James Wait, Thomas Pool, John Gladwin. (WRO D1/9/2/1)

**1375** 15 July 1833 (16 July 1833). East Hatch in Tisbury. The house of John Ford. Particular Baptist. The mark of John Ford of East Hatch, John Webb, Baptist minister, Edward Bracher, William James, Stephen Mullery. (WRO D1/9/2/1)

**1376** 9 Aug. 1833 (10 Aug. 1833). Allington [*near Salisbury*: see **1626**]. A dwellinghouse and premises. [*Primitive Methodist*: see **1506**]. The mark of James Coleman of Allington, John Young. (WRO D1/9/2/1)

**1377** 10 Aug. 1833 (31 Oct. 1833). Imber. A chapel or meeting house lately erected on part of a garden late Thomas Hayter's. Baptist. Edward Scammell, William Hayter, John Grant, Thomas Hayter, housekeepers in Imber. (WRO D1/9/2/1)

**1378** 11 Aug. 1833 (12 Aug. 1833). Aldbourne. A house and premises now occupied by Thomas Barrett junior. [*Baptist*: VCH 12, 85]. Stephen Gould, William Palmer, Joseph Orchard, Thomas Barrett. (WRO D1/9/2/1)

**1379** 21 Aug. 1833 (21 Aug. 1833). Marlborough. A house, warehouse, shops and premises with the appurtenances in the Marsh, St Mary's parish, now in the holding and occupation of Joseph Phelps. [*Primitive Methodist*: WRO 1150/286]. Joseph Preston of St Thomas's parish, Salisbury. (WRO D1/9/2/1)

**1380** 23 Sept. 1833 (23 Sept. 1833). Wilton. A building or chapel and premises in West Street, now in the holding and occupation of William Larkam. [*Primitive Methodist*: WRO 1150/286]. Joseph Preston of St Edmund's parish, Salisbury. (WRO D1/9/2/1)

**1381** 30 Sept. 1833 (18 Oct. 1833). Sherston. A building in the occupation of William Palmer. William Palmer junior, John Prior, Roger Gantlett. [*Pencilled at foot*] 'Mr Martin, New Sarum House.' (WRO D1/9/2/1)

**1382**   3 Oct. 1833 (12 Oct. 1833). Great Cheverell. A building in the possession or occupation of James Potter senior of Great Cheverell, bellfounder, William Sawyer of Great Cheverell, millwright, James Potter junior of Great Cheverell, agriculturist, William Price of Great Cheverell, miller, John Drover of Devizes, draper, Daniel Pomroy of Market Lavington, shoemaker, James Staples of Urchfont, grocer, William Dunford of Great Cheverell, brickmaker. [*Independent*: Oliver 58]. Mark Sawyer, James Potter. (WRO D1/9/2/1)

**1383**   3 Oct. 1833 (5 Oct. 1833). South Marston in Highworth. A dwelling-house and premises now in the occupation of John Kean. The mark of John Kean of South Marston, William Coller. (WRO D1/9/2/1)

**1384**   10 Oct. 1833 (18 Oct. 1833). 'Wraxall' (*Lower* [*deleted*] *Wraxall*). A building occupied by William Blake. Independent. John Wilkins, James G. Jones, S. Daniel, James Evuns. (WRO D1/9/2/1)

**1385**   17 Oct. 1833 (25 Oct. 1833). Keevil. A newly erected chapel. Wesleyan Methodist. William Sharpe of Melksham. [*Endorsed*] 'Revd J. Akerman, Wesleyan Chapel, Salisbury.' (WRO D1/9/2/1)

**1386**   29 Oct. 1833 (31 Oct. 1833). Shaw in Lydiard Millicent [*but dated from Swindon*]. The house of John Newth. John Newth, J.B. Moe . . . [*illegible*]. (WRO D1/9/2/1)

**1387**   29 Oct. 1833 (31 Oct. 1833). Zeals in Mere. A building intended as a chapel. Independent. James Little, Independent minister, Mere. (WRO D1/9/2/1)

**1388**   2 Nov. 1833 (21 Nov. 1833). Bishopstone [*north Wiltshire*: VCH 12, 11]. A chapel and premises now in the holding and occupation of a society of people belonging to the Primitive Methodist Connexion. Primitive Methodist. John Smith of Bishopstone, William Wiltshire, John Ride. (WRO D1/9/2/1)

**1389**   4 Nov. 1833 (12 Nov. 1833). Warminster Common in Warminster. A room and premises now in the holding and occupation of James Bigwood and George Parker. [*Baptist?*: see **748, 1377**]. William Turner of The Butts in Frome Selwood, Som., George Parker, Edward Lampard Scammell. (WRO D1/9/2/1)

**1390**   18 Nov. 1833 (23 Nov. 1833). Stanton St Quinton. The dwellinghouse and premises of Joseph Downham. Independent. James Henly, Thomas Simkins, the mark of James Smith, John To. .y [*illegible*], William Mortemor, Richard Smith, housekeepers in Stanton St Quinton. [*Endorsed*] 'To the Revd Mr. Williams, Minister of Endless St Chapel, Salisbury, paid.' (WRO D1/9/2/1)

**1391** 12 Dec. 1833 (12 Dec. 1833). Woodfalls Hill in Downton. A chapel now in the holding and occupation of the Society of Primitive Methodist, at Woodfalls Hill. Primitive Methodist. Joseph Preston of St Edmund's parish, Salisbury. (WRO D1/9/2/1)

**1392** 8 Jan. 1834 (10 Jan. 1834). Winterbourne Gunner. A dwellinghouse now in the holding and occupation of Job Sutton. Wesleyan Methodist. Thomas Ashton of Salisbury, Wesleyan minister. (WRO D1/9/2/1)

**1393** 24 Jan. 1834 (28 Jan. 1834). Cadley in Collingbourne Ducis. A dwellinghouse and premises now in the holding and occupation of Joseph Allen, labourer. John Rich of West Shefford, Berks. (WRO D1/9/2/1)

**1394** 27 Jan. 1834 (28 Jan. 1834). Great Bedwyn. A building now in the possession of William May, farmer, of Great Bedwyn. Wesleyan Methodist. William Pollard of Hungerford, Berks., Wesleyan Methodist minister. (WRO D1/9/2/1)

**1395** 27 Jan. 1834 (28 Jan. 1834). Rudge in Froxfield. A dwellinghouse now in the occupation of William Hobbs, labourer. Wesleyan Methodist. William Pollard of Hungerford, Berks., Wesleyan Methodist minister. [*Endorsed*] 'The Rev. Thos. Ashton, Wesleyan Minister, Salisbury, Paid,' (WRO D1/9/2/1)

**1396** 1 March 1834 (4 March 1834). Damerham. A building in possession or occupation of Mary Lanham. [*Independent*: see **1413**]. The mark of Mary Lanham, George Masters, William Baily. (WRO D1/9/2/1)

**1397** 3 March 1834 (10 March 1834). Box. A chapel in our possession. Catharine Rowe, Thomas Noble, of Box. (WRO D1/9/2/1)

**1398** 10 March 1834 (12 March 1834). Damerham. A new building on the premises of Stephen Percey. Stephen Percy, Edmund Sainsbury, William Rhodes, residing in Damerham. (WRO D1/9/2/1)

**1399** 29 March 1834 (7 April 1834). Baydon. A house and premises now in the holding and occupation of William Smith. George Price of West Shefford, [*Berks.*], William Smith. (WRO D1/9/2/1)

**1400** 5 April 1834 (9 April 1834). Derry Hill in Pewsham [*extra-parochial place*]. A dwellinghouse and premises now in the holding and occupation of Henry Cole. Henry Cole of Pewsham, the mark of John Cole, Vincent Sadler, Charles Robbins. (WRO D1/9/2/1)

**1401** 7 April 1834 (9 April 1834). Haydon Wick in Rodbourne Cheney. A dwellinghouse and premises in the holding and occupation of myself. The mark of Sarah Jacobs of Haydon Wick. (WRO D1/9/2/1)

**1402** 17 April 1834 (22 April 1834). Ashton Keynes. A dwellinghouse and premises in my possession. [*Primitive Methodist?*: see **1403**]. Henry Curtis of Ashton Keynes. [*Identical format to* **1403**]. (WRO D1/9/2/1)

**1403** 17 April 1834 (22 April 1834). Berwick Bassett. A dwellinghouse and premises in the possession and holding of Stephen Coleman. [*Primitive Methodist*: see **1626**]. William Wigley of Wootton Bassett. [*Identical format to* **1402**]. (WRO D1/9/2/1)

**1404** 17 April 1834 (18 April 1834). Salisbury. A building in St Martin's parish in the occupation of Richard Phillips. Richard Phillips, Thomas Elliott, Sidney Smith. (WRO D1/9/2/1)

**1405** 26 April 1834 (21 April 1834 [*sic*]). Chippenham. A dwellinghouse and premises now in the holding and occupation of Sarah Comly. [*Primitive Methodist*: see **1357**]. Sarah Comly of Chippenham. [*At foot*] 'Please direct for S. Turner P.M.T., Care of John Smith, Butts, Chippenham.' (WRO D1/9/2/1)

**1406** 28 April 1834 (29 April 1834). Maiden Bradley. A house and premises now in the holding and occupation of Samuel Daley. [*Baptist*: see **1389**]. William Turner of the Butts in Frome Selwood (Som.), the mark of Samuel Daly, Henry Bell. (WRO D1/9/2/1)

**1407** 17 May 1834 (17 May 1834). Townsend in Martin. A chapel and premises now in the holding and occupation of the Society of Primitive Methodists. Primitive Methodist. Joseph Preston of St Edmund's parish, Salisbury. (WRO D1/9/2/1)

**1408** 28 June 1834 (30 June 1834). Marlborough. A room in the Marsh in St Mary's parish, in the occupation of James Jennings, fruiterer. William White, James Jennings, John Maule, Thomas Liddale, James Looker. Jeremiah Pyke. (WRO D1/9/2/1)

**1409** 4 July 1834 (4 July 1834). Great Somerford. A house and premises now in the possession of John Porter, William Barnes and John Greeneway. Independent. Charles Williams of Salisbury, dissenting minister. (WRO D1/9/2/1)

**1410** 4 July 1834 (4 July 1834). Littleton Pannell in West Lavington. A chapel. Independent. Charles Williams of Salisbury, dissenting minister. (WRO D1/9/2/1)

**1411** 10 July 1834 (15 July 1834). Chippenham. A room now in the occupation of Mr Daniel Cheater in River Street. Baptist. Thomas Cawcutt, George Long, Henry Hunt, John Taylor, William Tayler, Robert Dowsall, Richard S Banks. (WRO D1/9/2/1)

**1412** 15 July 1834 (15 Aug. 1834). West Grimstead. A house and premises now in the holding and occupation of Henry Cook. [*Primitive Methodist*: see **1430**]. George Appleby of St Edmund's parish, Salisbury. (WRO D1/9/2/1)

**1413** (18 July 1834). Damerham. A building for public worship is erected. Independent. George Masters, John Main, William Bailey. [*Pencilled at foot*] 'To be attended to tonight, pd 2/6 to be called for.' (WRO D1/9/2/1)

**1414** 2 Aug. 1834 (2 Aug. 1834). Salisbury. A house in St Edmund's parish now in my occupation. 'The New Church signified by the New Jerusalem in the Revelations.' James Vile of St Edmund's parish, Salisbury. (WRO D1/9/2/1)

**1415** 9 Sept. 1834 (13 Sept. 1834). Froxfield. A dwellinghouse now in the occupation of Charles Akerman. Wesleyan Methodist. William Pollard of Hungerford, Berks., Wesleyan preacher. (WRO D1/9/2/1)

**1416** 9 Sept. 1834 (13 Sept. 1834). Pewsey. A newly erected building called the Wesleyan chapel. Wesleyan Methodist. William Pollard of Hungerford, Berks., Wesleyan preacher. [*Endorsed*] 'Rev. Jas. Akerman, Wesleyan Minister, Salisbury.' (WRO D1/9/2/1)

**1417** 17 Sept. 1834 (18 Sept. 1834). Chippenham. A chapel, house and premises now in the holding and occupation of John Garbutt and John Blackmore. Primitive Methodist. John Garbutt, John Blackmore, of Chippenham. [*At head*] 'NB Please to register it immediately and send the certificate back has soon as possible. Direct John Garbut, P.M. [*Primitive Methodist*] preacher, Back Lane, Chippenham. J. Garbutt.' (WRO D1/9/2/1)

**1418** 15 Oct. 1834 (11 Dec. 1834). Kington Langley in Kington St Michael. A house in the occupation of James Piniger. [*Independent*: see **1410**]. Charles Williams of Salisbury, dissenting minister. (WRO D1/9/2/1)

**1419** 12 Nov. 1834 (17 Nov. 1834). Shrewton. The meeting house newly erected. Baptist. Joseph Weare, Charles Blewden, James Grant, Thomas Killow. (WRO D1/9/2/1)

**1420** 6 Dec. 1834 (11 Dec. 1834). Compton Bassett. A dwellinghouse and premises now in the holding and occupation of Shadrack Ashe. Shadrack Ashe of Compton Bassett. (WRO D1/9/2/1)

**1421** 22 Dec. 1834 (23 Dec. 1834). Donhead St Andrew. An unoccupied room, the property of George Fricker. Methodist. George Lush, dissenting minister, Stephen Best, George Fricker. (WRO D1/9/2/1)

**1422** 2 Jan. 1836 [*recte 1835?*] (4 Jan. 1835). Wanborough. A house and premises now in the holding and occupation of John Shun. John Shun of Wanborough. (WRO D1/9/2/1)

**1423**   10 Feb. 1835 (12 Feb. 1835). Grittenham in Brinkworth. A building and premises now in the holding and occupation of Edward Hunt. Edward Hunt of Grittenham. (WRO D1/9/2/1)

**1424**   10 Feb. 1835 (12 Feb. 1835). Wanborough. A building and premises now in the holding and occupation of William Bourton. William Bourton of Wanborough. (WRO D1/9/2/1)

**1425**   10 Feb. 1835 (12 Feb. 1835). Wanborough. A building and premises now in the holding and occupation of John Russell. John Russell of Wanborough. (WRO D1/9/2/1)

**1426**   11 Feb. 1835 (20 Feb. 1835). Easton. A dwellinghouse now in the occupation of Robert Rew [*or Kew?*]. Wesleyan Methodist. William Pollard of Hungerford, Berks., Wesleyan preacher. (WRO D1/9/2/1)

**1427**   27 Feb. 1835 (28 Feb. 1835). Poole Keynes. A dwellinghouse and premises now in the holding and occupation of Charles Uzzell. [*Primitive Methodist*: see **1626**]. William Wigley of Wootton Bassett. (WRO D1/9/2/1)

**1428**   27 Feb. 1835 (28 Feb. 1835). Poulton. A dwellinghouse and premises now in the holding and occupation of Moses Wheeler. [*Primitive Methodist*: see **1626**]. William Wigley of Wootton Bassett. (WRO D1/9/2/1)

**1429**   28 Feb. 1835 (2 March 1835). Christian Malford. A building and premises now in the holding and occupation of William Compton. William Compton of Christian Malford Common. (WRO D1/9/2/1)

**1430**   7 March 1835 (7 March 1835). Fisherton Anger. A chapel and premises now in the holding and occupation of the Primitive Methodists. Primitive Methodist. George Appleby of St Edmund's parish, Salisbury. (WRO D1/9/2/1)

**1431**   1 April 1835 (6 April 1835). Ogbourne St Andrew. A dwellinghouse now in the occupation of Isaac Pryer. Wesleyan Methodist. William Pollard of Hungerford, Wesleyan minister. (WRO D1/9/2/1)

**1432**   8 April 1835 (8 April 1835). Salisbury. A room in High Street. Wesleyan Methodist. James Akerman of Salisbury, Wesleyan minister. (WRO D1/9/2/1)

**1433**   28 April 1835 (2 May 1835). Chapmanslade in Westbury. The building known as the Independent Chapel. Independent. James Angeon, pastor,

William Withey, William Grant, George Withey, Nathaniel Hains, Thomas Grant, residing in Chapmanslade. (WRO D1/9/2/1)

**1434**   6 May 1835 (15 May 1835). Fugglestone St Peter. Certain premises, the property of Mr William Smith. [*Baptist*: see **1356**]. James Butler of Salisbury, bookseller. (WRO D1/9/2/1)

**1435**   18 May 1835 (19 May 1835). Chute. An inhabited tenement and dwellinghouse in the possession and occupation of Henry Hopgood. Particular Baptist. John Boulton Walcot, Baptist minister, Ludgershall. (WRO D1/9/2/1)

**1436**   (6 June 1835). Kington St Michael. A building called Bethesda in the possession of Benjamin Rees, George Tanner and others. Independent. Charles Williams of Endless Street, Salisbury. (WRO D1/9/2/1)

**1437**   2 July 1835 (4 July 1835). Devizes. A building in St Mary's parish now used as a charity school. [*Congregational*: VCH 10, 298]. Robert Waylin, George Elgar Sloper, Samuel Whitchurch, Valentine Leach. (WRO D1/9/2/1)

**1438**   17 Sept. 1835 (17 Sept. 1835). Kington Langley in Kington St Michael. A newly erected building or chapel in the occupation of William Tanner, Benjamin Pegler and others. Independent. Benjamin Rees of Chippenham, Independent minister. (WRO D1/9/2/1)

**1439**   19 Sept. 1835 (24 Sept. 1835). Coate in Bishops Cannings. A house and premises now in my holding and occupation. John Willis of Coate. (WRO D1/9/2/1)

**1440**   3 Oct. 1835 (6 Oct. 1835). Cherhill. A chapel now in my possession. [*Primitive Methodist*: Blackford 252]. John Jordan of Cherhill. (WRO D1/9/2/1)

**1441**   13 Nov. 1835 (18 Nov. 1835). Rowde. A dwellinghouse and premises now in my holding and occupation. Thomas Dyke of Rowde. (WRO D1/9/2/1)

**1442**   1 Dec. 1835 (8 Dec. 1835). Sherston. A building in the possession or occupation of Samuel Stubbings, Roger Gantlett and others. Samuel Stubbings, Roger Gantlett, Stephen Gantlett. (WRO D1/9/2/1)

**1443**   9 Dec. 1835 (10 Dec. 1835). Salisbury. A building called the Masonic Hall in Crane Street now in the holding and occupation of Mr Truman and others. Jasper Peck of Salisbury. (WRO D1/9/2/1)

**1444**   5 Jan. 1836. Holt in Bradford on Avon. A room in the dwellinghouse lately in the occupation of Sarah Davis and now in my occupation. John Edward Davis. (WRO A1/250)

**1445** 5 Jan. 1836. Melksham. The house or building lately in the occupation of James Watson and now in my occupation in Watson's barton. [*Catholic Apostolic*: VCH 7, 163]. William Keene. (WRO A1/250)

**1446** 9 Jan. 1836 (11 Jan. 1836). Chisledon. A chapel and premises now in the holding and occupation of William Webb and others. Primitive Methodist. William Webb of Chisledon. [*At foot*] 'Direct for Mr Jno Garbutt, Wootton Bassett, P.M. [*Primitive Methodist*] preacher, Wilts.' (WRO D1/9/2/1)

**1447** 18 Jan. 1836 (19 Jan. 1836). Etchilhampton. A building in the possession or occupation of William Deighton. William Deighton, James Wheeler, Job Cox, Noah Rudman. [*At foot*] 'To E. Davies Esqr. Sir, Please to send the licence for the above place to T. Carter, Sidmouth St. Devizes.' (WRO D1/9/2/1)

**1448** 23 Jan. 1836 (25 Jan. 1836). Winsley in Bradford on Avon. A Wesleyan chapel belonging to Joseph Rawling[s] and others in trust. Wesleyan Methodist. John Knapp of Bradford. (WRO D1/9/2/1)

**1449** 25 Jan. 1836 (26 Jan. 1836). Thickwood in Colerne. A house and premises now in the holding and occupation of Henry Woodward. Henry Woodward of Thickwood. [*At foot*] 'Address, Henry Woodward, Thickwood, Near Collorn Near Ford, Wilts.' (WRO D1/9/2/1)

**1450** 8 Feb. 1836 (10 Feb. 1836). Biddestone St Nicholas. A dwellinghouse and premises now in the holding and occupation of William Hichens. Primitive Methodist. William Hichens of Biddestone. [*At foot*] 'Address, Samuel Wilshaw, Primitive Methodist Minister, Chippenham, Wilts.' (WRO D1/9/2/1)

**1451** 10 Feb. 1836 (23 Feb. 1836). Lyneham. A building in the possession or occupation of William Ingram. Baptist. William Engram, William Hewlet, William Hillier, John Martimore, Thomas Barrett, Abraham Simkins, William Simkins, Isaac Clifford, Jacob Hervey. (WRO D1/9/2/1)

**1452** 1 March 1836 (2 March 1836). Salisbury. Two rooms in the George Yard in St Thomas's parish. New Jerusalem Church. David Thomas Dyke of Wilton. (WRO D1/9/2/1)

**1453** 3 March 1836 (22 March 1836). Westrop in Highworth. A dwellinghouse now in the occupation of Thomas Titchener. [*Independent*: see **1129**]. Thomas Titchener, Samuel Brown, Samuel Flaister, Henry J. Larter. [*Endorsed*] 'Rev H. Larter, Highworth, Wilts.' (WRO D1/9/2/1)

**1454** 4 March 1836 (5 March 1836). Broad Chalke. A building in the occupation of Maisie Barnett and others. George Morris, Thomas Barnett, Thomas Burrough, Robert Barrett. (WRO D1/9/2/1)

**1455** 7 March 1836 (7 March 1836). Luckington. Two rooms in the occupation of Joseph Alexander. John Prior. (WRO D1/9/2/1)

**1456** 16 March 1836 (22 March 1836). Calne. A Wesleyan chapel in 'Mashlane,' the property of John Clark. Wesleyan Methodist. William Baker of Melksham, minister of the gospel. (WRO D1/9/2/1)

**1457** 2 May 1836 (4 May 1836). Warminster. A house at the junction of Pound Street and West End. John Scatter. (WRO D1/9/2/1)

**1458** 4 May 1836 (6 May 1836). Coombe Bissett. A cottage in the occupation of John Turner. Baptist. Philip John Saffery of Bodenham, Baptist minister. (WRO D1/9/2/1)

**1459** 9 July 1836 (14 July 1836). Crockerton in Longbridge Deverill. A house newly erected in Clay Street. John Scatter. (WRO D1/9/2/1)

**1460** 10 Sept. 1836 (13 Sept. 1836). Highworth Town tithing in Highworth. A dwellinghouse and premises now in the holding and occupation of William Godwin. Primitive Methodist. William Godwin of Highworth Town tithing. [*At foot*] 'Please to direct to Mr Jno Garbutt, P.M. [*Primitive Methodist*] preacher, Brinkworth, Wilts.' (WRO D1/9/2/1)

**1461** 11 Sept. 1836 (13 Sept. 1836). Littleton ?Pannell [*in West Lavington*]. A dwellinghouse and premises. Baptist. The mark of Thomas Davis of Littleton. [*Pencilled at foot*] 'Sep 13 1836 Mr Kellow Shrewton pd.' (WRO D1/9/2/1)

**1462** 16 Sept. 1836 (19 Sept. 1836). Castle Combe. My house and premises now in my holding and occupation. [*Primitive Methodist*: see **1450**]. John Baker of Castle Combe. [*Pencilled at foot*] 'S Wilshaw, Preachers house, Chippenham.' (WRO D1/9/2/1)

**1463** 16 Sept. 1836 (20 Sept. 1836). Edington. My house and premises now in the holding and occupation of myself. Thomas Coldrake of Edington. [*Pencilled at foot*] 'T Geach, Mr Lyne, Market Lavington.' (WRO D1/9/2/1)

**1464** 10 Oct. 1836 (14 Oct. 1836). Alton ?Barnes (*Great Alton*). A dwellinghouse now occupied by John Gale, labourer. Wesleyan Methodist. John Wilson of Devizes, Wesleyan minister. [*Endorsed*] 'Rev Wm. Jewitt, Wesleyan minister, Salisbury.' (WRO D1/9/2/1)

**1465** 17 Oct. 1836 (20 Oct. 1836). Longbridge Deverill. A room and premises now in the holding and occupation of Stephen Snelgrove of Longbridge Deverill. John Charlton of Longbridge Deverill, John Flower. (WRO D1/9/2/1)

**1466** 17 Oct. 1836 (20 Oct. 1836). Ramsbury. A house belonging to Mr John

Langfield. [*Baptist?*: see **1378**; Oliver 16]. C. Baker, Joseph Sheppard, James Kelson, John Jerun, the mark of Joseph Orchard, the mark of Stephen Gould, the mark of Thomas Barrett, the mark of Thomas Larance. (WRO D1/9/2/1)

**1467**   17 Oct. 1836 (20 Oct. 1836). Sherrington. A house and premises now in the holding and occupation of William Trowbridge of Sherrington. John Flower of Longbridge Deverill, William White. (WRO D1/9/2/1)

**1468**   17 Oct. 1836 (20 Oct. 1836). Warminster. A room and premises at Portway now in the holding and occupation of Mr William Long of Warminster. John Flower of Longbridge Deverill, Samuel West. (WRO D1/9/2/1)

**1469**   18 Oct. 1836 (25 Oct. 1836). Trowbridge. A room over a stable and coachhouse in the occupation of James Lucas in Wicker Hill. [*Baptist*: Doel 154]. Zechariah Dyer of Trowbridge, machine maker. (WRO D1/9/2/1)

**1470**   24 Oct. 1836 (25 Oct. 1836). Chute. An inhabited tenement occupied by Thomas Fowler. Particular Baptist. The mark of Thomas Fowler, C? B. Walcot of Ludgershall, Baptist minister. (WRO D1/9/2/1)

**1471**   2 Nov. 1836 (2 Nov. 1836). Hindon. A room and premises now in the holding and occupation of Walter Bartley for the Primitive Methodists. Primitive Methodist. Charles Day of Hindon. (WRO D1/9/2/1)

**1472**   5 Nov. 1836 (11 Nov. 1836). Chittoe [*in Bishops Cannings*]. The house and premises now in the holding and occupation of Charles Tylee. [*Primitive Methodist*: see **1450**]. Charles Tylee. [*At foot*] 'Your signature to the above as soon as possible will much oblige, your humble servant S. Wilshaw. Address S. Wilshaw, Chapel House, Chippenham, Wilts.' (WRO D1/9/2/1)

**1473**   18 Nov. 1836 (19 Nov. 1836). Salisbury. A house and premises in St Edmund's parish now in the holding and occupation of Joseph Sanger. [*Wesleyan Methodist*: see **1566**]. Joseph Sanger of Fisherton Anger. (WRO D1/9/2/1)

**1474**   23 Nov. 1836 (28 Nov. 1836). Elcombe in Wroughton. A house and premises now in the holding and occupation of Robert Hiles. The mark of Robert Hiles. (WRO D1/9/2/1)

**1475**   14 Dec. 1836 (12 Jan. 1837). Rudge in Froxfield. A dwellinghouse now in the occupation of Charles Edwards. Wesleyan Methodist. John Coates of Hungerford, Wesleyan minister. (WRO D1/9/2/1)

**1476**   17 Dec. 1836 (21 Dec. 1836). West Lavington. A preaching room and premises now in the holding and occupation of Daniel Oatley. Daniel Oatley of West Lavington. [*At foot*] 'By a very quick return of the licence will oblige, your humble st. T. Geach.' [*Endorsed*] 'Direct T. Geach, care of Mr Pinchens, White Street, M. Lavington.' (WRO D1/9/2/1)

**1477**   23 Dec. 1836 (27 Dec. 1836). Poulton. A house. Independent. John Cullen of Fairford, Independent minister. (WRO D1/9/2/1)

**1478**   31 Dec. 1836 (4 Jan. 1837). Cleverton in Lea and Cleverton. A chapel and premises in the possession, holding and occupation of Francis Day. [*Primitive Methodist*: see **1340**]. Francis Day of Cleverton. [*Identical format to* **1479, 1480**]. (WRO D1/9/2/1)

**1479**   31 Dec. 1836 (4 Jan. 1837). Purton. The house and premises now in the holding and occupation of William Ellison. [*Primitive Methodist?*: see **1478**]. William Ellison of Purton. [*Identical format to* **1478, 1480**]. (WRO D1/9/2/1)

**1480**   31 Dec. 1836 (4 Jan. 1837). Purton. The house and premises now in the holding and occupation of William Stealy. [*Primitive Methodist?*: see **1478**]. William Stealy of Purton. [*Identical format to* **1478, 1479**]. (WRO D1/9/2/1)

**1481**   10 Jan. 1837 (10 Jan. 1837). Warminster. A schoolroom belonging to the congregation of Independent dissenters assembling in Common Close, and situated in Common Close bounded on the east by the road and on the north by the chapel, to be used occasionally for worship. Independent. Robert Ashton, minister of the congregation. (WRO D1/9/2/1)

**1482**   19 Jan. 1837 (19 Jan. 1837). Salisbury. A dwelling and premises in Crane Street. James Compton of Fisherton Anger. (WRO D1/9/2/1)

**1483**   19 Jan. 1837 (19 Jan. 1837). Swallowcliffe. A dwellinghouse and premises now in the holding and occupation of Thomas Feltham. James Compton of Fisherton Anger. (WRO D1/9/2/1)

**1484**   27 Jan. 1837 (1 Feb. 1837). Leigh [*in Ashton Keynes*]. The house and premises now in the holding and occupation of Henry Curtus. Henry Cirtus. [*Endorsed*] 'Please direct for Mr Henry Elison, Leigh, Near Cricklade, Wilts.' (WRO D1/9/2/1)

**1485**   29 March 1837 (30 March 1837). Devizes. A building in New Park Street in St Mary's parish, in the occupation of Sarah Wyatt, to be used after the 30th March. Baptist. George Wessley, Baptist minister, Thomas Dangerfield, S. Wyatt, David Sinclair, inhabitants of Devizes. (WRO D1/9/2/1)

**1486**   1 April 1837 (10 April 1837). Ogbourne St George. A dwellinghouse belonging to me. Joseph Phelps of Marlborough. (WRO D1/9/2/1)

**1487**   23 May 1837 (25 May 1837). Bishops Cannings. A building in the possession or occupation of Thomas Bailey. Thomas Bailey, William Rose,

John Minty, William Offer, John Wilshire, James Merett. [*At foot*] 'Please to direct the licence to G. Randell, baker, New Park St. Devizes.' (WRO D1/9/2/1)

**1488** 3 June 1837 (6 June 1837). Etchilhampton. A dwellinghouse in the occupation of James Fishlock, to be used from 6th June 1837. Baptist. George Wessley, Thomas Fidler, Daniel Sims, James Fishlock, inhabitants of Etchilhampton. [*At foot*] 'PS Direct to George Wessley, Baptist Minister, Devizes.' (WRO D1/9/2/1)

**1489** 8 June 1837 (9 June 1837). Salisbury. A dwellinghouse in Greencroft Street in St Edmund's parish, in the possession of Thomas Smith. The mark of Thomas Smith of Salisbury, Frederick Tugwell. (WRO D1/9/2/1)

**1490** 30 June 1837. Melksham. The meeting house or chapel, vestry and premises near Old Broughton Lane called the Baptist chapel. Baptist. Joshua Russell, J.L. Phillips, John Moon, Thomas Allwood, John Giblett, inhabitant housekeepers in Melksham. (WRO A1/250)

**1491** 28 July 1837 (31 July 1837). Upavon. An inhabited tenement occupied by John Macklin, labourer, but purchased by William Smith on behalf of the Baptist church at Upavon, and intended to be converted into a meeting house for their use. Baptist. William Smith, deacon of the church, the mark of John Macklin, Stephen Offer of Netheravon, Baptist minister. (WRO D1/9/2/1)

**1492** 29 July 1837 (11 Aug. 1837). Melksham Town tithing. A building already licensed, but recently enlarged, called the Independent chapel. Independent. Alfred John Jupp of Melksham, John Cochrane. (WRO D1/9/2/1)

**1493** 7 Sept. 1837 (8 Sept. 1837). Salisbury. A building in Scots Lane. [*Independent*: HPCURCS 1–2]. Samuel Sleigh, J.C. Wheeler, John Toone, residing in Salisbury. (WRO D1/9/2/1)

**1494** 11 Sept. 1837 (11 Sept. 1837). Redlynch in Downton. A dwellinghouse and premises now in the holding and occupation of Jacob Everly. [*Primitive Methodist*: WRO 1150/286]. Henry Sharman of Fisherton Anger, Jacob Everly. (WRO D1/9/2/1)

**1495** 18 Sept. 1837 (27 Sept. 1837). Swallowcliffe. A premises now in the holding of John Burt of Swallowcliffe. James Compton of Fisherton Anger. (WRO D1/9/2/1)

**1496** 4 Oct. 1837 (18 Oct. 1837). Mere. A dwellinghouse now in the occupation of James Fry. Wesleyan Methodist. Henry Vyvyan Olver of Shaftesbury, Dorset, Wesleyan minister. (WRO D1/9/2/1)

**1497** 9 Oct. 1837 (18 Oct. 1837). Sutton Benger. A house in the occupation of John Pearce. John Pearce of Sutton Benger, yeoman, W. Vellis?, of Tytherton. [*Endorsed*] 'Mr John Cusse, grocer, Sarum.' (WRO D1/9/2/1)

**1498**  10 Oct. 1837 (10 Oct. 1837). Warminster. A dwellinghouse and premises now in the holding and occupation of Charles Day. [*Primitive Methodist*: WRO 1150/286]. Henry Sharman of Fisherton Anger. (WRO D1/9/2/1)

**1499**  19 Oct. 1837 (19 Oct. 1837). Hankerton. We have erected a building. [*Baptist*: Wiltshire Register 1827]. T. Martin, W. Walker, T. Sisum, J. Panter, J. Wigmore. [*At foot*] 'Sir, Please send the licence by return of coach and charge the same to the said Reynolds's probate. Yrs. H.G. Hanks, Oct. 19th 1837.' (WRO D1/9/2/1)

**1500**  5 Dec. 1837 (12 Dec. 1837). Fovant. A house and premises now in the holding and occupation of Solomon Goodfellow, Moses Goodfellow, Thomas Sanger and George Singleton. James Rumming of Hindon. (WRO D1/9/2/1)

**1501**  16 Dec. 1837 (18 Dec. 1837). West Lavington. A house and premises now in the holding and occupation of Daniel Oatley. Daniel Oatley of West Lavington. (WRO D1/9/2/1)

**1502**  Feb. 1838 (28 Feb. 1838). Limpley Stoke in Bradford on Avon. A house and premises now in the holding and occupation of Elizabeth Ford. William Walter of Freshford, Som., minister, William Head, Giles Ricketts, George Cable. (WRO D1/9/2/1)

**1503**  23 Feb. 1838 (28 Feb. 1838). Figheldean. A house, barn and premises now in the holding and occupation of Jacob Hulbert. [*Primitive Methodist*?: see **1506**]. George Wallis of Andover, Hants. [*Pencilled in margin*] 'Please to direct it to Mr Jacob Hulbert at Figheldean near Amesbury, Wiltshire.' (WRO D1/9/2/1)

**1504**  2 March 1838 (5 March 1838). Compton Bassett. A dwellinghouse and premises now in the holding and occupation of Thomas Tayler. Primitive Methodist. John Coxhead of Chippenham. [*Pencilled*] 'Revd Mr Coxhead, Primitive Methd. Pr'ing Ho. Casway, Chippenham.' (WRO D1/9/2/1)

**1505**  2 March 1838 (5 March 1838). Melksham. A dwellinghouse and premises now in the holding and occupation of Samuel Francklin, Samuel Wakeford and William Herns. [*Primitive Methodist*: see **1504**]. John Coxhead of Chippenham. (WRO D1/9/2/1)

**1506**  4 April 1838 (17 April 1838). Allington [*near Salisbury*: see **1626**]. A house and premises now in the holding and occupation of John Young. [*Primitive Methodist*: see **1626**]. George Wallis of Andover, Hants. (WRO D1/9/2/1)

**1507** 12 April 1838 (14 April 1838). Corton in Boyton. The Baptist chapel. Baptist. Thomas Hardick of Warminster. (WRO D1/9/2/1)

**1508** 21 May 1838 (22 May 1838). Burbage. A house and premises now in the holding and occupation of Henry Spackman. [*Primitive Methodist*: see **1506**]. George Wallis of Andover, Hants. [*Pencilled at head*] 'NB Please to direct Mr Henery Spackman, shoemaker, Burbage near Marlborough, Wilts.' (WRO D1/9/2/1)

**1509** 28 May 1838 (29 May 1838). Devizes. A building or chapel, called Salem Chapel, in New Park Street, St Mary's parish, to be used from June 24th. Baptist. George Wessley, minister, Thomas Dangerfield, Henry Ellen. (WRO D1/9/2/1)

**1510** 1 June 1838 (1 June 1838). Amesbury. A chapel. Wesleyan Methodist. Edward Usher of Salisbury, Wesleyan minister. (WRO D1/9/2/1)

**1511** 2 June 1838 (7 June 1838). Ashton Keynes. A house and premises now in the holding and occupation of William Saunders. [*Primitive Methodist*: see **1526**]. Joseph Preston of Brinkworth, John Maylard. (WRO D1/9/2/1)

**1512** 23 June 1838 (25 June 1838). Huish Hill in Wilcot. A house and premises now in the holding and occupation of Maria Penney. William Bell of Ogbourne St George. (WRO D1/9/2/1)

**1513** 23 June 1838 (25 June 1838). Marlborough. A house and premises in St Mary's parish now in the holding and occupation of James Whiteing. William Bell of Ogbourne St George. (WRO D1/9/2/1)

**1514** 23 June 1838 (25 June 1838). Savernake Park in Preshute [*recte extraparochial place*]. A house and premises now in the holding and occupation of Jane Stone. William Bell of Ogbourne St George. (WRO D1/9/2/1)

**1515** 11 July 1838 (11 July 1838). Chute Hatchett in Chute. A dwellinghouse and premises now in the holding and occupation of Anna Knight. Wesleyan Methodist. Edward Usher of Salisbury, Wesleyan minister. (WRO D1/9/2/1)

**1516** 18 Sept. 1838 (2 Oct. 1838). Bottlesford in Wilsford. An inhabited cottage occupied by William Hawkings. Baptist. The mark of William Hawkins, Stephen Offer of Enford, Baptist minister, John Batt of Bottlesford, carpenter. (WRO D1/9/2/1)

**1517** 2 Oct. 1838 (6 Oct. 1838). Southwick in North Bradley. A building in the possession or occupation of Job Bennett. Baptist. Absalom Bennett, William Hayward, John Bennett, Jonathan Syms, the mark of Joseph Baily?, William Wicks. [*Endorsed*] 'Mr John Bennett, Southwick, North Bradley, Trowbridge.' (WRO D1/9/2/1)

**1518** 5 Oct. 1838 (8 Oct. 1838). Poole Keynes. A house and premises now in the holding and occupation of William Reynolds. [*Primitive Methodist*: see **1526**]. Joseph Prenton [*recte Preston*] of Brinkworth, John Excell. (GRO GDR350)

**1519** 6 Oct. 1838 (8 Oct. 1838). Luckington. A house and premises now in the holding and occupation of William King. [*Primitive Methodist*: see **1526**]. Joseph Prenton [*recte Preston*] of Brinkworth, John Excell. (GRO GDR350)

**1520** 6 Oct. 1838 (8 Oct. 1838). Oaksey. A house and premises now in the holding and occupation of John Jefferis. [*Primitive Methodist*: see **1526**]. Joseph Prenton [*recte Preston*] of Brinkworth, John Excell. (GRO GDR350)

**1521** (18 Oct. 1838). Shrewton. The house of Charles Light. Baptist. Charles Light, John Feltham?, George Windsor, James Kellow. (WRO D1/9/2/1)

**1522** 31 Oct. 1838 (31 Oct. 1838). 'Noad Hill' in Downton. A dwellinghouse and premises now in the holding and occupation of James Shelly. [*Baptist*: see **1063**]. Samuel Wort of Redlynch in Downton. (WRO D1/9/2/1)

**1523** 3 Jan. 1839 (3 Jan. 1839). Great Wishford. A building in the possession of John Scamell. John Scamell, John Toone. (WRO D1/9/2/1)

**1524** 3 Jan. 1839 (5 Jan. 1839). Netheravon. A chapel and premises now in the holding and occupation of the Primitive Methodist connexion. Primitive Methodist. John Maylard of Allington. (WRO D1/9/2/1)

**1525** 9 Jan. 1839 (23 Jan. 1839). Bodenham in Downton. A building in the possession of Mrs Eliza Attwater. [*Baptist*: VCH 11,67]. Eliza Attwater, Maria Attwater. (WRO D1/9/2/1)

**1526** 27 Jan. 1839 (31 Jan. 1839). Highworth. A chapel and premises now in the holding and occupation of the Primitive Methodists. Primitive Methodist. Joseph Preston of Brinkworth, John Excel. (GRO GDR350)

**1527** 1 March 1839 (4 March 1839). Melksham. A room and premises now in the holding and occupation of Samuel Franklin, William Herns and John Woodbridge. [*Primitive Methodist*: see **1526**]. John Coxhead of Chippenham, Joseph Preston. (WRO D1/9/2/1)

**1528** 8 March 1839 (25 March 1839). Moredon in Rodbourne Cheney. A house or chapel. Independent. Thomas Strange, Lawrence Lawrence, Thomas Horne, Richard Strange, Nehemiah Lea, John Wheeler, housekeepers in Swindon. (GRO GDR350)

**1529** 8 March 1839 (25 March 1839). Swindon. A house or chapel. Baptist.

Stephen Barrett, John Price, Henry Jeffries, Charles Clark, John Wallis, William Kent, housekeepers in Swindon. (GRO GDR350)

**1530** 10 March 1839 (12 April 1839). Woodford. A dwellinghouse and premises now in the holding and occupation of James Saunders. [*Primitive Methodist*: WRO 1150/286]. Henry Sharman of Fisherton Anger. (WRO D1/9/2/1)

**1531** 11 March 1839 (18 March 1839). Sutton Benger. A dwellinghouse now occupied by James Watson, plumber and glazier, for occasional worship. James Huggins, labourer, James Watson, plumber, James Howell, blacksmith, resident inhabitants and householders of Sutton Benger. (GRO GDR350)

**1532** 18 March 1839 (20 March 1839). Sutton Veny. A house and premises now in the holding and occupation of Thomas White. Thomas White of Sutton Veny. (WRO D1/9/2/1)

**1533** 23 March 1839 (23 May 1839). Dauntsey. A house and premises now in the holding and occupation of Barnaby Kane. [*Primitive Methodist*: see **1526**]. Joseph Preston of Brinkworth, John Excell. (GRO GDR350)

**1534** 23 April 1839 (29 April 1839). Wroughton. A house and premises now in the holding and occupation of John Cook. [*Primitive Methodist*: see **1526**]. Joseph Preston of Brinkworth, Thomas Webb. (GRO GDR350)

**1535** 27 April 1839 (29 April 1839). Bishopstone [*near Salisbury?*]. A dwellinghouse and premises now in the holding and occupation of Charles Penney. [*Primitive Methodist*: WRO 1150/286]. Henry Sharman of Fisherton Anger. (WRO D1/9/2/1)

**1536** 13 May 1839 (22 May 1839). Trowbridge. A room formerly used as workshops in the Middle Rank, Conigre (*Conigree*). William Haines of Trowbridge, shoemaker. (WRO D1/9/2/1)

**1537** 25 May 1839 (28 May 1839). Pewsey. A dwellinghouse and premises now in the holding and occupation of Thomas Butler?, labourer. William Bell of Marlborough. [*At head*] 'My address is Mr Trueman wine merchant, Marlborough, with speed.' (WRO D1/9/2/1)

**1538** 6 June 1839 (7 June 1839). Ashton Keynes. A building called Bathesda Chapel. Congregational. John Stratford of Gloucester. (GRO GDR350)

**1539** 6 June 1839 (7 June 1839). Upper Stratton in Stratton St Margaret. A building called Providence Chapel. Congregational. John Stratford of Gloucester. (GRO GDR350)

**1540** 22 June 1839 (25 June 1839). Aldbourne. A house and premises now in the holding and occupation of Robert Farmer, blacksmith. George Price of Shefford, Berks. (WRO D1/9/2/1)

**1541** 26 June 1839 (1 July 1839). Bradford on Avon. A room over a storeroom for timber in the occupation of Postumus Bush on White Hill. Gideon Allen of Bradford on Avon, cordwinder. (WRO D1/9/2/1)

**1542** 24 July 1839 (26 July 1839). Broad Blunsdon in Highworth. A chapel and premises now in the holding and occupation of the Society of Primitive Methodists. Primitive Methodist. Joseph Preston of Brinkworth, William Bath. (GRO GDR350)

**1543** 26 July 1839 (27 July 1839). Ramsbury. A chapel erected expressly for religious worship, and properly invested in the hands of trustees, in the High Street. Thomas Odam, Charles Baker of Ramsbury, Samuel Chamberlain of Ramsbury, John Langfield of Ramsbury, James L. Luke of Ramsbury. [*At foot*] 'PS Please reply to Charles Baker.' (WRO D1/9/2/1)

**1544** 21 Sept. 1839 (21 Sept. 1839). Martin. A chapel and premises now in the holding and occupation of William Larkam, William Flemington and Robert Bailey. [*Primitive Methodist*: WRO 1150/286]. John Richards of Fisherton Anger. (WRO D1/9/2/1)

**1545** 1 Nov. 1839 (3 Nov. 1839). Steeple Ashton. A building called Bethel in Common Lane. Baptist. Joseph Spencer Watson, protestant dissenting minister, Shem Evans, Baptist minister, Joseph Pearce, George Parsons, James Morris, William Taylor, Edward Naile. (WRO D1/9/2/1)

**1546** 13 Jan. 1840 (14 Jan. 1840). 'Littelton.' A building or chapel called Ebenezer Chapel to be used from 15 Jan. 1840. Baptist. Samuel Davis, James Bartlett, James Davis, George Sainsbury, Richard Biffen, inhabitants of 'Littelton.' (WRO D1/9/2/1)

**1547** 21 Feb. 1840 (2 March 1840). Warminster. A building in Common Close recently erected to be called the Independent Chapel. Independent. Rev G.S. Tubbs, Thomas Browne, T.P. Ubsdell?, James D. Brodribb, John J. Case, William Young, William Payne, Richard E. Vardy, John Wilkins, Jab. Gaisford, George Haines, Thomas Moody, James Young, Uriah? Brodribb, William J. Aurt?, Nathaniel Lewis Butt, Robert D. Proviss, Edward Vardy, James Powell, John Cox. (WRO D1/9/2/1)

**1548** 26 Feb. 1840 (27 Feb. 1840). Manningford Bohun in Wilsford. A dwellinghouse and premises now in the holding and occupation of George Hawkins, labourer. [*Particular Baptist*?: VCH 10, 213]. William Bell of St Martin's parish, Marlborough. (WRO D1/9/2/1)

**1549** 2 March 1840 (19 March 1840). Corston in Malmesbury. A dwellinghouse, schoolroom and premises in my occupation. John Sealy. (GRO GDR350)

**1550**  9 March 1840 (10 March 1840). Homington. A chapel and premises now in the holding and occupation of William Larkam, Jacob Everley and William Sworn. [*Primitive Methodist*: WRO 1150/286]. John Richards of Fisherton Anger. (WRO D1/9/2/1)

**1551**  10 April 1840 (10 April 1840). Winterslow in Idmiston. A chapel. Wesleyan Methodist. John Knowles of Salisbury, Wesleyan minister. (WRO D1/9/2/1)

**1552**  14 April 1840 (15 April 1840). Woodrow in Melksham. A building and premises in Melksham Forest at the corner of the road from Calne to Melksham and of Sparlton [*recte Snarlton*: see **1554**] Lane. Baptist. Joshua Russell of Melksham, Thomas Allwood, Isaac Pocock, Jeremiah Harris, William Hawkins. [*Endorsed*] 'The Ark, Melksham, April 14 1840. Sir, Will you be so obliging as to register the enclosed and to return me a certificate of its being registered by the first post. I enclose half a crown which I believe is the proper fee. I am sir Yours very obed'tly, Joshua Russell.' (WRO D1/9/2/1)

**1553**  16 April 1840 (16 April 1840). Pitton [*in Alderbury*]. A chapel. Wesleyan Methodist. Thomas Hamson Walker of Salisbury, Wesleyan minister. (WRO D1/9/2/1)

**1554**  20 April 1840 (21 April 1840). Woodrow in Melksham. A building and premises at Melksham Forest at the corner of the road from Calne to Melksham and of Snarlton Lane. Baptist. Joshua Russell of Melksham, John Giblett, Jeremiah Adams, Thomas Allwood, John Moon, George James. [*Endorsed*] 'The Ark, Melksham, April 20th 1840. Sir, In writing out the former certificate I see I made a little mistake by putting Sparlton Row instead of Snarlton which it should be, and tho I do not think it would matter, it is better to rectify it. Please therefore to have this recorded and send me the certificate by post as before as early as possible which will oblige. Sir, Yours very ob'tly, J. Russell. I enclose half a crown.' (WRO D1/9/2/1)

**1555**  26 April 1840 (28 April 1840). Ashton Keynes. A chapel and premises now in the holding and occupation of the Primitive Methodist. Primitive Methodist. Joseph Preston of Brinkworth, John Goodwin. (GRO GDR350)

**1556**  1 May 1840 (5 May 1840). Collingbourne Ducis (*Lower Collingbourne*). A dwellinghouse and premises now in the holding and occupation of Joseph Butcher. [*Primitive Methodist*: see **1430**]. George Appleby of Andover, Hants. (WRO D1/9/2/1)

**1557**  20 May 1840 (21 May 1840). Salisbury. A room in the George Yard in the High St, St Thomas's parish. New Jerusalem Church. David Thomas Dyke of Wilton. (WRO D1/9/2/1)

**1558**  19 June 1840 (20 June 1840). Lockeridge in Overton. A dwellinghouse and premises now in the holding and occupation of Henry Bell. William Bell of St Mary's parish, Marlborough. (WRO D1/9/2/1)

**1559**  22 June 1840 (23 June 1840). Hawkeridge in Westbury. A building. [*Independent Methodist*: see **1594**]. William Curtis, John Gaisford. (WRO D1/9/2/1)

**1560**  24 June 1840 (24 June 1840). Westbury. A building near the Warminster road now in the occupation of William England senior. John Orchard, William England. (WRO D1/9/2/1)

**1561**  25 June 1840 (25 June 1840). Alderbury. A building. Wesleyan Methodist. John Knowles of Salisbury, Wesleyan minister. (WRO D1/9/2/1)

**1562**  25 Aug. 1840 (28 Aug. 1840). Hook in Lydiard Tregoze. A house and premises now in the holding and occupation of Henry Embling. [*Primitive Methodist*: see **1526**]. Joseph Preston of Brinkworth, Rowland Hill. (GRO GDR350)

**1563**  14 Sept. 1840 (16 Sept. 1840). Hilmarton. A dwellinghouse and premises now in the holding and occupation of Richard Lewis. [*Primitive Methodist*: WRO 1150/286]. Edward Foizey of Chippenham. (WRO D1/9/2/1)

**1564**  21 Sept. 1840 (24 Sept. 1840). Horningsham. A dwellinghouse and premises now in the holding and occupation of John Patient Carrington. John Patient Carrington of Horningsham. (WRO D1/9/2/1)

**1565**  12 Oct. 1840 (13 Oct. 1840). Trowbridge. A building called a Wesleyan chapel. Wesleyan Methodist. John Boyd of Bradford on Avon, Wesleyan minister. (WRO D1/9/2/1)

**1566**  15 Oct. 1840 (15 Oct. 1840). Salisbury. A building in Salt Lane, St Edmund's parish, heretofore known as the Presbyterian meeting house and for many years past used as a place of religious worship and schoolroom by a Wesleyan Methodist congregation, is still intended to be used by them for that purpose. Wesleyan Methodist. Joseph Sanger of Fisherton Anger, gentleman. (WRO D1/9/2/1)

**1567**  10 Nov. 1840 (13 Nov. 1840). Grittleton. A dwellinghouse now occupied by Philip Smith, plasterer and tiler, to be used for occasional worship. John Tilly, shoemaker, William Kimber, labourer, George Warner, draper, Philip Smith, plasterer, resident inhabitants and householders of Grittleton. (GRO GDR350)

**1568**   13 Nov. 1840 (16 Nov. 1840). Hook in Lydiard Tregoze. A house and premises now in the holding and occupation of the Society of Primitive Methodists. Primitive Methodist. Joseph Preston of Brinkworth. James Mathews. (GRO GDR350)

**1569**   8 Dec. 1840 (14 Dec. 1840). Little Bedwyn. A dwellinghouse and premises now in the holding and occupation of James Wentworth, labourer. William Bell of St Mary's parish, Marlborough. (WRO D1/9/2/1)

**1570**   2 Feb. 1841 (3 Feb. 1841). Blackland in Calne. A dwellinghouse now in the occupation of William Green. Wesleyan Methodist. Henry V Olver of Melksham, Wesleyan minister. (WRO D1/9/2/1)

**1571**   6 Feb. 1841 (8 Feb. 1841). Bromham. A chapel and premises at the Balls, now in the holding and occupation of trustees, John Smith, Isaac Hillier and others. [*Primitive Methodist*: WRO 1150/286]. Edward Foizey of Chippenham. (WRO D1/9/2/1)

**1572**   6 Feb. 1841 (8 Feb. 1841). Cherhill. My house and premises now in my holding and occupation. George Moss of Cherhill. (WRO D1/9/2/1)

**1573**   8 Feb. 1841 (9 Feb. 1841). Broad Street in Beechingstoke. A dwellinghouse and premises now in the holding and occupation of Isaac Tilley. William Bell of St Mary's parish, Marlborough. (WRO D1/9/2/1)

**1574**   13 Feb. 1841 (15 Feb. 1841). Bradford on Avon. A building called or known by the name of the Bradford Wesleyan Methodist Chapel. Wesleyan Methodist. Rev John Boyd, officiating Wesleyan minister. [*Endorsed*] Bradford, Wilts 13 Feb/41. Sir, I have to request you will send me without delay a licence agreeable to the prefixed certificate the fee for which is I understand 2/6 which sum I enclose. I am sir, Your mo–obt. servt. John Boyd.' (WRO D1/9/2/1)

**1575**   23 Feb. 1841 (24 Feb. 1841). Upton Scudamore. A building in the possession or occupation of Elizabeth Bainton. [*Baptist?*: VCH 8, 89]. Isaac New, John Stent, John Toone, Edward Davies. (WRO D1/9/2/1)

**1576**   27 Feb. 1841 (2 March 1841). Kingston Deverill. A chapel and premises now in the holding and occupation of James Brimble. James Brimble of Kingston Deverill. WRO D1/9/2/1)

**1577**   11 May 1841 (11 May 1841). Testwood in Whiteparish. A dwellinghouse called Testwood in the occupation of Charles Rose. [*Baptist*: see **1063**]. Samuel Wort of Downton. (WRO D1/9/2/1)

**1578**   22 May 1841 (24 May 1841). Aldbourne. A chapel and premises now in the holding and occupation of Robert Farmer, Thomas Barratt and others.

[*Primitive Methodist*: WRO 1150/286]. Henry Sharman of Newbury, Berks. (WRO D1/9/2/1)

**1579** (15 Oct. 1841). Box. A house. [*Primitive Methodist*: see **1555**]. Joseph Preston of Brinkworth. (PRO RG31/2 Gloucester diocese)

**1580** 5 Nov. 1841 (9 Nov. 1841). Seend Cleeve in Seend. A chapel and premises now in the holding and occupation of J. Flower, L. Miles and others as trustees. [*Primitive Methodist*: WRO 1150/286]. Edward Foizey of Chippenham. (WRO D1/9/2/1)

**1581** 5 Nov. 1841 (9 Nov. 1841). Stockley in Calne. A chapel and premises now in the holding and occupation of W. Strange, George Ruddle and others as trustees. [*Primitive Methodist*: WRO 1150/286]. Edward Foizey of Chippenham. (WRO D1/9/2/1)

**1582** 15 Dec. 1841 (22 Dec. 1841). Pinkney in Sherston. A building in the occupation of Absalom Hacker. Samuel Stubbings, John Mitchell, Absalom Hacker. (GRO GDR350)

**1583** 21 Dec. 1841 (21 Dec. 1841). West Harnham. A dwellinghouse in my occupation. Stephen Bell of West Harnham. (WRO D1/9/2/1)

**1584** (8 Jan. 1842). 'Purton Dorset.' [*This unidentified place may not be in Wiltshire, and is described as Gloucestershire in the 1852 return. However, it cannot be identified with either of the Purtons in Gloucestershire, and since it was certified at Brinkworth it may refer to a Wiltshire place.*]. A house. [*Primitive Methodist*: see **1555**]. Joseph Preston of Brinkworth. (PRO RG31/2 Gloucester diocese)

**1585** 26 Jan. 1842 (27 Jan. 1842). Plaitford. The dwellinghouse and premises now in the holding and occupation of Charles Moody. [*Primitive Methodist*: WRO 1150/286]. Robert Tuffin of Fisherton Anger. (WRO D1/9/2/1)

**1586** 12 Feb. 1842 (16 Feb. 1842). Cricklade. A chapel and premises in St Sampson's parish now in the holding and occupation of the Primitive Methodist. Primitive Methodist. Joseph Preston of Brinkworth, Edward Minton. (GRO GDR350)

**1587** 25 March 1842 (26 March 1842). West Lavington. James Baish's house and premises now in the occupation of William Chipman. Edmund Rawlings, minister. [*At foot*] 'PS I hope my form is correct if not let me know if you please and be so kind as to favour me with a certificate by return of post. ER. Address E. Rawlings, Market Lavington, Wilts.' (WRO D1/9/2/1)

**1588** 5 April 1842 (7 April 1842). Sherston. A house and premises now in the holding and occupation of John Bresington. [*Primitive Methodist*: see **1586**]. George Obern of Cirencester, Joseph Preston. (GRO GDR350)

**1589**   13 May 1842   (13 May 1842). Malmesbury. A hall and premises now in the holding and occupation of James Joseph Prior. John Cluer of Cheltenham, James Dawes. (GRO GDR350)

**1590**   23 May 1842 (24 May 1842). East Tisbury. A building on Zion Hill. [*Congregational*: Miles 37, 39]. John Combes of East Tisbury, Henry Bristol of West Tisbury, Matthew Combes of Wardour. (WRO D1/9/2/1)

**1591**   7 June 1842 (9 June 1842). Liddington. A chapel and premises now in the holding and occupation of James May. [*Primitive Methodist*: see **1586**]. Joseph Preston of Brinkworth. (GRO GDR350)

**1592**   1 July 1842 (1 July 1842). Bremhill. A house in the occupation of Benjamin Slade. Wesleyan Methodist. William Sharpe of Salisbury, Wesleyan minister. (WRO D1/9/2/1)

**1593**   14 July 1842 (16 July 1842). Ogbourne St George. A chapel. Independent. Richard Henry Smith, minister of the Independent chapel, Marlborough. (WRO D1/9/2/1)

**1594**   14 July 1842 (19 July 1842). Warminster. A building in Pound Street called an Independent Methodist chapel. Independent Methodist. John Gaisford, John Grist, William Brooks, John Tabor. (WRO D1/9/2/1)

**1595**   6 Sept. 1842 (7 Sept. 1842). Broad Hinton. A chapel and premises in Broadtown Lane now in the holding and occupation of the Primitive Methodist Connexion. Primitive Methodist. William Driffield of Brinkworth. (WRO D1/9/2/1)

**1596**   14 Sept. 1842 (16 Sept. 1842). Willesley in Sherston. My dwelling-house. John Clutterbuck of Willesley, labourer. (WRO D1/9/2/1)

**1597**   21 Sept. 1842 (24 Sept. 1842). Sopworth. A house and premises now in the holding and occupation of John Bressington. [*Primitive Methodist*: see **1588**]. George Obern of Cirencester. (GRO GDR350)

**1598**   27 Sept. 1842 (29 Sept. 1842). Shaw Hill in Melksham. A building in the possession or occupation of James Cannings. Baptist. James Cannings, occupier, William Blake, dissenting minister, John Wakely, James Shephard, James Angel, Stephen Smallcomb, Robert Weakly. [*Endorsed in pencil*] 'Please direct to Mr W. Blake, Baptist Minister, Broughton Gifford near Melksham.' (WRO D1/9/2/1)

**1599**   3 Oct. 1842 (4 Oct. 1842). Conock in Chirton. A house and premises now in the holding and occupation of Joseph Perry. Joseph Perry of Conock. (WRO D1/9/2/1)

**1600**   5 Oct. 1842 (7 Oct. 1842). Staverton in Trowbridge. A building called or known by the name of the Staverton Wesleyan Methodist chapel. Wesleyan Methodist. Rev Jacob Stanley, officiating Wesleyan minister. (WRO D1/9/2/1)

**1601**   13 Oct. 1842 (14 Oct. 1842). Ram Alley in Burbage [*recte Savernake Park extra-parochial place?*]. A cottage and premises now in the holding and occupation of Job Davies. Job Davies of Ram Alley. (WRO D1/9/2/1)

**1602**   23 Nov. 1842 (28 Nov. 1842). Aldbourne. A chapel in the Back Lane. [*Strict Baptist*: VCH 12, 85]. William Taylor, Stephen Gould, John Jervane. (WRO D1/9/2/1)

**1603**   28 Nov. 1842 (6 Dec. 1842). Hindon. A chapel and premises now in the holding and occupation of Thomas Merchant, Luke Turner, George Turner and Charles King. [*Primitive Methodist*: Sheard 29]. Thomas Merchant of King Hay in East Knoyle, Luke Turner, George Turner, Charles King. (WRO D1/9/2/1)

**1604**   4 Jan. 1843 (7 Jan. 1843). Melksham. A house and premises in Semington Lane in the occupation of . . . [*omitted*] Chivers. Baptist. Joshua Russell of Melksham, John Moon, James Butler, Thomas Allwood, Joseph Wallis. (WRO D1/9/2/1)

**1605**   7 Jan. 1843 (10 Jan. 1843). Atworth [*in Bradford on Avon*]. A chapel and premises now in the holding and occupation of John Smith and others. [*Primitive Methodist*: see **1357**]. Samuel Turner of Chippenham. (WRO D1/9/2/1)

**1606**   7 Jan. 1843 (10 Jan. 1843). Cherhill. A dwellinghouse and premises now in the holding and occupation of John Rivers? [*Primitive Methodist*: see **1357**]. Samuel Turner of Chippenham. (WRO D1/9/2/1)

**1607**   9 Jan. 1843 (19 Jan. 1843). Hullavington. A chapel and premises now in the holding and occupation of John Hitchcock. John Hitchcock of Seagry. (GRO GDR350)

**1608**   9 Jan. 1843 (10 Jan. 1843). Thornend (*Tharend*) in Christian Malford. A house and premises now in the holding and occupation of Joseph Cole. [*Primitive Methodist*: Tonks 91]. William Nation of Brinkworth. (GRO GDR350)

**1609**   20 Jan. 1843 (26 Jan. 1843). Marlborough. A chapel and premises in St Mary's parish, now in the holding and occupation of the Primitive Methodist Society at Marlborough. Primitive Methodist. Job Bodman of St Mary's parish, Marlborough. (WRO D1/9/2/1)

**1610**   20 Jan. 1843 (26 Jan. 1843). Ramsbury. A chapel and premises now in the holding and occupation of the Primitive Methodist Society at Ramsbury. Primitive Methodist. Job Bodman of St Mary's parish, Marlborough. (WRO D1/9/2/1)

**1611**   30 Jan. 1843 (30 Jan. 1843). Damerham. A house and premises now in the holding and occupation of John Keeping, Malachi Martin and William Flemington. [*Primitive Methodist*: WRO 1150/286]. Robert Tuffin of Fisherton Anger. (WRO D1/9/2/1)

**1612**   3 Feb. 1843 (6 Feb. 1843). Stanton St Quinton. A dwellinghouse and premises now in the holding and occupation of Geofford Hubbert. Thomas Knapp of Startley (*Starkley*) in Great Somerford. (GRO GDR350)

**1613**   9 Feb. 1843 (11 Feb. 1843). Stock Lane in Aldbourne. A cottage and premises now in the holding and occupation of John Davies. [*Primitive Methodist*: see **1609**]. Job Bodman of St Mary's parish, Marlborough. (WRO D1/9/2/1)

**1614**   23 Feb. 1843 (28 Feb. 1843). Purton. A chapel and premises in the Row, now in the holding and occupation of William Driffield. [*Primitive Methodist*: see **1595**]. Charles Gardner of Purton. (GRO GDR350)

**1615**   25 Feb. 1843 (25 Feb. 1843). Quidhampton in Fugglestone St Peter. A dwellinghouse now in my holding and occupation. Thomas King of Quidhampton. (WRO D1/9/2/1)

**1616**   18 March 1843 (18 March 1843). Ugford in South Newton. A dwellinghouse in my occupation. The mark of James Blake of Ugford. (WRO D1/9/2/1)

**1617**   3 April 1843. Trowbridge. A room being the third floor of a building in Silver Street, formerly a clothing factory belonging to and in the occupation of John Bell deceased. [*Baptist*: Doel 155]. John Cooper of Trowbridge, clothier. (WRO A1/250)

**1618**   8 April 1843. Marlborough. A dwellinghouse, number 8, St Martins Street, in my occupation. George Trueman of number 8, St Martins Street, Marlborough. (WRO D1/9/2/1)

**1619**   9 April 1843. Bottlesford in Wilsford. A building in the possession or occupation of John Keepence. [*Baptist*: Oliver 24]. William Freeman, John Keepence, Jonathan Waight, John Hitchcock, Isaac Stevens, Austin Oadie, Paul Tilly, Richard Pinchin, John Gillott, John Stratton. (WRO D1/9/2/1)

**1620**   4 May 1843. Holloway in East Knoyle. The house and premises now in the holding and occupation of Felten Burbidge. Felten Burbidge of Holloway. (WRO D1/9/2/1)

**1621** 9 May 1843. Milton Lilborne. A chapel and premises now in the holding and occupation of the Primitive Methodist Society at Milton. Primitive Methodist. Job Bodman of St Mary's parish, Marlborough. (WRO D1/9/2/1)

**1622** 19 May 1843. 'Crendle' [*Chandle Hill?*] in Damerham. A chapel. James Parkes of Ringwood, Hants. (WRO D1/9/2/1)

**1623** 23 May 1843. The Barton (*Borken*) in Clyffe Pypard (*Cliff Pipond*). A dwellinghouse and premises now in the holding and occupation of William Cumley. [*Primitive Methodist*: see **1595**]. William Driffield of Brinkworth. (WRO D1/9/2/1)

**1624** 23 May 1843. Bushton in Clyffe Pypard (*Cliff Pipond*). A dwellinghouse and premises now in the holding and occupation of James Turk. [*Primitive Methodist*: see **1595**]. William Driffield of Brinkworth. (WRO D1/9/2/1)

**1625** 24 May 1843. Wootton Bassett. A room in the occupation of Thomas Franklyne. Thomas Wiggins of Wootton Bassett. (WRO D1/9/2/1)

**1626** 25 May 1843. Allington [*near Salisbury*]. A chapel and premises now in the holding and occupation of the Primitive Methodist. Primitive Methodist. William Wigley of Andover, Hants. [*Pencilled at foot*] 'Mr Young, Allington, Boscombe, Wilts.' (WRO D1/9/2/1)

**1627** 12 June 1843 (21 June 1843). Swindon. A room belonging to Mr James Edwards adjoining the Golden Lion Inn near the Swindon Railroad Station on the Great Western Railroad. [*Wesleyan Methodist*: see **1697**]. Zephaniah Job of Swindon, dissenting minister, J.F. Payne. (GRO GDR350)

**1628** 28 Sept. 1843 (29 Sept. 1843). Bremhill. A house and premises now in the holding and occupation of Henry Alexander. [*Primitive Methodist*: see **1357**]. Samuel Turner of Chippenham. (WRO D1/9/2/1)

**1629** 11 Oct. 1843. Brixton Deverill. A building. George Norris, Jesse Brown. (WRO D1/9/2/1)

**1630** 10 Nov. 1843 (11 Nov. 1843). Corsham. A room and premises now in the holding and occupation of Solomon Hunt and Dinoh Sealey. [*Primitive Methodist*: see **1357**]. Samuel Turner of Chippenham. (WRO D1/9/2/1)

**1631** 10 Nov. 1843 (11 Nov. 1843). Reybridge (*Rawbridge*) in Lacock. A dwellinghouse and premises now in the holding and occupation of James Pagler. [*Primitive Methodist*: see **1357**]. Samuel Turner of Chippenham. (WRO D1/9/2/1)

**1632**   10 Nov. 1843 (11 Nov. 1843). Trowbridge. A chapel and premises now in the holding and occupation of John Smith and Joseph Riddick. [*Primitive Methodist*: see **1357**]. Samuel Turner of Chippenham. (WRO D1/9/2/1)

**1633**   20 Nov. 1843. Wardour. A room or building being part of a dwelling-house or tenement now in the holding and occupation of Mr Thomas Loder. James Jukes of Tisbury. (WRO D1/9/2/1)

**1634**   25 Nov. 1843 (27 Nov. 1843). Startley (*Starkley*) in Great Somerford. A building and premises now in the holding and occupation of William Driffield. [*Primitive Methodist*: see **1595**]. William Driffield of Brinkworth. (GRO GDR350)

**1635**   27 Nov. 1843 (29 Nov. 1843). Nettleton. A house and premises now in the holding and occupation of Joseph Davies. David Kent of Sherston. (GRO GDR350)

**1636**   30 Nov. 1843 (2 Dec. 1843). Hullavington. A building called Mount Zion Chapel. Particular Baptist. Thomas Ferries, watchmaker, Robert Seager, grocer, Aaron Sealey, blacksmith, Joseph Mallard, Abraham Angell, Simon Townsend, resident inhabitants and householders of Hullavington. (GRO GDR350)

**1637**   6 Dec. 1843 (6 Dec. 1843). East Grimstead. A dwellinghouse and premises in the holding and occupation of Charles Massey. Daniel Harding, saddler. (WRO D1/9/2/1)

**1638**   18 Dec. 1843. Kington Langley in Kington St Michael. A chapel and premises now in the holding and occupation of John Smith and others. [*Primitive Methodist*: see **1357**]. Samuel Turner of Chippenham. (WRO D1/9/2/1)

**1639**   18 Dec. 1843. Mountain Bower in West Kington. A dwellinghouse and premises now in the holding and occupation of James Vines. [*Primitive Methodist*: see **1357**]. Samuel Turner of Chippenham. (WRO D1/9/2/1)

**1640**   30 Dec. 1843. Little Bedwyn. A house and premises now in the holding and occupation of Frederick White. [*Primitive Methodist*: see **1610**]. Job Bodman of St Mary's parish, Marlborough. (WRO D1/9/2/1)

**1641**   29 Jan. 1844 (2 Feb. 1844). Sherston. A room and premises now in the holding and occupation of the Primitive Methodist Connexion. Primitive Methodist. Robert Moore of Sherston. (GRO GDR350)

**1642**   15 Feb. 1844 (26 Feb. 1844). Beckhampton in Avebury. A dwelling-house and premises now in the holding and occupation of Mary Amer. Joseph Phelps of Marlborough, ironmonger. (WRO D1/9/2/1)

**1643**   14 March 1844 (16 March 1844). Swindon. A house or chapel and burying ground at Prospect Place. Baptist. Thomas Lea [*or John Lea*: PRO RG31/2 Gloucester diocese], John Tarrant, Moses Day, Charles Clark, John Prince?, Stephen Barrett, housekeepers in Swindon. (GRO GDR350)

**1644**   22 March 1844. Collingbourne Ducis. A dwellinghouse and premises now in the holding and occupation of Joseph Lansley. [*Primitive Methodist*: see **1626**]. William Wigley of Andover, minister. (WRO D1/9/2/1)

**1645**   30 March 1844. Nunton in Downton. A dwellinghouse and premises in the occupation of William Joseph Andrews. [*Wesleyan Methodist*: Hall 206]. Levi Waterhouse of Salisbury. (WRO D1/9/2/1)

**1646**   30 March 1844. Sherston. My dwellinghouse. Jessy Hobbs in Sherston. (WRO D1/9/2/1)

**1647**   10 April 1844. Wexcombe in Great Bedwyn. A dwellinghouse and premises now in the holding and occupation of William Ching. [*Primitive Methodist*: see **1626**]. William Wigley of Andover, minister. (WRO D1/9/2/1)

**1648**   7 May 1844 (9 May 1844). Castle Combe. A dwellinghouse in the occupation of William Widcomb. William Widcomb, Giles Broom, Daniel Davies, Stephen Beazen, John Flewelling?, householders in Castle Combe. (GRO GDR350)

**1649**   25 May 1844. Netheravon. A dwellinghouse and premises now in the holding and occupation of William Snook. [*Primitive Methodist*: WRO 1150/286]. George Price of Fisherton Anger. (WRO D1/9/2/1)

**1650**   18 June 1844. Ebbesborne Wake. A dwellinghouse and premises now in the holding and occupation of Henry Parham. [*Primitive Methodist*: WRO 1150/286]. George Price of Fisherton Anger. (WRO D1/9/2/1)

**1651**   29 June 1844. Ludgershall. A chapel and premises now in the holding and occupation of Robert Dudman. [*Primitive Methodist*: see **1626**]. W. Wigley of Andover, minister. (WRO D1/9/2/1)

**1652**   17 July 1844. Lower Chute in Chute. A newly erected building known by the name of the New Wesleyan Chapel. Wesleyan Methodist. James Godden of Winton Street, Andover, minister. (WRO D1/9/2/1)

**1653**   1 Aug. 1844. Westbury. A dwellinghouse belonging to Martha Denniss in the occupation of David Hollaway. Congregational. The mark of Mrs Deniss, proprietor, David Hollaway, tenant, James Applegate, James Raines, Stephen Henry Applegate, John Wheeler, John Elkines, resident householders. (WRO D1/9/2/1)

**1654** 10 Oct. 1844. Wootton Bassett. A house and premises now in the holding and occupation of Thomas Wiggins. Thomas Wiggins of Wootton Bassett. [*At foot*] 'Direct Mr Thomas Wiggins, Wootton Bassett, Wilts.' (WRO D1/9/2/1)

**1655** 26 Oct. 1844. Donhead St Mary. A building, the Wesleyan Methodist chapel, in Donhead Street adjoining the premises of George Goddard, brewer. Wesleyan Methodist. Thomas Rogerson of Shaftesbury, Wesleyan Methodist minister. (WRO D1/9/2/1)

**1656** 30 Oct. 1844. Upper Studley in Trowbridge. A house and premises now in the holding and occupation of Samuel Slocomb. Henry Green of Trowbridge, James Pearce. (WRO D1/9/2/1)

**1657** 1 Nov. 1844. Salisbury. Two rooms in a void dwellinghouse belonging to Mr E. Vandenhoff in Castle Street, St Edmund's parish. [*New Jerusalem Church*: see **1557**]. David Thomas Dyke of Quidhampton [*in Fugglestone St Peter*]. (WRO D1/9/2/1)

**1658** 7 Nov. 1844. Alvediston. A dwellinghouse and premises now in the holding and occupation of James Adlam. [*Primitive Methodist*: WRO 1150/286]. George Price of Fisherton Anger. (WRO D1/9/2/1)

**1659** 7 Nov. 1844. Alvediston. A dwellinghouse and premises now in the holding and occupation of Thomas Jenkins. [*Primitive Methodist*: WRO 1150/286]. George Price of Fisherton Anger. (WRO D1/9/2/1)

**1660** 12 Nov. 1844. Froxfield. A dwellinghouse belonging to Mrs Sarah Nias of Newbury, Berks., and now in the occupation of George Evans of Froxfield. [*Independent*: see **1252, 1273**]. Richard Frost, William Moody, Ambrose Lanfear, Richard Lye. (WRO D1/9/2/1)

**1661** 30 Nov. 1844. Winsley [*in Bradford on Avon*]. A house and premises now in the holding and occupation of George Butt senior. [*Primitive Methodist*: WRO 1150/286]. Robert Tuffin of Abbey parish, Bath. (WRO D1/9/2/1)

**1662** 18 Jan. 1845. Trowbridge. A room and premises now in the holding and occupation of Henry Green. Henry Green of Trowbridge, James Pearce. (WRO D1/9/2/1)

**1663** 4 Feb. 1845. Broad Chalke. A chapel and premises now in the holding and occupation of the Primitive Methodist connexion. Primitive Methodist. George Price of Fisherton Anger. (WRO D1/9/2/1)

**1664** 1 March 1845. Farley [*in Alderbury*]. A barn and premises in the holding and occupation of Luke Phillips. Wesleyan Methodist. Thomas W. Smith of Salisbury, Wesleyan minister. (WRO D1/9/2/1)

**1665**  17 March 1845. Hurdcott in Winterbourne Earls. A building called or known by the name of the Wesleyan Chapel now in the tenure or possession of the trustees of the chapel. Wesleyan Methodist. Thomas W. Smith of Salisbury, Wesleyan minister. (WRO D1/9/2/1)

**1666**  4 April 1845. Ludwell in Donhead St Mary. A dwellinghouse and premises now in the holding and occupation of George Haskall. [*Primitive Methodist*: WRO 1150/286]. Henry Sharman of Motcombe, Dorset. (WRO D1/9/2/1)

**1667**  8 April 1845. Inglesham. A house and premises now in the holding and occupation of John Horton, farmer. Thomas Green of Highworth. (BRO EP/A/45/3)

**1668**  14 April 1845. Salisbury. Two rooms and premises in St Edmund's parish now in the holding and occupation of the committee of the Temperance Society. William Lane of St Edmund's parish, Salisbury. (WRO D1/9/2/1)

**1669**  7 May 1845. Avebury. A house in the occupation of Thomas Vickers. Joseph Phelps of Marlborough. [*Endorsed*] 'Mr Old, Oatmeal Row, Salisbury.' (WRO D1/9/2/1)

**1670**  26 May 1845. Downton. A new chapel and premises at Lode Hill now in the holding and occupation of trustees. Particular Baptist. John Janes of Downton. (WRO D1/9/2/1)

**1671**  12 July 1845. Charlcote in Bremhill. A dwellinghouse in the occupation of Jonas Haddrell. Thomas Freegard, Henry Woodward, Thomas King, James Wise, Stephen S. Jefferys, householders in Bremhill. (WRO D1/9/2/1)

**1672**  2 Oct. 1845. Woodsend in Aldbourne [*but dated from Hungerford*]. A chapel has recently been erected and is about to be used. Wesleyan Methodist. James Allen, Wesleyan minister. (WRO D1/9/2/1)

**1673**  3 Oct. 1845. Trowbridge. A room now in my occupation and formerly used as a workshop in Middle Rank, Conigre. [*Mormon*: WF 3(1), 34–35]. John Halliday of Trowbridge. (WRO D1/9/2/1)

**1674**  10 Nov. 1845. Bradford on Avon. The chapel and premises now in the holding and occupation of William Crook, John Smith and others. [*Primitive Methodist*: WRO 1150/286]. Robert Tuffin of St Peter's and St Paul's parish, Bath. [*Pencilled at foot*] 'Call tomorrow morn'g for it. (WRO D1/9/2/1)

**1675**  13 Nov. 1845 (14 Nov. 1845). Lowden in Chippenham. A dwelling-house in the possession of William Bairston? [*Altered in manuscript to Bainston or similar.* WRO A1/255 *appears to read Brinston*] Bailey. Joseph Hyatt of Gloucester. (GRO GDR350)

**1676** 18 Nov. 1845. Holt in Bradford on Avon. A house and premises now in the holding and occupation of Daniel Melsom. Henry Green of Trowbridge, Daniel Milsom. (WRO D1/9/2/1)

**1677** 27 Nov. 1845. Yarnbrook in North Bradley. A house and premises now in the holding and occupation of Arnold Joyce. Henry Green of Trowbridge, Arnold Joyce. (WRO D1/9/2/1)

**1678** 11 Dec. 1845. Upavon. A dwellinghouse and premises now in the holding and occupation of Benjamin Faggetter. James Ford of St Mary's parish, Marlborough. (WRO D1/9/2/1)

**1679** 12 Dec. 1845. Chilhampton in South Newton. A dwellinghouse and premises now in my holding and occupation. Stephen Wootton of Chilhampton. (WRO D1/9/2/1)

**1680** 28 Dec. 1845. Idmiston. A house and premises now in the holding and occupation of John Phillips. [*Primitive Methodist*: see **1506**]. John Young of Allington. (WRO D1/9/2/1)

**1681** 22 Jan. 1846. Easterton [*in Market Lavington*]. A house now in the occupation of William Draper. [*Mormon*: WF 3(1), 34–35]. John Halliday of Trowbridge. (WRO D1/9/2/1)

**1682** 26 Jan. 1846. Ogbourne St George. A house in the occupation of James Liddiard. Joseph Phelps of Marlborough. (WRO D1/9/2/1)

**1683** 9 Feb. 1846. West Harnham. A house and premises now in the holding and occupation of Frederick Hopkins. [*Primitive Methodist*: WRO 1150/286]. Charles Thomas Harris of Fisherton Anger. (WRO D1/9/2/1)

**1684** 11 Feb. 1846. Burcombe. A new chapel and premises now in the holding and occupation of the stewards of the Salisbury circuit. Wesleyan Methodist. Thomas White Smith of Salisbury, Wesleyan minister. (WRO D1/9/2/1)

**1685** 16 March 1846. Winterbourne Bassett *or* Winterbourne Monkton. A house in the occupation of William Hillier. Joseph Phelps of Marlborough. (WRO D1/9/2/1)

**1686** 27 March 1846. Ebbesborne Wake. A house and premises now in the holding and occupation of George Stephens. [*Primitive Methodist*: WRO 1150/286]. Charles Thomas Harris of Fisherton Anger. (WRO D1/9/2/1)

**1687** 30 March 1846. Berwick St John. A dwellinghouse occupied by George Green standing close by, and on the south side of, the brook which divides the parishes of Berwick St John and Donhead St Andrew. Wesleyan Methodist.

Thomas Rogerson of Shaftesbury, Wesleyan Methodist minister. (WRO D1/9/2/1)

**1688** 30 March 1846. East Tisbury. A chapel in a place termed the Quarry. Wesleyan Methodist. Thomas Rogerson of Shaftesbury, Wesleyan Methodist minister. (WRO D1/9/2/1)

**1689** 16 April 1846. Bullenhill in Steeple Ashton. A house now in the occupation of Thomas Dunsdon. [*Mormon*: WF 3(1), 34–35]. John Halliday of The Courts, Trowbridge. (WRO D1/9/2/1)

**1690** May 1846 (4 June 1846). Nettleton. A dwellinghouse in the occupation of William Strange junior. William Say, minister. (GRO GDR350)

**1691** 5 Sept. 1846. Upavon. A chapel and premises now in the holding and occupation of John Masterson. [*Primitive Methodist*: see **1702**]. The mark of John Masterson of Upavon, George Obern. (WRO D1/9/2/1)

**1692** 10 Sept. 1846. Rowde. The house of Mr Robert Mack at Trafalgar Place. Baptist. George Washington Anstie, Robert A Mack. (WRO D1/9/2/1)

**1693** 19 Sept. 1846. No Man's Land [*extra-parochial place*]. A chapel and premises now in the holding and occupation of the Primitive Methodist connexion. Primitive Methodist. William Brewer of Winterbourne. [*Pencilled in margin*] 'Elton Maidenhead.' (WRO D1/9/2/1)

**1694** 21 Sept. 1846. Hatch in West Tisbury. A dwelling and premises now in the holding and occupation of Luke Turner. [*Primitive Methodist*: WRO 1150/286]. Henry Sharman of Motcombe, Dorset. (WRO D1/9/2/1)

**1695** 21 Sept. 1846. Teffont Magna *or* Evias. A dwellinghouse and premises now in the holding and occupation of Henry Penney. [*Primitive Methodist*: WRO 1150/286]. Henry Sharman of Motcombe, Dorset. (WRO D1/9/2/1)

**1696** 13 Oct. 1846. Winterbourne Stoke. A dwellinghouse and premises now in my own occupation. George Eyers junior of Winterbourne Stoke. (WRO D1/9/2/1)

**1697** 15 Oct. 1846. 'Park' in West Overton [*in* Overton]. A building lately erected on a piece of ground at the west corner of a garden, conveyed by indenture of 18 May 1846 duly enrolled in chancery, by John Pye of Park to certain persons named as trustees. Wesleyan Methodist. Zephaniah Job of Marlborough, Wesleyan minister, H.G. McTier. (WRO D1/9/2/1)

**1698** 23 Oct. 1846. Stapleford. A house and premises now in the holding and occupation of John Feltham. Isaac White of St Edmund's parish, Salisbury. (WRO D1/9/2/1)

**1699**    28 Oct. 1846. Mere. A chapel and premises now in the holding and occupation of Charles Bell, Benjamin Perfect and others. [*Primitive Methodist*: WRO 1150/286]. Henry Sharman of Motcombe, Dorset. (WRO D1/9/2/1)

**1700**    3 Nov. 1846. Broad Hinton. A cottage now in the occupation of Edward Sadler. Joseph Phelps of Marlborough, Henry Page. (WRO D1/9/2/1)

**1701**    18 Nov. 1846. East Hatch in West Tisbury. A dwellinghouse and premises now in the holding and occupation of John Turner. [*Primitive Methodist*: WRO 1150/286]. Henry Sharman of Motcombe, Dorset. (WRO D1/9/2/1)

**1702**    18 Nov. 1846. Little Bedwyn. A chapel and premises now in the holding and occupation of the Primitive Methodist society. Primitive Methodist. George Obern of Marlborough, minister. (WRO D1/9/2/1)

**1703**    13 April 1847. Ogbourne St George. A building lately erected on a piece of ground belonging to Joseph Phelps. Joseph Phelps of Marlborough, William Thomas Carr. (WRO D1/9/2/1)

**1704**    20 April 1847. Fovant. The dwellinghouse of William Mills. John Gould of Sutton Mandeville, dairyman. (WRO D1/9/2/1)

**1705**    17 Nov. 1847. Steeple Ashton. A house now in the occupation of Robert Berrett. [*Mormon*: WF 3(1), 34–35]. John Halliday of Trowbridge. (WRO D1/9/2/1)

**1706**    5 Jan. 1848. Melksham. A room now in the holding and occupation of George Chandler. Philip Moss Westwood of Trowbridge. [*Endorsed in pencil*] 'Money order for 2/6 from Philip Moss Westwood, gent – trowbridge to Fitzherbert Macdonald esquire.' (WRO D1/9/2/1)

**1707**    14 Feb. 1848. Warminster. A room at the back of the Castle Inn, Silver Street, now in the holding and occupation of Philip Moss Westwood. Philip Moss Westwood of Trowbridge. (WRO D1/9/2/1)

**1708**    15 March 1848. Corsley. A room and premises now in the holding and occupation of the Primitive Methodist society. Primitive Methodist. William Harvey of Frome Sellwood, Som. (WRO D1/9/2/1)

**1709**    2 May 1848. Mere. A room on the premises in the occupation of John Toogood in Castle Street is about to be used. William Powley, William Perrett. (WRO D1/9/2/1)

**1710**    8 May 1848. Mere. A room on the premises in the occupation of Michael Baverstock in Castle Street is about to be used. George Godwin, William White. (WRO D1/9/2/1)

**1711**  20 May 1848. Quidhampton [*in Fugglestone St Peter*]. A barn and premises now in my occupation. John Young. (WRO D1/9/2/1)

**1712**  6 June 1848. Salisbury. A room in an unoccupied building in the George Yard, High Street, St. Thomas's parish, the property of . . . [*omitted*] Trowbridge. Thomas Lambert of Fisherton Anger. (WRO D1/9/2/1)

**1713**  15 July 1848. Salisbury. A room in the Black Horse Hotel, now unoccupied, in Winchester Street. John Shipway of Salisbury. (WRO D1/9/2/1)

**1714**  20 Oct. 1848. East Tisbury. A room and premises now in the holding and occupation of the Primitive Methodist society. Primitive Methodist. Charles Locke of Hindon. (WRO D1/9/2/1)

**1715**  7 Nov. 1848. Hilmarton. The house of James Rumming. James Rumming, Isaac Hart, William Hart, Richard Hillier, William Taylor, James Archard, inhabitants and householders in Hilmarton. [*At foot*] 'Please to direct – Isaac Hart, Hillmarton near Calne, Wilts.' (WRO D1/9/2/1)

**1716**  27 Nov. 1848. Rattle in Bremhill. A cottage and premises now in the holding and occupation of Thomas Ponting. [*Primitive Methodist*: WRO 1150/286]. Edward Foizey of Chippenham. (WRO D1/9/2/1)

**1717**  (30 Nov. 1848). Nettleton. A chapel. Samuel Stubbins, minister. (PRO RG31/2 Gloucester diocese)

**1718**  12 Dec. 1848. Berwick Bassett. A house in the occupation of Richard Cousins. Joseph Phelps of Marlborough, Arthur Page. (WRO D1/9/2/1)

**1719**  12 Dec. 1848. Marlborough. A room in St Peter's parish occupied by Henry and Arthur Page and others. Joseph Phelps of Marlborough, Arthur Page. (WRO D1/9/2/1)

**1720**  13 Dec. 1848. Kingston Deverill. A house and premises now in the holding and occupation of John Tudgay. [*Primitive Methodist*: see **1708**]. William Harvey of Frome Selwood, Som., the mark of John Tudgay. (WRO D1/9/2/1)

**1721**  20 Jan. 1849. Charlcote in Bremhill. A house now in the occupation of Richard Hatt. [*Mormon*: WF 3(1), 34–35]. John Halliday of Trowbridge. [*At foot*] 'I hearwith send An and order for two shillings and sixpence drawn by John Halliday in favour of Fitz Herbert McDonald.' (WRO D1/9/2/1)

**1722**  Feb. 1849. Steeple Ashton. A house now in the occupation of John Kingman. [*Mormon*: WF 3(1), 34–35]. John Halliday of Courts, Trowbridge. [*At foot*] 'Dear Sir, I have sent you 30 stamps to pay for the certificate and remain your humble servant, John Halliday.' (WRO D1/9/2/1)

**1723**   2 March 1849 (5 March 1849). Eastcott in Swindon. A chapel and premises now in the holding and occupation of John Pike and others, trustees for the Primitive Methodist connexion. Primitive Methodist. Edward Bishop of Brinkworth, Nathan Parrott. (BRO EP/A/45/3)

**1724**   17 March 1849. Lockeridge in Overton. A dwellinghouse now in the occupation of Thomas James of Lockeridge, labourer. Independent. Richard Henry Smith of Marlborough, Independent minister, Mr Neate of High Street, Marlborough, grocer etc., Thomas James of Lockeridge, labourer, Christopher Day of Marlborough, 'solr' [solicitor?]. [Identical format to **1725**]. (WRO D1/9/2/1)

**1725**   17 March 1849. Overton. A dwellinghouse now in the occupation of John Waite of Overton, labourer. Independent. Richard Henry Smith of Marlborough, Independent minister, John Neate of Marlborough, grocer, etc., Henry Froome of Marlborough, baker, John Wait of Overton. [Identical format to **1724**]. (WRO D1/9/2/1)

**1726**   24 March 1849. East Knoyle. A dwellinghouse in the holding and occupation of Sarah Laurance and Joseph Dewey. The mark of Sarah Laurance, Joseph Dewey, Thomas Evans. (WRO D1/9/2/1)

**1727**   26 March 1849. Hanging Langford in Steeple Langford. A chapel and premises now in the holding and occupation of Thomas Powell for the Primitive Methodist connection. Primitive Methodist. Thomas Powell of St Edmund's parish, Salisbury. (WRO D1/9/2/1)

**1728**   27 March 1849. Warminster. A house in West Street now in the occupation of William Bowring. [Mormon: WF 3(1), 34–35]. John Halliday of Trowbridge. (WRO D1/9/2/1)

**1729**   18 Sept. 1849. Rowde. A house in the occupation of William Bond. Baptist. Joseph Harford, William Bond, John Pyke, Aaron Duck. (WRO D1/9/2/1)

**1730**   21 Nov. 1849. Calne. A room in the occupation of Andrew Goodship in Wood Street. Robert Wicks Gibbons of Calne, linen draper. (WRO D1/9/2/1)

**1731**   28 Dec. 1849. Rushall. A building in our possession as trustees of the freehold, and in the occupation of Nathaniel Wise and others. General Baptist. William Henry Black, Thomas Whe. .nch? [illegible], W. Newling?, trustees. (WRO A1/250)

**1732**   Jan. 1850. Bradford on Avon. A few protestant dissenters intend to set apart the house of Jeremiah Batchelor. Baptist. Uriah Batchelor, John Penny, George White, George Steevens, Jeremiah Batchelor. (WRO D1/9/2/1)

**1733** 18 Jan. 1850. Bremhill. A house now in the occupation of Thomas Cleaverly. Joseph Phelps of St Peter's parish, Marlborough, Arthur Page. (WRO D1/9/2/1)

**1734** (29 Jan. 1850). Haydon Wick in Rodbourne Cheney. A building or chapel. Joseph Hyatt of Gloucester. (WRO A1/255; PRO RG31/2 Gloucester diocese)

**1735** 2 March 1850. Salisbury. A large room in the George Yard, High Street, St Thomas's parish. [*Mormon?*: WF 3(1), 34–35]. Jesse Griffen of Salisbury. (WRO D1/9/2/1)

**1736** 28 March 1850. Corsley. A building called or known by the name of the Wesleyan chapel in Forge Lane End. Wesleyan Methodist. Frederick Snelgrove of Corsley, shopkeeper. (WRO D1/9/2/1)

**1737** 12 April 1850. Cholderton. A dwellinghouse now in my holding and occupation. William Stephenson Scott of Cholderton, yeoman. (WRO D1/9/2/1)

**1738** (20 April 1850). Poole Keynes. A house occupied by William Reynolds. George Lee of Cirencester. (WRO A1/255; PRO RG31/2 Gloucester diocese)

**1739** (20 April 1850). Somerford Keynes. A house occupied by William Boulton. George Lee of Cirencester. (WRO A1/255; PRO RG31/2 Gloucester diocese)

**1740** (23 April 1850). Braydon (*Braden*) in Cricklade. A dwellinghouse occupied by William Millard. John Hutson and others. (WRO A1/255; PRO RG31/2 Gloucester diocese)

**1741** 5 Sept. 1850. Burbage. A room in the dwellinghouse of John Stagg. Martin Wright of Burbage. (WRO D1/9/2/1)

**1742** 21 Sept. 1850. Ramsbury. A dwellinghouse and premises in Oxford Street now in the occupation and holding of Thomas Mindelhall, labourer. Thomas Smith of Ramsbury. (WRO D1/9/2/1)

**1743** 10 Oct. 1850. Upton Scudamore. A building in the possession of Thomas Hardick junior and others is erected as a chapel. [*Baptist*: VCH 8, 89]. Charles Fryer, Thomas Hazell Reynolds, Thomas Hardick, John Vidler Toone, of Warminster. (WRO D1/9/2/1)

**1744** 12 Nov. 1850. Great Cheverell. A dwellinghouse in the occupation of Mr Thomas Dowding. John Chapman of West Lavington. (WRO D1/9/2/1)

**1745** 23 Nov. 1850. Redlynch in Downton. A dwellinghouse in the occupation of John Ford. [*Mormon?*: see **1735**]. Jesse Griffen of Salisbury. [*Pencilled at foot*] 'Call on Thursday.' (WRO D1/9/2/1)

**1746**   13 Dec. 1850. East Tytherton [*in Bremhill*]. The house of Thomas Smith. R.W. Gibbons. (WRO D1/9/2/1)

**1747**   13 Dec. 1850. Theobald's Green (*Tipple Green*) in Calne. The house of Henry Alexander. R.W. Gibbons. (WRO D1/9/2/1)

**1748**   (18 Dec. 1850). Wroughton. A house and premises occupied by George Gibbs. [*Primitive Methodist*: VCH 11, 251]. Thomas Cummin of Brinkworth. (WRO A1/255; PRO RG31/2 Gloucester diocese)

**1749**   30 Dec. 1850. Ridge (*Rudge*) in Chilmark. A dwellinghouse and premises now in the holding and occupation of Frank Roskinge Wood. Frank Roskinge Wood of Ridge. (WRO D1/9/2/1)

**1750**   (13 Jan. 1851). Chapel Knapp in Corsham. A house and premises. T. Mills junior, of Chippenham. (WRO A1/255; PRO RG31/2 Gloucester diocese)

**1751**   20 Jan. 1851. Little Cheverell. The dwellinghouse and premises of George Rideout. John Feltham. (WRO D1/9/2/1)

**1752**   29 Jan. 1851. Hilperton. A house and premises now in the holding and occupation of Eli White. Eli White of Timbrell Street, Trowbridge. (WRO D1/9/2/1)˙

**1753**   7 March 1851. Salisbury. I have taken a room in a house of Mr John Webb, in Green Croft Street, St Edmund's parish. George Spiller of Green Croft Street. (WRO D1/9/2/1)

**1754**   12 March 1851. Studley in Trowbridge. A chapel or meeting house lately erected. Baptist. Stephen Brown Clift of Trowbridge, gentleman. (WRO D1/9/2/1)

**1755**   29 March 1851. Stoke Farthing in Broad Chalke. A dwellinghouse and premises now in the holding and occupation of James Scammell. [*Primitive Methodist*: WRO 1150/286]. Henry Sharman of Fisherton Anger. (WRO D1/9/2/1)

**1756**   14 April 1851. Damerham. A chapel and premises now in the holding and occupation of John Ambrose and others. [*Primitive Methodist*: WRO 1150/286]. Henry Sharman of Fisherton Anger. (WRO D1/9/2/1)

**1757**   18 April 1851. East Knoyle. A chapel and premises now in the holding and occupation of Thomas Merchant and others. [*Primitive Methodist*: WRO 1150/286]. Henry Sharman of Fisherton Anger. (WRO D1/9/2/1)

**1758** 28 April 1851. Ridge (*Rudge*) in Chilmark. A large room in my dwellinghouse. John Mould of Ridge. (WRO D1/9/2/1)

**1759** 8 July 1851. Marlborough. A building lately erected on a piece of ground in St Mary's parish belonging to Montague Alexander. Montague Alexander of Marlborough, Thomas Liddall. (WRO D1/9/2/1)

**1760** (18 July 1851). Castle Eaton. The house and premises of Thomas Bond. Robert Esam Farley of Castle Eaton, Thomas Bond. (WRO A1/255; PRO RG31/2 Gloucester diocese)

**1761** 19 Aug. 1851. Wilbury in Newton Tony. A dwellinghouse and premises at the Wilbury Warren Farm now in the holding and occupation of myself. William Stephenson Scott of Wilbury. (WRO D1/9/2/1)

**1762** 16 Oct. 1851. Devizes. The front part of the premises belonging to Mrs Everett in Back Street, St Mary's parish, now in the holding and occupation of Thomas Billett. Thomas Billett. (WRO D1/9/2/1)

**1763** 7 Nov. 1851. Devizes. A building in St Mary's parish in the possession of John Weston. John Weston, occupier, Maurice Britton, minister. (WRO D1/9/2/1)

**1764** 12 Nov. 1851. Derry Hill in Pewsham extra parochial place. A chapel and premises now in the holding and occupation of William Hatherill and others, for the use of the Primitive Methodist connexion. Primitive Methodist. Robert Hartley of Victoria Cottage, Chippenham, John Smith. (WRO D1/9/2/1)

**1765** 13 Nov. 1851. Orcheston St Mary. The front part of a dwellinghouse and premises now in the holding and occupation of Catherine Wort. John Wallers James of Chippenham. (WRO D1/9/2/1)

**1766** 22 Jan. 1852. Rowde. A house in the occupation of William Bond. Baptist. Thomas Ferris, John Dyke?, William Bond. (WRO D1/9/2/1)

**1767** 25 Jan. 1852. Etchilhampton. A house in the occupation of Henry Bratchell. Baptist. Daniel Weston, James Fishlock, Henry Bratchell, Thomas Stevens. (WRO D1/9/2/1)

**1768** 28 Jan. 1852. Potterne. A building in the possession or occupation of Samuel Marshman. Samuel Marshman, occupier, George Dowse?, William Hampton. (WRO D1/9/2/1)

**1769** 10 Feb. 1852. Bradford on Avon. A club room rented by Mr William Harding on White Hill. Eli White of Timbrell Street, Trowbridge. (WRO D1/9/2/1)

**1770**   14 Feb. 1852. Calne. A dwellinghouse now in the holding and occupation of Abraham Clifford. Nathaniel Maslen of Calne. (WRO D1/9/2/1)

**1771**   19 Feb. 1852. Collingbourne Ducis. A room and premises now in the holding and occupation of Robert Blackmore. [*Wesleyan Methodist*: Hall 11]. George Beard of Andover, Hants., H.W. Carter. (WRO D1/9/2/1)

**1772**   (1 March 1852). Wroughton. A house. Henry Monday of Wroughton. (PRO RG31/2 Gloucester diocese)

**1773**   5 March 1852. Hilcott in North Newnton. The front part of a dwellinghouse belonging to John Weight now in the holding and occupation of William Spackman. Nathan Griffen, at Mr Isaac Smith's, Burbage. (WRO D1/9/2/1)

**1774**   5 March 1852. Ogbourne St George. A house and premises now in the holding and occupation of William Chun. John Blanchard of Ogbourne St George. (WRO D1/9/2/1)

**1775**   8 March 1852. Codford St Mary. A building in the possession or occupation of William Watts. William Powley, Samuel Badder, William Watts, occupier. (WRO D1/9/2/1)

**1776**   5 April 1852 Devizes. Newly erected buildings and premises in Sheep Street, St Mary's parish, now in the holding or occupation of trustees, but not yet delivered up by the building contractor. Richard Biggs of Devizes. (WRO D1/9/2/1)

**1777**   27 April 1852. Laverstock. A dwellinghouse and premises now in the holding and occupation of Harriet Phillimore. Edwin Whitlock of St Edmund's parish, Salisbury. (WRO D1/9/2/1)

**1778**   3 May 1852. Ogbourne St George. A chapel and premises now in the holding and occupation of Samuel Reev, James Duck, Charles Lowden and James Stratton, as trustees. Henry Platt of St Mary's parish, Marlborough. (WRO D1/9/2/1)

**1779**   3 May 1852. Upavon. A chapel and premises now in the holding and occupation of William Dance, Thomas Cruise, Jacob Shun, trustees. Henry Platt of St Mary's parish, Marlborough. (WRO D1/9/2/1)

**1780**   14 May 1852. Yatton Keynell. A house. Joseph Hyatt of Gloucester. (PRO RG31/2 Gloucester diocese)

APPENDIX

WILTSHIRE REGISTRATIONS UNDER THE DECLARATION OF INDULGENCE, 1672

As explained in the introduction (p.xi) the declaration of indulgence by Charles II enabled protestant dissenters to register their houses for religious worship. Over 4,000 houses in England and Wales were so registered between April 1672 and February 1673, although it is not certain that a licence was granted in every case. Two entry books among the State Papers Domestic (PRO SP44/27, SP44(38A) contain the registrations, and these, along with other documents of the period, were edited by G. Lyon Turner and published in 1911.[1] This work is scarce, and the following list of Wiltshire entries has been extracted from it, and arranged so far as is practicable in the same way as entries in the remainder of the present volume.

In the following list only registrations for religious meetings have been included; licences were issued also to teachers, but these have been omitted. Since every entry is taken from PRO SP44/38A only the folio number is given as a reference.

**A1**  20 April 1672. Salisbury. The house of Anthony Cooke. Presbyterian. (37)

**A2**  20 April 1672. Salisbury. The house of John Tombes. Presbyterian. (39)

**A3**  20 April 1672. Salisbury. The house of Thomas Taylor. Presbyterian. (40)

**A4**  20 April 1672. Salisbury. The house of Joseph Swaffield. Presbyterian. (40)

**A5**  20 April 1672. Salisbury. The house of Stephen Haskett. Presbyterian. (49).

**A6**  30 April 1672. Chippenham. The house of Benjamin Flower. Presbyterian. (49)

**A7**  30 April 1672. Broad Chalke (*Broadtholk*). The house of Henry Pen. Anabaptist. (55)

**A8**  1 May 1672. Donhead. The house of Compton South. Presbyterian. (56)

---

[1] Turner, G.L. *Original records of early nonconformity under persecution and indulgence*, 3 vols. 1911. All the information in the following list is taken from vol. 1, pp. 419–585.

**A9**  1 May 1672. Donhead. The house of Thomas Grove, esquire. Presbyterian. (58)

**A10**  1 May 1672. East Knoyle (*Knogell*). The house of Samuel Clifford. Presbyterian. (58)

**A11**  1 May 1672. Teffont. The house of John Phip. Presbyterian. (59)

**A12**  2 May 1672. Stoford in South Newton. The house of widow Blake. Anabaptist. (67)

**A13**  2 May 1672. Salisbury. The house of George Whitemarsh. Independent. (69)

**A14**  2 May 1672. Salisbury. Thomas Batt's house. Anabaptist. (75)

**A15**  2 May 1672. Amesbury. The house of Thomas Long. Anabaptist. (75)

**A16**  8 May 1672. Newton Tony. The house of John Girle. Congregational. (83)

**A17**  13 May 1672. Marlborough. The house of Nathaniel Bayly. Anabaptist. (98)

**A18**  13 May 1672. Marlborough. The house of William Hughes. Congregational. (98)

**A19**  13 May 1672. Devizes. The house of Edward Hope. Independent. (99)

**A20**  13 May 1672. Erlestoke (*Stoke*). The house of William Gough. Presbyterian. (101)

**A21**  13 May 1672. Newton Tony. The house of Francis Fines. Presbyterian. (101)

**A22**  13 May 1672. Ferne (*Ferme*) [*in Donhead St Andrew*]. The house of Robert Grove. Presbyterian. (104)

**A23**  16 May 1672. Durrington. The house of John Wells. Presbyterian. (114)

**A24**  16 May 1672. Salisbury. The house of John Hulatt. Presbyterian. (114)

**A25**  16 May 1672. Chilton Foliat. The house of Sir Bulstrod Whitelock at Chilton Lodge. Congregational. (115)

**A26**  20 May 1672. Trowbridge. The house of Edward Grant. Anabaptist. (132)

**A27** 10 June 1672. Ramsbury. The house of Thomas Freeman. [*Presbyterian*]. (153)

**A28** 10 June 1672. Westport St Mary? (*Westport in Marleborough*) The barn of Edward Brown. Presbyterian. (158)

**A29** [June 1672). Bower Chalke. The house of widow Randall. [*Baptist*]. (173)

**A30** [June 1672]. Nunton [*in Downton*]. The house of Elizabeth Clerke. [*Presbyterian*]. (173)

**A31** [June 1672]. Durnford. The house of Elizabeth Reeve. [*Presbyterian*]. (173)

**A32** [June 1672]. Bromham. The house of Nathaniel Webb. Presbyterian. (176)

**A33** [June 1672]. Warminster. The house of William Buckler. Presbyterian. (176)

**A34** [June 1672]. Stowford in Wingfield. The house of Joseph Bernard. Presbyterian. (179)

**A35** [July 1672]. Aldbourne. The house of Charles Gilbert. Presbyterian. (193)

**A36** [July 1672]. Calne. The house of Edward Parker. Presbyterian. (194)

**A37** [July 1672]. Bradford on Avon. The house of John Holton. [*Presbyterian*]. (195)

**A38** [July 1672]. Figheldean. The house of Henry Shipperd. [*Presbyterian*]. (195)

**A39** [July 1672]. Netheravon. The house of Richard Hearne. [*Presbyterian*]. (195)

**A40** 22 July 1672. 'Bedford' [*perhaps Bradford on Avon or Bulford*]. The house of John Lydiard. Baptist. (199)

**A41** 22 July 1672. Castle Combe. The house of James Organes. Presbyterian. (200)

**A42** 22 July 1672. 'Calden' [*perhaps Calne*]. The house of Edward Parker. [*Presbyterian*]. (203)

**A43**   22 July 1672. Salisbury. The house of John Haddissey. [*Presbyterian*]. (206)

**A44**   25 July 1672. 'Bredland.' The house of John Warren. [*Presbyterian*]. (213)

**A45**   25 July 1672. Maiden Bradley. The house of Matthew Morris. Congregational. (213)

**A46**   25 July 1672. Clack [*in Lyneham*]. The house of Robert Rowsall. Presbyterian. (214)

**A47**   25 July 1672. North Bradley. The house of widow Randall. Presbyterian. (215)

**A48**   25 July 1672. Idmiston. The house of John Reade. Anabaptist. (219)

**A49**   25 July 1672. 'Whitby' [*perhaps Whitley in Melksham: see* **32**]. The house of Abraham Little. Anabaptist. (219)

**A50**   25 July 1672. 'Weeke.' The house of William Lewse. Anabaptist. (219)

**A51**   25 July 1672. Southwick [*in North Bradley*]. The house of Robert Runwell. [*Congregational*]. (221)

**A52**   8 Aug. 1672. Erlestoke. The [*house of*] John Oxford. [*Baptist*]. (223)

**A53**   10 Aug. 1672. Ramsbury. The house of Henry Dent. Presbyterian. (232)

**A54**   5 Sept. 1672. Crockerton in Longbridge Deverill. The house of William Adlames. Baptist. (236)

**A55**   5 Sept. 1672. Westbury. The house of Thomas Edwards. Presbyterian. (241)

**A56**   5 Sept. 1672. Westbury. The barn of Thomas Edwards. Presbyterian. (243)

**A57**   5 Sept. 1672. Seend [*in Melksham*]. The house of Benjamin Rutty. Presbyterian. (245)

**A58**   [5 Sept. 1672]. Sutton Mandeville. The house of Salathiell Deane. Presbyterian. (245)

**A59**   [5 Sept. 1672]. Malmesbury. The house of Ann Smith. Baptist. (246)

**A60** 5 Sept. 1672. Trowbridge. The house of Thomas Tilson. Presbyterian. (248)

**A61** 5 Sept. 1672. Westport St Mary. The house of Ann Smith. Baptist. (249)

**A62** 30 Sept. 1672. Nettleton. The house of David Shouring. Presbyterian. (252)

**A63** [30 Sept. 1672]. Bradford on Avon. The barn of John Broome John [?*John Broome, junior*]. Anabaptist. (259)

**A64** [30 Sept. 1672]. Damerham. The house of Mary Harris. Presbyterian. (259)

**A65** [30 Sept. 1672]. Downton. The house of William Penny. Presbyterian. (259)

**A66** 30 Sept. 1672. Martin. The house of Dorothy Harris. Presbyterian. (259)

**A67** [28 Oct. 1672]. Westbury. The house of Philip Hunton. Congregational. (263)

**A68** [18 Nov. 1672]. Poulshot. The house of William Mayo. Presbyterian. (272)

**A69** [13 Jan. 1673]. Idmiston (*Edmoston*). The house of Richard Wort. Presbyterian. (284)

**A70** [3 Feb. 1673]. Upavon. The house of Andrew Biffen. Presbyterian. (288)

# INDEX OF DENOMINATIONS

For a general discussion of denominations see Introduction, pp. xxvii–xxxi

Anabaptist *see* Baptist

Arminian Methodist, 669; *see also* Methodist

Baptist (Anabaptist), 3, 6–7, 14, 16–7, 19, 21, 31–2, 38, 41, 43, 47, 55–6, 61, 67–72, 77B, 79, 89, 91, 98–9, 113, 119, 123, 142, 148, 151, 164, 167, 172–3, 178, 183, 189–90, 194, 196, 198, 200–1, 205–7, 229–30, 236, 242–3, 247, 257, 261, 263, 267, 271, 276, 278, 282, 291–2, 304–6, 308, 339, 345, 361–2, 369, 371, 377–8, 399, 405, 415, 418, 420, 446, 448, 462, 471–4, 475B, 479, 483, 484B, 491, 512, 517, 527–8, 540, 544, 547, 553, 557, 576, 583, 585, 588, 593, 604, 612, 618, 623, 632, 638–41, 644, 662, 668, 681–2, 691, 695–7, 704, 707, 709, 736, 739, 745, 748, 755–6, 761–2, 764, 777, 787, 798, 804, 808, 811, 823, 829, 831, 838, 843, 846–7, 853, 858, 868, 882, 894, 907–9, 915, 923, 931, 939, 952, 958, 965–6, 970, 972–4, 988, 1011, 1017, 1020–1, 1025–6, 1034, 1039, 1056, 1063, 1076, 1080, 1091, 1105, 1112, 117, 1121, 1125, 1150–1, 1157, 1181, 1183, 1194, 1202, 1204, 1223–4, 1226–7, 1232, 1247, 1256, 1267, 1269, 1284, 1288–9, 1292, 1295–6, 1302, 1315–6, 1318–9, 1324, 1344, 1356, 1372, 1377–8, 1389, 1406, 1411, 1419, 1434, 1451, 1458, 1461, 1466, 1469, 1485, 1488, 1490–1, 1499, 1507, 1509, 1516–7, 1521–2, 1525, 1529, 1545–6, 1552, 1554, 1575, 1577, 1598, 1604, 1617, 1619, 1643, 1692, 1729, 1732, 1743, 1754, 1766–7, A7, A12, A14–5, A17, A26, A29, A40, A48–50, A52, A54, A59, A61, A63; *see also* General Baptist; Particular Baptist; Strict Baptist; Trinitarian Baptist

Calvinist, 1266; *see also* Peculiar Calvinist

Calvinistic Methodist, 666, 670, 1175, 1193; *see also* Methodist

Catholic Apostolic, 1445

Congregational, 532, 663, 1437, 1538–9, 1590, 1653, A16, A18, A25, A45, A51, A67; *see also* Independent

Friends, Society of, *see* Quaker

General Baptist, 403, 404, 1208, 1731; *see also* Baptist; Unitarian

Independent, 8, 101, 224, 228, 233, 235, 253, 273–4, 279–80, 289, 310, 312, 314, 316–9, 322, 329–31, 334, 337–40, 342–3, 346–9, 352–7, 359–60, 366–8, 370, 373, 375–6, 379–84, 386–7, 389–96, 400–2, 406, 408–9, 413–4, 416–7, 422–31, 433–9, 441–2, 447, 450, 452–3, 456, 459, 464, 466–70, 475A, 477–8, 480–2, 484A, 487–90, 493–5, 498–507B, 510–1, 514–6, 518–9, 522–4, 526, 529–30, 532–3, 535–8, 541–3, 549, 552, 554–6, 559, 561, 563–7, 569–71, 575, 577–9, 581–2, 584, 586–7, 589–90, 595–6, 599–600, 603, 609–10, 612–3, 615–6, 623–8, 631, 633–4, 636, 640, 642–4, 648, 655–6, 658–9, 661, 663, 671, 679, 682, 690, 699, 708, 722, 724–5, 733, 736, 743, 746, 754, 758, 761, 767–8, 770, 776, 778, 784, 788–93, 796, 799–800, 803, 810, 814–8, 820–1, 830, 848–52, 863, 869–71, 889, 893, 895, 898, 904–5, 914, 920–1, 929–30, 933, 935, 944, 947, 949, 955, 968–9, 976, 978–9, 981–2, 987, 993, 997, 999A-1001, 1003, 1014–5, 1024, 1029–33, 1050, 1055, 1067, 1069, 1072, 1079, 1085–9, 1093–4, 1100, 1107, 1111, 1113, 1115–6, 1119, 1128–9, 1131–2, 1135, 1147–9, 1152–4, 1156, 1166, 1169, 1178, 1182, 1184, 1191, 1198, 1203, 1205, 1207, 1210, 1214–5, 1222, 1230, 1252, 1254, 1260, 1268, 1272–3, 1275, 1290, 1299–1300, 1305, 1326, 1333, 1338–9, 1355, 1382, 1384, 1287, 1390, 1396, 1409–10, 1413, 1418, 1433, 1436, 1438, 1453, 1477, 1481, 1492–3, 1528, 1547, 1593, 1660, 1724–5, A13, A19

Independent Methodist (Tent Methodist), 957, 964, 967, 971, 977, 983, 1004–5, 1007, 1027–8, 1036–8, 1040–2, 1044, 1047, 1053–4, 1081, 1108, 1130, 1142, 1559, 1594; *see also* Methodist

Latterday Saints, Church of, *see* Mormon

Methodist, 309, 311, 321, 327–8, 332–3, 336, 341, 350–1, 358, 363–5, 372, 374, 388, 407, 421, 443–4, 454–5, 457–8, 460–1, 463, 465, 476, 485–6, 508–9, 520–1, 525, 534, 545A, 548A, 550, 560, 562, 568, 573, 580, 591–2, 594, 598, 601–2, 605, 607–8, 611, 614, 617, 620, 622, 629–30, 635, 637, 645–7, 650–3, 657, 660, 664–5, 667, 673–8, 680, 683–8, 692, 694, 700, 702–3, 705–6, 710–21, 723, 726–31, 734–5, 737–8, 740–2, 744, 747, 749–50, 752–3, 757, 759, 763, 766, 769, 771–5, 779–83, 785–6, 794–5, 797, 801, 805, 807, 812–3, 824, 826–8, 832–7, 839, 841, 844–5, 856–7, 859–61, 864–5, 872–3,

# INDEX OF OCCUPATIONS

# INDEX OF PERSONS AND PLACES

Arabic numbers refer to entries, small romans to pages. Entries prefixed by 'A' occur in the appendix. Places are in Wiltshire unless otherwise stated. Place-names beginning with East, Great, Little, Lower, North, South, Upper and West appear under the main part of the name. No attempt has been made to distinguish between persons of the same forename and surname. Frequently occurring forenames are abbreviated as follows:

| | | | |
|---|---|---|---|
| Alex | Alexander | Jn | John |
| Bart | Bartholomew | Jos | Joseph |
| Ben | Benjamin | Margt | Margaret |
| Chas | Charles | Mic | Michael |
| Chris | Christopher | Nic | Nicholas |
| Dan | Daniel | Phil | Philip |
| Edm | Edmund | Ric | Richard |
| Edw | Edward | Rob | Robert |
| Eliz | Elizabeth | Rog | Roger |
| Fred | Frederick | Sam | Samuel |
| Geo | George | Thos | Thomas |
| Hen | Henry | Wm | William |
| Jas | James | | |

Allright, Jn, 732; M, 604; Mary, 593
Allwood, Thos, 1490, 1552, 1554, 1604
Allworth, Jn, 979
Alton Barnes (Alton, Aulton Barnes, Great Alton), 489, 1008, 1464
Alton Priors in Overton, 489
Alvediston (Alvideston), 574, 954, 1658, 1659
Amber, Jn, 625
Ambrose, Jn, 1756
Amer see Amor
Amesbury, 226, 346, 464, 637, 826, 834, 922, 1510, A15; Marlborough St, 844; see also Amesbury, West; Ratfyn
Amesbury, West, in Amesbury, 792
Amor (Amer), Mary, 1642; Ric, 463
Andover, [Hants], 736, 814, 1045, 1058, 1110, 1503, 1506, 1508, 1556, 1626, 1644, 1647, 1651, 1771; Winton St, 1220, 1652
Andrews (Andres). . . . , 1228; B, 1174, 1190; Benjamin, 1163; David, 316; Jas, 323; Jn, 74, 871, 962, 1021, 1082; Sam, 581; Thos Wills, 617, 630; Wm, 438; Wm Jos, 1645
Angear (Angeon, Anger), Jas, 987, 1085, 1433; Jn, 706
Angel (Angell), Abraham, 1636; Jas, 1598; Jn, 663; Jn, jun, 414; Jn, sen, 414; Jos, 414; Thos, 409
Angeon; Anger see Angear
Anmlin, Luke, 548A
Ann, Abbots, [Hants], 914, 949
Annetts, Jas, 896
Anns, Thos, 409
Anstie, Ben, 1232; Ben Webb, 377; Geo Washington 1232, 1692; Jas O, 1312, 1318; Jn, 434; Paul, 1232; Peter, 377, 988, 1076, 1121
Anstridge, Wm, 1215
Ansty (Anstey), 840, 1158
Antram, Jn, 374
Appleby, Geo, 1412, 1430, 1556
Applegate, . . . , 1199, 1225, 1226; Jas, 1011, 1653; Stephen Hen, 1653
Archar see Archer
Archard, Jas, 1715; Wm, 281, 441
Archer (Archar), G.J., 982; Isaac, 314; Jacob, 369; Jacob, jun, 628; Jas, 314, 369; Jas, sen, 628
Arman, Wm, 360
Arnald see Arnold
Arnell, Wm, 706
Arney, Wm, 737, 744
Arnold (Arnald), Geo, 235; Jn, 52, 236, 900; Wm, 177
Arthurs, Geo, 799
Ashe, Shadrack, 1420
Asher (Aisher), Jn, 464
Ashley (Ashly), Jn, 63, 338

Ashley, Little (Little Ashely, Little Ashly), in Bradford on Avon, 2, 4
Ashton Keynes (Ashton, Ashton Kaines), 258, 347, 720, 753, 1031, 1402, 1511, 1538, 1555; see also Leigh
Ashton, Rob, 1481
Ashton, Steeple (Steple Ashton, Steple-Ashton), xxvi, 43, 143, 775, 852, 879, 1121, 1224, 1247, 1705, 1722; Common Lane, 1545; see also Ashton, West; Bullenhill; East Town; Hinton, Great; Littleton; Semington
Ashton, West, in Steeple Ashton 513, 791, 1125
Ashton, Thos, 455, 1392, 1395
Asphens, Francis, 169
Atkins, Jn, 164, 660
Attwater (Attwaters), . . . , 362; Anna, 345; Eliza, 1525; Maria, 1525; Thos, 362
Attwood (Atwood), Ann, 918; Thos, 560; Wm, 557, 1223
Atworth (Atford), in Bradford on Avon, 31, 32, 295, 418, 564, 1605
Auckland (Aucland), Thos, 195
Aurt, Dan, 1305; Wm J, 1547
Aust, Hen, 1205; Ric, 25; Thos, 493, 554, 1087
Austin, Jn, 598, 629; Wm, 598
Avebury (Abury), 159, 160, 235, 386, 417, 930, 1080, 1227, 1669; see also Beckhampton
Aver, Wm, 601
Avon, in Christian Malford, 1185
Awdry, Geo, 115; Sam, 115
Axford, in Ramsbury, 906
Axford, Hen, 72; Isaac, jun, 122; Jn, 3, 72, 869, 1324; Thos, 43; Wm, 261, 430, 431, 439; see also Oxford
Axton, Abraham, 645
Ayliffe (Ailiff, Aylife), Jas, 799; Rob, 1258, 1287; Thos, 286, 480
Ayres (Aires), Cornelius, 537

Baber see Barber
Backer see Baker
Badbury, in Chisledon, 1064, 1234
Badder, Sam, 1775
Badminton [recte Beaufort], Duke of, see Somerset, Hen. Chas
Baeley see Bailey
Baggs, Jn, 318
Bagnell, Jos, 618
Bagshot (Baggshot), in Shalbourne, 1353
Baiden, Jas, 1002; Matthew, 1081
Bailey (Baeley, Baili, Baily, Balley, Bayly), Edw, 324, 326; Jas, 660; Jn, 325; Jos, 409, 1517; Nathaniel, A17; Ric, 159, 160; Rob, 796, 1544; Sam, 403, 404; Sarah, 320; Thos, 177, 677, 685, 1265, 1487; Wm,

'Bedford,' A40

Bedwyn Common (Bedwin Common), in Great Bedwyn, 1130

Bedwyn, Great (Great Bedwin), 815, 825, 949, 1394; see also Bedwyn Common; Grafton; Wexcombe; Wilton

Bedwyn, Little (Little Bedwin), 1569, 1640, 1702; see also Chisbury

Beeby, . . . , 830, 908; Sam, 853, 868

Beechingstoke (Beachen Stoke) see Broad Street

Begbie, Jas, 310

Belcher, Jane, 1303

Bell, . . . , 1051, 1052, 1071; Chas, 1699; Hen, 1406, 1558; Jn, 4, 1617; Stephen, 256, 686, 687, 693, 703, 713, 1583; Thos, 379, 679; Thos, jun, 687; Wm, 420, 1512, 1513, 1514, 1537, 1548, 1558, 1569, 1573

Belton, Jn, 7, 38

Bemerton [in Fugglestone St Peter], 500

Bence, Thos, 77E

Bendall, Jn, 708

Bendy, Jas, 412

Benger, Geo, 452

Benjamin, Jn, 541

Bennen, Jas, 736

Bennett (Bennet), Absalom, 808, 1517; Enoch, 808; Joan, 102; Job, 1517; Jn, 373, 541, 566, 595, 1517; Jos, 795; Thos, 259, 262; Wm, 426

Berkshire, place in, see Hungerford; Newbury; Shefford; Shefford, West

Berley see Burley

Bernard see Barnard

Berrett see Barrett

Berry, David, 1131; Jas, 413; Thos, 9

Berryman, Anthony, 307

Bertholomew see Bartholomew

Berwick Bassett (Barwick Basset, Berwick), 8, 930, 1403, 1718

Berwick St James (Berwick St James's), 473, 790, 831

Berwick St John, 699, 1159, 1288, 1687

Bessant, Thos, 1014

Best, Stephen, 1421; Thos, 955; Thos, jun, 733

Beth, Thos, 498

Bethel, Thos, 554

Bevan; Beven; Bevin see Beaven

Bevis (Beavis), Jas, 842; Thos, 842; Wm, 890

Bewley Common, in Lacock, 698

Bewley (Bewly), in Lacock, 170, 312

Biddelcom; Biddelcombe see Biddlecombe

Biddestone (Biddeston, Biddistone, Bitson, Bittlestone), 77B, 85, 86, 117, 982, 1107; St Nicholas's parish (Biddestone St Nicholis), 1450; see also Slaughterford

Biddiscomb, Henry, 961

Biddlecombe (Biddelcom, Biddelcombe, Biddlecom), Chris, 201, 210; Eliz Anne, 1178; Thos, jun, 509; Thos, sen, 509

Bidmead, Dan, 603, 659, 666, 1175, 1182; Jas, 1182

Biffin (Biffen), Andrew, A70; Jn, 557; Ric, 1546; Rob, 442, 649

Biggs, Edm, 419; Geo, 401; Jas, 401, 701; Ric, 1232, 1776; Wm, 401

Bignell, Walter, 227

Bigwood, Jas, 748, 1246, 1389; Matthew, 932

Billett (Billet), Abraham, 725; Mic, 92; Ric, 284; Thos, 463, 1762; Wm, 725

Billing, N, 1192

Bird, Wm, 402

Birdbush (Bird-Bush), in Donhead St Mary, 234

Bishop, Ben, 611; Chas, 705; Edw, 1723; Geo, 475B, 1045; Jas, 545B; Jos, 346; Wm, 637

Bishops Cannings see Cannings, Bishops

Bishops Knoyle see Knoyle, East

Bishopstone (Bishoppstone, Bishopston), [unidentified], xvii, 149, 612, 677, 783, 1214, 1271, 1303; Pontons, 627

Bishopstone, [in Ramsbury hundred, north Wiltshire], 1181, 1183, 1372, 1388

Bishopstone, [in Downton hundred, south Wiltshire], 955, 1535

Bishopstrow, xxviii, n3

Black, . . . , 736; Wm Hen, 1731

Blackland, in Calne, 1570

Blackman, Jas, 571

Blackmore (Blackmor), Jn, 837, 1417; Rob, 1771

Blagdon (Blagden), Jn, 405, 406

Blake, . . . , A12; Ben, 853; Geo, 64, 65, 66, 480, 657, 747, 1096; Grace, 546; Jas, 418, 485, 657, 883, 1616; Jn, 9, 742, 761; Jos, 306, 386, 417, 747; Sam, 735; Sarah, 885; Stephen, 883; Thos, 823; Wm, 462, 807, 1384, 1598

Blanchard, Eliz, 831; Issachon, 831; Jas, 831; Jn, 1774; Thos, 831

Bland, Jas, 363

Blandford (Blanford), Hen, 477; Thos, 300

Blatch, Ben, 316; Hen, 316, 317, 464, 556, 626, 633, 642, 987; Hen, jun, 556; Jas, 316, 317, 556; Jn, 261; Sarah, 1085; Wm, 316, 317; Wm S, 763

Blatchley, Jn, 418

Blewden, Chas, 1419

Blewett, Wm, 495, 674

Blundell, Thos, 426

'Blunsdon,' 855

Blunsdon, Broad (Broad Blunsdon St

Kingswood, xxi, 77E, 127, 548B, 548C

Kington Langley (Langley, Tangley) in Kington St Michael, 287, 1046, 1418, 1438, 1638

Kington St Michael (Kineton St Michal, Kingston St Michaell, Kingston St Michal, Kingston St Michals, Kingston St Michel, Kington St Michel), xv, xxviii, 73, 112, 120, 470, 1033, 1088, 1089, 1250, 1436; see also Kington Langley

Kington, West (West Keynton, West Kineton, West Kinton), 88, 102, 158; see also Mountain Bower

'Kinton,' 24

Kirby (Kerby), Jn, 300; Jos, 1111; Ric, 1015; Wm, 1289, 1296, 1347

Kittin, Wm, 1094

Knackston (Knackstone), Stephen, 27, 209; Thos, 1

Knapp, Jn, 372, 1448; Thos, 1612

Knee, Thos, 698

Kneepence see Keepence

Knight, . . . , 1178, 1223; Anna, 1515; Geo, 1302; Hen, 671; Isaac, 71, 89; Jane, 38; Jn, 470; Mary, 493, 554; Patience, 293; Ric, 434; W, 1203; Wm, jun, 557

Knock, Thos, 949

Knook, 871

Knowl Common (Knowle Common), in Mere, 1148

Knowles, Jn, 1551, 1561

Knoyle, East (Bishops Knoile, Bishops Knoyle, East Knogell East Knoile, Eest Knoyle), xxviii, 17, 75, 229, 257, 416, 501, 516, 636, 972, 1128, 1166, 1191, 1322, 1364, 1726, 1757, A10; see also Hay, King; Holloway; Upton

Knoyle, West, 523, 710, 1118, 1123, 1364

Laburn, Jn, 83

Lacock (Laycock), xxvi, n3, 41, 69, 161, 663, 1165; White Hart, 414; see also Bewley; Bewley Common; Bowden Hill; Notton; Reybridge

Lacy, Wm, 549

Ladd (Lad), Ben, 281, 298; Thos, 428

Lake, Sarah, 885

Lambert (Lamberd), Jane, 475A; S, 707; Thos, 1712

Lambourn (Lamborn), Rob, 1372; Wm, 509

Lampard (Lamppard), Ann, 501; Edw, 501, 516; Geo, 507A; Jn, 416; Jonathan, 443; Sam, 894; Thos, 277, 443, 507A

Lamton, Wm, 60

Lanan, Jas, 1268

Lancaster, Thos, 218, 238

Landers, Jas, 1029

Landford, 833

Lane, Hen, 823; Jas, 842; Jn, 140, 210; Wm, 487, 1668

Lanfear, Ambrose, 1273, 1333, 1660

Lang. . . , Wm, 303

Langfield, Jn, 1466, 1543

Langford, Hanging, in Steeple Langford, 1727; Bennitts, 1269

Langford, Steeple, see Langford, Hanging

Langley (Langly), Dorothy, 453; Edw, 470; Francis, 264, 290; Hen, 290

Langley Burrell (Langley Buriell, Langly Burrell), 92, 162, 244, 293

Lanham, Edw, 345; Hen, 80, 217; Jn, 600; Mary, 1396; Wm, 80

Lanning, . . . , 1167

Lansdell, Jas, 192

Lansham, Wm, 104

Lansley, Jos, 1220, 1644

Larance see Lawrence

Large, Wm, 1347

Larkham (Larkam), Edw, 735; Wm, 524, 741, 1327, 1380, 1544, 1550

Larrance see Lawrence

Larter, H, 1032; Hen, 1111, 1299; Hen J, 1129, 1453

Lasbury, Jn, 368; Thos, 368

Lass, Ric, 270

Latton, xxviii, n3, n4

Laurance; Laurence see Lawrence

Laverstock, 465, 1777; see also Ford; Milford

Lavington, Market (Lavington, Lavington Forum, Markett Lavington), 4, 24, 212, 238, 459, 575, 609, 624, 767, 849, 1382, 1463, 1587; White St, 1476; see also Easterton

Lavington, West, 165, 610, 1476, 1501, 1587, 1744; see also Littleton Pannell

Lawes (Law, Laws), David, 349; Edm, 54; Geo, 581; Hen, 1238; Jas, 349, 595; Jn, 16, 167; Leonard, 830; Rob, 1175; Thos, 584; Wm, 77G, 587, 830, 1238

Lawrence (Larance, Larrance, Laurance, Laurence, Lawrance), Ben, 520, 614; Elisha, 697; Jn, 450, 594, 614, 648, 1152; L, 1055; Lawrence, 1014, 1528; Levi, 1071; Marion, 327; Sarah, 520, 614, 1726; Thos, 365, 1151, 1466; Wm, 155, 282, 650

Laws see Lawes

Lea (Lee), . . . , 1270, 1271; Geo, 612, 627, 1738, 1739; Jas, 591; Jn, 267, 282, 1643; Nehemiah, 1528 Peter, 181, 288; Rob, 581; Thos, 267, 282, 1155, 1643

Lea and Cleverton, see Lea; Cleverton

Lea (Lee), in Lea and Cleverton, 24, 505, 603, 666, 1126, 1175

Leach, Jas, 764; Sam, 242; Valentine, 1437

Leader, Jas, 817

# WILTSHIRE RECORD SOCIETY

(As at 31 August 1985)

*President:* C.R. ELRINGTON, F.S.A.
*Honorary Editor:* J.L. KIRBY, F.S.A.
*Honorary Assistant Editor:* DR JANE FREEMAN
*Honorary Treasurer:* MICHAEL J. LANSDOWN
*Honorary Secretary:* JOHN H. CHANDLER

*Committee:*
E. BRADBY
D.A. CROWLEY
MISS S. EWARD
DR. P.M. HEMBRY

MRS N.D. STEELE (*co-opted*)
K.H. ROGERS, F.S.A., representing the Wiltshire Archaeological and Natural History Society

*Honorary Auditor:* MAURICE G. RATHBONE
*Correspondent for the U.S.A.* CHARLES P. GOULD

## PRIVATE MEMBERS

APPLEGATE, MISS J. M., 55 Holbrook Lane, Trowbridge

ASAJI, K., 3–1–44–709, Minatojima, Naka-machi, Chuo, Kobe, Japan

AVERY, MRS S., 23 Saxonhurst, Downton

BADENI. THE COUNTESS, Norton Manor, Malmesbury

BAKER, M., 73 Easton Royal, Pewsey

BALL, S. T., 19 The Mall, Swindon

BAUGH, G. C., 28 Oak Street, Shrewsbury

BEARD, MRS P. S., "Bracken", Booilushag, Maughold, Isle of Man

BENDLE, MRS EDITH, 22 Shady Bower Close, Milford Hill, Salisbury

BERRETT, A.M., 22 Linacre Road, Barton, Torquay

BERRY, G. B., Burton Grange, Mere

BIDDULPH, G. M. R., c/o Personnel Records, British Council, 65 Davies Street, London W1

BISHOP, J. N., 112 Thornhill Road, Streetly, Sutton Coldfield, W. Midlands

BLAKE, T.N., 16 West Hill Road, London SW18

BLUNT, C. E., O.B.E., F.B.A., F.S.A., Ramsbury Hill, Ramsbury, Marlborough

BONNEY, MRS H. M., Flint Cottage, Netton, Salisbury

BOX, S. D., 73 Silverdale Road, Earley, Reading, Berks.

BRADBY, E. L., Beech House, Seend

BRAND, P. A., 2 Theed Street, London SE1

BRIGGS, MISS M., Glebe Cottage, Middle Woodford, Salisbury

BROOKE-LITTLE, J. P., M. V. O., F.S.A., Norroy and Ulster King of Arms, College of Arms, Queen Victoria Street, London EC4

BROWN, W. E., The Firs, Beckhampton, Marlborough

BUCKERIDGE, J. M., 104 Beacon Road, Loughborough, Leics.

BURGESS, I. D., 29 Brackley Ave, Fair Oak, Eastleigh, Hants.

BURGESS, J. M., Tolcarne Wartha Mill, Por-kellis, Helston, Cornwall

BURNETT-BROWN, MISS J. M., Lacock Abbey, Chippenham

BUXTON, E. J. M., F.S.A., The Grove, East Tytherton, Chippenham

CALLEY, SIR HENRY, D.S.O., D.F.C., D.L., Overtown House, Wroughton, Swindon

CAREW HUNT. MISS P. H., Cowleaze, Edington, Westbury

CARTER, MRS B. J., J.P., 28 Okus Road, Swindon

CARTER, PROF. J. M., Dept. of History, East Carolina Univ. Greenville, N. Carolina

CAWTHORNE, MRS N., 47 London Road, Camberley, Surrey

CHANDLER J. H., 27, Park Street, Trowbridge

CHURN, R. H., 5 Veritys, Hatfield, Herts.

CLARK, G. A. 51A Brook Drive, Corsham

CLARK, V., Pembroke House, London Road, Marlborough

COLE, MRS J. A., 113 Groundwell Road, Swindon

COLLINS, W. GREVILLE, Luckington Manor, Chippenham

COOMBES-LEWIS, R. J., 18 Bishopthorpe Road, Sydenham, London SE26

CORAM, J. E., 51, The Street, Hullavington, Chippenham

COULSTOCK, MISS P. H. 15 Pennington Crescent, West Moors, Wimborne

COULTAS, MICHAEL, 36 Vicarage Street, Warminster

COVEY, R. V., Lower Hunts Mill, Wootton Bassett, Swindon

COWAN, COL. M., 24 Lower Street, Harnham, Salisbury

COX, MISS P. M., 6 Silverbeech Avenue, Liverpool

CRITTALL, MISS E., F.S.A., 22 Church Street, Kelvedon, Essex

CROUCHER, MRS B., 25 Ashley Piece, Ramsbury, Marlborough

CROWLEY, D. A. 10, St. Margaret's Villas, Bradford on Avon

CUFFE-ADAMS, E. J., 1 Northfields Close, Lansdown, Bath, Avon

DANIELS, C. G., 81 Goffenton Drive, Oldbury Court, Fishponds, Bristol

D'ARCY, J. N., The Old Vicarage, Edington, Westbury

DAWNAY, CAPT. O. P., C.V.O., Flat 5, 32 Onslow Square, London SW7

DIBBEN, A. A., 18 Clare Road, Lewes, East Sussex

DUNLOP, THE REVD CANON I. G. D. 24 The Close, Salisbury

DYKE, P. J., 35 Buckleigh Avenue, London SW20

EDE, DR. M. E., 12 Springfield Place, Lansdown, Bath

EGAN, T. M., Vale Cottage, Stert, Devizes

ELKINS, T. W., 42 Brookhouse Road, Cove, Farnborough, Hants

ELRINGTON, C. R., F.S.A., Institute of Historical Research, University of London, Senate House, London WC1

FISHLOCK, M., 1 Grove End Lane, Esher, Surrey

FLOWER-ELLIS, J. G. K., Swedish University of Agricultural Sciences, 590183 Umea, Sweden

FORBES, MISS K. G., Bury House, Codford, Warminster

FOY, J. D., 28 Penn Lea Road, Bath, Avon

FREEMAN, DR J., Institute of Historical Research, University of London, Senate House, London WC1

FROST, B. C., 12 Ham Road, Upper Wanborough, Swindon

FULLER, MAJ SIR JOHN, Bt., Neston Park, Corsham

GHEY, J. G., 18 Bassett Row, Bassett, Southampton

GIBBONS, M. E., 47 Stockwood Road, Chippenham

GIBBS, MRS. E., Sheldon Manor, Chippenham

GODDARD, MRS G. H., The Boot, Scholard's Lane, Ramsbury, Marlborough

GOODBODY, E. A., 12 Clifton Road, Chesham Bois, Amersham, Bucks.

GOUGH, MISS P. M., 39 Whitford Road, Bromsgrove, Worcs.

GOULD, C. P., 1200 Old Mill Road, San Marino, California, U.S.A.

GOULD, L. K., 263 Rosemount, Pasadena, California, U.S.A.

GRANT, THE REVD A. E., 42 Sedgebrook, Liden, Swindon

GRIFFITHS, T. J., 29 Saxon Street, Chippenham

GUIDO, MRS M., 44 Long Street, Devizes:

HALFHEAD, MRS M. D., 30 High Street, Wootton Bassett, Swindon

HALL, MRS J., Netherdene, Shrewton, Salisbury

HALLWORTH, F., O.B.E., F.L.A., F.R.G.S., Northcote, Westbury Road, Bratton, Westbury

HAMILTON, CAPT. R., West Dean, Salisbury

HANCOCK, J., 25 Millbank court, 24 John Islip Street, London, S.W.1.

HARE, DR. J. N., 7 Owens Road, Winchester, Hants.

HARTCHER, THE REVD G. N., Holy Cross College, Mosgiel, New Zealand

HATCHWELL, R.C., The Old Rectory, Little Somerford, Chippenham

HAWKINS, M. J., 121 High Street, Lewes, Sussex

HAY, PROF. D., University of Warwick, Coventry

HAYWARD, MISS J. E., Pleasant Cottage, Crockerton, Warminster

HELMHOLZ, R. H. University of Chicago Law School, 1111, East 60th Street, Chicago, Illinois, 60637 U.S.A.

HEMBRY, DR P. M., Pleasant Cottage, Crockerton, Warminster

HILLMAN, R. B., 18 Carnarvon Close, Chippenham

HORNBY, Eileen, 41 Silverwood Drive, Laverstock, Salisbury

HUGHES, Robert, 60 Hurst Park Road, Twyford, Berks

HUMPHRIES, FLT LT A. G. Officers' Mess. R.A.F. Finningley, Doncaster, S. Yorks.

JACKSON, R. H., 67 Queens Road, Tisbury

JAMES, J. F. 3 Sylvan Close, Hordle, Lymington, Hants.

JEACOCK, D. The Old Laundry, Hungerdown Lane, Lawford via Manningtree Essex

JELLICOE, THE EARL, D.S.O., M.C., Tidcombe Manor, Tidcombe, Marlborough

JENNER D. A., 98 Princes Avenue, Palmers Green, London N13

KEEN, A. G., 37 South Street, Aldbourne, Marlborough

KEMPSON, E. G. H., Sun Cottage, Hyde Lane, Marlborough

KENT, T. A., New Garden House, 78 Hatton Garden, London, EC1

KIRBY, J. L., F.S.A., 209 Covington Way, Streatham, London SW16

KITCHING, MRS W. M., Willow Cottage, Pitton, Salisbury

KNEEBONE, R., 20 Blind Lane, Southwick, Trowbridge

KOMATSU, PROF Y., Institute of European Economic History, Waseda University, Tokyo 160, Japan

KUMIKATA, K., c/o Department of Economics, Yamagata University 1-4-12 Kojirakawa-machi, Yamagata-shi, 990, Japan

LANSDOWN, M. J., 53 Clarendon Road, Trowbridge

LAURENCE, MISS A., Arts Faculty, Open University Milton Keynes

LAURENCE, G. F., St Cuthberts, 20 Church Street, Bathford, Bath

LEVER, R. E., Reads Close, Teffont Magna, Salisbury

LIGHT, L., 19A Moor Road, Broadstone, Dorset

LITTLE, J. E., The Pantiles, Chapel Lane, Uffington, Berks.

LONDON, MISS V. C. M., 55 Churchill Road, Church Stretton, Shropshire

LONG, S. H., 90 Southfield Road, Oxford

MCCREE, PETER, Hill Cottage, Reybridge, Lacock

MACKECHNIE-JARVIS, C., The Granary, Milford Mill Road, Salisbury

MARSH, R., 13 Sudeley Street Brighton

MAY, JOHN, Arundell House, Tisbury

MERRYWEATHER, A. F., Frithwood Cottage, Bussage, Stroud

MOLES, MRS M. I., 40 Wyke Road, Trowbridge

MONTAGUE, M. D., 15, Ryrie Street, Mosman, N.S.W. Australia 2088

MOODY, R. F., Harptree House, East Harptree, Bristol

MORIOKA, PROF K., 3–12–4 Sanno, Otaku, Tokyo, Japan

MORLAND, T. E., 47 Shaftesbury Road, Wilton, Salisbury

MORRIS, MISS B., 9 Cleveland Gardens, Trowbridge

MOULTON, A. E., The Hall, Bradford on Avon

NEWMAN, MRS R., Tanglewood, Laverstock Park, Salisbury

NOKES, P. M. A. 14 Market Street, Wells

O'DONNELL, J. A., 1 Mill Green Cottages, Newbridge, Yarmouth, Isle of Wight

OGBOURNE, J. M. V., 14 Earnshaw Way, Beaumont Park, Whitley Bay

OSBORNE, MAJ R., c/o Lloyds Bank, Westbury-on-Trym, Bristol

OULD, MISS E. M., 12 Coxstalls, Wootton Bassett, Swindon

PAFFORD, J. H. P., D. Lit., F.S.A. Hillside, Allington Park, Bridport, Dorset

PARKER, P. F., 45 Chitterne Road, Codford St Mary

PASKIN, LADY, Wishford, Salisbury

PATRICK Sharon, 69 Wain-a-long Road Salisbury

PERRY, S. H., 11 Petersham Place London SW7

PHILLIMORE, MISS M. G., 18 Queen Street, Worthing, West Sussex

PINCHES, MRS R. V., Parliament Piece, Ramsbury, Marlborough

RADNOR, THE EARL OF, Longford Castle, Salisbury

RAMSAY, G. D., 15 Charlbury Road, Oxford
RANCE, H. F., 38 Grove Road, Beaconsfield, Bucks.
RATHBONE, M. G., Craigleith, Snarlton Lane, Melksham Forest
RAYBOULD, MISS F., 20 Radnor Road, Salisbury
REEVES, MISS M. E., F.B.A., 38 Norham Road, Oxford
ROGERS, K. H. Silverthorne House East Town, West Ashton, Trowbridge
ROOKE, MISS S. F., The Old Rectory, Little Langford, Salisbury
RUNDLE, MISS P., 55 The Rank, Maiden Bradley, Warminster

SANDQUIST, PROF T. A., Department of History, University of Toronto, Canada
SANGER, MRS J., 46 Woodside Road, Salisbury
SAWYER, L. F. T., 51 Sandridge Road, Melksham
SHELBURNE, THE EARL OF, Bowood House, Calne
SHELDRAKE, B., 26 Bowood Road, Swindon
SHEPPARD, M. J., 1 Jubilee Road, Newbury, Berks.
SHEWRING, D. G., 4 Clifton Street, Treorchy, Rhondda, Glam., Wales
SLOCOMBE, MRS P. M., 11 Belcombe Place, Bradford on Avon
SOMERSET, JANE, DUCHESS OF, Bradley House, Maiden Bradley, Warminster
SOPP, G. A., 23952 Nomar Street, Woodlands Hills, California, U.S.A
STEELE, MRS N. D., Milestones, Hatchet Close, Hale, Fordingbridge, Hants.
STEVENAGE, M. R., 31 Brooklyn Court, High Road, Loughton, Essex
STEVENSON, MISS J. H., F.S.A., Institute of Historical Research, University of London, Senate House, London WC1
STEWART, MRS J. D., Folly Cottage, Lower Rudloe Lane, Corsham
STEWART, MISS K. P., 16 Beatrice Road, Salisbury

STOKES, M. E. J., 40 New Zealand Avenue, Salisbury
STRATTON, J. M., Manor Farm, Stockton, Warminster
SWEET, C. F., 20 Fairdown Avenue, Westbury
SYKES, B. H. C., Conock Manor, Devizes

TAYLOR, A. J., C.B.E., D. Litt., F.B.A., F.S.A., Rose Cottage, Lincoln's Hill, Chiddingfold, Surrey
TAYLOR, C. C. F.S.A., Royal Commission on Historical Monuments (England), 13 West End, Whittlesford, Cambridge
TOMLINSON, MRS M. Hill Cottage, Little Easton, Dunmow, Essex
TSUSHIMA, MRS JEAN, 'Malmaison', Church Street, Great Bedwyn.
TURNER, I.D., 222 Nottingham Road, Mansfield, Notts.

VERNON, MISS T. E. Summerhouse Cottage, 86 Coxwell Court, Coxwell Street, Cirencester, Glos

WAITE, R. E., 18A Lower Road, Chinnor, Oxon.
WALL, MRS A. D., Department of History, University of Sydney, N.S.W., Australia.
WARNEFORD, F. E., New Inn Farm, West End Lane, Henfield, West Sussex
WARREN, P., 8 Stephens Close, Harnham Meadows, Salisbury
WATKIN, B. W., New Barn, Bull Lane, Crockerton, Warminster
WEINSTOCK, THE LORD, Bowden Park. Lacock, Chippenham
WOODHEAD, B., 47 High Street, Ramsbury, Marlborough
WORDSWORTH, MRS G., Quince Cottage, Longbridge Deverill, Warminster
WRIGHT, D. P., Haileybury, Hertford

YOUNG, C. L. R., 25 Staveley Road, London W4

## UNITED KINGDOM INSTITUTIONS

Aberdeen. Kings College Library
Aberystwyth. National Library of Wales
   "            University College of Wales
Bangor. University College of North Wales
Bath. Reference Library

Birmingham. Central Public Library
   "         University Library
Boston Spa (Yorks.). British Library Lending Division
Brighton. Brighton Polytechnic, Falmer

Brighton. University of Sussex Library, Falmer
Bristol. Avon Central Library
" University Library
Cambridge. University Library
Canterbury. University of Kent Library
Chippenham. Technical College
Coventry. University of Warwick Library
Devizes. Wiltshire Archaeological and Natural History Society
Dorchester. Dorset County Library
Durham. University Library
Edinburgh. National Library of Scotland
Edinburgh. University Library
Exeter. University Library
Glasgow. University Library
Gloucester. Bristol and Gloucester Archaeological Society
Hull. University Library
Leeds. University Library
Leicester. University Library
Liverpool. University Library
London. British Library
" College of Arms
" Guildhall Library
" Inner Temple Library
" Institute of Historical Research
" London Library
" Public Record Office
" Royal Historical Society
" Society of Antiquaries
" Society of Genealogists
" University of London Library

Manchester. Rylands University Library
Marlborough. Memorial Library, Marlborough College
Marlborough. Savernake Estate
Norwich. University of East Anglia Library
Nottingham. University Library
Oxford. Bodleian Library
" Exeter College Library
" New College Library
Reading. Central Library
" University Library
St Andrews. University Library
Salisbury. Cathedral Library
" The Museum
" Bourne Valley Historical Society
" Royal Commission on Historical Monuments (England), Manor Road
" Salisbury College of Technology
Sheffield. University Library
Southampton. University Library
Swansea. University College of Swansea Library
Swindon. Swindon College Library
" Wiltshire Family History Society
" The Library, Burmah Oil Trading Ltd.
Taunton. Somerset Archaeological and Natural History Society
Trowbridge. Wiltshire County Library and Museum Service
" Wiltshire Record Office, County Hall
York. University of York Library

## INSTITUTIONS OVERSEAS

### AUSTRALIA

Adelaide. Barr Smith Library, University of Adelaide
Canberra. National Library of Australia
Kensington. Law Library, University of New South Wales
" Baillieu Library, University of Melbourne
Melbourne. Victoria State Library
Nedlands. Reid Library, University of West Australia
St Lucia, Brisbane. Main Library, University of Queensland
Sydney. Fisher Library, University of Sydney

### CANADA

Halifax, Nova Scotia. Dalhousie University Library

Kingston, Ont. Douglas Library, Queen's University
London. Ont. D. B. Weldon Library, University of Western Ontario
Montreal, Que. Sir George Williams University Library
Ottawa, Ont. Carleton University Library
St John's, Newf. Memorial University of Newfoundland Library
Toronto, Ont. Pontifical Institute of Medieval Studies
" " University of Toronto Library
Vancouver, B.C. Main Library, University of British Columbia
Victoria, B.C. MacPherson Library, University of Victoria

DENMARK
Copenhagen. The Royal Library

GERMANY
Göttingen. Niedersächsische Staats– und Universitätsbibliothek

REPUBLIC OF IRELAND
Dublin. Trinity College Library

JAPAN
Osaka. Institute of Economic History, Kansai University
Sendai. Institute of Economic History, Tohoku University

NEW ZEALAND
Wellington. National Library of New Zealand

SWEDEN
Uppsala. Royal University Library

UNITED STATES OF AMERICA
Ann Arbor, Mich. General Library, University of Michigan
Athens, Ga. University Library, University of Georgia
Atlanta, Ga. The Robert W. Woodruff Library for Advanced Studies, Emory University
Baltimore, Md. George Peabody Dept., Enoch Pratt Free Library
Berkeley, Calif. University of California
Bloomington, Ind. Indiana University Library
Boston, Mass. Public Library of the City of Boston
    "      " New England Historic and Genealogical Society
Boulder, Colo. University of Colorado Libraries
Cambridge, Mass. Harvard Law School Library
    "      " Harvard College Library
Charlottesville, Va. Alderman Library, University of Virginia
Chicago, Ill. University of Chicago Library
Chicago, Ill. Newberry Library
Cleveland, Ohio. Public Library

Dallas, Tex. Public Library
Davis, Ca. University Library
De Kalb, Ill. Northern University of Illinois, Swen Franklin Parson Library
East Lansing, Mich. Michigan State University Library
Eugene, Oreg. University of Oregon Library
Evanston, Ill. The United Library, Garrett/Evangelical Seabury Western
Fort Wayne, Ind. Public Library of Fort Wayne and Allen County
Hattiesburg, Miss. University of Southern Mississippi Library
Haverford. Pa. Haverford College Library
Iowa City, Iowa. State University of Iowa Library
Ithaca, N.Y. Cornell University Library
Las Cruces, N. Mex. New Mexico State University Library
Los Angeles, Calif. Public Library of Los Angeles
    "      " University Research Library, University of California
Minneapolis, Minn. Dept of History, Minnesota University
Newark, Del. University of Delaware Library
New Brunswick, N.J. Rutgers State University Library
New Haven. Conn. Yale University Library
New York, N.Y. Columbia University of the City of New York
    "      " Public Library, City of New York
Notre Dame, Ind. Notre Dame University Library
Philadelphia, Pa. Pennsylvania University Library
Princeton, N.J. Princeton University Library
Salt Lake City, Utah. Genealogical Society of the Church of Latter Day Saints
San Marino, Calif. Henry E. Huntington Library
Santa Barbara, Calif. University of California Library
South Hadley, Mass. Mount Holyoke College Library
Stanford, Calif. Stanford University Library
Statesboro, Georgia Southern College Library
Tucson. Az. University of Arizona Library
Urbana, Ill. University of Illinois Library
Washington, D.C. Library of Congress
    "      " Folger Shakespeare Library
Winston-Salem, N.C. Wake Forest University Library

# LIST OF PUBLICATIONS

The Wiltshire Record Society was founded in 1937, as the Records Branch of the Wiltshire Archaeological and Natural History Society, to promote the publication of the documentary sources for the history of Wiltshire. The annual subscriptions is £10 for private members, £12 for institutions. In return, a member receives a volume each year. Prospective members should apply to Dr. J. H. Chandler, 27 Park Street, Trowbridge, Wilts. Many more members are needed.

The following volumes have been published. Price to members £10, or £12 and to non-members £15, postage extra. Available from the Hon. Treasurer, Mr M. J. Lansdown, 53 Clarendon Road, Trowbridge, Wiltshire.

XXVII *Wiltshire returns to the bishop's visitation queries, 1783.* Edited by Mary Ransome (1972). Folder

XXVIII *Wiltshire extents for debts Edward I-Elizabeth I.* Edited by Angela Conyers (1973)

XXIX *Abstracts of feet of fines relating to Wiltshire for the reign of Edward III.* Edited by C. R. Elrington (1974)

XXX *Abstracts of Wiltshire tithe apportionments.* Edited by R. E. Sandell (1975)

XXXI *Poverty in early-Stuart Salisbury.* Edited by Paul Slack (1976)

XXXII *The subscription book of Bishops Tounson and Davenant, 1620–40.* Edited by Barrie Williams (1977)

XXXIII *Wiltshire gaol delivery and trailbaston trials, 1275–1306.* Edited by R. B. Pugh (1978)

XXXIV *Lacock abbey charters.* Edited by K. H. Rogers (1979)

XXXV *The Bradenstoke cartulary.* Edited by Vera C. M. London (1980)

XXXVI *Wiltshire coroners' bills 1752–1796.* Edited by R. F. Hunnisett (1981)

XXXVII *The Justicing Notebook of William Hunt, 1744–9.* Edited by Elizabeth Crittall (1982)

XXXVIII *Two Elizabethan women: Correspondence of Joan and Maria Thynne, 1575–1611.* Edited by Alison D. Wall (1983)

XXXIX *The Register of John Chandler, Dean of Salisbury, 1404–17.* Edited by T.C.B. Timmins (1984)

## VOLUMES IN PREPARATION

*Wiltshire glebe terriers,* edited by Susan Avery; *The Edington cartulary,* edited by Janet Stevenson; *The Wiltshire tax roll of 1332,* edited by D. A. Crowley; *The Baynton commonplace book,* edited by Jane Freeman; *Crown pleas of the Wiltshire eyre, 1268,* edited by Brenda Farr; *Abstracts of feet of fines relating to Wiltshire, 1377–1422,* edited by J. L. Kirby; *Papist returns and estate enrolments, 1705–87,* edited by J. A. Williams.

A leaflet giving full details may be obtained from Dr J. H. Chandler, 27 Park Street, Trowbridge, Wilts.